PRAISE FOR *THEY WERE SOLDIERS*

"Nearly three million young Americans served in the Vietnam War and came home to no welcome and no respect in a nation divided and angry over that war. Hollywood and much of the media branded this generation, as great in every way as their fathers' generation, with all the sins of a very few. It was a time of bitterness and sadness. Now old Vietnam hands Marvin J. Wolf and Joe Galloway have interviewed and profiled half a hundred Vietnam veterans to paint a much more accurate picture of a generation that came home determined to do well for their communities and our country. From Colin Powell and Barry McCaffrey, who soldiered on to four-star rank and high political office; to marine Fred Smith, who founded and built FedEx; to Diane Carlson Evans, an army nurse who demanded that the sacrifices of the women also be recognized—these riveting stories in *They Were Soldiers* are an important contribution to the national weal. I challenge you to read these stories of a Great Generation with dry eyes."

—STEVEN PRESSFIELD, *New York Times* BESTSELLING AUTHOR OF *The War of Art*

"We have conveniently and collectively erased the Vietnam War from most of our memories—it didn't work out the way our myths tell us American wars should—but we cannot erase the experiences of those who fought in it. They are brought to life magnificently in *They Were Soldiers*, which is a vivid and heroic reminder that we forget at our own peril."

—KEN BURNS, AWARD-WINNING FILMMAKER

"I loved reading *They Were Soldiers*. It was like hanging around with my veteran friends at a reunion listening to them tell me not what they did in the war, but what they did with their lives, which is far more interesting."

—KARL MARLANTES, *New York Times* BESTSELLING AUTHOR OF *Matterhorn*

"An impressive assembly of inspiring stories of our Vietnam generation who went and did what our nation asked in combat with as much intrepid courage, skill, fierce devotion to each other, sacrifice, and a will to win as any generation in our nation's history."

—FRED FRANKS, GENERAL, US ARMY (RET.)

THEY
WERE
SOLDIERS

BOOKS BY JOSEPH L. GALLOWAY

*We Were Soldiers Once . . . and Young: Ia Drang—the Battle That
    Changed the War in Vietnam* (with Harold G. Moore)

*We Are Soldiers Still: A Journey Back to the Battlefields
    of Vietnam* (with Harold G. Moore)

BOOKS BY MARVIN J. WOLF

Nonfiction

*The Japanese Conspiracy: The Plot to Dominate Industry
    Worldwide—and How to Deal with It*

Fallen Angels: Chronicles of L.A. Crime and Mystery
    (with Katherine Mader)

Platinum Crime (with Armand Grant)

Beating the Odds: The Untold Story Behind the Rise of ABC
    (with Leonard Goldenson)

Rotten Apples: True Stories of New York Crime and Mystery
    (with Katherine Mader)

Family Blood: The True Story of the Yom Kippur Murders
    (with Larry Attebery)

Perfect Crimes (with Katherine Mader)

*Where White Men Fear to Tread: The Autobiography of
    Russell Means* (with Russell Means)

Buddha's Child: My Fight to Save Vietnam (with Nguyen Cao Ky)

Abandoned in Hell: The Fight for Vietnam's Firebase Kate
    (with William Albracht)

Fiction

For Whom the Shofar Blows

A Scribe Dies in Brooklyn

A Tale of Two Rabbis

M-9: A Chelmin and Spaulding CID Mystery

THEY WERE SOLDIERS

THE SACRIFICES AND CONTRIBUTIONS
OF OUR VIETNAM VETERANS

JOSEPH L. GALLOWAY
AND MARVIN J. WOLF

NELSON
BOOKS

An Imprint of Thomas Nelson

Published in Nashville, Tennessee, by Nelson Books, an imprint of Thomas Nelson. Nelson Books and Thomas Nelson are registered trademarks of HarperCollins Christian Publishing, Inc.

Thomas Nelson titles may be purchased in bulk for educational, business, fund-raising, or sales promotional use. For information, please e-mail SpecialMarkets@ ThomasNelson.com.

Any Internet addresses, phone numbers, or company or product information printed in this book are offered as a resource and are not intended in any way to be or to imply an endorsement by Thomas Nelson, nor does Thomas Nelson vouch for the existence, content, or services of these sites, phone numbers, companies, or products beyond the life of this book.

ISBN: 978-1-4002-0883-8 (TP)

Library of Congress Cataloging-in-Publication Data

Names: Galloway, Joseph L., author. | Wolf, Marvin J., author.
Title: They were soldiers : the sacrifices and contributions of our Vietnam veterans / Joseph L. Galloway and Marvin J. Wolf.
Description: Nashville : Thomas Nelson, 2020. | Includes bibliographical references. | Summary: "Joseph Galloway and coauthor Marvin Wolf bring to life the inspirational stories of Vietnam veterans who returned home from the "lost war" to enrich America's present and future"-- Provided by publisher.
Identifiers: LCCN 2019036793 (print) | LCCN 2019036794 (ebook) | ISBN 9781400208807 (hardcover) | ISBN 9781400208814 (ebook)
Subjects: LCSH: Vietnam War, 1961-1975--Veterans--United States--Biography. Veterans--United States--Biography.
Classification: LCC DS559.73.U6 G35 2020 (print) | LCC DS559.73.U6 (ebook) | DDC 959.704/34092273--dc23
LC record available at https://lccn.loc.gov/2019036793
LC ebook record available at https://lccn.loc.gov/2019036794

Printed in the United States of America

22 23 24 LSC 10 9 8 7 6 5 4 3 2 1

With great respect and admiration, the authors dedicate this book to the memory of a great soldier and a true American hero, Cyril R. "Rick" Rescorla. Decorated for valor in the Ia Drang valley battles in Vietnam, Rescorla became a hero again on September 11, 2001, when he saved the lives of some twenty-seven hundred people in the World Trade Center's South Tower. After shepherding those individuals to safety down forty-four flights of stairs, Rick Rescorla went back up those stairs with firefighters to look for stragglers and perished with them in the collapse of the building.

Greater love hath no man than this, that a man lay down his life for his friends.

—JOHN 15:13 KJV

Veteran Reflections at the Wall

Remains of casualties were sent back home;
Their names now in Optima typeface in granite.
The whys and wherefores of war end in tomes
While inscribed in this black wall, mirrored and mammoth,
Tapered head to foot and full:
58,000 who signed up or were summoned.
For the vets who come here there's never a lull
In remembrance of Nam nor their shabby homecoming.
Faces lined with living through generations
Sons turning into fathers; the American dream.
Though others still wounded seek compensation
Denied the proverbial peaches and cream.
"Those who forget history . . ." we know the rest
Sloughing through rice paddies they passed that test.

—RON VAZZANO[1]

CONTENTS

CONTENTS

PART TWO: HEALERS

PART THREE: OFFICEHOLDERS

PART FOUR: GOVERNMENT SERVICE

CONTENTS

FOREWORD

The Vietnam War came up on my radar in early 1963 through the dispatches of David Halberstam of the *New York Times*, Neil Sheehan of United Press International, and Malcolm Browne of the Associated Press. Somehow I knew then that this would become an American war and my generation's war, and I had to go there and cover it.

At the time I was covering the statehouse in Topeka, Kansas, for UPI but began a campaign of begging and pleading to be sent to Asia and to that developing war. Against all odds, I succeeded, and in late 1964 I was transferred to UPI Asia Headquarters in Tokyo. In March 1965, the first battalion of US Marines landed in Da Nang in Vietnam, and three weeks later I was on a plane bound for Saigon and the war. This would be the first of four tours in Vietnam for me: 1965–66, 1971, 1973, and 1975 for the end. Since then I have been back to Vietnam five times.

As a kid I had read the collected works of World War II correspondent Ernie Pyle and dreamed that someday I might follow in his footsteps and chronicle the lives and deaths of American troops in combat, however lofty an ideal that might be.

Now I had arrived and a long, painful journey began. The marines and I began to learn the hard lessons of both war and Vietnam that spring of 1965. They were fighting Viet Cong[1] guerrillas and finding it hard, hot work in the rice paddies, jungles, and mountains. They pursued a wily, wispy foe on his home turf and seldom caught him.

I wore jungle fatigues and little else. The Nikon cameras dangling from my neck and the lack of a rifle over my shoulder distinguished me from the marines and, later, army soldiers. I was twenty-three, only a bit older than the grunts, and I would hook up for a few hours or a few days with a company on patrol. When we came to a halt, the guy next to me would look me over and ask who I was.

"A reporter."

"You a civilian?"

"Yes."

"And you're out here with me?"

"Yes."

"They must pay you a helluva lot of money!"

"No. I work for UPI, and they are the cheapest outfit in the world."

"Then you are *crazy,* man!"

The guy next to him would ask who I was. "Some crazy reporter," he would reply. Then all was clear and good. Nobody understands crazy like infantrymen.

The learning curve in combat is very steep, and failures are punished with wounds or death. I learned from the officers, sergeants, grunts, and such veteran war correspondents as Dickey Chapelle of *National Geographic,* Jack Foisie of the *Los Angeles Times,* Keyes Beech of the *Chicago Daily News,* and others who had also covered World War II and Korea. I also learned by observing, by watching the troops in the field in the crushing heat as they carried packs and weapons and ammo weighing up to sixty or seventy pounds on their backs. I saw men felled by heatstroke in the 118 degrees of the tropics, white foam around their mouths as their bodies convulsed. When a man began to stagger and seemed about to collapse, his buddies would take some of his equipment to ease the burden and help him keep up. All the time they would scan the jungle or the tree line in a never-ending 360-degree sweep like owls. In Vietnam, the enemy was everywhere and nowhere, and nothing could be overlooked or ignored on pain of death and destruction.

This was a time long before laptop computers and satellite phones and Wi-Fi connections. Getting your story to the bureau in Saigon and shipping your precious film weren't the easiest chores. I would dictate a story through the military phone system—a shaky, overburdened linkage of old-fashioned switchboards that snaked from north to south and east to west. Each switch had a code name: Tiger Switch, Puma, Lion. All who used that system were ranked by priority, one being the highest, four being the lowest. Civilian reporters were a four, at the very bottom, and could be disconnected by any- one with a higher priority—that is, until we learned to be "Colonel Smith Priority Two." But even then, it could take hours to dictate five hundred words to the home office. For photos, we wrote caption[2] data on the manila envelopes that contained our 35mm film canisters and then headed to the air base at Da Nang to find a "pigeon," someone traveling to Saigon who would be willing to carry an envelope in exchange for a ride to their hotel or quarters from the UPI messenger who met their flight. The film would be developed, edited, printed, and then taken to the *Saigon Post and Telegraph* for transmis- sion by radiophoto machine to UPI in Tokyo, Hong Kong, or Manila for relay to New York and the world.

By covering troops in combat, I learned to be a very careful, methodical reporter, double-checking the spelling of a soldier's name and hometown and quoting him honestly. I never knew when my reporting would show up in Vietnam. I could spend an hour or a day or two with an outfit; then I'd leave to get my story and film out. Because we were a worldwide news agency, the odds were high a hometown newspaper of one or more troops would print my story, and a soldier's mom would cut it out and put it in her next letter to her son. Or it might be printed in *Stars and Stripes*, the military newspaper that circulated widely in Vietnam. Either way, the troops would read my sto- ries, and chances were good I would hook up with that unit again weeks or months later. You do not make mistakes in stories about men who are armed and dangerous.

During my tours in Vietnam, I marched with and befriended young lieu- tenants, captains, and majors, soldiers I would meet again and again in that war and other wars that followed. In August 1965, I met and marched for a day with a newly promoted major named Norman Schwarzkopf in the Central Highlands out of Duc Co Special Forces Camp. Norm was an adviser to a battalion of South Vietnamese airborne troops. A quarter century later, in the first Persian Gulf War, he was the commanding general of US Central

Command (CENTCOM). He reminded me that my coauthor Lt. Gen. Hal Moore had been his tactical officer when Norm was a West Point cadet. Norm called me to his headquarters in Riyadh, Saudi Arabia, two weeks before the invasion of Kuwait and Iraq and pulled the cover off his battle map and briefed me on what he was planning to do. Then he assigned me to "the division which has the most challenging and dangerous mission in my battle plan— and the commander who is most like Gen. Hal Moore." Ten days before the invasion, I reported to the Twenty-Fourth Infantry Division, Mechanized and its commander, Maj. Gen. Barry McCaffrey. I was given total access to a division preparing for war.

In all my dealings with American troops, I was never turned away or turned down. I was generally welcomed as the only civilian those young soldiers and marines would ever see sharing their hardships and horrors. I was always willing to lend a hand in combat—to carry water and ammunition or a wounded man. I never presented myself as a neutral observer, aloof from what was happening all around me. These young men America had sent to war, in return, were willing to share what little they had—a drink from their last canteen of water or half a cup of the last coffee.

In November 1965, I stumbled into the bloodiest battle of the Vietnam War, where an understrength battalion of the First Cavalry Division (Airmobile) was surrounded by two regiments of North Vietnamese Army regulars. For three days and two nights, it was a bloody struggle to survive against an enemy determined to kill all of us. And on the following day and night, two miles away, another battalion was ambushed and slaughtered in the tall elephant grass. These were the battles of Landing Zone X-Ray and Landing Zone Albany. Some 234 Americans were killed and another 250 were badly wounded. More than 2,000 enemy dead lay all around those two small clearings in the jungled forest.

Those battles changed my life, changed my heart. I left Ia Drang valley with an abiding love for our soldiers and a lifelong debt owed those young Americans who gave their precious lives so I might survive to tell their stories to the world. Men died all around me; others were horribly wounded. Not one of us left that place unchanged from the men who arrived there just days before. I did what I could to help, even unlimbering an M-16 and helping to fend off the enemy. For a brief time I stopped being a reporter and became a soldier. In the process, I found and made the best, most loyal friends of a lifetime and earned the lasting respect and trust of the military family.

Joseph L. Galloway
Concord, North Carolina
April 2019

INTRODUCTION

On April 5, 1962, the morning I thought would be my last day in the army, I met our company clerk in the unit orderly room at Fort Benning, Georgia. As we shook hands, he said this was also *his* last day in Delta Company; his next duty station was Saigon, South Vietnam.

Though I was only twenty, I had served a year in South Korea and had visited Japan. I had also excelled in high school geography, but I had no idea where South Vietnam was. Before going home, I went to the post library and found Saigon in an atlas. I wondered why we had troops there, even clerks, but then I put it out of my mind. I was headed for civilian life. I had more important things to think about.

I wasn't alone in my ignorance and apathy. In the early 1960s, before the low-level insurgency in Vietnam's rural provinces blossomed into an enormous shooting war, in the period when only a few thousand US soldiers were in South Vietnam, few Americans were aware of the fighting there and fewer could have found Vietnam on a map.

There was plenty to distract us. This was the dawn of the civil rights era, when bold Freedom Riders, blacks and whites together, rode interstate buses into the Deep South in defiance of segregation laws. A time when black students staged sit-ins at segregated lunch counters across the South. A time when black churches were burned and bombed. A time when many African

Americans heard Martin Luther King Jr.'s call for nonviolent protest and others listened to Malcolm X and sought racial justice by any means necessary.

The sixties also spawned a sexual revolution. Birth control pills became legal for contraceptive use in 1960. Suddenly, men and women no longer waited for marriage to experiment with sex. Within a few years, millions of mostly young Americans were enjoying sexual freedoms that often shocked and offended their parents.

It was also the era when millions of young people began experimenting with marijuana, LSD, peyote, psychedelic mushrooms, and other consciousness-altering substances. In just a few years, many of them would be in Vietnam, where marijuana was cheap and readily available.

According to Jeremy Kuzmarov, author of *The Myth of the Addicted Army: Vietnam and the Modern War on Drugs* (Amherst: University of Massachusetts Press, 2009) and an American history professor at the University of Tulsa, serving in the war did not cause American soldiers to begin using drugs: many were smoking, snorting, injecting, or swallowing mind-altering substances before they joined the military.

And most of all, during the early sixties, millions of young Americans fell in love with rock 'n' roll, with its beat, its seditious lyrics, and its shaggy-haired outlaw artists who expressed the frustration, loneliness, alienation, and anger of youth. Americans who came of age during the Great Depression—the generation that defeated fascism and built the interstate highway system, the atomic bomb, the Hoover Dam, and a great deal more—never grooved on rock 'n' roll, sensing in its rhythms not a cultural revolution but taboo racial overtones. Even more than sex and drugs, rock music widened the divide between the Greatest Generation and their children, a generational gap like few before.

Few outside Washington thought much about South Vietnam either, even though during World War II the United States had important interests in Vietnam. While France was battling Nazi Germany, Japan invaded France's Indochina colonies—present-day Laos, Cambodia, and Vietnam. In a few weeks the French surrendered, and Germany ceded Indochina to its Japanese ally as a prize of war. Those subtropical, agrarian regions were rich in rice, rubber, tea, coffee, and minerals and were strategically positioned at China's back door at a time when China was fighting both a Communist revolution and an invading Japanese army.

INTRODUCTION

For decades prior to World War II, the United States had enjoyed a brisk trade with Japan in scrap steel and raw petroleum, but Japan's seizure of Indochina led the United States to embargo both commodities. Since Japan's oil stockpiles could fuel a naval war for only one year, they attacked the enormous American naval base at Pearl Harbor, Hawaii, hoping for a knockout blow. Thus the spread of World War II into the Pacific was partly the result of events in Vietnam.

World War II included covert operations in south China and in Tonkin—as North Vietnam was then known—by agents of the Office of Strategic Services (OSS), the forerunner of the CIA. Ho Chi Minh, a French-speaking Vietnamese nationalist, and Vo Nguyen Giap led a guerrilla campaign against the Japanese and sought American help. A small team of OSS officers was inserted by parachute into Tonkin's mountainous border area with China. Their mission: advise and support Ho and Vo in their fight against the Japanese. The OSS arranged for some arms and ammunition to be parachuted to the guerrillas. When the OSS team was withdrawn, they told their superiors the United States should do much more to help Ho and Vo.

But the US government declined to provide additional help, so Ho accepted arms and other aid from Chinese communists fighting both Japan and the Chiang Kai-shek regime. At the end of the war, when Germany and Japan surrendered separately, France sought to reestablish control over its former colonies. Ho begged the United States to press France to allow the people of Indochina to determine their own political fate.

France, however, is America's oldest ally. Bled white by the Nazi occupation, France's factories and transportation networks were in shambles, and France expected its Indochina colonies to help fuel the recovery of its national economy. It came as no surprise when French president Charles de Gaulle threatened to leave NATO and expel NATO's Paris headquarters unless US president Harry Truman supported France's fight to regain control of its Indochina colonies. America had become actively engaged with covert efforts to stop the Soviets from building an iron curtain across Eastern Europe. Communist guerrillas were fighting to take over Greece, and Truman, seeking to keep the Allied coalition together, acceded to de Gaulle's demands. Because of Ho's wartime embrace of the Chinese communists in their joint struggle against the Japanese, anti-communist elements in the US State

Department and Congress declared him a communist and decided Ho could not be trusted.

The French returned to Indochina, to their mines, plantations, and other economic interests, and Ho's guerrilla army, the Viet Minh, turned its efforts against them. For several years, US support for the French in Indochina offset 70 percent of France's war effort, but France was eventually defeated by this peasant army. As part of the 1954 Geneva Accords, France agreed to withdraw from its former colony and to split the country along the seventeenth parallel until formal elections could be held to determine future governance. Under French rule there had been three autonomous colonies; now Vietnam became two countries, with North Vietnam led by Ho Chi Minh. Roman Catholics and many affluent Buddhists headed south—as did some of Ho's guerrilla cadres, who became known as the Viet Cong.

The Catholic refugees were mostly an educated group whose interests were more aligned with the West than with their countrymen. They were aided by well-connected American and French Catholics who saw not only business opportunities but also a chance for more converts to Christianity. Within months, Ngo Dinh Diem, a devout Catholic, was elevated to power over the South, brushing aside its Buddhist majority and refusing to sign the 1954 Geneva agreements. Insurgency grew in the South, and a few thousand and then tens of thousands of US advisors were sent to train the South Vietnamese military to defend against the spread of communism from the North. Diem's inept, corrupt, and brutal regime ended in 1963 with his murder during a military coup that was carried out with tacit CIA assistance. Over the next seventeen months, a succession of coups, failed coups, and government reorganizations kept the Saigon government in a perpetual state of flux, a vacuum eagerly filled by the Viet Cong.

In August 1964, a US warship was collecting radio intelligence in the Gulf of Tonkin, along the coast of North Vietnam, and reported an attack by North Vietnamese torpedo boats, which supposedly triggered an extended battle between the torpedo boats and the warship and supporting US aircraft. Two days later, a second American ship in the same area reported a similar attack. In a 2003 documentary film, former secretary of defense Robert S. McNamara admitted the first attack *may* have happened, but there was no shooting, no sea battle, no US aircraft involved. The second attack was a Department of

Defense fabrication.[1] Nevertheless, President Lyndon Johnson asked Congress for war powers in Vietnam and was rewarded with authority to deploy US troops, aircraft, and ships in and around both Vietnams.

In February 1965, a Viet Cong battalion attacked the US Army base at Camp Holloway, near Pleiku, in the Central Highlands. Eight GIs were killed and 126 wounded.

In June 1965, cocky, flamboyant thirty-four-year-old Nguyen Cao Ky, commander of the South Vietnamese Air Force, assumed power as prime minister.[2] Ky knew that tens of thousands of North Vietnamese Army (NVA) troops had infiltrated South Vietnam through the mountainous Central Highlands. When he saw his own generals were unable to stop them, he realized his country was in danger of being cut in half at its narrow waist. Military defeat would follow, so he appealed to President Johnson for more US troops.

Johnson sent the Third Marine Division and its supporting air wing to Da Nang on the northern coast and the army's 173rd Airborne Brigade to Bien Hoa Air Base near Saigon. He also ordered the newly formed and untried First Cavalry Division (Airmobile) to pack up its fifteen thousand men, their weapons and equipment, including 437 aircraft, and go to Vietnam.

In August 1965, First Cavalry troops boarded transport ships and departed from East Coast ports, bound for South Vietnam's South China Sea port of Qui Nhon. Converted World War II aircraft carriers followed the troops, carrying most of the division's helicopters.

Simultaneous with these departures by sea, a 1,030-man First Cavalry advance party flew out of Warner Robins, Georgia. Their mission was to seize an abandoned dirt airstrip near the Song Ba River, midway between Qui Nhon and Pleiku, and clear the adjacent jungle to disperse the division's helicopters. On August 27, the first of the advance party's fifty C-130's landed on that nine-hundred-foot dirt strip and disgorged a rifle platoon.

Minutes later, a second C-130 landed. It carried jeeps with machine guns and recoilless rifles, long-range radios, operators, and the command group.

Armed with an M-16 rifle and a camera, I accompanied the command group. For the next twenty-eight days everyone from Brig. Gen. John M. Wright Jr., the assistant division commander, to me, the lowest-ranking private, spent our daylight hours clearing the dense, triple-canopy jungle that abutted the landing strip. We had machetes, shovels, axes, handsaws, and flamethrowers. Building the world's largest helicopter landing field without heavy equipment was backbreaking work.

I did not have to be there. I did not have to go to Vietnam. I had fulfilled my military obligation by serving three years and two months active duty, all of it as an infantryman, between 1959 and 1962, followed by three years in the inactive reserve. In March 1965, having realized US combat troops would soon be in Vietnam, I reenlisted as a private (three stripes being the cost of my three-year hiatus), armed with a silly and precarious plan to land a berth as a combat photographer and "see the elephant" through a camera viewfinder long and well enough to launch a career in photojournalism.

I also had deeply personal reasons for reenlisting: my parents had thirteen siblings between them. Neither they nor any of their siblings nor their siblings' spouses, who were all children of European immigrants, had fought in World War II. Only my father's youngest brother, Bill, had served in uniform, but the war ended before he finished aviator training. America had been good to my family, and I felt an obligation to contribute. At least five of my cousins felt as I did and enlisted in the army, marines, or air force.

I didn't want to miss what I knew would be the greatest adventure of my generation, and I didn't think I would live into old age anyway. None of my grandparents had lived to see fifty, and my uncles, who were approaching or barely beyond that milestone, were in poor health.

In hindsight, my thinking was very mushy.

Against all reason, I succeeded in the first part of my plan. In July 1965, Maj. (later Lt. Col.) Charles Siler, the division public information officer, plucked me from a doomed rifle platoon[3] and made me his photographer and later his press chief. Over a fifteen-month period, I accompanied elements of all nine infantry battalions into the field on combat operations. Ditto for the recon squadron, all division artillery battalions, and most of the combat support outfits as well. I worked with the cream of the international press corps. I earned air crewman's wings and a few colored ribbons. I stopped a piece of shrapnel. I saw the elephant, and I saw it through a camera lens.

Ultimately the success of my plan derailed it. It was never my idea to become the indispensable man, but by May 1966 I again wore sergeant's stripes. Six months later I was offered an appointment to infantry second lieutenant. I would not learn for another thirty years how lucky I was: the army and the marines together awarded only sixty such appointments, and most went to helicopter pilots and Special Forces noncoms.

The offer was a personal validation. Eight years earlier, as a seventeen-year-old high school senior, I had won an appointment to West Point but was four inches short of minimum height. A year later, as an eighteen-year-old specialist 4, I had competed for and won one of a hundred annual presidential military academy appointments for active-duty soldiers—but I was two inches short. In early 1962, I applied for officer candidate school, but I was an inch too short and wasn't allowed to take the entrance exam.

Accept a direct appointment? Yes, indeed. And nobody asked how tall I was.

Two years later I accepted a promotion to captain and agreed to extend my term of service indefinitely at the pleasure of the president.

The last US combat troops left Vietnam in 1973. My service under President Richard Nixon ended in August 1974, and I returned to civilian life and a precarious but stimulating career as a self-employed journalist.

US Army Lt. Col. Peter Dewey, serving with the OSS during World War II, was the first of many thousands of American fighting men to die in Vietnam. After the Japanese surrendered in August 1945, Dewey led a team gathering intelligence and searching for missing American pilots. On September 26, 1945, he was shot at a roadblock by a Viet Minh guerrilla who mistook him for a Frenchman.

Between 1964 to 1975, about 9.7 million Americans served in uniform, a little less than 10 percent of our male generation. Two-thirds of them were volunteers, and together they comprised the best-educated army our country had ever sent to war. Some 2,709,918 Americans actually served in Vietnam—on land, in its waters, or in the skies above them. More than 58,000 of these men and women were killed, a little over 2 percent of those who served in-country. Sixty-one percent of the dead were twenty-one years old or younger.[4]

About a quarter of the men and women who served were draftees, conscripted by the Selective Service System that until nearly the end of the war operated under rules favoring the affluent over the poor and whites over minorities, allowing the privileged to avoid the draft. Before 1965, many National Guard and reserve units were as much a uniformed fraternity as a component of national defense. New applicants were unofficially restricted to friends and relatives of members and former members. It's no surprise that when the first combat troops left for Vietnam, many chronically understrength guard and reserve units filled up within weeks. Nevertheless, personal, political, or business connections could still shoehorn a well-connected youth into an overstrength reserve unit. Every Major League Baseball team and many NFL teams protected their top talent by pulling political strings to get them into National Guard or reserve units, where they would be safe from the perils of combat in Vietnam. Only a handful of major league players saw the combat zone.

There were other ways to avoid the draft. While few working-class Americans of that era had a family doctor, the more affluent could sometimes persuade a personal physician to write a letter stating their son suffered from a condition that precluded military service. Some doctors coached their patients in ways to fail a draft physical; a few went so far as to prescribe medication that allowed them to present a disqualifying medical symptom.

Scholarship students and those affluent enough to afford four years of college and graduate school often escaped the draft through successive deferments. Until Congress eliminated most graduate school deferments, thousands remained enrolled until they were considered to be too old to serve or the war ended. Deferments for those studying for religious ordination remained in place throughout the war years, and many affluent men enrolled in a divinity school with no intention of serving as clergy. Every man who went on an overseas mission for the Church of Jesus Christ of Latter-Day Saints was exempted from the draft.

Three-fourths of the American troops in Vietnam were volunteers, though many had enlisted in the hope they might get better or safer duty than a draftee. In practice, the route by which a soldier entered service mattered much less than what skill sets were needed at that moment. My best friend in high school, Kenneth Dean Smith, was drafted at age twenty-five. An accomplished photographer, he was trained as a mortar gunner. In high school, Ken took a typing class and wisely reminded his superiors of this fact at every opportunity. In Vietnam, he served with distinction as an infantry company clerk.

The gulf between those whose only choices were between military service, prison, or exile to Canada or Sweden and those whose circumstances allowed them to pursue a promising civilian career path grew wider as the war wore on. A handful of those who evaded military service launched careers that in later years brought them into positions of national prominence and authority. For many who fought in Vietnam, this wound never healed.

From beginning to end, many Americans supported the war. Patriotic and fervently anti-communist Americans insisted it was a fight that had to be won. Many Catholics supported their Vietnamese coreligionists who were overrepresented in the Saigon government. But as the war went on and the draft's unfairness became more apparent, and as thousands upon thousands of men came home in caskets, many Americans turned against the war. In 1971, the *New York Times* published information from a trove of stolen classified documents that revealed long-suppressed information about the war, its origins, and its conduct. The Pentagon Papers made it plain the Johnson administration had lied early and often about the war, and the Nixon administration was no better in this regard.

On April 30, 1975, the day Saigon fell to the victorious North Vietnamese Army, David Brinkley, NBC's widely respected evening news anchor, broadcast a commentary from Arlington National Cemetery, the thousands of graves behind him calling silent attention to the terrible cost of the Vietnam War. "America did not lose this war," Brinkley said, "because we never tried to win it. Instead, we tried to help our ally, South Vietnam, until we decided not to."

Whether the Vietnam War was a colossal mistake, a noble cause, or something else, for decades the patriotism and personal sacrifice of the men and women who fought in this war were largely ignored by the American public. More than a few returning soldiers were vilified as baby killers and war criminals, including me, by no less than Norman Mailer. The wounded and broken among us were shamefully ignored by our countrymen and government. Our individual struggles to reintegrate with society were magnified by merciless media attention. For decades, a staple character in Hollywood films was the crazed Vietnam veteran. If a Vietnam veteran assaulted his wife, if another was homeless and mentally ill, if a third was arrested for a crime, then every Vietnam veteran was assumed to be dangerous, demented, or damaged in some way. The kindest labeled us as soldiers of a lost cause.

In the November 13, 2015, issue of the *New York Times*, Pulitzer Prize–winning author Neil Sheehan, who had reported from the 1965 Ia Drang valley battlefield, wrote:

INTRODUCTION

It always galls me when I hear or read of the men who fought the Second World War as "the greatest generation." On the first day of the battle [of Ia Drang], Nov. 14, [1965,] . . . C ("Charlie") Company [of the First Battalion, Seventh Cavalry, was assigned to defend] the south and southwest sides of the [battalion] perimeter. . . . None of the officers and men of the company had ever seen serious combat before. Shortly after dawn the next morning, hundreds of North Vietnamese soldiers . . . rose out of the elephant grass and rushed C Company's foxhole line, seeking to overwhelm it. When the fight was over, Charlie Company had ceased to exist. Of the approximately 100 men who had seen daybreak, fewer than 40 were not wounded. There were gaps in the foxhole line where the dead and wounded lay. But the North Vietnamese attackers never [broke] through that line in sufficient numbers to threaten the battalion position, because the men of C Company, First Battalion, Seventh Cavalry, fought and died like the young lions they were.

They, and so many others who fought in Vietnam, were as great as any generation that preceded them. Their misfortune was to draw a bad war, an unnecessary war, a mistake by American politicians and statesmen, for which they paid.[5]

If Vietnam *was* a lost cause and "a bad" and "unnecessary war," that was hardly the fault of those who left homes and loved ones behind to fight for objectives that a lawfully elected government chose to pursue. Nevertheless, the false and misleading generalization persists that Vietnam veterans are a legion of broken soldiers, sailors, and marines, a lost generation, warped and wounded by wartime experiences and rejected by the greater society.

Only now, some fifty-five years after the first of our fighting men went off to that war, is it possible to see the real accomplishments of America's Vietnam generation. Like our parents, the so-called Greatest Generation, our efforts have transformed America in myriad ways: America is immeasurably richer, fairer, and better because of the Vietnam generation's contributions.

In the following pages, you will meet some Vietnam veterans, men and women who sacrificed for their country, who returned to a nation that turned its backs on them, and who nevertheless went on with their lives, made further sacrifices and important contributions to their families, to their communities, and to the commonweal. We are living proof that the Vietnam generation is every bit as worthy of respect and admiration as the generations that preceded us.

Marvin J. Wolf
Asheville, North Carolina
April 2019

PART ONE

ARTISTS AND
PROFESSIONALS

CLOVIS JONES

The Vietnam War spawned thousands of pilots, many of whom left their service and went on to fly commercial aircraft. Unlike soldiers in the air force, navy, and marines who were mostly trained to fly fixed-wing aircraft, most army pilots flew helicopters. Few army combat soldiers became aviators. Clovis Jones was likely the most notable exception. He first served a combat tour as an enlisted infantryman and then flew helicopter gunships. He went on to become one of the most unusual and accomplished pilots in American civil aviation.

Clovis Jones was born in Dawson, Georgia, in 1945. From his earliest years, he wanted to be a pilot, to soar through the air. During his last year of high school, he went to see an army recruiter.

"I wanted to enlist in the high school to flight school program," he recalled. "I'm a young black kid from Georgia, thinking, *Hey, I'm going to flight school*. I passed every test. I didn't realize these particular recruiters didn't get credit for recruiting aviators; those were inducted through other recruiting stations. I think he put 'Airborne Infantry' on my contract to fool me."

Jones finished basic training and advanced infantry training. He went on to jump school and earned the silver wings of a paratrooper. He thought he was going to flight school until he went to the 101st Airborne Division at Fort Campbell, Kentucky, where he was assigned to a rifle squad. Then his "good test scores and good attitude" caught the attention of Command Sgt. Maj. Herbert P. McCullah, who wanted him to be a clerk, pushing him further from his goal. Jones recalled, "I didn't want to sit behind a typewriter." Nevertheless, Jones was sent to take clerk-typist classes at night, after his normal duty day, and then became a clerk at headquarters.

More than a year later he was transferred to the Eleventh Air Assault Division, which later became the First Cavalry Division (Airmobile). Jones was assigned to Charlie Company, First Battalion, Eighth Cavalry (C/1/8) where he was designated his squad's point man—the soldier who leads his squad or patrol through dense foliage as they seek to make enemy contact. It was a job more dangerous than most and one that suited Jones well.

By coincidence, McCullah continued as the battalion command sergeant major as he transferred from the 101st to the First Cavalry, and when that division deployed to Vietnam, tensions rose over the battalion mail clerk's stingy hours. When men who had been in the field for weeks returned to base camp, they hoped to find mail from home. "Even before a shower, clean clothes, something to eat, and sleep, they wanted their mail," Jones explained. The clerk, however, refused to deliver mail if it was after 1700; he insisted they wait until the next morning at 0800. Jones remembered, "The troops locked and loaded. They would happily have killed him."

The next day McCullah solved the issue by designating Jones as the battalion "field" mail clerk. Again Jones objected. He wanted to stay with his buddies as the squad's point man. McCullah, however, had the final say. From that day forward, whenever the battalion was in the field, Jones would drive the day's mail, along with any official correspondence, from the base camp to the battalion's forward command post (CP), where it would be distributed to the respective companies. If it was too far or too dangerous to drive, Jones hopped a Huey and was flown to the battalion CP. From there, he went to each company and distributed the mail, bringing comfort from home to the men.

Jones had other duties as well. "On November 12, 1965, I drove one of our S-2 sergeants to the Catecha Tea Plantation House to speak with the French manager. The manager confirmed the previous evening a battalion of North Vietnamese Army (NVA) troops had moved through the plantation on their way to Ia Drang.

"Patrols from the 1/8 reported that the NVA moving through the plantation had Chinese and Cuban advisors," Jones said. "As NVA intentions were unknown, the 1/8 went on full alert." The next morning, the 1/8 was pulled out of Ia Drang and ordered to their base camp at An Khe where they stayed for two days. Then, on November 15, they were redeployed to Plei Me, not far from Ia Drang, where the fighting raged.

One of Jones's friends was hit, an experience that changed him forever. Jones said, "He took a bullet in his left temple. It was protruding from his right temple. I knelt and tried to pull the bullet out of his head to bring him back to life. When I realized what I was doing, it seemed as if I had been cut from my left shoulder down to my right ankle. A part of me wanted to mourn my friend. The other part said, 'You've got a job to do.' That was one of the pivotal moments in my life. A change came over me. It was the realization that when it's time for fun, let's have fun. When it is time to work, let's get the job done. In a word, I matured."

Jones had the sad duty of identifying the remains of other men killed in action. He was almost the only man in the battalion who knew every soldier's name and face, and the casualties he witnessed took a toll on him. "To quote a line from a movie about Ray Charles, 'This much killing just ain't natural,'" he said.

Later, during the Ia Drang battle, Jones flew from the Plei Me Special Forces Camp to the base camp at An Khe. His pilot was Capt. Ed "Too Tall to Fly" Freeman, who some forty-four years later was awarded the Medal of Honor for his repeated flights into LZ X-Ray during the heaviest fighting there, bringing in vital ammunition and taking out the wounded. Jones and Freeman's flight to An Khe included a short stop at X-Ray.

"I told him that I wanted to be a pilot—I told *everybody* that I wanted to be a pilot," Jones recalled. "Freeman encouraged me. He put me in the copilot's seat and asked if I knew how to fly a helicopter. All the way from X-Ray to An Khe, he told me how much he respected infantrymen. He said, 'We will bring you support, even if we have to bring it to you at grass-top level. I know you are going to do the same thing when you become a pilot.'

"That was very encouraging," Jones said. "I had repeatedly applied for flight school and heard nothing at all. Of course, many people thought I was a little deranged, so hearing that from Ed Freeman was encouraging."

In June 1966, Jones was honorably discharged and felt frustrated with the army. "For almost three years, I tried to go to flight school and nobody listened to me," he said. He returned to his home in Georgia, but that didn't work either. "I didn't fit in back there. I couldn't relate to anybody. Then I heard from Jim Hutchison, my foxhole buddy, who lived in Chicago. He invited me to come to Chicago.

"He was press secretary for a gentleman running for Congress against Bill Dawson, the incumbent, a black congressman from Chicago's South Side. I worked with my friend during the summer of 1966," he said.

He also reconnected with Martin Luther King Jr., whom he had met during the Albany movement, a desegregation and voter's rights coalition formed in Albany, Georgia, in November 1961. While in high school, he had been one of the students to attend and speak at the mass meetings in Albany. Then, after joining with King's Chicago Freedom movement, which brought his civil rights movement from the South to northern cities, Jones and some Vietnam buddies led King's march to city hall in August 1966.

A man of valor, Jones believed in the dignity of every person, no matter where they were. He went to Soldier Field to watch a game with some friends who had also served in Vietnam. They were sitting toward the top of the stadium, he said, "with no one behind us and a good field of vision. We were laughing and joking, acting like the silly twenty-year-olds we were, and a college kid overheard us reminiscing about Vietnam.

"He said, 'You guys were soldiers in Vietnam? You're baby killers.'"

Jones recalled, "He spat on me." Then Jones picked him up over his head and climbed toward the top of Soldier Field "to throw him off. But my buddies grabbed both of us and pulled us down. From that day forward, I avoided crowds unless I was *required* to go to any arena for some important reason. I avoided busy sidewalks and street corners. If I had to catch a bus, I never stood on the corner but a short distance away," he said, describing the precautions he took to keep himself in check.

During his time in Chicago, Jones continued to help with the civil rights movement. He attended meetings between King and other civil rights leaders held at a doctor's house. "I got a chance to meet many of the civil rights leaders who had been in Albany. It turned out that the minister of my church in Dawson was a classmate of Dr. King at Morehouse College. I asked Dr. Benjamin Mays for a premed scholarship at Morehouse, and after I made application, it was granted."

Jones left Chicago and went to Atlanta, where he enrolled in Morehouse. "Toward the end of my first semester, I got a call from the army aviation department. They wanted to know if I was still interested in flight school," Jones said. Surprised by the question, Jones learned he had been accepted the previous year, but, he explained, "The First Cavalry wouldn't let anybody out for a school, so I was never informed. If I still wanted to go to flight school, I had to reenlist." Jones called Commnad Sgt. Maj. McCullah for advice, who told him to reenlist for Fort Campbell, Kentucky, and he would make sure Jones actually went to flight school.

"I finished my semester, took another flight physical, and then reenlisted for Fort Campbell," Jones recalled. McCullah was as good as his word. By May 1967, Jones was at Fort Wolters, Texas, for basic helicopter training. Then he went to Fort Rucker, Alabama, for advanced training and learned to fly Hueys.

"I expected to go directly to Vietnam," Jones recalled. "Instead, I was assigned to Fort Sill, Oklahoma, and transitioned into the Cobra."

Comparatively speaking, if the Huey is your mother's station wagon, the Cobra is a Corvette with teeth and claws. "We had two pods of 7.62mm miniguns, each firing up to 4,000 rounds per minute, and four pods of nineteen 2.75-inch folding-fin rockets with high explosive warheads. In the nose was an automatic grenade launcher, firing up to 225 40mm grenades a minute," Jones recalled.

Jones was among the first members of Alpha Battery, Fourth Battalion, Seventy-Seventh Aerial Rocket Artillery, which was activated on September 1, 1968. When the battalion joined the 101st Airborne (Airmobile), Jones flew the older, slower, and less lethal UH-1C gunship for a few months until the new Cobras were delivered. "I took a three-week refresher course at Qui Nhon, where I became an instructor pilot on the Cobra," Jones recalled.

One afternoon while giving an in-country orientation and a check ride to a new pilot, Jones's Cobra suddenly handled oddly. "We were down to about five hundred feet above ground level, and then on one of the turnarounds, the nose tipped forward," he recalled. "I took the controls to see if there were any vibrations, any unusual feeling. There were none, but shortly afterward, when we returned to Camp Eagle and our skids were maybe twenty feet off the ground, the ninety-degree gearbox and the tail rotor left the aircraft.

"We immediately went into a spin. The Cobra's nose went from nose up to nose down, and I was looking at the ground. It spun to the left as if it wanted to roll on its back. For the next ten seconds I thought I was dead three times," Jones recalled. "It was pure instinct, plus what I learned the last day of flight training at Fort Wolters, that enabled me to get that bird safely on the ground."

Jones's first primary flight instructor had told him African Americans didn't make very good pilots. His next instructor, Dick Strauss, however, showed him things the helicopter could do that were not in the instruction manual. He told Jones, "It may come in handy one day." It came in handy *that* day.

Throughout his second year in the war zone, Jones did much more than fly. "I was the section commander," he recalled. "I was an instructor pilot, the safety officer, and assistant operations officer, all as a W1, and then as a W2." Ten days before Chief Warrant Officer 2 Jones went home, his superb leadership skills were recognized with a direct appointment to second lieutenant, field artillery.

From Vietnam, he went to the artillery officer basic course and then to Fort Rucker as an instructor at the Warrant Officer Career College. After completing his service commitment, Jones left active duty but retained his reserve commission. He recalled, "I joined the Georgia National Guard and, after fixed-wing transition training, I flew an OV-1 Mohawk in the 159th Military Intelligence Company."

Because he was rated for both helicopters and fixed-wing aircraft, in 1975 Jones found his first civilian flying job with the Flight Test Department at Hughes Helicopters, working on the Apache program. Then Howard Hughes died and much of the Apache program was put on hold. "When my pay stopped, I went back to Morehouse for a year of premed. I believed I could be a good doctor," he said.

But his passion was flying. Jones left school again and took a job piloting the Falcon 10 and Gulfstream 1 for Xerox Corporation. In 1978, he found a job flying passenger jets for Western Airlines, now part of Delta. "I started on a 737. My job was to sit on the jump seat, make announcements, and do the preflight," he said. It was a role that was an insult to a man with Jones's experience. After about three months, though, he was promoted to second officer, and then to flight engineer. In 1980, he was furloughed. Jones found a better job flying for Air California, based at John Wayne Airport in Newport Beach, California.

At the end of 1983, he was offered a job at FedEx. He started there in January 1984 and remained with the company, flying MD-10 and MD-11 cargo jets all over the world for almost twenty-two years.

In 1998, concerned there were so few African American airline pilots, he helped found a group now known as the Organization of Black Aerospace Professionals and served as its first president. "I had to raise a lot of money for the organization," he recalled. "We worked with the airlines, and we now have about three thousand black airline pilots."

While he was with FedEx, Jones bought a house in Scottsdale, Arizona. The day he retired, he had knee surgery, which led to a series of medical crises. "It took six years to recover because, during surgery in a civilian hospital, I contracted four strains of salmonella plus Lyme disease. It took years of effort before my doctors figured it out and put me on the road to recovery."

When Jones was finally back in good health, he suffered two more setbacks in rapid succession. "I was rear-ended by a tractor-trailer truck," he recalled. "I recovered from that and then was rear-ended by a drunk driver." Five years of surgery and rehab followed.

Most men—even most pilots—who reach age seventy and have suffered the pain and frustration of recovering from multiple surgeries slip into quiet retirement and are content with their memories. Not Clovis Jones. Near the end of 2017, he passed a Federal Aviation Administration flight physical. "I have been passionate about flying since I was four years old," he explained. "I wasn't ready to give it up."

His new job is flying for JetSuite, a short-hop airline serving smaller airports in the Pacific and Southwest regions.

Today, septuagenarian Clovis Jones, combat infantryman, attack helicopter pilot, airline captain, and instructor pilot, shows no sign of heading for the hangar.

DON
RAY

Long before medicine and science were able to recognize and diagnose the physical and mental conditions collectively called learning disabilities, people struggled with them, often frustratingly unaware their difficulties were the result of something they were not responsible for and couldn't fix on their own. Many gave up, condemning themselves to stigma and a second-class life. Others applied their remaining powers to invent work-arounds. In no profession is this more difficult than the military.

The son of two Lockheed employees, Don Ray was born in Hollywood and grew up in the eastern parts of the San Fernando Valley, the huge, football-shaped valley that is mostly the northern half of the city of Los Angeles. Both his father and later his stepfather physically abused Don and his siblings. By the time Don started high school, he exhibited the symptoms of what is now called post-traumatic stress disorder. He was also moderately dyslexic.

Despite his reading disorder, Don made his way through high school by devising strategies that hid his problem from teachers. To create a science report, he would copy text from an encyclopedia and then rewrite it. For a bibliography, he gambled the teacher wouldn't check the book titles and authors he invented. He made it to graduation and immediately enlisted. After basic training at Fort Ord, California, he went through MP training at Fort Gordon, Georgia. Then he was sent to Okinawa for training with a canine partner, Fritz.

"We met our dogs, all German shepherds, on Okinawa. Then, after six weeks of training together, we all went to Vietnam," Ray recalled.

He was sent to Soc Trang, deep in the Mekong delta, where he volunteered with the Soc Trang Civic Action Group to teach English. "In our free time, we helped rebuild schools and orphanages," he said. At night, Ray and Fritz were tasked with patrolling the airfield perimeter. Within two months, many of the dog handlers who were old-timers went home, and Ray became the ranking dog handler in the detachment. "Then the sergeant in charge of our unit and our veterinarian technician were both arrested for black marketing," Ray explained. And he suddenly found himself in the role of the detachment's acting veterinarian technician.

The nearest qualified veterinarian technician was a helicopter ride away in Dong Tam. Ray wrote to friends at home and asked them to send books on the care of dogs. "I used an old encyclopedia and those books to try and learn anything about canine health issues. Just before I became the acting vet tech, one of our dogs got sick. His nose started bleeding, and he was sent to the veterinary hospital at Tan Son Nhut Air Base in Saigon. That was when I learned there was a disease going around that affected only American dogs. They called it idiopathic hemorrhagic syndrome, or nosebleed disease. No one knew what caused it."

Before a cure was found, this disease took the lives of some 250 army dogs. One night, another of Ray's dogs began to bleed. "Our dogs had priority over soldiers when it came to an emergency medevac," he explained. "I demanded the medevac take me and this dog to Saigon."

For some reason, the pilot said he could take them only as far as Dong Tam. Ray awakened the duty officer there and asked for a helicopter to take his dog to Saigon. When the duty officer declined, Ray demanded that the commanding officer be awakened. "He ordered two pilots to fly us to Saigon in a gunship."

By the time the gunship landed at Tan Son Nhut's hospital, the dog had stopped breathing. "This was the hospital that treated people, and it caused a stir. Everyone came to see my dog. I had my books, and I ran through the encyclopedia to see how to give artificial respiration to a dog," he continued. This involved lifting the dog's leg while pushing on its chest. But first, Ray had to cut the gauze tied around the dog's legs to prevent him from jumping off the helicopter. Ray called out for help. "A nurse pushed her way through the crowd and asked what she could do." He told her to cut off the leg restraints. When the dog's legs were free, "I pushed on his chest and the nurse lifted his leg—and suddenly the dog was breathing again," Ray recalled. Veterinarian clinic doctors sent a Jeep to fetch the dog. "I never got to thank that nurse or find out who she was," Ray recalled, still grateful for her help.

During his brief stay at the hospital, Ray saw the full effects of this ailment and vowed to do something about it. The dog he brought to Saigon, however, died of the disease as well.

Ray had made it through high school with a mixture of hard work and cunning ideas to hide his limited reading skills. Now he took it upon himself to find a way to save not only his beloved Fritz but every American dog in Vietnam.

Back in the delta, at Can Tho, he met with a veterinarian who explained the first symptom of this disease was inflammation of the nose, but by then it was too late to save the dog, because they had not yet identified the particular virus or bacterium that caused the disease. A dog could be saved only if the disease was discovered before the symptoms appeared. That meant taking blood from the dogs every week to measure the ratio of red blood cells to the total volume of blood, the hematocrit. Soc Trang had no veterinary facility, but Ray asked the doctor to teach him how to take the dogs' blood.

"The next day I took blood from a dog and went to a dispensary at the airfield where technicians could test it," Ray recalled. He asked a technician to give him a red blood cell count and a hematocrit for the blood he had drawn.

When the technicians examined the sample, they realized it wasn't human blood and refused to test it. Ray asked them to teach him how to examine the blood and determine the hematocrit for each sample. "I told them I had twelve dogs and needed to get their individual hematocrits every week."

One of the technicians said, "What do *we* get out of this?"

They struck a bargain. The technicians were required to give weekly blood samples that could be compared with other blood cultures. If Ray would give his own blood every week, they would teach him how to determine hematocrits and allow him to use the lab to work up his dogs' blood. Ray agreed.

He began by charting each dog's hematocrit. After three or four weeks he noticed one of the dog's white cell count had dipped, so he sent it to Tan Son Nhut Air Base.

When Ray was transferred to Vung Tau, a seaside community where American soldiers took in-country R & R, he was assigned a new dog, Ralph, and returned to patrolling the perimeter of the local ammunition dump. In February 1969, the enemy launched a second Tet Offensive, and Vung Tau was hit with dozens of rockets and mortar rounds. Ray and Ralph survived.

Shortly afterward, the dog handlers were ordered to clean their dogs' teeth, a complicated and sensitive procedure that few handlers knew how to do. But Ray knew. One of his peers asked where he had learned to do it, and he explained he had been a vet tech at Soc Trang.

"Then you're the one whose dog survived," said another MP. "The dog you sent was the first dog ever to survive nosebleed disease."

Because Ray had detected the decrease in white blood cells before the symptoms had started, the dog had survived, and Ray's work gave other doctors the opportunity to isolate the offending bacterium and develop a vaccine to protect the dogs from infection. The cure was tetracycline, a broad-spectrum antibiotic often used to cure human infections.

In his own offbeat, dogged way, Don Ray opened the door to saving thousands of valuable dogs. He said, "There are many people who hold a pipe in their hand and say, 'Ah, I'm not sure that's such a good idea,' but many Vietnam veterans just solve the problem and don't wait for the pipe smokers. So I solved that problem myself."

Although he didn't pursue a medical career, Ray's experience in Vietnam became the foundation for his lifelong interest in research. When he was honorably discharged in 1972, he had his heart set on becoming a veterinarian. It was not to be. The preveterinary classes he needed to take at Pierce College in Los Angeles were full.

Still, it was during this period Ray learned his reading problem had a name. "I had scotopic sensitivity syndrome, and that prevented me from being able to read for more than five or ten minutes without my eyes watering and the words jumping all over the page," he recalled. He was also diagnosed with attention deficit hyperactivity disorder. "I wasn't the hyperactive kind," he explained. "I was just disorganized."

Rising to the challenge, Ray remembered an eleventh-grade experience. As part of a journalism class, he was on the staff of the school newspaper. One day he learned the teacher had assigned the students to write an editorial. He hadn't brought any research materials, had done no reading, and knew he would flunk the class if he didn't turn in some kind of editorial.

"I had taken notes and paid attention in class. I knew all the elements of an editorial, but I didn't have a topic," Ray recalled. "I looked up at the clock. Next to it was the American flag, which I already knew had forty-eight stars. But this was 1966. Alaska and Hawaii had joined the union years earlier.

"So I wrote an editorial noting that we daily pledged allegiance to the flag of the United States of America," Ray continued. "But every day thousands of Burbank students pledged the allegiance to a flag that is not the flag of the United States, because that flag has fifty stars and ours had only forty-eight."

Outraged parents called the board of education and were told that, no, the flags were all fifty stars. The teacher/publisher of the paper demanded to know how Ray had researched his editorial. He said he had counted the stars on all the flags in all his classes. The editor sent people to every school in the district; none found a fifty-star flag.

The fifty-star flags were eventually found in a district warehouse.

Ray got an A in the class.

That memory prompted him to enroll at California State University, Northridge, where he studied journalism. When he graduated, he accepted a job as an administrator with the US Postal Inspection Service. He didn't much care for the work, but in his spare time, he began working on recovering the history of the 1928 St. Francis Dam flood, California's second-worst disaster after the San Francisco earthquake of 1906.

The *Los Angeles Times* published a lengthy account of the disaster, including the following facts. Built under the direction of William Mulholland, the thirteen-hundred-foot-long concrete dam held a reservoir of some twelve billion gallons of water. At midnight on March 12, 1928, the dam burst, sending a ten-story-high wall of water toward the Pacific Ocean. Several towns, dozens of ranches, an Edison construction camp, an Indian reservation and trading post, and an enormous electrical powerhouse were flooded. Twelve hundred houses were demolished and ten bridges were destroyed.

No one knows how many died. In August 1928, the official toll was 385, but the remains of victims continued to be found; though many victims were swept out to sea, so far their remains have not been recovered. Some were washed ashore as far south as Mexico. The remains of those lost turned up along the California coast into the 1990s.

Among those assumed to have perished was the wife of the dam keeper, Tony Harnischfeger. As part of the volunteer project to recover the lost history of this disaster, Ray went looking for the former Mrs. Harnischfeger. He learned she had died, but he found some of her relatives, which led him to a few survivors.

The volunteer project then planned a fiftieth anniversary banquet for the handful of survivors. The event received national publicity and 175 people showed up.

"We realized each of these survivors had an incredible story of their survival fifty years earlier—an unknown and unsuspected history. And we decided we needed to record their accounts," Ray said.

This and other discoveries Ray made for the project led to a job at the NBC station in Los Angeles, the start of a long career in journalism. Ray became widely known as the go-to guy to teach anyone how to mine data from the public records.

As part of a Channel 4 investigative team, Ray scored many scoops, the first of which involved Jim Jones, the charismatic cult leader of the 1978 Jonestown massacre in which 909 followers died, all but two from cyanide poisoning. While researching the event shortly after it happened, Ray discovered that Jones had been previously arrested for lewd conduct, but the case had never gone to trial, and the records had been sealed. He realized that if this arrest had been public knowledge, Jones might never have been able to take his followers out of the country, and their lives might have been saved.

Over the next decades, Ray uncovered other scoops while working at a variety of TV stations, including:

- a 1993 accusation of child abuse by entertainer Michael Jackson;
- a price-fixing conspiracy by America's largest oil refiners;
- an unreported partial meltdown and release of radioactive gas by a Southern California nuclear reactor in 1959;
- a music teacher who led a group that staged fraudulent auto accidents to collect insurance money;
- a legal error that allowed attorneys to unseal boxes of documents related to the infamous Skid Row Stabber, revealing a possible second suspect;
- a scheme whereby President Ronald Reagan's friends bought an expensive home in elite Bel Air and, through an elaborate sequence of events, transferred ownership to Reagan in such a way that he paid nothing for a house valued at more than $3 million[1];
- a prominent man who for years falsely claimed to have flown in combat over North Korea during the war.

For some forty years, Ray trained law enforcement officials, paralegals, reporters, and private investigators from coast to coast in the intricacies of searching every sort of public record to find facts relevant to civil and criminal cases and to investigations of every sort. Long before it became easy and fashionable, he self-published *A Public Records Primer and Investigator's Handbook*, a book on accessing public records. Even today there's a copy of this book on the desk of every reporter in Southern California.

Today, he's still dedicated to preserving important records. He created the nonprofit The Endangered History Project Inc., which preserves "almost anything of possible historical value, including old films, old recordings, old photos, manuscripts, letters, World War II letters, and so forth," he explained.

He's now working on a book about finding lost relatives by researching public records.

JAMES CACCAVO

Among humanity's unsung heroes are those who are quick to recognize someone else's problem and who need no prompting to render aid in any form. Lesser men wait to be asked, but a very few require no such prompting. Capable, endlessly inventive, curious to a fault, they dive into the deep end and do whatever is needed. And they do so time and time again.

A slim, fair, compact man who favors a pencil mustache, Jim Caccavo is in many ways an ordinary American. More accurately, he's a regular guy who does extraordinary things the way most of us tackle the humdrum tasks of our daily routine.

But let's start at the beginning.

Jim's dad, Edward, spent a long career in the US Air Force, rising to the rank of master sergeant. Like most military families, Jim's lived here and there and there and then here again. He spent his juvenile years in the Philippines, suburban Maryland, rural Massachusetts, Dayton (Ohio), and Winter Park (Florida), among other places.

In 1962, during his junior year at Winter Park High School, he took art classes (he had drawn and sketched since childhood) and wrote a play titled *Only a Visitor*, which was similar to ABC's sitcom *Mork & Mindy*. The play was produced by the drama class and caught the attention of the chairman of the theater arts department at nearby Rollins College. "He recommended me for a playwriting scholarship," Caccavo said.

After graduating high school in 1963, though, Caccavo enlisted in the army. He wanted to fulfill his military service obligation and earn GI benefits that would allow him to finish college and eventually go on to a career in writing.

After basic training, Caccavo went to Fort Jackson, South Carolina, for personnel administration training. His next assignment was to an element of the First Cavalry Division, which was then in South Korea. The Second Battalion, Eighth Cavalry, was stationed north of the Imjin River very close to the demilitarized zone. This was a time when North Korean infiltrators and saboteurs roamed the area during an undeclared, low-intensity war. Caccavo's unit was in one of the US Army's most perilous locations. Despite his training and job title as a clerk, Caccavo sometimes found himself on recon patrols in this hazardous region.

In his spare time, Caccavo wrote plays and made drawings of his surroundings. He also bought a cheap 35mm camera and learned to use it. He gave some of his plays to a civilian Special Services official, who drafted him to play a part in a touring drama company performing *Stalag 17* for GIs across South Korea. The travel was a revelation. All he'd seen of the country was the gritty military area north of the Imjin. Now he saw almost the whole country.

When he met a member of the First Cavalry Division's public information office who worked on the newspaper, Caccavo told him he could draw and paint. "He suggested I see his boss," Caccavo recalled.

In short order, Caccavo was transferred to the newspaper staff, and soon afterward began taking photos for the publication.

Some of his work appeared in the Pacific edition of *Stars and Stripes*. When he finished his thirteen-month tour, Caccavo was assigned as a clerk to the Thirty-Eighth Transportation Battalion in Worms, West Germany. "I was only a PFC, but when I showed my clips and a portfolio to the sergeant major, I became the de facto battalion public information officer." He made his own schedule, and to the delight of his commanding officer, much of his work, especially his photo stories, appeared in the pages of Europe's *Stars and Stripes*.

"I had virtually an entire transportation battalion at my disposal. I was doing all kinds of things and learning more and more as I went along," he recalled. One of his photos won a top award in the National Press Photographers 1965 Pictures of the Year competition.

Caccavo took his discharge in Germany and spent a year working for *Overseas Weekly*, a tabloid that covered both the US military and American civilians living abroad. In his spare time, he enrolled in an art school and decided that when he got back to the States he'd enroll in the ArtCenter College of Design (a world-class institution in Pasadena, California) and then pursue a career in art.

On his way to the West Coast, Caccavo spent a couple of weeks in New York, rounding up photo assignments in South Korea from the United Nations and the American Korean Foundation. En route to Seoul, he stopped in Tokyo and visited the Associated Press office, where journalists shared contacts in Korea and South Vietnam with him.

In Seoul, on his UN assignment, Caccavo met Sung-Hee, who was working for the UN Housing Corporation. Within a few years, they married.

Caccavo was having so much fun, making money and learning so much, he elected to postpone his enrollment in the Pasadena school. He accepted a yearlong assignment from the American Red Cross to document its humanitarian work in South Vietnam. During what became almost two years in the country, he was periodically loaned out to the Red Cross of other nations. He worked for the French, German, Australian, New Zealand, and even the Vietnamese Red Cross.

While on assignment in Vietnam, he was wounded and received the Purple Heart from the American Red Cross. Shortly after, he returned to California, where his family then lived.

While visiting Pasadena, Caccavo met Charlie Potts, the head of ArtCenter's photography department. All Caccavo knew about Charlie was that he was a World War II navy veteran who had photographed the surrender of the Japanese on the battleship *Missouri*. Afterward, he had gone on to a successful career as a commercial photographer. In his last decades, Potts turned ArtCenter's photo department into the nation's premier school for professional photographers. Under his tutelage, a generation emerged who documented the civil rights movement, created the images used by Madison

Avenue agencies to sell every sort of product and service, and served architects, engineers, and scientists no less than newspapers and magazines.

Of the hundreds of students Potts taught, few became closer to him than Caccavo. After graduation, during a short, successful stint at the *Los Angeles Times*, while handling freelance work for *Newsweek*, Time Life, and a dozen other publications, Caccavo made time to teach one day a week at ArtCenter.

When Potts planned to retire in 1984, Caccavo built a scale model of the USS *Missouri*, the battleship on which Potts had served and where Japan had signed the unconditional surrender documents ending World War II. He displayed it at Potts's retirement party and included battery-powered lighting on the bridge and other locations. Mysteriously, two years later, at the hour of the day when Potts lost a long battle with cancer, those lights ceased to work.

Caccavo knew that Potts wanted to be buried at sea, and he knew the USS *Missouri* had been upgraded and returned to active service in 1984. Its home port was nearby Long Beach, California. So Caccavo wrote the *Missouri's* captain and the US Navy's Office of Information, where he found people who had known Lt. Comdr. Charles Potts, USNR (Ret.), better than he had. During World War II, Potts had been the navy's premier photographer in the Pacific. His still photos and motion pictures were featured in *Victory at Sea*, a twenty-six-part documentary first broadcast on NBC in 1952 and 1953.

The navy readily agreed to facilitate Charlie Potts's burial at sea from the deck of the *Missouri*. On July 4, 1987, a burial detail of 110 sailors in dress whites filled the battleship's fantail, the very deck boards where the surrender documents of World War II had been signed. As the mighty ship rode the ocean swells fifteen miles northwest of Catalina Island, the remains of Lt. Comdr. Potts and five other World War II navy veterans went into the sea. Caccavo documented it all for *Time* magazine.

Before any of the remains were released to the sea, the ship's senior chaplain, Comdr. Victor Smith, prayed, "Unto almighty God, we commit his body to the deep in the sure and certain hope of his resurrection unto eternal life."

Caccavo said, "I didn't look when the urn went over the side." He closed his eyes, remembering all his conversations with Charlie. "The pain and despair he went through during World War II. The meaning of the service. There was a feeling of mourning but also of joy that this man was, at last, receiving the honor due him for what he had given so many during his lifetime. At that moment, I felt all the pain and anguish he had carried in his soul since World War II was released."

———◇———

A few years after Caccavo graduated from ArtCenter, he and Sung-Hee bought a house near Fairfax Avenue and First Street in Hollywood. One of their favorite places to eat is a nearby Thai restaurant called Chao Krung, owned by Thai immigrants Supa and Boon Kuntee. The food was excellent, but the drab dining area, while spotless, lacked the sort of character most successful dining establishments boasted. Chao Krung was barely profitable.

In 1991, the televised beating of black motorist Rodney King by several white Los Angeles policemen led to rioting in a mostly African American section of Los Angeles. When these officers were found not guilty by an all-white jury, the city exploded again. Hundreds of businesses were burned or looted. Among them was the Kuntees' other enterprise, a modestly successful shoe store. Lacking insurance, the family transferred ownership of Chao Krung to their daughter and filed for bankruptcy.

Caccavo's studies at ArtCenter had included interior design, so he decided to lend that expertise to redecorating the restaurant. He selected new carpeting, gold wallpaper, and wood paneling. He suspended his photography career for a month while he painted the walls with original murals of a Bangkok evening. Applying paint that glowed under black light, he worked at night and slept by day. The result was a stunning and totally original interior that presented a nighttime illusion that the restaurant overlooked the Chao Phraya River that runs through Bangkok.

In the hostess area, Caccavo built a semblance of joined roof corners that is typical of Buddhist temples. Scattered atop the shingles of one roof are dozens of gold leaves. Each bears the name of a journalist killed in Vietnam—Americans, South Vietnamese, Japanese, British, Australian—men and women from every country who died while covering the war.

On the facing roof are more leaves, painted black with gold letters. These represent the North Vietnamese journalists who died while documenting the war. A gilded statue of the Buddha, a beat-up typewriter, a battered camera, and a notebook were added to the area where the roofs met. In 1996, monks from a Buddhist temple came to chant prayers, light incense, and dance to consecrate the restaurant as a shrine to Buddha.

News reports of this unique restaurant circulated worldwide. For many years Southern California–based reporters, photographers, and other newsies who had covered the Vietnam War met frequently at Chao Krung for casual get-togethers, to greet visiting colleagues, or to celebrate special occasions. Chao Krung prospered as never before.

The only compensation Caccavo accepted for his efforts on behalf of a bankrupt immigrant family was a modest discount on his meals. "I helped them because I could and because it was the right thing to do," he explained.

———◇———

While Caccavo was working for the Red Cross in Vietnam, a friendly military intelligence officer gave him a few diaries collected from battlefields, the work of North Vietnamese soldiers. They no longer had intelligence value, but to Caccavo these small, bound booklets were priceless. "I was mesmerized by their delicate calligraphy and watercolors of flowers," he recalled. "Who were the writers? What were they like? How did they die? What were the messages written in them?"

One diary contained small photographs of a group of Vietnamese, among them a beautiful young woman. "I couldn't help but wonder about their fates," Caccavo said. "As I looked at the photos, I could sense the presence of these individuals as if they were coming in from the other side and thanking me for saving their memories. Charlie Potts once referred to enemy journals as 'the souls of men' and suggested I should someday return them to their families."

When the war ended in 1975, Caccavo had lost thirteen friends, including several Vietnamese. The flood of Vietnamese refugees that followed the war included several old friends, and he spent time and money helping them settle into new homes in Southern California. "They were all grateful for my help, but when I asked them to translate the diaries of enemy soldiers, all politely refused," he recalled.

Eventually he found a Vietnamese woman to translate two of the diaries. One had belonged to Tran Ke Dat; the other was the property of Hoang Le Sao. The latter had written the addresses and the names of his wife and mother on the back of the diary with a request to return it to them in Cao Bang, a province north of Hanoi. "I decided someday I would do just that," Caccavo recalled.

The translations revealed these were not diaries but notebooks where friends and loved ones wrote poetry and remembrances for one another. One poem in Hoang's notebook described a young woman being comforted by the diary's author as she confides to him the loss of her family.

In 1996, Caccavo was notified by the Red Cross that they had found Hoang's family in Cao Bang—and Hoang Le Sao was very much alive!

Jim Caccavo bought a plane ticket to Hanoi, where the Vietnamese Red Cross took him to meet a thin, bespectacled man in his fifties, clad in a military uniform without rank or insignia. Their meeting was documented by Vietnamese television; Caccavo's gallantry in finding and returning the notebook was noted as an act of deep friendship.

The camera also caught Hoang turning away, his eyes filled with tears and so overcome with emotion he couldn't speak. Caccavo experienced almost identical feelings of joy mixed with the melancholy thoughts of Hoang's wartime suffering.

When both could speak, Hoang invited Caccavo to visit his home in Cao Bang, and then, unprompted, made an emotional appeal to his countrymen to assist Americans in recovering the remains of missing servicemen.

In their subsequent meetings, Hoang explained he had served as a lieutenant in the 761st Regiment and had been wounded three times. By an amazing coincidence, Hoang recalled he had been in the Cu Chi area on the night Caccavo was wounded there by shrapnel from a 122mm rocket.

Mustered out in 1976, Hoang had since worked in construction and farming to support his wife and three daughters. The war had left him with sometimes painful wounds, and it was obvious to Caccavo that he also suffered from symptoms associated with PTSD: flashbacks and nightmares, especially about the horrifying times he had spent cowering in the earth while hundreds of bombs dropped by American B-52's exploded all around him. "It was like the world coming to an end," Hoang said.

Hoang and Caccavo have remained friends over the decades since their first meeting, and Caccavo has returned to Vietnam several times and made the long overland journey to Hoang's home in Vietnam's far north. They also correspond via the Red Cross email system.

JAN
SCRUGGS

It is often the most ordinary of people who see a need and, with no under-standing of the myriad obstacles in their paths, move to help, attracting more skilled people along the way. Then, together, they accomplish the dif-ficult in such a way that others think it looks easy.

Jan Scruggs was born in Washington, DC, in 1950 and grew up primarily in Bowie, Prince George County, Maryland. His father had suffered a prewar injury and was not accepted for World War II military service. The baby of the family, Jan had two older brothers who had served in the army and marines in the years before the Vietnam War.

In 1968, Scruggs volunteered for the draft along with tens of thousands of other men eager to get their military service out of the way and then get on with their lives.

"It worked out much bigger than I even planned. It seems like my entire life has revolved around my year in Vietnam," he said.

In Vietnam, Scruggs was a gunner on an 81mm mortar team. "Most of the fire missions were at night, so during the day we just sort of wandered around our firebase. From time to time I was called upon to be a rifleman."

His worst day in Vietnam came when soldiers unloading a truck carrying 81mm mortar rounds somehow caused three rounds to explode, resulting in twelve dead and several wounded.

"I was about a hundred yards away. I grabbed my first aid gear and ran over there. And they were in just this big mass of people with brains sticking out and arms missing and everything. And to make things even worse, they were on fire," he recalled.

The cause of the accident was never made public.

Scruggs was wounded in action on May 28, 1969. "I had a lot of grenade fragments in my legs and right arm. The morning before I was hit, I had put my folded poncho on my pistol belt, like we used to do in basic training. And when I *was* wounded, it probably saved my spine from being cut in half," he recalled.

After two months in field hospitals and then a convalescent center at Cam Ranh Bay, Scruggs returned to his unit for duty. "I finished my tour with the same guys I started with. It wasn't much fun, but we were on a firebase and had hot meals almost every day."

Scruggs was honorably discharged in 1970. He was twenty years old, too young to vote or buy a beer. "I flew back to Maryland and moved in with my brother, Ron, who lived in a little town called Cheverly. For a while, I worked as a security guard. I had a lot of problems sleeping; it was a very transitional time in my life."

When he was about twenty-two, Scruggs nearly committed suicide. "I was going part-time to a community college and working part-time as a janitor in a department store. On one of those nights, I said to myself, *You know what? I think I'm done.* My revolver was already loaded. So I pulled the hammer back and put it to the side of my head. But I wanted to look in the mirror. I was kind of curious, wondering if once I shot myself if I would actually see the bullet come out of my head. I wasn't thinking rationally. Then suddenly I said to myself, *This is kind of a bad idea.* And I took the gun away from my head, put my thumb on the hammer, and released the tension on the trigger spring to slowly lower the hammer to a safe position."

He continued, "I wanted to get a college education, but I wasn't sure if I'd ever have the money for it. Then, in 1971, I think around October, I met the woman who is now my wife. Rebecca Fishman was from Boston; her father was a Harvard lawyer, and she came from a nice Jewish family. We've been married a long time, and she's my whole world then and now. Rebecca worked to help put me through college at American University, and after earning a bachelor's degree, I went to graduate school there. And I became an expert on post-traumatic stress disorder."

Scruggs studied for a master's in education in counseling psychology. He knew he had PTSD. He explained, "I would wake up thinking about these guys who got blown up. I would think about getting wounded. I would think about these different things that happened to me. They weren't going away. So in graduate school, I began to study this phenomenon. I did a research project which was published in *Military Medicine*, an academic journal." The results of his project showed that people who had seen a lot of combat had a more general kind of psychopathology than those who saw a small amount of combat in Vietnam.

Scruggs graduated in 1976. His study was published in the *Washington Post*, and he testified before the US Senate. At twenty-seven years old, he explained, he was "sort of a small-time celebrity—and I didn't have a job." He found work digging ditches. Eventually, Scruggs found a better job with the US Department of Labor.

At this time in his life, Scruggs began to confront some of the antiwar sentiment and the ugliness directed against Vietnam veterans. "One guy said, 'Look, I didn't go to Vietnam, and I would not go to Vietnam because it goes against everything I learned in school and in church, from my parents, "Thou shalt not kill." It's very simple. I would not go there.'

"So there was that kind of smug behavior that many of the antiwar people had. And my other friends as well. They weren't heavy antiwar movement people, but none wanted to go to Vietnam, possibly get his legs blown off, although everybody I know cooperated when they were drafted and ended up going over there. And I think they're all proud they did," he added.

Once a friend wanted to introduce him to a girl he knew. They all had lunch, and Scruggs recalled, "Halfway into the conversation, the girl said, 'One of the things I would never do is ever go out with anybody who had been in the Vietnam War. I was just watching the Lieutenant Calley trial[1] for his role in the My Lai Massacre and reading about it in *Time* magazine. Because you never know, am I dating one of these guys who bayoneted some little baby?'"

Scruggs knows there is a wide variety of outcomes among Vietnam veterans, ranging from somebody who came back more confident and more self-assured to somebody who came back with raging PTSD, who, now at age seventy, still has not gotten his life together. He said, "Some people came back drug addicts. Some returned to become ministers. It's amazing.

"But one study showed that those who went to the Vietnam War as opposed to those who did not, they tended to be more financially successful. In part, maybe, because the military gave them some job skills or opportunities to attend college," Scruggs concluded.

Somewhere during these first years after Scruggs returned from Vietnam, he decided what this country and specifically its Vietnam veterans needed more than sympathy or educational opportunities was a monument. But how did that idea enter Jan Scruggs's mind?

"It came from my studies of Carl Jung, a student of Sigmund Freud," he said. "Jung wrote about the collective psyche. We all have certain feelings and emotions and things that are sacred to us as part of society. And I thought that having a memorial engraved with the names of the war dead would work because of that very reason, because of the work of Carl Jung."

He embarked on a campaign in April 1979. Because of his limited knowledge about how to accomplish such a goal, he said, "It never should have worked. But because ignorance is bliss, instead of being afraid, I was just the opposite. I wasn't afraid at all. I was more than happy to jump in and do the work."

He says his biggest hurdle was H. Ross Perot, a billionaire who didn't want the memorial to be built. "He put a lot of resources into it, and there were a lot of controversies. He launched a public relations campaign by enlisting some dissatisfied veterans and getting members of Congress to call Secretary of the Interior James Watt in 1982 on the same morning that we were scheduled to receive our construction permit."

The public became aware of Scruggs and his quest to build a monument to Vietnam veterans when he called his first press conference in May 1979.

Then he appeared on *60 Minutes, Good Morning America*, and the *Today* show to appeal for funds. Contributions great and small rolled in.

The legislation was introduced in November 1979. And in November 1982 the memorial was completed. It was beyond anything Washington had seen or will ever see again. It changed all the rules. And Scruggs did it in three years.

But Scruggs gives credit to a group of men who orchestrated the details. He said, "The heroes of this saga are the guys who saved me from myself. They are graduates of the US Military Academy, led by John P. Wheeler III, who was also a graduate of the Harvard Business School and a Yale Law School graduate. A very brilliant fellow."

Wheeler was a Vietnam veteran who recruited some other Harvard men. Scruggs explained, "They put this whole idea together, just like a Harvard Business School class problem. 'What do we need here? We need a site. We need a design. We need money. We need construction.'" Wheeler became chairman of the board of the Vietnam Veterans Memorial Fund who, according to Scruggs, "planned the whole thing out so that it would be built by November 1982. And astoundingly, we succeeded," Scruggs explained.

From the start, Scruggs decided that any monument to a war that could never be won must be a monument to the fallen. On it, then, he wanted to place the name of every man and woman who gave his or her life in Vietnam during the many years of US involvement in the war. It was the only requirement he had in the call for designs that went out to architects nationwide.

Since Washington, DC, is a city of monuments, the designs that came in all looked like all the other white marble memorials: men on horses, men with guns, men putting up the flag. Only one design concentrated on the names, and it was the one chosen. When it turned out the Vietnam Veterans Memorial (the Wall) was to be of black marble and the designer was Asian American, a firestorm of protest ensued, chiefly among those who thought the architect was Vietnamese.

As it happened, Maya Lin, then still an architectural student, was part of a distinguished Chinese American family that has called themselves Americans since 1940. But that didn't seem to matter to those who wanted a more traditional monument. To mollify them, John Wheeler added a stand-alone sculpture, *The Three Soldiers*, by Frederick Hart, to the memorial grounds.

When the stark black marble of the Wall was unveiled in November 1982, however, the power of the design became apparent to all. It is the names, row after row after row of names of dead Americans, that bring tears to all who view it. Adding to that power was the ability of the highly polished black marble to reflect the grounds and the people who approached the Wall.

After the Wall attained national recognition and became the most honored monument in the city, Scruggs went back to school and earned a law degree at the University of Maryland. "I didn't want to really become a lawyer," he said. "I just always wanted to have a law degree. I felt I would become very interested in law and I would be a very capable lawyer. But by the time I got out of law school, I was forty years old. Everyone else was getting out at age twenty-three. I just decided there's only one thing I really care about. I have a passion for the Vietnam Veterans Memorial and the Vietnam War. And so I went back to the Vietnam Veterans Memorial Fund, and we began raising money for the tenth anniversary of the Vietnam Veterans Memorial in 1992. And I stayed there until I retired in 2015."

The foundation paid Scruggs a modest salary to serve as president, and as the years went by, Scruggs turned to the foundation to raise money for an assortment of causes, including removing land mines and other unexploded ordnance in South Vietnam.

In 2017, he suffered a massive heart attack and was placed in a medically induced coma. He had long suffered from endocarditis, an infection of the inner lining of the heart's chambers and valves. After he was in a coma for a month, doctors advised Scruggs's wife that he was unlikely to survive and she should consider withdrawing life support. Shortly after that, Scruggs opened his eyes and began a swift recovery.

Scruggs had been under a lot of stress prior to his heart attack. He said he was largely ignored by the people in charge of the Vietnam Veterans Memorial Fund during the thirty-fifth anniversary of the memorial. Nevertheless, his place in history is secure. Described by *Time* magazine's Hugh Sidey as "indefatigable," Scruggs was responsible for the creation of the monument that has seen one hundred million visitors since 1982. So many of his peers and fellow veterans venerate the Wall that it has become a living shrine to the memory of the otherwise forgotten warriors of a war that America never tried to win.

JAY
MANCINI

Real estate developers are often characterized as greedy or are referred to in other unkindly terms in part because they bring sweeping change. The collections of magnificent and highly functional buildings that populate our national skylines, however, do not sprout from the ground like trees. Each structure is the product of an enormous number of work hours by people with a multitude of skills, ranging from carpenters, electricians, earth-movers, glaziers, and masons to architects, accountants, attorneys, bankers, and engineers. Conducting this enormous orchestra of diverse talents usually falls to one person. Someone like Jay Mancini.

Jay Mancini grew up in an affluent family in San Mateo, California. In 1964, he graduated from the Shattuck School, a military prep school near Minneapolis, and then enrolled in Lawrence College in Appleton, Wisconsin, where he majored in modern European history. He was also a competitive wrestler and played football.

As a freshman, he decided to deal with the "first job after college" issue immediately. He interviewed with recruiters from all four branches of the military. He wore glasses, and the army, navy, and air force all told him, "Your eyesight is a problem." He asked, "What does that mean?"

"The army told me I could be a supply officer or some such," he recalled. Then he went to the marines, and they said, "We'll buy you all the eyeglasses you want. Did you say you're a wrestler? While you're here, why don't you take this test?"

He took the test, and they said, "We'd like to introduce you to the platoon leaders course program. You'll really like it. It's live action, and you get to go in the summer."

Mancini went to Quantico the summer between his freshman and sophomore years and again the summer between his junior and senior years. He was commissioned a second lieutenant in the Marine Corps soon after his graduation in 1968. Mancini flew to Okinawa in January 1969 to join the First Marine Division and then to Da Nang, South Vietnam, and the First Battalion, Twenty-Sixth Marines.

As his plane was approaching the coastline, Mancini recalled, the pilot came on the public address and said, "'We're going to be performing an unusual maneuver. We're going to dive down toward the airport and then level off to land.' Then as though to answer the unspoken question, he added, 'To avoid antiaircraft fire.'" Mancini thought, *This is a secure airfield, right?*

From his window seat, Mancini watched the frenzied activity on the air base below: camouflaged A-1E Skyraiders lifting off, their wing racks chockablock with rockets, bombs, and napalm canisters; sinister-looking F-4 Phantoms trailing black smoke as they roared into the sky; helicopters darting around; and men in flak vests and steel helmets scurrying between sandbagged bunkers.

"As I'm seeing all this, I'm trying to make the mental adjustment from two weeks earlier when I was a civilian watching the Rose Bowl," Mancini confessed.

"Our 707 landed and rolled toward a sandbagged terminal. The pilot is back on the PA, saying, 'As soon as you're off the plane, you are to run to the bunker that you'll see. You'll be waved into the bunker.'"

Mancini ran to the bunker and saw signs with regimental numbers. He found the Twenty-Sixth Regiment and identified himself. "Within about twelve hours, I'm standing in front of my platoon," he recalled. "I'm looking at the scraggliest, meanest, toughest guys I've ever seen. About a third of them had been at Khe Sanh. And they were thin, maybe 85 percent of their normal weight, because they'd been in the field for so long. And they're looking at me like, 'You're gonna get us all killed, aren't you?'

"I introduced myself to the platoon sergeant and the squad leaders. Then the XO said, 'Mancini, you're gonna take the patrol out tomorrow night.'"

Mancini's first combat patrol was to interdict Viet Cong that sometimes came under the cover of darkness to get food from a nearby village. He had the feeling this was a low-risk operation intended to help him adjust to his new circumstances and new challenges.

He continued to lead night patrols for a while. Within two weeks he was in his first firefight. "Nobody hit anything. It's pretty hard to shoot accurately at night," he said.

Soon after that, his battalion boarded some ships for an amphibious assault north of Da Nang. His company was in reserve, so Mancini climbed to the ship's bridge to watch a classic, picture-perfect Marine Corps amphibious operation roll out.

He recalled, "At 0400 the ships went to general quarters and we passed out ammunition, rations, and such. Then they boarded either CH-46 Sea Knight helicopters or went down to the well deck and got on amphibious assault vehicles. About 0700 the helicopters took off and circled above us. Then the amphibious assault vehicles rolled, one by one, into the sea and headed for the beach.

"The helicopters flew over the beach and headed inland. A frigate (primarily an antisubmarine vessel) was firing its three-inch gun at the beach. A little before 0800, I saw the tracked amphibious assault vehicles pull up on the beach. The frigate stopped firing, the ramps went down, the guys charged the shore.

"There was no opposition. One company seized the beach and two companies went in after them," he continued. "Pretty soon they were in a fight. The next morning, we saddled up and went in to reinforce."

Mancini's battalion had four such landings.

Over the first half of his tour, Mancini saw several of his men die and many others wounded. The Twenty-Sixth was operating in enemy-held areas and took heavy casualties. Mancini was wounded when a sliver of shrapnel buried itself in his chest not far from his heart. Fortunately, it didn't penetrate deeply.

A religious Catholic, Mancini carried rosary beads and prayed for himself and his men whenever he had a few minutes to spare.

During these operations, his battalion was reinforced by a reconnaissance platoon and an artillery battery. When the recon platoon leader finished his tour, Mancini volunteered to take his place.

"We went in before the first infantry company came ashore," he explained. "Then we'd go inland and secure the LZs and so forth. We did that a couple of times, and then all the ships sailed back to Pearl Harbor. The scuttlebutt was that the Twenty-Sixth Regiment would saddle up and go home."

That would take some time, however. But while the marines were preparing to draw down this force, the battalion recon platoons were detached and sent to the First Force Reconnaissance Company, which supported all Marine Corps combat units in Vietnam.

Mancini's recon platoon began running long-range patrols into the mountainous area west of Da Nang, looking for enemy infiltration routes, ammunition caches, weapons, food, and vehicles.

"We did that for three or four months, six or seven men at a time, no flak jacket or helmet, just a pack, forty rounds of ammunition, four grenades, and for some reason a gas mask," he recalled. "Each patrol was inserted by helicopter. Once on the ground, we moved away from the LZ as fast as possible for two hours and then went to ground, set up a perimeter, established radio contact with headquarters. Once we were certain the enemy wasn't looking for us, our patrol moved cautiously toward an objective, avoiding trails and ridgelines. At the objective, we saw what there was to see, reported it to HQ, and after moving some distance away, we were picked up by helicopter."

There came a patrol whose mission was to make their way to a particular ridgeline from where they could observe a narrow valley through which, from time to time, intelligence suspected large enemy formations would pass. Weather permitting, they were to observe the target; when the enemy appeared, they were to adjust fire for a 175mm gun battery many miles distant.

Despite heavy rain, Mancini's patrol was inserted without incident. They made their way unobserved to the ridge and remained there for the next eight days as the rain continued. Visibility was limited to twenty feet.

"The coldest I've ever been was on that ridge at night," Mancini recalled. He had two men on the radio while the others paired off to sleep and share body heat. The radio watch rotated every two hours.

Their food ran out on the fifth day. On the ninth, the rain ended but fog settled on the ridge. "We heard NVA units moving down the trail below. As each unit passed, their road guards fired a shot," Mancini said. "We radioed headquarters and reported we could hear movement, but the fog prevented us from adjusting artillery." Mancini was told to stand by and remain in place.

He realized, "If we start firing artillery at them, the enemy will realize that somebody is adjusting it, and they must be up by one ridge or another. They'll come looking for us. When that happens, how are we going to get out of here?"

The rain returned, and Mancini radioed his concern to headquarters. He was told to abort the mission and head for the pickup point. Moving down the hillside in poor visibility, he became disoriented. He found a river that seemed familiar, so he decided to look for an open area nearby, report his approximate location, and let the helicopters find him.

His men spread orange panels to guide the pilots, but they missed it. The patrol started back up the ridge until its rear guard reported two enemy soldiers were following at a distance.

"We set up an ambush, but they must have figured that out and backed off," Mancini recalled. The NVA were now aware of their presence. He realized it was only a matter of time before the area would be swarming with enemy patrols.

Mancini hid his patrol in a jungle bamboo grove and radioed headquarters. Night fell.

At intervals throughout the night, the sound of rifle shots echoed through the hills, coming from varying directions, suggesting they were surrounded, although none of the shots were nearby.

Then word came they would be rescued by SPIE (special patrol insertion/extraction). A helicopter would hover over the jungle and drop a heavy line with D rings spaced along its length. Every man in the patrol had a parachute rig sewn onto his jacket with a D ring. All they had to do was click their rings onto one on the line, and the helicopter would ascend and carry them to safety, while they dangled beneath the aircraft.

Mancini said his prayers.

The rescue bird arrived shortly after dawn, escorted by a pair of gun birds that circled overhead. As he was pulled up through the jungle canopy and into the bright light, Mancini feared they would draw fire. Wet, hungry, and miserable, the patrol was finally set down at a friendly firebase after thirty minutes of flight.

As his yearlong tour ended, Mancini was offered the opportunity to return for a second. A senior officer told him, "You're now very experienced patrolling here. We'd like you to re-up and come back for a second tour. And to make it all square, we'll send you to jump school."

Mancini considered this offer for all of two seconds. "If it's all the same to you, sir, I think I'll go home," he said. "Because it had come to me on that ridgeline that if I called in fire from the 175 battery, I was playing Russian roulette with getting my guys out alive."

Mancini's final duty station was Camp Pendleton, California, where he taught squad tactics in the infantry training regiment to recent graduates of boot camp. He was honorably discharged in 1971. But the Jay Mancini who went to Vietnam as a recent college graduate and rookie platoon leader was not the man who came home, and he knew it.

"Over about the next ten years—I call them my bad years—I had a lot of mood swing issues. I'd shift from ebullience to depression, and in between I was angry. I kept thinking about Vietnam and that at least one of my guys was killed because, as a young lieutenant, I'd made a mistake. Those things stay with you," he said.

"And then there was the antiwar atmosphere at that time. People were very antimilitary," he recalled. "I remember being at a dinner party where nobody knew my background, and this kid turns to me and says, 'I've really been thinking about the war, and anybody who served ought to be tried as a war criminal.'"

Mancini said, "I held my fire for about five seconds," and after "a few curses directed at the boy," he left. "Stopped the party cold," he said.

Throughout those ten hard years, Mancini often sought solace in alcohol. "I did some serious drinking," he recalled. He also went to confession often. "It was helpful having someone to talk to about my problems."

This miasma of the mind gradually lifted, although there were setbacks.

"After 9/11, I made a point of not watching any news or reading the newspaper. But the very knowledge of 9/11 sent me into a downward tailspin. I ran into a depressive cycle, and Marion, my wife, made me see a psychiatrist.

"When I went to his office, he said, 'Tell me about yourself.' So I mentioned a few things and said, by the way, I was an infantry officer in Vietnam.

"He stopped me right there and said, 'You're the third in the last two weeks. The good news is, I can fix this. I've got a medication that will really help this. But you can really help me, which is to say, help yourself. You need to get exercise every day. I want you doing something. I don't care what it is, but you've got to get cardiovascular exercise every day.'"

Mancini did as he was told, and the regimen helped. After he'd left the Marine Corps, he followed in his father's footsteps and worked as a commercial leasing agent, specializing in San Francisco office space. Still struggling with what we now know as PTSD, he decided to apply to the Wharton School. After he convinced the dean of admissions to admit him, he took extra law classes and earned an MBA.

Mancini has held senior positions with Perini Land and Development Company and Bramalea Pacific, where he acquired a broad range of skills, including managing large construction projects, partnering with and directing the work of contractors, architects, engineers, designers, and many other specialty consultants. He developed an expertise in negotiating contracts, administering construction loans, managing costs and schedules, controlling budgets, and overseeing quality control throughout the process of acquiring suitable land, building attractive and useful structures on it, and then leasing space to tenants.

By 1991 he had been entrusted with the management of large-scale, fast-tracked projects and was known as a leading expert in the integrated design-build process. He started his own firm, G&M Realty Ventures LLC. "I invest people's money in properties. I do consulting work. And I built up a small portfolio of rental properties to support us between major projects," he explained.

Mancini is especially proud of his work on the Presidio of San Francisco. The oldest continually operating military base in the United States, the Presidio was established by the Spanish army in 1776. In 1989, Congress ordered the US Army facility to close.

By long-existing law, decommissioned military bases become the property of the National Park Service (NPS), a division of the Department of the Interior. The NPS, however, while capable of managing former bases that include many thousands of acres of forest, grassland, and marshes, was not prepared to manage the Presidio's eight hundred structures, many of them historic treasures, or its more than two thousand units of residential housing. When Congress refused to appropriate the funds necessary to maintain the Presidio's historic nature, developers from thousands of miles around began salivating at the possibility they could obtain the seaside property at auction. Dozens of lobbyists began chatting up California's congressional delegation and top Department of Defense officials. The Presidio's fifteen hundred acres could easily hold dozens of high-rise office and residential buildings. Enormous profits could be reaped.

Mancini and some friends had a different idea. With the help of Representatives Nancy Pelosi and Phillip Burton, laws were passed to create a unique trust into which fourteen hundred acres of the Presidio were preserved. The Presidio Trust Act calls for "preservation of the cultural and historic integrity of the Presidio for public use."[1]

In 1993, Mancini joined Jerry Keyser, a noted land economics professional, and Dean Macris, former head of San Francisco city planning, to create a strategy whereby 80 percent of the Presidio—the interior area adjacent to the city of San Francisco—could achieve financial stability. Mancini's team was tasked to determine what enterprises and activities could be attracted to the Presidio while preserving its historic buildings.

The balance of the land, which included a wildlife habitat, along with hiking and picnicking areas that offered breathtaking ocean and Golden Gate Bridge views, would be deeded to the city and county of San Francisco for public use as a seaside recreational area. Revenue to support its maintenance would come from the leased properties.

Their plan was published in October 1993. Because he was responsible for income and cost analysis, Mancini was asked by Pelosi to brief congressional staffers and then testify before House and Senate committees about the potential to make the Presidio economically self-sufficient. "My testimony was offered in support of legislation introduced by Representative Pelosi to create a federal corporation, the Presidio Trust, to implement the strategy and take control of the fifteen-hundred-acre Presidio," he explained.

In 1994, before the trust could be created, Mancini assembled a multidisciplinary team to begin implementing the strategy. Working with the NPS, Mancini's team negotiated several leases to renovate vacant historic buildings for productive use. These leases began to generate revenue to defray the cost of the Presidio operations. Mancini's team also began planning the major infrastructure improvements necessary for the Presidio to be attractive to a broad base of tenants. Legislation creating the trust passed in 1996, and in 1997 Mancini's team turned control of their projects over to trust personnel.

By 2004 about half the Presidio's eight hundred buildings, many of historic significance, were restored and partially remodeled. By 2016 some two thousand units of badly needed residential housing had been leased out at market rates. A seven-acre great lawn was opened to the public as well as a trampoline park in a former aircraft hangar. The Presidio's residents include the Bay School of San Francisco, a private coeducational college preparatory school, the Gordon and Betty Moore Foundation, Tides Foundation, Arion Press, Sports Basement Presidio, and the Walt Disney Family Museum. Many commercial enterprises also lease buildings on the Presidio.

Lucasfilm built the Letterman Digital Arts Center (LDAC) in the Presidio, which became Lucasfilm's corporate headquarters. The $300 million development includes nearly 900,000 square feet of office space and an underground parking garage with a capacity of 2,500 vehicles. Lucasfilm's Industrial Light and Magic, Lucas Licensing, and Lucas Online divisions share the site.

Beyond his professional accomplishments, Mancini is a religious man. As a member of the Order of Malta, he takes seriously ill people on pilgrimages to Lourdes, France, and to Guadalupe, Mexico. "We take very sick people to Lourdes, for what generally is emotional healing. But every so often there really is a miracle cure," he added.

Not through miracles but with decades of hard work and the acquisition of expertise in a panoply of related fields, Jay Mancini has clearly left his mark on San Francisco and nearby cities as few others have. For generations to come, a legion of landmark structures will stand as monuments to his vision, skill, and industry.

JOHN BALABAN

According to the Roman philosopher Seneca, "Luck is what happens when preparation meets opportunity."¹ Surely there was no one among the legions of Americans in South Vietnam during the war years less prepared to be a soldier than John Balaban. And no one more prepared than Balaban to make a unique and important contribution to Vietnamese history and culture.

Born in Philadelphia in 1943, John Balaban was the youngest in a hard-scrabble family of Romanian immigrants. He grew up in one of the city's toughest neighborhoods, and his childhood memories include kids being battered, stabbed, shot, and killed by other children, siblings, or parents in an atmosphere of pervasive violence and perpetual peril. Undersized and asthmatic, Balaban retreated from this dangerous world into conversations with invisible companions and became a diligent student.

At sixteen, Balaban and his father had a brief fistfight, after which Balaban ran away. He left with two dollars and a faint notion about hitchhiking to California. The temperature was in the teens and the drifts of snow were taller than his head.

Fortunately, he was taken in by one of his high school teachers and her husband, and he did chores and chopped firewood to earn his keep. In the six months before his graduation, Balaban began attending the monthly Southampton Friends Meeting. Among these Quakers, he found a refuge from violence.

During the next four years he attended Penn State and became involved in the early antiwar movement. He went to the 1964 March on Washington to hear Martin Luther King Jr. speak. Among his closest friends were war protesters who burned their draft cards and joined sometimes bloody anti-war demonstrations. Balaban sympathized with his friends' sentiments, but he was too focused on his studies to join them. He was also dismayed by the violence and the threat of yet more to come. Before he graduated, Balaban won a Woodrow Wilson Fellowship, which he used for tuition-free graduate study at Harvard. He immersed himself in Ovid, Chaucer, and the Scottish poets of the late Middle Ages.

In mid-1967, at a time when four hundred thousand American troops were in South Vietnam and more than two hundred body bags arrived in the States every week, Balaban approached his draft board. They asked if he was willing to go to Vietnam. He was, he told them, but not as a soldier. He was a conscientious objector, but instead of the usual fates of conscientious objectors—emptying bedpans in a veterans hospital, serving as an army medic, or going to prison—he would go to Vietnam for two years of alternate duty with the International Voluntary Services (IVS), a nonprofit organization founded by the Mennonite, Brethren, and Quaker churches that sought to improve living standards in underdeveloped countries. It was funded by both private and government organizations, the bulk of which came from the US Agency for International Development. Volunteers were mostly college graduates schooled in economics or other humanitarian fields.[2]

While American soldiers served one year in Vietnam, Balaban served two with IVS. At his two-week boot camp in Vietnam, Balaban was the only conscientious objector.

After boot camp, Balaban and three female volunteers were flown downcountry to Cao Lanh, a provincial capital on the east bank of one of the mighty Mekong River's many branches, for a month's orientation and tutoring in basic Vietnamese.

Sleepy Cao Lanh was near the North Vietnamese sanctuaries in the so-called Parrot's Beak region along the Cambodian border. The IVS volunteers were billeted in a three-story brick-and-stucco house—no air-conditioning—between a building housing a CIA officer and another where a USAID advisor lived. A Vietnamese language teacher flew down from Saigon, took one look at the setup, consulted with some of the local high school teachers, and flew back to Saigon, fearful for his safety.

Instead of sending the volunteers back to Saigon, they remained, with little to do except avoid street demonstrations and worry over warnings about imminent Viet Cong attacks.

While Balaban was exploring the area on a solo jaunt, he encountered several men in a village. Their leader, an older man, listened to the American's earnest attempt to speak Vietnamese. Perhaps he was amused by Balaban's guileless display of chutzpah, but whatever his reasons, he turned him loose. A week later, Balaban learned that, later that day, Viet Cong had ambushed a US Army jeep very near where he had been temporarily detained.

One night during the third week in August 1967, the Viet Cong attacked. It began with mortars and rockets and small-arms fire. It ended with the arrival of an AC-47 gunship, a version of the World War II DC-3, dubbed Spooky, that was equipped with Gatling guns capable of firing six thousand rounds a minute. The IVS volunteers survived unscathed.

In September, Balaban was sent to Can Tho, another provincial capital and the largest city in the Mekong delta. Once an architecturally charming center of French colonial agriculture, the region was now the unlovely regional headquarters for the US Army, Navy, Air Force, Special Forces, and their South Vietnamese counterparts. There, Balaban taught English four hours a week at Can Tho University, which left plenty of time to be tutored in Vietnamese and to explore the area. As he did, he realized the war's terrible effects on civilians. The area's hospitals were filled with those wounded by stray munitions or whose homes had been bombed or strafed by US or Vietnamese forces battling the Viet Cong.

That same month, Balaban joined more IVS volunteers—none of whom were conscientious objectors, but most of whom were firmly opposed to the war—in signing a letter to President Johnson protesting the manner in which the war was being carried out, especially the spraying of herbicides (including

Agent Orange) on crops, the establishment of free-fire zones, the millions of refugees created by the fighting, and the horrific toll on civilians. Much to their surprise, the letter was published on the front page of the *New York Times*, which did not endear its signers to the IVS, USAID, or the State Department. Viet Cong leaders sent word that the IVS volunteers would be safe from attack but asked them all to go home; they were told their good works helped ordinary Vietnamese but confused them about the ultimate US goals in Vietnam.

Shortly after the letter was published and the Viet Cong had weighed in, Balaban helped some local men build a dike through an abandoned paddy field that had long functioned as a sort of community outdoor latrine. Disregarding the field's deadly microbes, Balaban waded into the muck and went to work. A few days later he fell ill. Weeks later, he had recovered and was staying in the IVS building when someone stole his wallet. Balaban decided to move to a tiny apartment in the home of a lay Buddhist nun some distance from the IVS building.

At the start of the Vietnamese New Year on January 30, 1968, the Viet Cong and North Vietnamese launched a nationwide assault on cities and major military installations, known as the Tet Offensive. Balaban was awakened by the sound of exploding mortar rounds and small-arms fire. He huddled in his apartment for a day before retrieving his Vespa motorbike. His neighbors offered to shelter him from the Viet Cong, but Balaban, aware of the danger his presence brought to the neighborhood, set off on his motor scooter for the imagined safety of the IVS building.

He avoided two small pitched battles, reached his destination, and with other volunteers, went to the Military Assistance Command Vietnam (MACV). There, American advisors to the Army of the Republic of Vietnam (ARVN) units were handing out a ragtag collection of weapons. With mixed feelings, he took a .45-caliber M-3 submachine gun, known as a grease gun, and returned to the IVS house, where he found a fragmentation grenade and a concussion grenade in a bathroom. He put them in a shaving kit and tied it to his belt.

The Viet Cong assault continued, and the next day, going against a fleeing stream of refugees from the city, some of the volunteers moved to the hospital and discovered the Vietnamese doctors had all fled. Remaining were some Vietnamese nurses, all of them Catholic nuns, a few US Air Force doctors, and hundreds of wounded and dying civilians. The sound of gunfire drew closer.

"I was utterly confused and perplexed," Balaban recalled. "I am totally opposed to killing. If I hadn't been able to make arrangements with my draft board, I would have gone to jail or fled to Canada. I felt very strongly about that. But *that* day the war came to my city, and only those American military surgeons could save the wounded civilians, . . . dozens of whom were literally dying in the dirt around the hospital. It was like that scene in *Gone with the Wind* in Atlanta, in the rail yard, where people lay bleeding out on the ground."

He recalled the day vividly. "The battle was going on around us. A surgeon said the Viet Cong or North Vietnamese were trying to get into the hospital. The doctors were afraid to stay there. They said, 'We will stay and continue to operate if you guard the hospital.'"

With Balaban was another volunteer, an Idaho farm boy. "We both had grown up with guns and hunted as kids," he recalled. "Probably he was good at it. I was. I won a sharpshooter's medal when I was a kid. And it was either help these people or walk away. I had the grease gun and the grenades. He had a carbine. We went around the hospital grounds together, looking for the Viet Cong purportedly trying to get in over the wall. There were none."

They patrolled most of that morning and then moved to guard the operating room. Balaban recounted, "Just above me was a water tower that had been riddled with bullets. The water sprayed out in all directions. Then a Vietnamese Catholic nun knocked very timidly at the door. I was surprised that she was still there. She had a Red Cross armband that she wanted to tie around my arm. I thought that I shouldn't be holding a gun while wearing a Red Cross armband. But I let her tie it on—it was a moment of utter confusion. I had agreed to guard that operating room for those American doctors. I sure didn't want to shoot anybody. But these were circumstances that I had never anticipated. I was sure then, and I'm sure now, that I would have shot someone before I let him shoot me or a doctor."

Balaban didn't have to shoot anyone. By late afternoon a Special Forces team arrived, and he was pressed into service as an orderly, carrying out the dead, putting wounded people on operating tables, and then, after a quick class on sterilizing technique, cleaning wounds and picking debris out of them.

The battle for Can Tho raged for several more days, and through most of it Balaban worked in the hospital, seeing an unimaginably horrific stream of mutilated children and women. On the next-to-last day of fighting, Balaban and other volunteers moved to the comparative safety of an air base at the edge of Can Tho. Just down the road, the North Vietnamese Army (NVA) massed for an attack. The consensus among the base's defenders was that, without air support, they were doomed; they had too few men and guns to stop the NVA. But thick, low clouds covered the area, making it impossible for accurate bombing or low-level strafing.

Miraculously, a few hours into the NVA's night attack, the clouds masking the air base and environs cleared, and an AC-47 Spooky arrived to break the back of the attack, saving the base and hundreds of US and ARVN defenders and unarmed civilians.

Around noon the following day, Balaban and some IVS volunteers returned to inspect their building. Perhaps a quarter mile away, an aircraft dropped a cluster bomb, maybe on some remnant of the retreating enemy. A fragment from one of its bomblets flew across the city and buried itself in Balaban's shoulder.

He was treated in Vietnam but went home to recuperate and find a new job—the University of Can Tho had been destroyed. Six weeks later, his shoulder nearly healed, Balaban returned to Saigon to work for the Committee of Responsibility to Save War-Burned and War-Injured Vietnamese Children (COR). His job was to find injured and/or disfigured Vietnamese children and take them to the United States for surgical treatment. After they healed, the children would be reunited with their families. With plenty of supporting evidence, COR believed that lacking such medical care, these children would never live full lives. Many would likely soon die. And so Balaban and Richard Berliner, another volunteer who was more fluent in Vietnamese, along with an American volunteer doctor, roamed Vietnam and persuaded the parents of each injured child—if the parents could be found—to allow them to take their children to the States. Then they had to battle South Vietnam's corrupt, sclerotic, and Byzantine bureaucracy to obtain exit visas one child at a time. On occasion, they resorted to shaming officials by forcing them to look at photos of hideously mangled children. They did whatever they had to do. At times they also had to argue with US military physicians who suspected, without evidence, that COR was a communist front intent on making anti-American propaganda with these horribly disfigured children. It was true that Balaban and his colleagues believed that when Americans saw these children, they would be horrified that such innocents were the majority of those injured in the war, but these children were not propaganda.

Despite these formidable obstacles, Balaban and his colleagues ultimately sent dozens of children to the United States for treatment. A few, with no living relatives, remained in the States. The rest were repatriated to their dangerous and unstable homeland and to their parents. Sharing in the joy of reuniting a child with his or her parents was often the only thing that kept Balaban going.

What Balaban accomplished in his time with COR was admirable and remarkable, but he was not alone. Thousands of American and third-country nationals came to Vietnam as volunteers, including Catholic organizations too numerous to list and other organizations affiliated with the Seventh-day Adventists, Quakers, Baptists, and Mennonites. There were volunteer medical teams from South Korea, the United States, Britain, Thailand, France, the Philippines, Switzerland, Germany, Iran, Spain, and even the United Nations Educational, Scientific and Cultural Organization (UNESCO). Their contributions to saving lives, working for peace, and healing the wounded are comparable to what Balaban accomplished working for COR.

———◇———

When he finished his alternate service, Balaban returned to his home in June 1969. He had earned none of the benefits conferred on those who served in the military. But he was no longer the same man who had left Harvard two years earlier.

"I came back angry," he recalled. "Angry at my fellow Americans. I would get into fistfights. Road rage came my way again and again. I still have to watch my temper.

"But how could I not have come back changed? Seeing children maimed and burned and killed as I did as part of my daily work, angry at the country that mostly did that damage—you'd be pretty dead if you weren't stirred up a bit by that.

"The other thing is that I came back braver. I had no doubts about myself, as I think I would have if I had just stayed at Harvard studying Old English.

I was taking seminars in Middle Scots poetry. I would have probably been very good at that, but I don't think I'd ever known things about myself that I learned by doing what I did."

Vietnam was under Balaban's skin, if not actually in his blood. In 1970, while teaching English at Penn State, a friend sent him a collection of folk poetry and proverbs collected in northern Vietnam in the 1930s, during the era when French colonizers had decreed that Chữ Nộm (Vietnam's written language using large characters that resembled Chinese but were unique to Vietnam and dating from the thirteenth century) would no longer be taught. Instead, *chu quoc ngu*, a Romanized alphabet created by French Jesuits in the sixteenth century, would be taught exclusively. The book of poetry was written in the more modern language.

Working with a young Vietnamese acquaintance, Balaban translated some of the poems. This oral poetry, known to Vietnamese as *ca dao*, was purely Vietnamese and as ancient as the nation itself. But very few of these anonymous poems had been written for posterity; they were unknown in the West. And no one had ever recorded them.

"Hoping that Vietnamese culture would survive long enough for me to record this loveliest of its aspects," Balaban wrote in his memoir, *Remembering Heaven's Face*, he applied for a National Endowment for the Humanities fellowship.

In 1971, after taking a leave of absence from Penn State, Balaban and his wife, Lonny, moved to Honolulu, where he studied Vietnamese. That August they flew to Vietnam.

Funded with a modest grant and equipped with an early Sony cassette recorder, Balaban set out to record as many poems as he could. He had also lined up a part-time teaching post at Hue University in English grammar and linguistics. After a short trip to the Mekong delta, the Balabans headed north. Hue's prewar charms had been all but obliterated by the war, and adequate housing was scarce. There was also the issue of security: Hue was not safe for Americans.

So the Balabans established a home in Saigon. Every month, Balaban flew to Hue for four days of teaching. In Saigon, he spent weeks fruitlessly searching for ca dao to record. He listened to folk singers, to a blind singer accompanied by a six-string steel guitar, but none of it was ca dao. Composed by ordinary peasants and passed on orally, ca dao "had existed through the millennia from the distant origins of the Vietnamese, when they called themselves the Lac and lived in diminutive agrarian kingdoms in the deltas of the Red and Black Rivers of the north," Balaban observed.

He asked folk singers and city dwellers a few generations removed from their rice-farmer ancestors if ca dao was still sung in the countryside. The people shook their heads. Balaban felt panic about his quest. Had he won a fellowship, with a year's salary, to study something that no longer existed?

He hoped the displaced northerners who sang modern folk songs and came from privileged families were wrong. He hoped that ca dao was still alive in the countryside. What drove Balaban more than the thought of losing his grant was the fear it would die out and be lost forever.

"In Saigon lived about four million people who had been driven from the countryside to live in shanty towns," Balaban explained. "I figured that everything that held those people together culturally was gone. But it wasn't! Those traditions go on. What kills them, ironically, is a culture of the electronic kind. If you have a radio or a TV, why sit around a kerosene lamp and sing poetry to other people? That's what kept it alive for more than a thousand years. It's still there, but not as vibrant, maybe dying.

"As long as there were Vietnamese living in the traditional rice-growing rhythm of the land, they sang ca dao," Balaban noted. Few of these poems had been written down, and few of those who wrote them were literate. Balaban says the poems were sung because the way they were arranged created a melody and turned the musical tones of the Vietnamese language into a natural melody line sung by a single person to the cricket-churning backdrop of the delta. No guitar. No piano. No chorus. Nothing but an unstudied voice offering its plaints of love and yearning to the trees in the family orchard, to the baby being rocked in a woven hammock, to the river sliding off into the horizon. This singing of ca dao joined with the rhythms and rhymes to make those delicate vanishing artifacts—more than any monsoon-crumbled monument—the clearest record of Vietnamese culture.

Balaban made a temporary base on Con Phung island (also known to foreigners as Phoenix island), deep in the Mekong delta. It was and remains a unique place. In Balaban's time, a mystic called Ong Hai ("Older Brother") or the Coconut Monk had established a religion that drew pilgrims from across the entire delta. It also drew many foreigners, and for reasons never clear, the war avoided this island, though gun battles were often heard nearby.

Ong Hai welcomed this conscientious objector, and Balaban became known to all who visited. Farmers from every region of the delta, each visiting for their own reasons, shared their poems with him. Sometimes he left the island and went deeper into the delta.

"I had this wonderful sense of doing something really remarkable, really special, that no one else, not even the Vietnamese, had done before," Balaban recalled. "For centuries, a few literary scholars would write them down. But here I was, taping these people. I would walk up to them—in those days my Vietnamese was pretty fluent. And I would ask simple questions: 'Would you sing me your favorite poem?' And most people did it. It was not, in that culture, a strange question at all. Their reaction was more like, 'Finally, the Americans sent somebody to ask something important of us.' And I don't think I ever met anybody who didn't know these poems."

After this time in the delta, Balaban, often accompanied by his wife, traveled around the country. In Hue, he found an eighty-year-old scholar who had served as a mandarin at the last imperial court. In Buon Ma Thuot, he recorded a schoolteacher, a riverboat merchant, farmers who plowed with water buffalo, mothers singing to their babies, young children, a shipwright—people from every walk of life and strata of society. "I tapped into something very special, a record of Vietnamese humanistic belief that went back a thousand years to the period when Vietnamese broke apart from its cousin language, Muong.

"When I was getting my precious tapes out of the country," Balaban recalled, "I went through customs at Tan Son Nhut Airport. The customs authorities asked, 'What's in here, what do you have?' They probably wanted a bribe. I told them what was on my tapes, and they wanted to open the cassettes to see what was inside. I said, 'No, you can't open them. You'll destroy the tapes.' That made them even more suspicious. One of the officers said, 'If you can't open the cassettes, why don't you sing us one of the poems?' And I did. And that was it. That was my passage out of Vietnam with my tapes."

Balaban wasn't done. Over the next decades he made several trips to Vietnam, even during the immediate postwar era, when the two countries had no diplomatic relations. Working with a few dedicated scholars and spending much of his time raising money, Balaban set out to bring access and attention to the nearly lost and uniquely written language called Chữ Nôm.

"Chữ Nôm is a writing system . . . developed on the Chinese model," he explained. "But it represents Vietnamese speech, not Chinese speech."

Chữ Nôm was in use perhaps as early as the ninth century. Almost its entire word stock is Vietnamese, with very few words borrowed from Chinese. All over Vietnam, stone monuments and tomb inscriptions can be found in Chữ Nôm. "Its heyday was the 1800s," Balaban explained. "There is a period from around 1775 to 1809 or so when it was the official script of the Vietnamese government." That government was the rebel government that expelled the Chinese from the country and ended the division between north and south, namely, the Trinh clans in the north and the Hue clans in the south.

When Balaban's first translations of folk poetry appeared in print, two Vietnamese scholars suggested he next translate the works of Ho Xuan Huong (1772–1822). "She may have been the most brilliant writer in this tradition," Balaban explained. The woman's life, however, was mysterious. Was she beautiful or plain? Dark-skinned or fair? Tall or petite? A concubine? History doesn't say. Her work was often erotic or bawdy. "Ho Xuan Huong turned to the common wisdom alive in peasant folk poetry and proverbs," Balaban observed. "Common people . . . could hear in her verse echoes of their folk poetry, proverbs, and village common sense."

But all the translations of her work were done in modern Vietnamese. To translate her work from the original texts, Balaban had to learn enough Chữ Nôm to verify those translations.

That took him ten years.

In the process, he found all sorts of things—medicine, history, religion, and literature—had been written in the old script that no more than a hundred people, all quite elderly, could still read with any fluency.

In 1999, with two Vietnamese computer experts, Balaban started a foundation whose purpose was to make the ancient script widely available by printing it using modern methods. From this came *Spring Essence*, Balaban's translation of Ho Xuan Huong's poems, which appeared in Chữ Nôm.[3] The key to that was creating TrueType fonts of Chữ Nôm characters, which took the work of a man Balaban called a genius.

Balaban and his two Vietnamese collaborators resurrected a language that had not been used since 1919, but the importance of their work is not limited to translating poetry.

"Throughout Vietnam, rotting away in libraries, are thousands of volumes written in Chữ Nôm," Balaban explained. "And they're disappearing. Some have been burned or eaten by rats, mice, and insects, or succumbed to mildew. Our next project was to digitize them one by one. We dealt with the director of the National Library of Vietnam—a one-armed veteran of the war—and he did something brave and remarkable: he opened up the national library to this American foundation that we had created. We worked with scholars, some from Cornell University, and digitized the texts, page by page. We put them in an online library that could be read anywhere in the world. It's a wonderful collection of history, culture, and literature that was for the first time available to scholars worldwide."[4]

And Balaban led the effort to raise the funds to make that happen.

In November 2000, President Bill Clinton went to Vietnam. At a state dinner in Hanoi, he gave a speech in which he mentioned Balaban's *Spring Essence*, to the surprise of the Vietnamese present. "That created a big stir and helped us raise money," Balaban recalled.

Balaban offered his time and to do what few, if any, could have accomplished let alone attempted. And it was only possible because Balaban was and remains a poet and saw the value and the virtue of poetry in any language. Balaban now lives in Cary, North Carolina. He is poet-in-residence and professor of English at North Carolina State University.

His foundation's work continues.

JIM
GRAHAM

In America, as elsewhere, elected and appointed officials come and go, and often they fail to understand or deal with the issues that are important to their constituents. This is as often due to a lack of interest as it is to a lack of appropriations. Governments cannot do everything that needs to be done. There are, therefore, a multitude of issues, large and small, that often are dealt with by the people themselves, usually through civic organizations. It can take years, even decades or centuries, but the power of the American people to address vital issues remains one of our nation's great strengths.

The ringing awakened Jim Graham, a reporter for the Columbus, Georgia, *Ledger*. He eased out of bed, hoping not to disturb his sleeping wife, Patty. Glancing at the clock on his nightstand, he grabbed the phone.

"You the guy who wants to know about the cops and those burglaries?" said a low, raspy voice.

"Yeah," Jim replied. "Who is this?"

"Never mind. Meet me in half an hour," the caller said, naming a parking lot in an industrial area of town.

"Who is this?" Jim repeated, but the line went dead.

It was the autumn of 1966. Jim was twenty-five, just months out of the army and back from Vietnam. He was tall and lean, with deep-set brown eyes and a receding hairline. He wasn't sure he wanted to meet a guy with no name and a raspy voice at 3:00 a.m. in a dark, deserted neighborhood of factories and warehouses.

He picked up the phone and awakened his boss, Bob Lott, the city editor. Jim asked what he should do.

"You gotta go meet the guy," said Lott.

"I'm not sure that's such a good idea."

"You won't be alone," replied Lott. "Now get moving."

Several weeks earlier Jim had sat in the back row of a nearly empty courtroom in the Columbus police station and watched a stream of arraignments. Occasionally someone would appear on a charge that might fill a few inches of copy on one of the *Ledger*'s back pages. One day, Jim sat up when a vaguely familiar vagrant shuffled in.

The man was charged with burglary as part of a ring that had been active in Columbus and the surrounding environs for months. He was the first of the gang to be arrested.

"How do you plead?" asked the judge.

"Guilty but with an explanation," replied the man. "I was the lookout, but they made me do it. The cops, I mean. They were the burglars, and they made me be their lookout."

Ignoring this assertion, the judge set a date for the man's trial.

But Jim's curiosity was piqued, and he spent the next few months asking his sources in the police department about the progress of their investigation into the burglary ring. He got nowhere—that is, until the night of the mysterious call summoning him to a meeting in a dimly lit parking lot.

When Jim pulled into the lot, he saw two other cars nearby. Lott was in one, and two other reporters were in the other. Feeling a little more confident, Jim parked, got out, and walked to the only other car in the lot.

The driver's door swung open and a man got out. In the dim light, Jim saw a face he recognized. He was a cop. The officer said he had been ordered to investigate a burglary ring suspected to be operating out of the Columbus police department. After he submitted his findings to his boss, he expected some kind of follow-up, but nothing happened. After a while, he was told to forget about the investigation; the chief would handle everything in his own way.

The detective handed Jim a thick file. "This is a copy of my investigation," he said. "Take it and get out of here."

Jim's multipart story ran on page one of the *Ledger* for several days. As soon as the first story was released, his car—whether in traffic or parked—was ticketed daily. Police officers he knew and had worked alongside for years greeted him with stony stares. In the end, twenty-three officers lost their jobs, and the chief suffered a fatal heart attack.

———◇———

In 1942, Jim Graham was born in Cincinnati, Ohio. His father was too old to serve in World War II; he worked as an auditor at military post exchanges until he was convicted of embezzlement and sent to prison. After he was paroled, his big family moved to Dayton, a busy, prosperous manufacturing center.

When the Korean War began in 1950, Jim's oldest brother, Frank, enlisted in the navy. A standout recruit, he was encouraged to apply to the Naval Academy and graduated in 1956 from Annapolis.

Jim admired Frank, but his ambitions didn't include the military. "After high school, I got a job with WHIO, a television station, as a floor director," he recalled. "It was mostly stuff like running cables, turning on lights, positioning microphones—easy to learn, and the first step in what I thought might be a good career in broadcasting."

Shortly after his twenty-first birthday, in May 1963, Jim began to feel the hot breath of the draft board on his neck. "I had not gotten a draft notice, but at age twenty-one, I felt I was a prime candidate," he recalled. "I knew that if I enlisted, the army would guarantee that I got the school I wanted."

Still looking forward to a career in television, Jim signed up with a guarantee that after basic training, he would attend the Defense Information School at Fort Slocum, on Davids Island off New Rochelle, New York. He requested the radio and television basic course. But when he finished basic training, he learned the course was full. He was offered instead a spot in the journalism course. The alternative was infantry training. Jim took the journalism course.

"It was great. Most of our instructors were graduate students at Columbia. New York City was a half hour away by train, and our weekends were free," he recalled. "A great duty station."

Eight weeks later, after learning the basics of news reporting and copy editing, Jim was offered the opportunity to request a geographic area for his first duty assignment. "I was hoping I might get to stay in the New York area, so I put in for the East Coast," he recalled.

He was assigned as the information specialist for the Third Brigade of the Second Infantry Division at Fort Benning, Georgia. "I was devastated. I had enlisted in the army to avoid being drafted and becoming an infantryman— that's not my idea of fun. So, Fort Benning, Georgia, was a real shock. I pissed and moaned for days until a guy I met at a party in Manhattan gave me a simple philosophy: take your life with you wherever you go."

After about a year at Benning, Jim was reassigned to the Eleventh Air Assault Division (Test). This was the army's test bed for the then-unproven concept of air mobility. Senior generals thought it might be possible to free combat soldiers from the tyranny of the terrain, to fly them to hilltops to fight their way downhill, instead of approaching the enemy from the bottom and fighting their way up as infantrymen had done since warfare began. The Eleventh tested this concept, inventing methods and the means of employing Bell's new UH-1 helicopter. In the process, they sought to demonstrate that air mobility might work on the battlefield.

The division information officer decided that Jim would become editor of the division's section of the *Bayonet*, the post newspaper. Jim recalled, "I had no idea what I was doing. I had never edited even a term paper, but I guess he saw something that I didn't know was there. He was a great teacher and guided me fairly gently. He had me promoted to specialist 4 and then specialist 5 in the span of about a year. I worked with Spec/5 Jim Baker, a professional editor before he was drafted, in the composing room of the *Ledger* and the *Enquirer*, which printed the *Bayonet*. He taught me all I ever knew about writing headlines and laying out pages."

In July 1965, the colors of the Eleventh Air Assault were retired, and its men and equipment merged with those of the Second Infantry Division. Then the Second sent its colors to South Korea, and the First Cavalry sent its colors from Korea to Fort Benning. After sending the troops and heavy equipment not needed in the world's first airmobile infantry division to other army units, the First Cavalry Division (Airmobile) was created. A month later, President Johnson sent the new and untried division to Vietnam.

Soon after arriving in-country, Jim Graham accompanied an infantry unit on a search-and-destroy mission. After an unopposed air assault, he followed the unit commander toward a village. A machine gun opened fire from the village, and the approaching troops took cover in the rice paddies and continued to advance. Nobody was hit, and when the Americans entered the village, they found only a teenage boy chained to a gun that had been carefully arranged to fire over the heads of any approaching troops and delay their advance until the Viet Cong could escape.

"Thus ended my war," recalled Jim. "We waited for the choppers and rode back to base camp in silence."

But this was not the end of his combat tour. He was posted three hundred miles farther south. In Saigon, he wore civilian clothes and worked in the office of a Vietnamese printing company. Every week he received a packet of stories and pictures from the First Cav's public information team and assembled this material into an edition of the *Cavalair*, the division's weekly newspaper. His assignment was not without danger. During Jim's time there, Viet Cong bombs destroyed Saigon hotels where US troops were billeted and blew up restaurants where they were known to visit. From time to time, a GI was abducted or shot in the streets.

When his enlistment was up in April 1966, Jim returned to the States for an honorable discharge. He went back to Columbus, where his wife, Patty, lived, and immediately went to work for the *Ledger*. But after exposing the police burglary ring, Jim and Patty found living in Columbus very uncomfortable. They decided to move to Athens, where Jim used his veteran's educational benefits to enroll at the University of Georgia's Henry W. Grady College of Journalism and Mass Communication. "The dean looked at my clippings and said, 'I don't think there's a hell of a lot we can teach you.'" The dean nevertheless told Jim to take the few core classes that he personally taught and any other courses he wanted until he had enough credits to graduate with a degree in journalism.

After Jim earned his degree at the end of 1969, he and Patty divorced. He sent out dozens of résumés and received two offers. He accepted a job as a general assignment reporter at the *Detroit News* for $101 a week.

For the next decade Jim covered every sort of story, including a few notable scoops. He helped organize a chapter of the Newspaper Guild, a move the *News* had resisted for more than a century. And he married Molly Abraham, the *News*'s restaurant critic, adopted her six-year-old son, Jimmy, and fathered another son, Rob.

Throughout his reporting career, the one area that Jim never covered was politics, even though, like all big cities, Detroit offered much to report about. Perhaps this omission is why in 1978, at the start of his second term, Detroit mayor Coleman Young asked Jim to serve as his press secretary. Regarded as one of America's leading African American politicians in the 1950s, Young rose to national prominence after confronting Wisconsin senator Joseph McCarthy. Then a labor organizer, Young told the senator, "You think I'm a crook, but I think it's *you* who is the crook." Although Young served five terms in office, Jim lasted only two years as his press secretary before the mayor decided he needed "somebody more political."

If Jim was insufficiently political for the mayor, his two years in city hall made him *too* political for another Detroit journalism job. "My wife was well established in her job, and we didn't want to leave the area," explained Jim. "I took a corporate media relations job, which I hated, but it paid well enough."

After five years he quit and became a freelance media consultant. Around that time, his second marriage fell apart. "I probably should have taken the opportunity to leave Detroit and find a decent job, but my sons were there and so was everybody else I knew," he explained.

Jim remained single, meanwhile struggling with the feast-or-famine life-style that is the freelancer's lot. His clients included the county government and Ogilvy & Mather Advertising, for whom he wrote newsletters for a division of the Ford Motor Company. Over his ten years as a freelance writer, Detroit's business community changed drastically. Many companies folded or moved away.

In 1991, Jim decided he needed a better job. He answered a blind ad and became the executive director of Friends of the Rouge, an organization formed to raise awareness about the need to clean up the Rouge River in southeast Michigan. The Rouge River meanders for twenty-two miles through Detroit and its suburbs, and in 1991 it was one of the most polluted rivers in the country. The biggest polluter was the enormous complex built by the Ford

Motor Company between 1915 and 1930. It was said that raw materials went in one end of the Rouge River complex and finished cars came out the other. More than a square mile was covered by ninety-three structures, including steel furnaces, coke ovens, rolling mills, glass furnaces, and plate-glass rollers, factories for manufacturing tires, casting engines, building and assembling frames, manufacturing transmissions and radiators, a soybean conversion plant that turned soybeans into plastic auto parts, and even a paper mill. A massive coal-burning power plant produced enough electricity to light the city of Detroit.

Much of the waste generated by this facility went into the river. So had the garbage and trash of three generations. Even worse, the area's sewer system was built to carry both sewage and stormwater. That meant that whenever it rained, the pipes overflowed and dumped both rainwater and raw sewage into the river.

For decades, little maintenance was performed on the region's storm drains and the drinking water pipes that ran within them. In 1992, an Environmental Protection Agency program, the Detroit Project, was initiated to deal with the sewer overflows into the river and to cope with other pollution sources, including sanitary sewer overflows, stormwater runoff, and discharges from illicit connections and failed septic systems.

Jim's new job was to recruit thousands of volunteers to help remove trash and logjams from the river and to design and initiate a variety of education programs for adults and schoolkids about their local environment. With Friends of the Rouge, he launched public involvement and education programs. He tripled the organization's budget, raising large sums to help fund its programs. And he hired several people who have remained with the organization today. The organization continues to educate schoolchildren and adults and has recruited more than fifty thousand volunteers, given thousands of workshops, and produced vast quantities of printed material. In Wayne County alone, almost seven hundred schools have joined the state's green school program.

Jim said, "The ten years I spent at Friends of the Rouge were some of the most satisfying and fulfilling of my career." He was fifty when he got that job, and he said, "I often told people that it had taken me fifty years to find the right job."

Sewage no longer runs in the Rouge River. Acres of native plant zones were created throughout the watershed, and thousands of native plants, trees, and shrubs were planted. Fourteen tons of contaminated fish were removed from two small lakes along the river, along with more than a half million tons of contaminated sediment. Trout, catfish, largemouth bass, and carp have returned to the river, along with other long-vanished aquatic life, including several species of insects that are vital to the river's ecology. In 2014, for the first time in more than a century, salmon swam in the Rouge River.

———◇———

In 1990, Jim joined a choir because he loved to sing and because it seemed like a good place to meet someone who shared his interest in singing. It worked. Gail Reagan and Jim dated for almost ten years. In 1999, he had a quadruple heart bypass; Gail was his caregiver all the way. "That operation opened my heart and my eyes," said Jim. "Nobody else had taken such good care of me." They were married soon after he recovered from surgery.

In 2009, Jim Graham retired from his last job, fund-raising for Walsh College, a business school. In retirement, he continues to volunteer for Friends of the Rouge by writing fund-raising letters and emails.

MICHAEL REAGAN

We cannot know what heaven is, but we should hope that when we stand before our Creator to be judged, we will not be asked how numerous were our good deeds. Instead, we will be asked, "How much love did we put into what we did?"

Michael Reagan was born and raised in Seattle in an impoverished household. His parents were abusive alcoholics. Though his years of fear and anger are now long past, he remembered, "I was the oldest son, so I was kind of the family's caretaker, and I got tired of it."

When his close friend Bill Denhoff was killed in Vietnam, Reagan grew angry and wanted to join the Marine Corps. He thought it might be fun to travel, but he confessed, "Tell the truth, I thought that living in Vietnam might actually be less dangerous than where I lived. So four of us, all friends from the neighborhood, decided to join up. Two joined the army, and two the marines. We all went to Vietnam to avenge Bill's death."

After boot camp, Reagan went to Camp Pendleton for a couple of months. Confident that his training had been top notch, he said, "I'd been trained as a marine to fight in a war. I felt that I was totally prepared, as a good marine should be, and I was a good marine. I didn't even think about life or death." But when he got off the plane, his attitude abruptly changed.

"When I got off the plane," he said, "it was hotter than Hades. I smelled things that no one wants to smell. My first thought was that maybe this wasn't the best idea. I dropped my bags off at Dong Ha, at a place called Con Thien, in midsummer 1967. When I first heard the word *incoming* I thought I'd pee my pants. It was the scariest thing I've ever seen, and we got a ton of that every day.

"All of a sudden I went from knowing everything I needed to know to survive to being a novice and having to learn all kinds of new stuff to stay alive—not to fight, just to stay alive. Over that year we learned more stuff, things that you never thought you'd ever want to learn. Good things and bad things," Reagan recounted.

He was assigned as a rifleman to Kilo Company, Third Battalion, Fourth Marines. It was hard, hot, dangerous work. "When I landed, my squad leader had some advice for me," Reagan remembered. "'You want to stay alive, listen to what I have to say.' I listened to every word. My platoon commander was the same way. He said, 'I'm gonna teach you how to stay alive.' I followed all their directions."

Combat for Reagan's platoon was steady and deadly. Within two or three months, his squad leader went home.

"The platoon commander called me over and said, 'I want you to take over the squad.'"

Kilo Company and Reagan spent most of his tour on or near the demilitarized zone (DMZ). "One day in March 1968 we were moved to Cam Lo regional headquarters," he recalled. "We were told this new area would be a lot safer than where we had been, even though it was still near the DMZ. We were tired, short-staffed, and hungry for food, mail, and sleep. We needed a rest," Reagan explained.

For reasons rarely explained to American civilians, the Vietnamese DMZ was anything but demilitarized. An international treaty prohibited military activities or equipment within the DMZ, but the North Vietnamese ignored the treaty and used it to park men, equipment, and all sorts of weapons with little fear of being attacked. US and Allied forces, on the other hand, observed that strip of land near the seventeenth parallel that was two kilometers deep, running east from the Laos border more than a hundred kilometers to the South China Sea.

At their new location, Reagan's platoon was assigned to the DMZ's perimeter guard. "Most of the others were out on patrol," he recalled. "Early that morning we were hit by rockets and mortars. A lot of them. And because we were still near the DMZ, we were pounded by very large rockets that had been fired at a steep angle and so seemed to drop out of the sky without warning—no one knew where they would hit. We had holes to hide in, but we knew the enemy sometimes snuck up on us under their own incoming. If they caught us in our holes, they'd kill us. We had to be ready to jump out once the incoming stopped, then fight to stay alive.

"Because of our patrols, there was a delay in the enemy's attack. We were able to get to our wounded. There were two men I knew well. Peder Armstrong went to my high school in Seattle. Vincent 'Vinny' Santaniello was from Queens, New York. He was our company driver. Peder was soon dead and Vinny was badly injured—his leg was almost blown off and his femoral artery cut. We didn't know that once that artery is cut, you're dead. Our medics, John Nunn and Tony Milazzo, and I went to Vinny and tried to stop the bleeding.

"I held Vinny in my arms and tried to calm him, although it didn't appear to me, as I remember it, that he was feeling a lot of pain. Both medics went at him as vigorously as anyone could, trying to keep him alive. As I held him in my arms, all I could do was tell him that he would be okay. I also wanted to be sure that he knew he wasn't alone," Reagan continued.

"We all knew that our battle wasn't over. We expected the enemy to come and the fighting to resume. Meanwhile, our attention was on Vinny.

"And that's when my life changed," Reagan said. "Suddenly Vinny looked up at me and said, 'Mike, I just want to go home!' Then he closed his eyes and died. He went home. I've seen his face every day since then for more than fifty years."

When Reagan's year in the war zone was up, he had to leave the battlefield alive before he could be on his way home. A Chinook came to take him and his squad. The big twin-rotor helicopter approached the pickup point near the DMZ and immediately came under fire. Reagan and his men began shooting back, hoping to keep that helicopter aloft long enough for them to escape. There was so much incoming fire, the pilot couldn't land. He hovered toward the ten waiting men, five going on R & R and five going home. Reagan sent the others ahead, and one by one, with Reagan going last, the Chinook's door gunner grabbed them and threw them into the copter. "We were told to stay on the floor," Reagan recalled. "As we rose, bullets came through where the windows had been—there was no glass in them—and were ricocheting around inside, over our heads, until we were at altitude. I was at the door and watched the ground disappear and prayed we'd keep going up," he recounted.

Reagan flew from Da Nang to Okinawa on a KC-130. Flag-draped coffins were placed down the center aisle; homebound troops were in canvas-strap seats along the sides. "My plan was to pick up my extra seabag, which I had stored before I went into Vietnam a year before. Then I could change into better clothes for the rest of the trip. But my bag was among the many that couldn't be found. They seemed to lose a lot of seabags," Reagan recalled, still annoyed after so many years.

"Five of us coming out of the field had buddied up, and two had bags that were found. We were all about the same size, so we dumped everything out of the bags and put on whatever we could find." From Okinawa, the marines flew first to Midway Island, refueled, and then went on to Hawaii.

On the leg to Hawaii, a marine colonel noticed Reagan was out of uniform and said so. "At first I was sarcastic about it," Reagan recalled. "That was stupid. Then I told him why I had no clothes. He asked for my name and serial number." The colonel disappeared for some time. When he returned, he told Reagan that, when they landed in Hawaii, he was to go with the MPs who would be waiting for him.

"We landed in the middle of the night, and I went with the MPs," Reagan continued. "They took me to an airport bathroom and secured the door. They told me to clean myself up. The colonel had called from the plane and had gotten a uniform made up for me, from underwear to ribbons. And they gave me bathing materials—a towel, soap, razor, and shaving cream. They held the plane for me.

"Back on the plane, when I passed the colonel, he smiled," Reagan recalled.

The marines flew to Travis Air Force Base near Sacramento, where they were given civilian clothes and ordered to change before taking a bus to San

Francisco International Airport. "They told us there were people who would not welcome us back home. We had to conceal that we had been in Vietnam," Reagan recalled. "I flew to Seattle, where there were more antiwar folks to spit on us and call us names. Still no welcome home. I got home, and around 7:30 a.m., my friend Maynard Tapp, may he rest in peace, knocked on the door. When I answered, he hugged me and said, 'Thanks for coming home from Vietnam.'

"*Now* I was home.

"I knew that while I was in the war, I had crossed over some kind of threshold. The world I knew when I left had been changed to something else. I didn't know what it was, and it didn't feel safe. I didn't hide from being a Vietnam vet, but I didn't make it something I wore on my shirt either. When I left, I was a nineteen-year-old child. Now my childhood was gone. I was back in Seattle as a twenty-one-year-old adult, and I felt alone. When we were in Vietnam, we were never alone. We had our brothers with us. Whether they lived or died, they were always there with us," he said.

Reagan's adjustment to being out of combat was less than smooth. "I started seeing all the antiwar stuff that was going on, seeing uncensored television and reading uncensored newspapers, and all the stuff we'd experienced wasn't what they were talking about. And the brotherhood of my unit, the security, and support—that was all gone. I began to question if I knew enough to be able to survive this transition. I'm sure a lot of us were asking ourselves those questions. Many came up with the wrong answers, but fortunately for me, I ran into people who didn't understand who I was and where I'd come from and what I was doing or what it had made me. They just knew that I seemed to be worthwhile enough to keep straight, to keep out of doing stupid stuff and wrong stuff."

Reagan met some of those people after enrolling in Seattle's Burnley School of Professional Art. It was a three-year program, paid for with his GI Bill education benefit.

In high school, Reagan had often gotten into trouble for drawing on everything and everybody. "I like to tell people I was a straight C student, except in art, where I got a B+, and the only reason I didn't get an A was that my art teacher told me that I wasn't trying hard enough. He told me I had more talent than I was using."

In Vietnam, Reagan had spent some of the time between combat engagements drawing portraits of the men in his squad and platoon. "I used to tear open the C-ration boxes and use those and a grease pencil to draw portraits," he recalled. "They'd send those home, and they'd pay me, and I'd send the money home. By then I knew that I wanted to become an artist when I got home. But a lot of the guys whose portraits I drew didn't come home. Their pictures were the only thing that came home."

"I graduated in late 1973," he explained. "My first freelance job was to do a cartoon book for special education for the Seattle school district. The person in charge of special education was a retired marine colonel who'd served in Vietnam. He called me to his office and asked if I needed a job. I did. I was twenty-seven and freelancing wasn't working for me." The colonel told Reagan about the Comprehensive Employment Training Act (CETA) and that he was teaching people how to use computers. "I could use some of your design sense," he said.

After he learned to program computers, Reagan was hired by the University of Washington to combine his computer and graphic art skills in a new office called trademarks and licensing. He worked for UW as director of trademarks and licensing while also serving as the unofficial artist-in-residence.

For Reagan, it was the perfect job. He designed trademarks and logos while also creating posters and artwork for UW. He retired in 2005 with a pension. During those thirty years, he earned a reputation as a first-class portrait artist. Reagan has drawn portraits of seven US presidents (Richard Nixon, Gerald Ford, Jimmy Carter, George H. W. Bush, George W. Bush, and Donald Trump) plus a pope and three prime ministers. He has created artwork for the Seattle Seahawks, the National Football League, and many celebrities.

In 2004, Sharise Johnson, the widow of a medic who had been killed in Iraq, called to ask what Reagan would charge for a portrait of her husband. The image of the dying Vincent Santaniello flashed through his mind. Without a moment's hesitation, he said, "I can't charge you. I'm a Marine Corps Vietnam veteran."

"At that moment I understood that the final moment of Vincent's life on March 28, 1968, was the moment I was actually born for. As he died in my arms, Vinny was telling me that we would be doing this work someday. He said he wanted to go home. For more than fourteen years I've been trying to keep Vinny's wish for a lot of other fallen heroes: getting them home. It's changed my life," he said. "I know my soul has come home from Vietnam.

"Mrs. Johnson called me after she received the portrait and said that when she saw it she was for the first time able to talk to her late husband about everything they had left unfinished," Reagan recalled. "She told me that she loved him and that she felt him tell her that he loved her back. She said, 'In the year that my husband's been dead, I haven't slept through a full night. But after I saw his portrait, I slept all night.'"

Reagan keeps a towel on his drawing board because the act of drawing each portrait brings tears to his eyes. He has now drawn more than fifty-three hundred pencil portraits for the families of soldiers killed in Iraq and Afghanistan and of all the victims of the 2018 Marjory Stoneman Douglas High School shooting. Each takes five to six hours. This is now Reagan's unpaid full-time job. They provide closure for the families and for himself.

"Something changed me in Vietnam," he observed. "God has blessed me. God had a purpose for me even before I went to Vietnam, and this is that purpose. When I'm tired or I've got a cold or the flu, and I still have to finish a picture, it's Him doing it. I know now that I did all those celebrity drawings so I could prepare my skills to do portraits of all these soldiers.

"People ask how I pay the bills. Nobody makes any money from my portraits. Not my attorneys, not my accountants, not me. We're all volunteers," he explained. "I'm a 501(c)(3) and we can't get any corporate help. But every time I've needed something, it shows up. A company in Germany gives me pencils. Another company called me to say, 'You'll never have to order more drawing boards.'" He only pays for mailing tubes and postage to send his drawings to gold star parents and widows.

Reagan and his wife, Cheryl, have modified their lifestyle to live on less. He used to buy a new car every other year; now he drives a twelve-year-old compact. "I spend a lot of time doing talks and sending posters out and letting people know about the Fallen Heroes Project." In 2018 NBC ran a story about Reagan, and the next month donations poured in.

In March 2015, Reagan's work was recognized by the Congressional Medal of Honor Foundation. He was awarded the Civilian Service Before Self medal in a ceremony at Arlington National Cemetery.

"Every day, all across America, ordinary citizens perform extraordinary acts of courage and service," said Ron Rand, president and CEO of the foundation. "The Citizen Honors Program was created by our nation's truest heroes, the recipients of the Medal of Honor, to recognize and celebrate the amazing deeds of America's citizen heroes."

After the ceremony, Reagan and Cheryl flew back to Seattle. Cheryl is a nurse, and she had to return to her regular shift, and Michael, days behind in his work of love, had to return to his board to resume drawing another fallen hero.

OLIVER STONE

Motion pictures combine multiple technologies with multiple art forms. No amount of technology, however, replaces a compelling story. Through his many powerful films, Oliver Stone has demonstrated his mastery of the art of using fiction to convey reality.

Oliver Stone's first trip to Vietnam was in 1965. He was nineteen and fluent in his French-born mother's native tongue; he found a job teaching the children of affluent ethnic Chinese in the Free Pacific Institute, a Catholic school in Cholon, Saigon's Chinese neighborhood. "This was my first teaching experience, and it taught me a lot," Stone recalled. "I worked two semesters; I had my hands full with forty to fifty kids in each class. I taught several subjects. If I flunked a kid, he'd show up next semester in my higher classes anyway; they never repeated a class, because the parents were paying for their kids to attend. I'd say there was a lack of integrity, but because the country was at war, the school's administrator was grateful the parents could afford to send their kids there."

In that period before great numbers of US troops began arriving in

Vietnam, Stone was one of the few Americans in Cholon. He nevertheless traveled around Saigon on a motorbike and never felt threatened.

Stone worked for his return passage on the *Red River*, a US-flagged freighter, by serving as a wiper, keeping the engine room and boiler tubes clean. "We came back on a very rough trip through the North Pacific to Coos Bay, Oregon. After that, I had no desire to go back to sea," Stone said.

Born William Oliver Stone in 1946, he was the only son of Louis Stone, a successful stockbroker and financial writer, and Jacqueline Goddet. His parents met in Paris in 1945, while his father, a lieutenant colonel, served as a finance officer on Gen. Dwight D. Eisenhower's staff.

Stone grew up in New York but spent his summers with his maternal grandparents in France. He attended Trinity School, the oldest continually operated school in New York City, and later spent four years at the Hill, a Pottstown, Pennsylvania, boarding school. He went to Yale but dropped out and joined the merchant marine. Stone traveled widely, but his last overseas port of call was Saigon.

Returning to the States, Stone reenrolled in Yale and again dropped out because "I was writing a book. I wanted to be a novelist. I admired Mailer and Hemingway and Joyce and Jack London and above all Joseph Conrad," he told Bill Moyers.

Writing as Oliver Stone, his book was rejected by publishers, so he gave up "trying to be different" and went back to his birth name. "I joined the army as William Stone," he said. "I wanted to be anonymous. I wanted to be, as I said in *Platoon*, to be like every other person. I didn't want any special breaks. I just wanted to be infantry. I didn't want to be a lieutenant. I wanted to be a PFC and get it from the bottom. And if God had a meaning for my life, He'd sort it out. Otherwise, I'd be dead. That was my approach in 1967."

Trained as an infantryman, Stone arrived in Vietnam during the last part of the 1968 Tet Offensive. He served with the Twenty-Fifth Infantry Division, then deployed near the Cambodian border. He was wounded twice and awarded the Bronze Star for valor.

"I was feeling my way. I don't think I am of the warrior class, but I did my job. Eventually, I did well as a soldier. At first, I was a typical grunt. I made mistakes. The first time I was wounded, this idiot behind me threw a grenade at night when he didn't know what he was doing. It landed close to me, and I was hit by shrapnel."

When he first went into combat, he said, he was afraid at times, especially in the beginning. "You learn to crystallize the fear. You have to lose the fear, get past it because, otherwise, you're going to freeze up. Sometimes you get angry, and that's not a good emotion either. You get numbed out, you reach a place of desensitization. You shoot without thinking. And you shoot because it's an instinct," he added.

He honed his skills, though, and said, "We were losing men. I saved some people."

One day a sniper, half-hidden in a spider hole, was systematically killing men in Stone's platoon. From a distance Stone remembers as twenty to twenty-five yards, he threw a grenade that landed in the hole and killed the sniper. It was a difficult toss. The sniper was almost as far away as home plate is to first base, and the M-26 grenade Stone threw was three times as heavy as a baseball and only two-thirds its diameter. Moreover, had he thrown the grenade too far or not far enough, he might have killed someone in his own platoon.

"I will always remember that sniper. I saw his body. I did my job as a soldier, and he was doing his job. He's still there as a spirit in my mind," Stone added.

What Stone encountered in Vietnam was nothing like what he had imagined. A writer by instinct, he said, "I couldn't take notes in the field because it was so wet." Being wounded a second time made everything real. "I realized what war really was. I think that getting real was the best thing that ever happened to me," he explained.

After recovering, he went to the Auxiliary Military Police in Saigon and got into a fight with a sergeant. But instead of the usual punishment, Stone was allowed to volunteer to return to a combat unit. He joined the First Squadron, Ninth Cavalry, the First Cavalry Division's reconnaissance unit. Seven months later he completed his tour. He was honorably discharged and returned to New York City.

Like many Vietnam veterans, he found adjusting to civilian life difficult. "I came back desensitized. I was another person," he recalled. "Speaking another language. Thinking another way. Not believing in anything I saw in Vietnam. I was an angry young man and had violent thoughts. It took me a while, a few months, to get into any kind of situation where I could be social and integrate."

Only six months after his return, he went back to college on the GI Bill. He said, "I was very lucky in the sense that I went to the NYU film school, and I got a chance to make films. That was a release, an artistic expression, and I did three Vietnam movies. Over the course of those three movies, I learned a lot more and I worked out some of my deepest feelings that I didn't even recognize at the time."

Before graduating from NYU with a bachelor's in fine arts, Stone worked at various jobs. He drove a cab, served as a messenger, became a salesman, and then worked as a production assistant. All the while, he wrote screenplays. Then he wrote a long treatment—an industry term for a description of a screenplay, sometimes with a scene or two—that was optioned by a producer. The treatment never went anywhere, but the producer, recognizing talent, helped Stone find an agent.

To all but cinephiles, Stone's career began in 1986 with *Salvador* and *Platoon*. But he labored in obscurity for many years before those films, making his living as a screenwriter, starting with a pair of horror movies, *Seizure* (1974) and *The Hand* (1981), and two short films, *Last Year in Viet Nam* (1971) and *Mad Man of Martinique* (1979).

But almost ten years earlier, when he was in his late thirties, Stone began to get noticed with a series of screenplays adapted from novels: *Midnight Express* (1978); *Conan the Barbarian*, written with director John Milius (1982); *Scarface*, also with Milius (1983); and *Year of the Dragon* (1985), written with director Michael Cimino.

Midnight Express had a bare-bones budget but was an enormous commercial success worldwide. It was nominated for six Academy Awards. For his work on the film, Stone won an Academy Award, for best adapted screenplay, and also a Golden Globe Award.

In 1976, Stone wrote *Platoon*, which was loosely based on his experiences in Vietnam. Over the next decade it was turned down or picked up but not made so many times that Stone began to think of the script as a stale joke.

He had written the screenplays for *Midnight Express*, *Scarface*, and *Conan*, but he was a director at heart. Stone told Bill Moyers, "I wanted to break through. I'd had two failures up to then, two horror films. . . . I vowed never to do a horror film again."

While working with Michael Cimino on *The Year of the Dragon*, Cimino convinced him to show the *Platoon* script to Dino De Laurentiis, who never followed through on producing the film. It took a lawsuit for Stone to reclaim the rights to his work.

In 1986, he met English producer John Daly, who had read both *Salvador*, Stone's most recent work, and *Platoon*.

As he told the *Guardian*'s Mark Lawson in 2006, "Daly asked which one I wanted to do first," Stone recalled. "To a young filmmaker, it was like a dream." Stone chose *Salvador* because he was convinced *Platoon* was cursed and, like so many times before, something would happen in preproduction that would be the end of it. "God bless the English for making those two movies," Stone said. "They were made almost fraudulently in Mexico. *Salvador* was made on a letter of credit issued for an Arnold Schwarzenegger movie."

Stone won his second Oscar for directing *Platoon*. With that, he had arrived and had the status to make almost any movie he wanted to make. His filmography includes two more films about Vietnam, *Born on the Fourth of July* (1989) and *Heaven and Earth* (1993), each exploring different dimensions of the war.

As with his earlier work, Stone's later films use fiction to illuminate the truth as Stone saw it. In *JFK* (1991), for example, he rejected the findings of the Warren Commission and searched for an answer to the puzzle of John F. Kennedy's assassination that made sense to him.

Stone has been nominated for an Oscar eleven times and has been awarded three Oscars, two for directing, *Platoon* and *Born on the Fourth of July*, and one for screenwriting, *Midnight Express*.

He has returned to Vietnam several times. "They are a mix of amazing people, resilient, a new generation that in a sense has forgotten the war," Stone said. "They didn't make a big deal about it, it was another . . . war for them. Between the French, the Americans, and the Chinese . . . they have a history of warfare. They're warriors. On the other hand, I do have some qualms about the commercialization of the place and the spirituality of it. I don't understand the Vietnamese. . . . There are things in modern Vietnam that elude me. They still seem to me to have a collective strength and also a collective judgment. In other words, everyone is judged in that society. There is more freedom here, freedom of choice, in America."

In many ways, Stone's story is typical of Vietnam veterans. He went to war as a naive young man and came back angry, embittered, and lost in his own land. Then he pulled himself together and, still struggling against inner demons, finished his formal education, found a vocation, worked through years of failures and rejection until an opportunity presented itself. Like so many of his brothers in arms, Stone rallied his inner resources, summoned what he had learned in both war and peace, and rose to the occasion. Thus, he found his niche in life, in American society. While few Vietnam veterans have earned the worldwide recognition Oliver Stone has, most have followed this path to find their place in the world.

At the suggestion of the subject, portions of this profile are drawn from his interviews with Bill Moyer in 2009 and with Mark Lawson in 2006 for the *Guardian*.[1]

PAUL
LONGGREAR

Are there such things as miracles, or are they merely unexplained natural phenomena? Does God still speak to humans? Can people change their character almost overnight? Paul Longgrear would say yes to all those questions. Is Longgrear a saint or merely a spinner of tall tales? He has never laid any claim to sainthood, but he is likely the finest, most humble, and genuinely devout man you will ever meet.

Paul Longgrear was thirty-five years old when he met his father for the first time. He had grown up without a father in a hardscrabble household headed by a single mother in Jonesboro, Arkansas.

"We didn't go to church," he recalled. "My mother worked all the time just to feed me and keep me in clothes. But I'm an American, and back then, people prayed in school. Some kids I knew invited me to church. I didn't want to go, but I believed there was a God."

This is odd talk from a man who would over many years earn his living as the pastor of four Baptist churches. A man who led Georgia state prison inmates in Bible study. A salaried Christian counselor at Liberty University.

Someone who gave Bible lessons in a Columbus, Georgia, rescue mission for the homeless and indigent. A person who spent a good part of his life helping destitute Jews in Eastern European nations emigrate to Israel.

Before that work, though, when he was just twenty-two years old, Longgrear received a draft notice in the mail. "I was physically healthy, I was sound of mind, I knew I was going to have to serve in the army," he recalled. "And I didn't really mind going. I wanted to see the world. I was pretty wild at that time. *Really* wild, to be honest."

Longgrear took to the army like a termite to a log. "I grew up wanting to be Sergeant Rock," he recalled, referring to a popular comic book character. "That's all I wanted: to lead American kids into battle."

After basic training at Fort Polk, Louisiana, where he was selected as the outstanding trainee in his company, Longgrear went to Fort Ord, California, for advanced infantry training. He graduated fourth in his class. Then he was sent to officer candidate school at Fort Benning, Georgia, where he was the distinguished graduate in his class. Along with his commission as a second lieutenant came a two-year commitment from the date of his commissioning. "They kept me there as a tactical officer," he recalled. A tactical officer is the OCS equivalent of a basic training drill instructor; his job was to train new candidates.

But Longgrear was not a happy camper. He wanted to go to Vietnam. He called a Pentagon personnel officer five weeks in a row until that officer suggested Longgrear volunteer for parachute training and then apply to become a Green Beret. Lieutenant Longgrear was married in December 1966, then he went to the special warfare school. The following October he left for Vietnam.

"My wife, Patty, was a Christian. Before I left for Vietnam, she went to live with her parents in Alabama. The last thing she said to me before I left was, 'I'll be praying for you.'"

In Vietnam, he was assigned to the Fifth Special Forces.

The Special Forces are force multipliers. By recruiting and training local fighters from Vietnam's scores of minority groups, a dozen Green Berets could lead an army of hundreds into battle against the Viet Cong or the North Vietnamese.

Instead of leading American soldiers into combat, Longgrear was assigned to the Mike Force. "Mike" meant mercenaries, and each unit had several hundred troops that were stationed at four strategic sites in Vietnam. They were a mixture of Vietnam's minorities, including Cambodians, Laotians, Chinese, and the thirty different indigenous tribes collectively known as Montagnards ("Yards" for short; "people of the mountain" in French) or *Degar*. Led by American and Australian officers, they were an elite force, highly trained, well-equipped, and used as a fire brigade to reinforce Special Forces units that encountered more trouble than they could handle.

In October 1967, as a first lieutenant, Longgrear led the Twelfth Company of the First Corps, Mike Force, a unit of four forty-man platoons of Rhe Montagnard tribesmen to reinforce the Special Forces camp at Lang Vei in South Vietnam's northwestern corner.

The A-Team commander was Capt. Frank Willoughby, Longgrear's classmate in the Special Forces qualification course. Willoughby invited Longgrear into his camp but insisted that the Rhe tribesmen remain outside. He feared there would be trouble between Longgrear's men and his own Bru Montagnards.

Willoughby said, "Why don't you come in so I can introduce you to the guys?"

Longgrear responded, "If my Yards aren't invited inside your camp, *I'm* not invited inside your camp."

Intelligence reports suggested the North Vietnamese Army (NVA) would soon attack Lang Vei. For the next four months, Longgrear and his men went on long-range patrols, looking for signs that an attack was imminent.

"The enemy's rule at that time was to avoid engagement," Longgrear explained. "They were building up their forces for what would become known as the Tet Offensive and didn't want to draw attention to themselves. So every once in a while, when one of our long-range patrols bumped into the NVA, they'd literally take off running, no matter how many of them there were. And we kept feeding the intel back."

In late January a senior officer ordered Longgrear and Willoughby to bring Longgrear's Rhe inside the perimeter. Soon after that, the NVA began probing the camp, mounting small, brief attacks designed to reveal the camp's strong points, locations of automatic weapons, and other intel.

Longgrear recalled, "Every night at about 1700 and lasting about an hour, the NVA fired artillery at us from over the border in Laos. They seemed to be zeroing in. Then we got reinforcements: a Laotian battalion run by the CIA. I had no respect for them, and I didn't trust their loyalties. My battalion commander ordered me to disarm them and keep them outside the camp. I did that, and the State Department complained. I was almost relieved of command, but then the attack began."

The NVA moved on the camp with a vanguard of sixteen Soviet PT-76 light tanks followed by more than a thousand infantry and sappers. "I told my men, 'Fight the ground soldiers. Don't worry about the tanks. They're not going to bother you. If you can keep the enemy off the tanks, we can kill the tanks.' Our 106mm recoilless rifle knocked out the first three tanks. We managed to immobilize all but five of the rest before we ran out of light antitank weapons (LAWs)."

The battle raged for hours, until the enemy penetrated the camp walls.

Longgrear said, "About two o'clock in the morning we retreated eight kilometers from the camp into the tactical operations center, which had been built by the Seabees. It was underground, below an eight-foot tower, and hardened. We numbered thirteen: eight Americans and five Vietnamese Special Forces.

"Our written plan was that once we abandoned the camp, the marines would come at daylight to reinforce us. At 0500 we radioed. I said, 'Okay, we've got them fixed. Got 'em surrounded from the inside. Come and get us.'

"The marine battalion commander told Willoughby, 'There's only eight Americans left alive. More of us than that would be killed trying to rescue you. So good luck. We're not coming.'"

With daylight, the enemy attack resumed. "They found the camp's armory and took all its weapons and ammunition. They shot flamethrowers in. They threw hand grenades, and then they planted a shaped charge, blew a big hole in the wall, trying to get inside and kill us," Longgrear remembered.

"I didn't know it, but my radio operator, Frankie Dooms, had been saying, 'They're killing us, they're killing us, please somebody help us.' We were shooting back, there was fighting everywhere around us. I didn't even know that he was on the radio.

"Fortunately, an FAC came over the radio. He had control of a squadron of A-1E Skyraiders[1] from the carrier *Coral Sea*. But it was overcast, and they couldn't see the ground.

"The FAC heard Frankie and conveyed our situation to the Skyraider flight commander. The FAC said, 'I can't get you down; you can't get down to see.'

"The flight leader said, 'Look, I can't leave those guys. I just can't do it. Not and sleep tonight. Find me a sucker hole.'

"The FAC found a sucker hole—a small opening in the clouds. By the grace of God, that hole was right over us. They swooped down and put bombs right on top of us. We could hear the enemy screaming.

"That gave us a chance to regroup. Then they were shooting flamethrowers in through a hole in the concrete wall and throwing white phosphorous grenades and tear gas at us. At one point, I was on the floor and just trying to breathe. I got my rifle knocked out of my hand, I was hit in the head, my ankle was hit with a grenade fragment."

When the Skyraiders ran out of bombs, they left. Then a three-man team of Americans came through with some Laotian fighters and fought their way toward the ops center.

Longgrear remembers that one of them, Sgt. Eugene Ashley, helped keep the enemy from getting in while his men were regrouping. After they were organized, they took up fighting positions at the holes that they'd blown in the tower above the bunker.

"The Skyraiders were gone. The marines are not coming," Longgrear continued. "I kind of got in a corner by myself, and suddenly running through my head is what Patty said just as I left home. *I'll be praying for you.* Those five words are rolling through my head. *I'll be praying for you.* Over and over.

"I got down on one knee and emptied the bullets from my last magazine. As I took them out, I was praying. I said, *Look here, God, let me tell You something. I've never asked anything from You. I'm prepared to die the way I lived, so I'm not going to ask for anything. But my wife is a Christian, and my baby's never hurt anybody. I expect You to take care of them. You understand that?*

"I had nineteen bullets left," Longgrear continued. "One by one, I jammed them back in the magazine. Eighteen for the enemy, the last one for me. I wasn't gonna be captured.

"After I put my magazine back together, I stood up. I had two of my men with me, and Captain Willoughby had four of his. I said, 'You people can stay down here and die like worms if you want to. I'm going to take my men and we're going outside and die like men.'

"Willoughby said, 'Wait a minute. Calm down, Lieutenant. Calm down.'

"'I'm tired of this crap,' I said, 'I can't take it anymore. I'm about to go crazy. I'm running out of ammo, haven't had any water to drink, I'm bleeding. I'm out of here.'

"Willoughby said, 'If the lieutenant's going, we're all going.'

"The captain radioed his headquarters and told a colonel that our little group was leaving."

The colonel said the enemy was using the camp's old fighting positions for protection from the bombers. He said he would call the orbiting Skyraiders and have them make three more bombing runs. That would be all the bombs they had left. But after those three runs, they would make a few more passes, hoping this would keep the enemy's heads down long enough that they wouldn't see the small American force come out.

"We all went to the door. Three of the men were wounded and couldn't walk. So three men carried them. I was the point man. We moved to the door, and I asked, 'Everybody ready?'

"They said, 'We're ready.'

"'Who's going first?'

"And this kid Frankie says, 'Hell, Lieutenant, it's your idea. *You* go first.'

"I looked at him for a second and thought, *He's right. It's my idea.*"

The steps had been burned away, but the risers, the wood that supported the steps on either side, were intact. Longgrear slung his rifle over a shoulder, wedged his back against one riser and his feet against the other, and slowly made it to the top, all the while hoping no enemy soldier would drop a grenade through the top of the tower. "One hand grenade, they'd get us all," he said.

When he got to the top, he found that someone had left some barrels near the structure. "I got behind a barrel and looked all around," Longgrear remembered. "I didn't see anybody."

At that moment, one of the Skyraiders appeared, no more than fifty feet off the ground and roaring toward him at over 200 mph. For an instant Longgrear and the Skyraider pilot locked eyes. "His name was Ron Brand," Longgrear recalled. "Many years later, we met at a reunion.

"I looked at that dude, and he waggled his wings.

"When I saw that, a jolt of something, maybe adrenaline, shot through me. I'd never done drugs, but I couldn't have been any higher. I mean I was like, *God, if I could jump fifty feet, I'd be out of here.*"

The men still in the tower pushed the wounded up and out. One by one, Longgrear dragged them behind the barrels. And then the other three came up.

Eugene Ashley opined they should move uphill, toward the ruins of a supply bunker. When they got there, they should drop over the next hill to the road, which he thought wouldn't be guarded.

"We didn't actually know what was going on at that moment. We're the only ones left alive. Everyone else is dead on the ground around us. Ashley, his men Allen and Johnson, and I left the barrels and started out. I said, 'If you hit the ground, stay where you lay. I'm trying to get as many of us out of here alive as possible.'"

Everyone knew from training and experience that if he were hit, he was to raise his arm so the next man, as he ran by, could grab his hand and keep running. "That was so you don't have to stop and come back," Longgrear explained.

"So we ran until I saw a tank. A knocked-out tank. Now, two days earlier I had paid all my men. But the battle started the next day, and my men's pockets were full of money. As I came around the tank, I found two NVA soldiers behind a machine gun. They had a pile of South Vietnamese money stacked in front of them. I immediately spun around and fired a burst of four rounds before my rifle jammed. At the same time, my ankle popped—it was very loud—and I landed on my back. I put my hand up, but everyone was gone. The fall had knocked the wind out of me. I struggled to get my breath and at the same time tried to clear the jam in my rifle. Again Patty's words ran through my head, *I'll be praying for you . . . I'll be praying for you . . . I'll be praying for you.*

"I said to myself, *I've got to quit thinking about that.*"

Longgrear looked up. "This airplane was passing, and it seemed to stop in midair," he recalled. "Aloud, I said, 'What is *that?*' And then I noticed the sky was full of artillery rounds. The enemy had been firing them to prevent us from bringing in reinforcements. But now there were no more explosions, but I could see the shells, stopped in midair, as though time had paused.

"And still Patty's words ran through my head: *I'll be praying for you.*

"I heard footsteps behind me, so I took my rifle, still jammed, and rolled around to hit the guy with it.

"Then came a blinding light so bright I had to shut my eyes. And I thought, *That's God!*

"He—God—said, *What are you going to do?*

"I said to myself, *What do I say to God?* I thought, *Uh-oh, I'm in trouble.* And then, *Come on, man, be straight, be cool. I can always talk my way out of stuff.* But what do you say to God?

"That was me, talking to myself, trying to deal with this, trying to figure out what's going on. Then something warm began moving down my head. And I thought I was dying. I'd never died before, so I didn't know how it worked. I told myself this is the way you die. I didn't hurt. I wasn't in pain. I just lay there. I caught my breath. I remember the warm feeling washing over my body. I lost all sense of motion. I lost my hearing. I figured, in a moment, I'll be blind. Then I won't be able to speak. I'll just be dead. And I thought, *This isn't bad.* I took a breath and relaxed. I thought I was a dead man.

"And then God said again, *What are you going to do now?* But when He said it that second time, it sounded exactly like my mom when she was fed up with me.

"I realized that the warmth I felt was love. I'd never felt love like that. I'd had a lot of lady friends, and I'd felt that part of love, but I'd never known real love. Never had a daddy. I had five stepdaddies, and they were all a bunch of losers. Momma worked all the time; she was a hard woman. She loved me, and I loved her, but it wasn't like this. This was breathtaking. I knew that God loved me. I began to weep. I didn't know any prayers, any of the stuff they teach in church. Bawling like a baby, I said, *God, I don't want to die, not now.*

"A feeling of great peace came over me. I laid back. Artillery shells screamed overhead and a Skyraider zoomed past me. I thought to check if my rifle was still jammed. It was. I thought, *God didn't say to stay here.* I looked around. I couldn't see any enemy soldiers. I got up and started hobbling until I made it over the hill, to the military crest, and my guys were there. They thought I'd been hit, that I was maybe dead."

His men urged him on, and together they walked to the rendezvous point and met up with the troops sent to escort them to safety.

———◇———

Paul Longgrear received the Silver Star for his actions at Lang Vei. He was so seriously wounded he was medevaced from Vietnam.

When he recovered from his wounds, he volunteered to return to Vietnam. In July 1969, he joined the Fifth Battalion, Forty-Sixth Infantry, part of the 198th Light Infantry Brigade. This time he led American troops, and he again distinguished himself in battle.

The pull of military service remained strong, but after seven years on active duty, Longgrear elected to continue his service as a reserve officer. He retired from the US Army Reserve as a colonel, with twenty-six years of service.

During those years, Longgrear earned a bachelor's in mass media communications at Florida Southern College in Lakeland. While attending college, he also served as the assistant professor of military science and tactics for the school's ROTC program.

The focus of Longgrear's life became serving God in a variety of unusual ways. In addition to earning a living over the years as pastor to four churches, Longgrear slowly came to direct his faith in an unusual direction.

"When I began to study the Bible, I came to understand the Jews' relationship with God," he explained. "God, for whatever reason, had given His heart to the Jews. So I began to realize that, as a Christian, I was sort of adopted into His family. Patty and I eventually became convinced to move to Israel with an organization called the International Christian Embassy, an international Christian Zionist organization based in Jerusalem."

The Longgrears were in Israel for two years. After the fall of the Berlin Wall in 1989 and the subsequent breakup of the Soviet Union, Paul Longgrear went to Russia and then to several of the former Soviet republics for the Ebenezer International Fund.

He and his colleagues looked for Jews who wanted to move to Israel but lacked the means to do so. At one point he was in charge of a camp near Odessa, on the Black Sea, where some five hundred Jews were housed for several months before they boarded a ship to Israel.

"Before they could go to Israel, we first had to prove that each of them was Jewish. We had to hire people to find proof of their heritage. It was difficult. During World War II, while the Nazis were murdering six million European Jews, many Jewish families destroyed anything that might show they were

Jewish," he explained. "We helped them find records in synagogues, proof of a bar mitzvah or of a Jewish marriage. Or a letter from a rabbi, attesting to their Jewish ancestry." Longgrear and his colleagues helped about one hundred thousand Jews emigrate to Israel.

In his later years, Longgrear directed his religious efforts closer to home, teaching the Bible to prison inmates, to the homeless, and to fellowship groups at many different churches. He founded a youth camp, took Christian tour groups to the Holy Land, served as a guest instructor at Bible colleges in Jerusalem and London, and served on the lay staff of several churches. He also coached college football, boxing, and soccer.

But most of all, this graying warrior maintained a deep spiritual relationship with God.

On a blood-drenched battlefield, God had gotten his attention. Longgrear said, "He doesn't speak audibly, but He has nevertheless made it clear to me what He wanted me to do. Go to Israel. To Russia and Ukraine. Teach the poor, the incarcerated, the homeless. God has taught me, mentored me, helped me understand the Scriptures."

Paul Longgrear is in the Officer Candidate School Hall of Fame, the Army Ranger Hall of Fame, and the Arkansas Military Veteran Hall of Fame. He owns an international shipping business and built with his own hands a comfortable home in southern Georgia that he and Patty share.

QUANG X. PHAM

Every person's life is a series of challenges, potential pitfalls, and forks in the road of opportunity. Ripped from a comfortable life in his native country to live in America, Quang X. Pham was forced to learn a new language, adapt to new customs and laws, and make his way in life as he grew to adulthood without the advice and backing of his father, who spent decades in a Communist reeducation camp in Vietnam. No doubt Quang was lucky. But he was also confident enough in his own abilities to embark on two risky courses of action, the first as a Marine Corps aviator and the second as an entrepreneur.

The son of a South Vietnamese Air Force (VNAF) pilot, ten-year-old Quang Pham left Vietnam with his mother and three sisters eight days before the war ended.

"On the night of April 22, my mom woke us. My father told us to pack and get ready to leave," he recalled.

With two suitcases (one containing his father's military records), Quang and his family arranged themselves on a motor scooter, and Lt. Col. Hoa V.

Pham drove through Saigon's darkened streets to Tan Son Nhut Air Base. The family joined a group of perhaps a hundred, mostly women and children, and filled a bus at the air terminal.

"We sat in that bus for more than an hour," Quang recalled. "It was hot and suffocating inside." He saw his father outside, in conversation with various men. Then his father beckoned his mother. She left the bus and returned with fifty dollars in US currency.

The bus abruptly pulled away from the terminal, and Quang saw his father wave in silhouette. "A few minutes later we boarded a C-130. Six hours later we woke up at Clark Air Force Base in the Philippines," he recalled.

"It was our good fortune that my father was among the most senior officers in the VNAF," Quang said. "When President Nguyen Van Thieu resigned on April 21, my father knew Saigon would not hold out much longer." The Phams were on the first or second C-130 refugee flight—mostly filled with the families of VNAF officers and airmen—to leave the country.

After enlisting in the VNAF and rising to sergeant, Quang's father had been selected for flight training in the United States. He was in the last B-25 Mitchell medium bomber class to graduate from Reese Air Force Base in Lubbock, Texas. His first combat missions against the Viet Cong came in 1962, when he was assigned to a fighter squadron based at Da Nang. In 1964, Lieutenant Colonel Pham was flying an A-1E Skyraider in close support of US Marines during a pitched battle at Do Xa when he was shot down by Viet Cong antiaircraft fire. Too low to bail out, he crash-landed and climbed out of his burning aircraft. A marine CH-46 Sea Knight helicopter landed under small-arms fire to rescue him. In 1969, when the US Air Force began transferring newer aircraft to an expanding VNAF in preparation for US withdrawal, Pham commanded a C-123 squadron that flew critical resupply missions during the 1972 Battle of An Loc. During the last two years of the war, he trained VNAF pilots to fly C-130's.

In April 1975, Lieutenant Colonel Pham elected to remain in Vietnam and fight with the slim hope that somehow the North Vietnamese communists would be defeated. "We didn't see my dad again until 1992," Quang Pham added.

From the Philippines, the five Phams were flown to Andersen Air Force Base, Guam, where they stayed for seven days. Saigon fell on April 30, and resettlement officials told the family they would be leaving the next day because the base was expecting many thousands of refugees.

On May 1 or 2, the Phams were among the hundreds who boarded C-141 transports bound for Little Rock, Arkansas, with a refueling stop in Hawaii. In Arkansas, they were bused to Fort Chaffee. They stayed in a makeshift refugee camp for ten weeks until a sponsor family was found for them. Near the end of June, they were flown to Oxnard, California, where Quang began life as an American.

Near the coast and surrounded by strawberry farms, Oxnard is a city of minorities. Mexican Americans and Filipino Americans had their own, largely homogeneous communities, while African Americans mixed with Korean and Thai immigrants and a more affluent white minority.

Because he was new, spoke little English, and was different, Quang was teased and pushed around, but he quickly adapted to his new life. A tall, handsome boy, he learned to play basketball, baseball, and soccer and soon became the equal of his peers and a better athlete than most. In high school, Quang captained the basketball team and dated cheerleaders. He was an American kid who ate different food at home and could get along in three languages.

Through all the years since leaving Vietnam, however, Quang mourned the loss of his childhood dream: to become a pilot like his father. From 1972 to 1975, when his life in Saigon so abruptly ended, the Pham family lived on Tan Son Nhut Air Base. "I was hooked on flying," Quang recalled. "I saw my father go to work in a flight suit. I saw planes land and take off around the clock from the air base and the civilian airport. When my father had duty, I visited the flight line. The first Americans I met were the advisors in my father's squadron. When we fled in 1975, those dreams went out the window."

A decade later, thoroughly Americanized, Quang had no difficulty getting accepted to study at the University of California, Los Angeles, only a hundred miles south of Oxnard.

One day Quang strolled by a small city of booths, a job fair that was part of career day at UCLA. There he met Capt. Doug Hamlin, USMC, who was responsible for recruiting officer candidates out of UCLA, Long Beach State, and a number of other colleges in Southern California.

Quang recalled, "He was in dress uniform and I was intrigued. But I was very timid. I never thought I could become an American military officer or a pilot—those dreams ended after I left Vietnam. I was a twenty-year-old UCLA undergraduate, and when Hamlin presented a brochure about the Marine Corps officer candidate school, it had pictures of airplanes and helicopters on it. But I kind of walked away."

Hamlin called him back over but Quang kept walking. Hamlin persisted: "Yeah, I'm talking to you. You know who I'm talking to."

Quang went back to the booth. "He gave me the whole pitch about the platoon leader's course at Quantico and made it clear that I had to become a marine before I could learn to fly. I had to learn to shoot a rifle, complete infantry training, and be able to lead marines before I could go to flight school in Pensacola. If I passed all the required tests for the pilot program, finished OCS, and became a basic marine officer, flight school was guaranteed."

The recruiter failed to mention that only half of those who start the marine platoon leader's course are able to complete it. Quang was in the half that succeeded. Completion opened the door to fulfilling his dream of flying. After the platoon leader's course, he went to flight school and was assigned to fly the CH-46 Sea Knight dual-rotor helicopter.

"I served on active duty for seven years and in the reserve for six," he explained. He was twice deployed overseas, first during Desert Storm in 1990 and early 1991. "In the summer of 1992, I was embarked aboard the USS *Tarawa* with a four-ship amphibious ready group. We returned to the Gulf in the summer of 1992.

"Between other flying assignments in the reserve and before I left active duty, I served as an aide-de-camp in 1993 to Third Marine Aircraft Wing commander Joe Paul Feder Angelo. General Angelo was a great leader, and I learned a lot as his aide," Quang recalled.

It is rare that a marine general officer reaches his or her lofty position without having previously served as an aide-de-camp. And a great percentage of those selected for aide go on to wear stars on their collar. While on this assignment, Quang, by then a captain, was offered the opportunity to remain on active duty indefinitely, indicating a strong possibility that he would eventually rise to the Corps' senior ranks. Working for a general who had been a marine for thirty years, including three tours in Vietnam, Quang was given the rare opportunity to see what a longtime career would entail. He said, "I could see what the general did, how he spent his days. Also, what his staff did, his chief of staff, and all the other command and control positions in a marine air wing."

Most who spend a year as a general's aide become career officers, but Quang went the other way. He wanted to prove himself in another milieu and avoid "the very rigid military career track of school, deployment, command, more school, and staff jobs" that required twenty to twenty-five years before earning the responsibility he desired.

When Quang left active duty at the end of 1994, he discovered corporate America was very high on junior military officers (JMOs). He connected with a recruiting firm looking for lieutenants and captains ready to enter the private sector. "They had jobs in sales, operations, and finance," Quang recalled. "After serving as an aide, I did not want to be in a corporate headquarters. I wanted to be in sales. I wanted to make the most money I could. I wanted to have the autonomy to plan each day—the opposite of the military lifestyle. You may be the best captain in the marines, but you're going to make the same pay as every captain who served in the marines as long you had."

Quang received several offers. "I could have worked as an executive recruiter or as a chemical salesman, and I had two offers in medical sales and pharmaceutical sales. I accepted the pharmaceutical job for a joint venture between Astra and Merck. It was called Astra Merck, and my job was to sell the big purple pill, Prilosec."

This was the first proton pump inhibitor to be clinically introduced, a prescription-only drug that treated damaged esophagi, stomach ulcers, acid reflux disease, and chronic heartburn. When he was offered the job at the end of 1994, Prilosec was already on its way to being a blockbuster. This was Quang's entrée to the pharmaceutical industry, and he found he enjoyed selling, which was a surprise. "When I was in college or the marines, I had no idea that that was the field I would pursue," he explained.

The two most important tools in a salesman's kit are the ability to think on his feet and a willingness to accept risk—exactly what a marine aviator has for breakfast. In 1998, Quang went from Astra Merck to a rising new San Francisco biotech company, Genentech, then and now one of the world's top biotech companies. "Merck was more oncology oriented, selling purple pills for acid reflux and other GI diseases. Genentech," he said, "had a breast cancer drug, Herceptin, and a lymphoma drug. These were important drugs based on biotechnology, which was different technology than most standard drugs."

After five years in the industry, however, he realized it wasn't as different from the military as he had thought. "Corporate America is career track–oriented too," he explained. "You had to do tours in the field, but in order to get promoted, you had to come inside the corporate headquarters."

Quang did very well at Genentech and was selected for a promotion that would require him to work in the San Francisco headquarters. At that point, he decided to leave the company and become an entrepreneur.

Within two months he raised $5 million in venture capital, and in March 2000, he founded Lathian Systems, a database marketing company that helped drug companies promote their products to doctors. Two years later he sold Lathian to a direct marketing company in New Jersey. While he was running Lathian, Quang started another company that went nowhere fast. "Like any investor, you might make out on one investment but lose and shutter the second one," he explained.

He decided to lean on what he knew best. "Pharmaceuticals are a highly regulated, capital-intensive industry that is usually started by insiders. The value of the company is in its ownership of intellectual properties and the necessary complexity of manufacturing them, which discourages copycat drugs from China, India, and Mexico," Quang explained. "It's difficult but necessary to ensure the quality of products and being able to bear the liability costs if your products don't work or harm people.

"I spent almost twenty years as a consultant, an adviser, and a commercial partner for many different drug companies, taking part in product launches, meeting many people, and networking with them. During those years I was able to get some products into companies and acquire some capital. I invested a lot of my own money and then was able to take part in mergers and acquisition deals to get promising new products into testing and trials before I started my own pharmaceutical firm."

In 2014, Quang started Espero Biopharma. Four years later it was the fastest-growing company in northeast Florida. "Cardiovascular disease is the number one killer globally," he explained. "We have two products in the market that treat angina—chest pain from heart artery blockage. One is a blood thinner called Tecarfarin." The drug is currently in head-to-head human trials with warfarin, presently the industry standard. With its narrow therapeutic window, warfarin interacts with more than 130 drugs. "If you want to get into the market, you've got to beat the standard of care," Quang explained.

The company's other product treats atrial fibrillation. If clinical trials confirm its properties, budiodarone will be marketed as a better alternative to amiodarone, the present standard drug for this condition. Budiodarone works in a similar manner as amiodarone, but it acts faster and is less toxic to the body, resulting in fewer and less severe adverse side effects.

Quang credits Vietnam and the US military for helping him achieve what he wanted to do. "It made my life very rich," he said.

The scared little boy who came to America grew up to realize his dream of flying. Then, after decades of hard work, he became one of America's most valuable and successful resources: an entrepreneur. Now in his early fifties, Quang Pham believes his best may be yet to come.

RUSSELL
BALISOK

According to the New York Times, *most nursing homes had fewer nurses and caretaking staff than they reported to their state and county governments.*[1] *In the fifty states, nearly 1.4 million people are cared for in skilled nursing facilities. When such nursing homes are short-staffed, nurses and aides scramble to deliver meals, ferry bedbound residents to the bathroom, and answer calls for pain medication. Essential medical tasks such as repositioning a patient to avert bedsores may be overlooked when workers are overburdened, and this may lead to an otherwise avoidable hospitalization. So who is looking out for the elderly, taking their abusers to court, forcing nursing homes, hospitals, and HMOs to maintain state-mandated staffing levels, and compelling these institutions to compensate their patients when they fail to follow the law? Men like Russell Balisok rise to the occasion.*

Russell Balisok of Los Angeles is one of the few attorneys in his field. In the state of California, none have done more to force the medical and long-term care community to live up to their legal obligations. He's also authored enforcement legislation and helped guide it through the state assembly and senate into law.

But let's start at the beginning.

Balisok was born and raised in South Central Los Angeles in 1946, when its neighborhoods were an ethnic stew of whites, Mexican Americans, and African Americans. After high school, he enrolled at California State University, Los Angeles.

"I grew up in a one-parent home with a schizophrenic older brother. It was pretty brutal, and it took me quite a long time to really deal with all of that," Balisok said. "I was a poor student from a middle-class family, hence I enrolled in Cal State LA."

He didn't stay long, however. "Rather than quit, I took the easy way and flunked out," Balisok recalled. "I was not interested in school."

On February 15, 1966, Balisok received a draft notice and was sent to basic training at Fort Hood, Texas. He volunteered for advanced infantry training and emerged from this eight-week course as a heavy-weapons infantryman.

He believed he would soon be sent to Vietnam, so he volunteered for officer candidate school and thought the war would be over by the time he graduated. He became an infantry second lieutenant on March 27, 1967, at Fort Benning, Georgia. "That was the worst time of my military career; that was brutal."

Thus, the US Army, as it has for centuries, took a feckless schoolboy and in less than a year turned him into a man and then an officer and a gentleman. As much as Balisok had expected to delay his visit with South Vietnam's unfriendly environs long enough to avoid them altogether, the war continued to boil on. So he applied for flight school. He thought the conflict would be resolved before the next eight months passed, before he learned to fly a helicopter well enough for the army to risk sending him to war.

While his application went through channels, Balisok returned to Fort Hood for four months of seasoning in a mechanized infantry company of the First Armored Division. Then his application was approved, and Balisok went to Fort Wolters, Texas, for primary helicopter training as part of Flight Class 68-4, with graduation scheduled for April 1968. Just before he completed flight training at Fort Rucker, Alabama, Balisok was promoted to first lieutenant, and the war in Vietnam showed no sign of ending. His orders for the war zone came almost immediately after graduation.

By then, Balisok's wife, Dorothy, was pregnant. "She wrote to President Johnson complaining that the war would take her husband away at a time when he should be there for the birth of his first child," Balisok recalled. "I was diverted to Fort Riley, Kansas, to allow me to be present for the birth," he said. "My job there was to find outdated post regulations, figure out who to circulate them to for comment, then take the comments, redraft them, and then circulate them again. Once they came back clean, I sent them to somebody to sign, and we had our new post regulations."

He was also required to maintain flight status by flying one of the post's few helicopters four hours a month. And as an additional duty, Balisok inspected all military funeral details in the state. "The remains of men killed in action were returned to their homes in Kansas. I flew to each locale and observed the funeral detail, then reported any irregularities. That was not good training for a young man on his way to Vietnam, I can assure you," he added.

"My daughter was born in July 1968," he recalled. "There were two other officers from my flight class who were in the same situation, with new kids."

Weeks went by after his daughter's birth with no word about his new assignment. "We met and called the Pentagon's infantry aviation assignments desk to find out why we were still at Fort Riley," Balisok explained. "That was, of course, the first really major mistake of my military career. Had I not called, I might still be there."

The army had somehow lost track of Balisok and the two other new fathers. "This was well before computers," he explained. "I spoke to a lieutenant colonel named Kastner, who was in charge of infantry aviation assignments. I said, 'I'm here with my two buddies, and we're interested in finding out what's going on.'"

Kastner said, "What's your name again?"

Balisok told him, and three minutes later Kastner came back on the line and yelled, "Where are you?" When Balisok said he was at Fort Riley, Kastner said, "You've got orders to Fort Bragg and you're AWOL."

Balisok responded that he had not received those orders, and after a certain amount of swearing, Kastner said, "Okay, okay, okay. Who are the other two guys?" After Balisok told him, Kastner said, "They're AWOL too! We've got to get this cleaned up."

The three of them shipped out to Fort Carson, Colorado, where they joined an aviation battalion being formed to round out the 101st Airborne

Division in Vietnam, which had deployed to the war zone as an airborne unit. It was then in the process of being reconfigured as an airmobile division, which included adding hundreds of helicopters. The division was redeploying from the Central Highlands to an area near the DMZ to allow some marine units that had taken a beating at Khe Sanh to move south, where they would refill their depleted ranks with replacements. Balisok was a tiny part of a huge, strategic reconfiguration of all US forces in South Vietnam.

At Fort Carson, Balisok was assigned to the 158th Aviation Battalion. "Our unit, Bravo Company, was the last of the four companies to deploy." An aviation battalion was then comprised of three Huey "lift" companies, with the mission to transport infantry into battle, and one gunship company. Balisok said, "When I reported to the battalion, Major Robinson, the S1,[2] assigned me to the gunship unit, which flew heavily armed Cobras. I asked to go instead to a lift company. I didn't want to go home to my family after flying Cobras for a year and have images of killing people in my mind. I would be happy just to take troops in and out and support them. I accepted the risks of that, but I didn't want to fly a Cobra."

Robinson understood. One of the other new guys, Billy Higgins, wanted to fly Cobras. So they switched.

Balisok's most dangerous mission came soon after deployment.

"My second mission was to take a Special Forces team comprised almost entirely of Montagnards and Chinese Nung mercenaries across the border into Laos. That required ten aircraft from different units. I flew number seven, call sign NAT 7. We were led by NAT 1. The mission commander decided that one ship at a time would approach over the open field to a hole in the jungle canopy, hover down into a bomb crater, drop our passengers, and then climb out."

What could go wrong? "Well," Balisok explained, "the open area was a free-fire zone for an NVA battalion. I heard the first guy taking hits. It sounded like someone banging on his aircraft with a hammer really fast. The pilot was yelling and screaming as he made the approach. Once below the canopy level, he was fine. Then he had to hover down *into* the bomb crater; otherwise, the helicopter was too high for people to jump safely.

"That was the first guy. I was number seven. Everybody before me was shot up. I took hits all the way over and down into the hole. One shook the aircraft so hard it seemed like we were inside an unbalanced washing machine. Finally, we're in the crater, and we dropped off our people.

"As I climbed out, I got a radio call, 'Any NAT aircraft, NAT 1.'

"Nobody answered. He called again. No answer. Finally, I responded. 'NAT 7.'

"'NAT 1 . . . NAT 4 chickened out. He put his folks off to the east someplace. Go pick them up and deliver them.'

"So we went back a second time, but it wasn't so bad because the NVA had pretty much run out of ammunition.

"We put the second bunch down, went back, and set the aircraft down and found thirty-eight 7.62mm bullet holes and one .50-caliber hole—fired from a hilltop above the jungle canopy—six inches from the main rotary tension pin through the main spar of the rotor blade. There were also two bullet holes, four inches apart, in the bulkhead, just above my door gunner, right where his face would have been."

Balisok's worst experience in Vietnam, however, didn't involve his own peril. In the first days of his tour, before his company's aircraft arrived, he and his men spent most of their days filling sandbags and building revetments to protect their sleeping area and their parked aircraft.

"One day I had some extra time, so I went to the MARS station[3] and called my wife. Waiting my turn, I sat next to Lt. Col. Weldon Honeycutt, commander of the Third Battalion, 187th Infantry. He said this was his second tour and that the men now fighting the war didn't know what they were doing. Didn't know what it meant to be in a real combat situation. Didn't know what it meant to be tough. While he was talking, I was thinking that I hope we never find out, but if we do I'm sure we'll do our job."

For ten days after May 10, 1969, Balisok and his aviation company supported Honeycutt's battalion, 3/187, and other US units as they fought at Hill 937, which came to be known as Hamburger Hill. While the hill was of no strategic importance, atop that hill and in bunkers all the way up its steep slopes was a large NVA force.

Before the first American or South Vietnamese soldier set foot on the hill, it was bombarded for two hours by close-support aircraft. That was followed by ninety minutes of artillery fire.

Then the 187th and the First ARVN Division's Second Battalion, Third

Infantry attempted to take the jungled height by frontal assault. "On Honeycutt's orders, his battalion continuously sought to assault Hamburger Hill," Balisok recalled.

Balisok and his platoon brought in ammunition, food, and water. They also ferried reinforcements into the battle and evacuated the dead and wounded.

"He just kept sending his guys into a meat grinder," Balisok recalled. The result was predictable: squad by squad, platoon by platoon, company after company, the Third Battalion, 187th Infantry took frightful casualties.

It required ten days and four additional US and ARVN infantry battalions to clear the hill. The ARVN 2/3 reached the crest of Hamburger Hill at 10:00 a.m. on May 20. Instead of attacking the NVA troops below them from the rear, an enemy formation then punishing what was left of Honeycutt's battalion, the 2/3 was ordered to withdraw from the summit. Artillery then pounded the hilltop. After taking still more casualties, the 3/187th broke through the NVA and occupied the hilltop, which created the illusion they alone had taken Hamburger Hill. The battle became a subject of congressional hearings, and the commander of US forces, Vietnam, changed his strategy to prevent another such senseless loss of American lives.

Honeycutt, however, was rewarded for his men's sacrifice. He went on to become a major general.

"Three weeks later, after we abandoned Hamburger Hill, the enemy walked back onto it without firing a shot," Balisok explained. "It had no military significance except that it was there and there were people there to defend it, so we had to attack it. That was the story of Vietnam.

"Later I made friends with some of the guys who were on Hamburger Hill," Balisok recalled. "I'm certain anyone in that battalion would have killed Honeycutt if they got a chance.

"That part of my Vietnam experience followed me around for twenty-seven years," Balisok continued. "I had a nightmare about this guy every night during those years: I crouched outside Honeycutt's quarters with my pistol, and at 4:00 a.m. he comes out, and I kill him and then walk away. Same nightmare for twenty-seven years. I finally put that away."

Balisok lost one man, a crew chief hit by a rocket-propelled grenade (RPG) during an assault landing on his first combat mission. He completed his tour without another man killed or wounded, surely a testament as much to leadership as to luck.

After completing his service in Vietnam, Balisok returned home. Things were different. "I lost almost all my friends," he recalled, "because they disapproved of my Vietnam service." And Balisok was "quite dedicated and interested in school. I persuaded Cal State University to accept me on probation. I made straight As from then on. After I graduated, I was lucky enough to talk my way into Southwestern University (a Los Angeles law school) at the last minute."

Which brings us back to Balisok's career as an advocate for the abused elders of California and elsewhere. In 1975, he graduated from law school and passed the bar. He couldn't find a job with a law firm, because Vietnam veterans were pariahs and because Southwestern Law School graduates were regarded as only a little better than Vietnam veterans.

He opened an office and joined the lowest class of attorney: sole practitioners. He also took a job at Southwestern, teaching first-year students research library and legal writing skills. "It was kind of like a homeroom for law students," he joked.

In the 1980s he made a living with a practice that was mostly real estate and "meat-and-potatoes" business litigation. "One day in 1982," he said, "in walked two families referred to me by my secretary's mother, who worked for Jewish Family Services in Los Angeles (a free, nondenominational social services organizational). They told me what had happened to each of their mothers in nursing homes that led to their deaths.

"I was struck dumb that this could even happen. Until then I hadn't handled personal injury cases, but their stories were so affecting that I almost cried with them," he said. Then he went home and told Dorothy about it, and this time he did cry. "I was shocked by the depraved conditions those two mothers were subjected to. I decided that I would try to make a career suing nursing homes."

Balisok worked for nearly seven years before winning a case. "Two years later, coincidentally, the California legislature enacted the California Elder Abuse Act, which made the cases I had been handling economically viable." *Barely* viable, but enough to allow Balisok to continue. "As time went by, I realized I could sue all the nursing homes in the world—and their doctors, for that matter—under the Elder Abuse Act, but nothing would change unless I could make the Elder Abuse Act apply to the people who were actually paying for the care, namely, the HMOs and hospitals that provide Medicare nursing home benefits to enrollees and sometimes prefer profit over providing contracted services.

"The difference between collecting from one nursing home and collecting from the much deeper pockets of HMOs was that the HMOs actually select the nursing homes they place patients in. In effect, they are encouraging or tolerating policies that no nursing home should tolerate.

"They hid behind a California statute called the Knox-Keene Health Care Service Plan Act of 1975. It's complicated, but HMOs are basically protected from the misconduct of the entities to whom they delegate care, which would ultimately be the nursing home," he continued.

"To find a way around that, I filed four lawsuits, each questioning whether the Medicare preemption condition on which they were relying actually applied. I established two court of appeals opinions that it did not," Balisok explained. "Six years after establishing in the state supreme court that the Medicare Act did not preempt a lawsuit, Congress enacted a different Medicare law. So I went at it again."

After working his way through the courts, Balisok received published opinions from the California Courts of Appeal that established his claim that his clients should be allowed to sue HMOs who used Medicare funds to pay for nursing home care.

"The two cases I referred to basically established that one can sue an HMO for the misconduct of those it delegates care to. State laws and regulations that might serve to protect HMOs no longer apply," he said.

"That's how I got started," Balisok explained. "Because I started early and because I learned just what to do for the Elder Justice Act and how to avoid some other limitations that apply under state law, I became quite a celebrity in certain circles. People kept inviting me to put on programs and explain things to them. I took an interest in the development of the law. There are several state supreme court opinions and court of appeals opinions in this area that I worked on and helped with.

"I managed to make a living doing that. Most people don't, but there are others much more successful than I. I don't advertise. I'm happy with my little career of picking and choosing the cases and the issues I want to litigate."

How big a problem is elder abuse in America?

"There's neglect of elders in others' care and custody. There's physical abuse not requiring care or custody. And there is financial abuse, which includes doing something that would impair the interest of an elder and a piece of real or personal property," Balisok explained. "Those three things are huge throughout the country, but financial abuse particularly. 'Impairing the interest of an elder and a piece of real or personal property' is quite common."

Some of the cases on Balisok's docket now are ugly but unfortunately typical of those he chooses. "A guy goes to a nursing home after a stroke. He has a G tube, a little tube in his stomach. One night he pulls it out. They reinsert it without verifying that it's actually in his stomach and that the seal that prevents it from leaking into his abdomen is intact. It's not. It's leaking all over the place, and it's what they do then that constitutes elder abuse. They didn't send him to the hospital. They did not discontinue the feeding. And they didn't order an X-ray immediately because it was after the X-ray technician's regular hours. To save a hundred dollars, they waited until the next morning. After the X-ray, they waited another three hours to call an ambulance, and they lied to the paramedics about the cause of the patient's drop in blood pressure, which was all that fluid in his abdomen and not in his stomach. That slowed the process of assessment and correction by the hospital staff."

Another case also involved a man who suffered a stroke. In the hospital, he had a tracheotomy and was placed on a ventilator. He was sent to an attached skilled nursing facility and suffered a series of events that left him brain-dead. When his wife realized he was brain-dead, wore a diaper, and was still on a ventilator, she knew he didn't want to live like that. She asked the nursing home to take him off the ventilator and let him die.

"For the next sixty or seventy days, they came up with one excuse after another to keep him alive, just so they could continue to collect for his critical care treatment from Medicare," Balisok explained. "On the hundredth day, following his discharge from the hospital, when Medicare payments ended, they said, 'Okay, we'll disconnect him.'"

Balisok has several other cases, including a few against the biggest and most prestigious hospitals west of the Mississippi.

He's in his seventies now. His wife of some fifty years, Dorothy, who long ago wrote a letter to the president, would like him to retire and enjoy his golden years while they are both in good health. But Russell Balisok is not ready.

"I saw a lot of killing in Vietnam," he said. "Bodies laid end to end, stacked like cordwood after an unsuccessful assault by the NVA. Friends killed in action. I understand that. I don't understand killing for profit. Taking my wartime experiences and trying to make sense of them in terms of what I see in my professional life has been difficult, because everything that affected me so greatly in Vietnam was, for the most part, the fortunes or misfortunes of war. I saw what I can say was stupidity and should never have happened, but so be it.

"But now we have all this killing going on for profit, and it seems to be okay. Everybody knows it's going on. And nobody wants to talk about it. Nobody will say anything. Whistle-blowers are few and far between. So that's kind of what I tell my wife every time she says, 'Why aren't you retired? Why are you still doing this? Why don't you take more profitable cases?'"

STUART STEINBERG

If there's a combat job more dangerous than walking point for an infantry unit or flying an unarmed helicopter, it is EOD—explosive ordnance disposal, what police departments call the bomb squad. The job is defusing, rendering harmless, or safely exploding things that go boom. Little, brightly painted bomblets, dispensed by a giant metal seed pod called a cluster bomb, can blow a hand or an arm off or blind or even kill an adult. Larger ordnance range from unexploded hand or launcher grenades to mortar shells, artillery shells up to eight inches in diameter, bombs filled with up to a ton of TNT, and a devil's toy box of land mines and booby traps. They can and likely have killed at least one EOD expert, and in Vietnam, there was a seemingly endless supply of ordnance. What kind of masochist volunteers to spend a year or more playing with death? It takes all kinds. Men with a death wish, sure, but more often they are men of great courage and greater compassion, willing to risk life and limb to make the battlefield a little safer for other troops. Men who are detail-oriented, smarter than average, with prodigious memories, keen eyesight, and the hand-eye coordination of a major leaguer. Men with just enough self-confidence to know when to stop and when to go. Men like Stuart Steinberg.

100

S tuart Steinberg was born in Washington, DC. When he was five or six, his family moved to Falls Church, Virginia, which today is an endless suburb of housing developments, but then it was mostly trees, a town so small that Steinberg's Hardware doubled as the post office.

"When I was about fifteen, we moved into a new suburban development in Fairfax County," he recalled. "I graduated from high school in 1966 and went out to Eastern New Mexico University, in a little place called Portales, and almost immediately flunked out of school. By the time I returned home, I had a notice from my draft board."

Draft calls were ramping up nationwide to staff new units going to Vietnam and replace the two hundred or more men returning every week in coffins.

"On July 27, 1966, with Murphy, my best friend in high school, I went into DC and got staggeringly drunk. Neither of us has any memory of getting from DC and the Georgetown area to the Army Navy Country Club golf course, where I had crashed through a fence. We were asleep in the car in the middle of a fairway. When we woke up, way down the course we could see a golf cart or something coming toward us, so we beat him out of there and went down to Alexandria. We went into a Waffle House for breakfast. Murphy had his back to the street, and I was looking past him, out to the other side of the street, which was where all the military recruiters hung out their shingles. I said, 'Well, man, you know neither of us wants to get drafted.' Because back then, if you got drafted you knew where you were going.

"So we went across the street to the marines. But they were closed, so we went next door to the army, and I got talked into this Nike Hercules crewman thing. We were set to leave for the induction station down in Richmond that night. So I drove out to my parents' country club. They had been playing golf, and I found them in the restaurant. And I told them I had enlisted, that I needed to be at the train station in Alexandria at midnight.

"My mom completely freaked out. She knew that Vietnam was really heating up around that time. But my dad, in World War II he was an infantry company commander. He went to the South Pacific—Borneo, New Guinea, the Philippines—and he was actually in one of the few army units on Guadalcanal. I think he was kinda proud of me. He took me to the train station, and Murphy and I went to Richmond and had our physical and got sworn in. Then we took the train to Fort Jackson, South Carolina.

"We got there on July 29. They got everyone lined up, and then they called me and Murphy out. A captain was with a couple of other guys. They told Murphy they had discovered he had a pilonidal cyst, a growth at the base of his spine. It's often caused by an ingrown hair. The captain said, 'This is a waivable defect. We can send you right over to the hospital and have it squared away, and then you can continue on to basic training.'

"But Murphy said, 'Now that I think about it, I think I want to get out.' And then they told me that because we had enlisted on the buddy program, if I wanted out, I could get out too. I said, 'Look, man, I'm not doing that. I don't want to be drafted.'

"Then the captain told me that Fort Jackson's training center was full. So they put me in a car and drove me to a unit at Fort Gordon, Georgia. We went into the day room, and I handed my orders to the clerk, and he said, 'Wait just a minute. The CO and the reserve sergeant want to talk to you.' I was escorted to see the commanding officer—I'm still in civilian clothes. He told me that I was the only regular army enlistee in an entire company of enlisted reservists that had been called to active duty.

"It was explained to me that this whole company was full of highly educated men, including several lawyers, who had joined the army reserve to keep from being drafted while they were in school. But they had each been ordered to active duty, and now they were in this company.

"Because I was the only regular army person in the company, I was immediately promoted to acting sergeant and acting platoon sergeant. They gave me an armband with sergeant's stripes to wear over my fatigue jacket.

"I really ate basic training up. All the things like the low crawl under barbed wire, I aced all of those things. I was the number-one guy in all of that stuff in my company, probably because these enlisted reservists didn't much care about doing well."

After basic training, Steinberg was assigned to a missile battery deep in the Everglades, where he received on-the-job training in maintaining the Nike Hercules air defense missile. "My job was to push the missiles out of the silo, clean them with acetone or whatever else we were using, inhaling all these fumes of course. And then push them back into the silo."

At this remote base, some eighty miles from Miami, Steinberg, who is Jewish, encountered a clique of anti-Semitic noncommissioned officers. "Two of these jerks were actually running a loan-sharking operation. I'm pretty sure the CO and the first sergeant knew about it. When I complained about the anti-Semitic remarks and about those sergeants riding me for weeks, I was told to suck it up," he said.

Steinberg put up with this treatment for nearly a year. Then he went to see a career counselor at Homestead Air Force Base and reenlisted for one of the few army specialty schools available to a soldier without a college degree: explosive ordnance demolition (EOD) school.

His reenlistment came with a thousand-dollar bonus and an additional fifty-five dollars a month in hazardous duty pay. It seemed like a fortune to Steinberg, whose PFC pay after taxes and an obligatory savings bond amounted to only ninety dollars.

Steinberg's first stop was Fort McClellan, Alabama. For three weeks he learned about chemical and biological weapons, particularly nerve agents. Then he went to the EOD school at Indian Head, Maryland, near the Naval Surface Warfare Center.

Basic EOD was a five-month school. Of the twenty-eight students who started in August 1967, twelve graduated. "When they pinned that badge on me, it was one of the best days of my life," Steinberg said. He and a good friend from that school, Tom Brown, received orders for Dugway Proving Ground in Utah.

Not long after his arrival, a unit at Dugway accidentally leaked a ton of lethal VX (sarin) nerve gas that fell like a curtain of death onto the fields of a nearby sheep ranch. It killed all six thousand sheep, the sheepherder's horses and herd dogs, and everything that walked, crawled, or flew in that area. The Skull Valley sheep ranch incident happened on a Thursday, and by sheer chance, all the ranch's herders had Thursdays off, so there were no human casualties.

Steinberg's job, along with several other men from EOD, was to clean up the mess.

"It was a really traumatic experience," he said. "Seeing all these dead animals, birds, snakes, Gila monsters, cockroaches, whatever. And while we were doing this, they brought in heavy equipment guys from some engineering unit. We dug a huge pit, and then they scraped everything into this pit. And then we filled it with old tires. Then we laid out thousands of blocks of C-4, tied them all together with detonating cord, soaked the thing with thousands of gallons of jet fuel, and then set it off. It burned for two or three days.

And then they covered it up. They scraped the earth and filled in the hole with dirt, covered it up, fenced it off, and paid the owners of this land a lot of money.

"We were done after about ten days. We got back to Dugway, and the next day I went with four others on our team to personnel and volunteered for Vietnam. We thought we would be safer there, because in addition to nerve gas, at that time, almost all US chemical and biological weapons, going all the way back to World War I, including mustard and phosgene gasses, were stored at Dugway. Thousands and thousands of containers. It was part of our job to find leakers and destroy them safely. We thought it was only a matter of time before all of us died."

Steinberg served eighteen months in Vietnam, much of it in areas with heavy fighting, from September 4, 1968, until March 24, 1970. "By the time I got orders for Vietnam, 32,549 soldiers were dead. I had followed the siege at Khe Sanh on television virtually nonstop. None of that translated into 'That might happen to me' when I saw bodies in flag-draped coffins or wounded loaded onto medevac choppers.

"I was EOD and we were invincible. In the back of your mind you knew that even a tiny mistake could kill or maim you. You also believed this would not happen to you. If you thought that way, you could not do your job. You had finished school when many others had not. That meant something in itself. Wearing that silver badge with the bomb and the lightning bolts was impressive, especially to me.

"We flew to Vietnam in a charter. After we landed, walking down the ramp felt like walking into a blast furnace. It was like nothing we had ever experienced, even in the blazing, skin-blistering heat of the Utah desert. The air was thick and hot. It was like inhaling molten syrup. It burned my throat as I tried to swallow. It was hard to adjust my vision, because the heat seemed to sear my eyes. Even my eyebrows were sweating, and the humidity meant it was like taking a bath without the tub.

"By the time I left Vietnam, I was immune to the weather, the heat, the humidity, the everlasting monsoons, the cold—yes, it was cold during the monsoons—the bugs, the snakes, the leeches, and the bats. I had also gotten used to the enemy, because they were everywhere, just like the bugs, snakes, leeches, and bats. Yet I never got used to the spiders, which always seemed to be huge and hiding under my bed or climbing out of one of my boots or dropping on me from a tree in the bush.

"During my time in Vietnam, I detonated several tons of plastic explosives and TNT, destroying booby traps, dud ordnance, and ordnance that needed blowing up for strategic reasons. In addition, I helped blow two hundred feet or so off the top of a mountain, destroying an enemy cave complex. Later, I probably helped change the environment forever in a large area of the South China Sea off the coast near Vung Ro Bay, where we dumped thousands of tons of bad ammunition.

"I participated in more than seven hundred 'incidents,' disarming and destroying chemical and biological weapons, booby traps, grenades, mines, dud artillery projectiles, rockets, and aircraft-dropped bombs from 250 to 2,000 pounds. I also dealt with anything else that could explode or burn or kill or maim people in the most horrible ways imaginable, which they often did.

"Somehow, the regular, everyday dud or booby trap was usual, and the duds and booby traps where the enemy was trying to shoot us at the same time, well, these were unusual.

"We lost forty-two men in Vietnam. Our EOD teams in Vietnam were no-bull, no-nonsense outfits. Everyone's life depended on everyone else doing his job correctly. Every time we went out, there was absolutely no margin for error. On many occasions we went into hot landing zones with the infantry, often flying in by helicopter during a combat assault. There we were, trying to do our job, while the war raged all around us, and we had to ignore it."

Walking into still-burning ammo dumps after an enemy attack, battle-hardened infantrymen called him crazy to his face. Steinberg accepted that as the highest praise.

"One of our other tasks—one that I would perform again and again at locations all over Vietnam—was to clear the bodies of dead enemy soldiers. This involved checking the bodies for booby traps and unexploded ordnance.

"They were my first dead bodies, other than relatives in a casket, including several that were blown to pieces, shot many times, missing limbs and heads. Blood and gore were everywhere. That night, I pretty much stopped sleeping, and that has not changed in the years since, at least, not without medication."

Steinberg returned from Vietnam a changed man. Life and death no longer had the usual meanings to him. He had been wounded a few times, and his healed wounds still sometimes hurt.

Steinberg finished his army service in a small town in Ohio. Ravenna

Arsenal stored the propellant used by artillery to hurl huge warheads dozens of miles. "We had a great duty station, and most of what we did was Secret Service details. If the president or vice president or some other high-ranking muckety-muck was in our area of operations, we would attach to the Secret Service. We wore civilian clothes, carried hidden arms. We looked like the Men in Black."

He turned down a promotion to staff sergeant and took an honorable discharge in June 1971. Soon afterward, Steinberg enrolled in a community college, then moved to Vermont to attend Goddard College in Plainfield. He graduated with a bachelor of arts in July 1976. Then he was accepted by the University of New Hampshire School of Law in Concord and graduated in 1980 with a juris doctor degree.

Steinberg's first job as an attorney was learning to be an investigator for a husband-and-wife practice, after which he accepted a teaching fellowship at Georgetown University Law Center in Washington, DC, and was granted a master of law degree in 1982.

"Then I returned to New Hampshire with my first wife and our newborn son. I took the Massachusetts bar exam, passed it. I was hired to be the criminal defense guy in a very heavyweight law firm outside of Boston. One partner had been a former attorney general. Another was a Kennedy lawyer. A third partner was a former county district attorney. It seems their very wealthy clients' kids were always doing something stupid. I did that for about a year. Then my wife and I split up. I went to western Massachusetts and ended up as a partner in a firm with one of my former law school buddies and another lawyer. I did that for the next six or seven years. And then I just woke up one day and said, 'I can't do this anymore.'

"I thought the whole criminal justice system was screwed up. In the 1980s I was lucky if I could get the money to hire an expert witness. I certainly couldn't get money for an investigator, so I was doing all my own investigations as well as trying these felony cases. And I got tired of dealing with lying cops and dishonest DAs who didn't care about justice. They cared only about convictions."

Steinberg packed his car intending to move to California, where his parents and two sisters lived. It never happened.

"I was driving across Michigan, and I saw the exit for Traverse City," Steinberg recalled. "I knew one of my best friends from law school was practicing law there. So I thought I'd stop and see her. I stayed in Traverse City and started clerking for her. Then I met Steve McDiamond, a private investigator, and we became friends and eventually partners. I did that from late 1989 or early 1990 until 1995. By then I had remarried, and my wife and I moved to Oregon," he recalled.

"On February 26, 2007, I entered a substance abuse rehabilitation and recovery program at a Washington State VA Medical Center. I withdrew from prescribed morphine on January 8, after being on prescription narcotics for many years. I had used painkillers for some damage to my right knee, caused by an exploding mortar round, and my left knee, caused by another Vietnam incident. Many people helped while I was in rehab, not just the staff, but also the veterans in this program after I decided I could not spend the rest of my life as an addict," he recalled.

In 2009, Steinberg spent six months in Afghanistan as an adviser to the Afghan border police on counternarcotics operations along the Iranian border. "I would have stayed longer, but my wife said I had to come home after the bad guys twice tried to bomb my driver and me," he said.

Between 2005 and 2010 Steinberg worked with a nonprofit group originally made up of Vietnam combat veterans. "Our primary task was to assist homeless veterans, those at risk of becoming homeless, disabled, poor, or a combination of all of those. Many had substance abuse, alcohol, and mental health problems. Maybe that has something to do with why I wrote a book—hearing the stories of other people, day after day, tale after twisted, brutal tale. I tried to tell their stories in the hope that America will finally understand how the Vietnam War destroyed lives and continues to do so. I guess it destroyed my life a little. Or maybe it was a lot. I am trying now to have a good third marriage, mend my relationship with my son, and to a large extent, save my own life," he said.

Steinberg retired from his law practice and now spends most of his time as one of Vietnam Veterans of America's leading service officers, assisting veterans in getting their full benefits. In 1974, a fire destroyed thousands of veterans' records, including medical records, at the National Personnel Records Center in St. Louis. This has presented complications for veterans seeking treatment or compensation for service-connected injuries. Steinberg has applied his years of experience as an investigator to find work-arounds for these cases and has often been successful. He has also written a book, *This Is What Hell Looks Like: Life as a Bomb Disposal Specialist During the Vietnam War*, which was published in 2018 by Fonthill Media.

TED GOSTAS

Among the hundreds of American fighting men who survived years as prisoners or war, few, if any, were tortured as long and as cruelly as Ted Gostas. His strong desire to live led him to inhabit an alternate reality as a shelter from the madness of his cruel treatment. His survival and return to active duty, even in a limited capacity, were nothing short of a miracle.

It was an ordinary house in an upper-class neighborhood in the ancient imperial capital of Hue, some sixty miles north of Da Nang.

The neighbors said the man living there was a German architect. He spoke German fluently, but Ted Gostas was an American. And he was no architect. Capt. Theodore Gostas, US Army Intelligence, was a spymaster, recruiting locals to spy on their neighbors. Gostas was interested in many things about Hue, but mostly about pinpointing Viet Cong agents and sympathizers and learning their plans.

Ted Gostas was born in 1938 in Butte, Montana. His mother was from Czechoslovakia, and his Greek-immigrant father owned a restaurant. In 1941, the family and the restaurant moved to Bayard, Nebraska, and two years later to Cheyenne, Wyoming.

Gostas studied English literature at the University of Wyoming. He also enrolled in the ROTC program. As graduation and army commissioning approached, the ROTC department secretary noted his college major by writing ENG on his Form 66, the document that launched his army future.

"Someone thought ENG meant engineering," Gostas said, and he was sent to Fort Leonard Wood, Missouri, where he underwent basic combat engineer training. He learned to drive a bulldozer and build Bailey bridges over streams as he was trained in the duties of a combat engineer. While visiting St. Louis one night, someone broke into his car and stole his briefcase with his notes from his classes, and he barely passed the final exam.

US Army combat engineers also fight as infantry, so Gostas went to Fort Benning, Georgia, for infantry training. "The infantry was really tough," he recalled. "I had a hard time at Fort Benning, but the commanding general gave me an extra three points for the leadership program, and I graduated as a second lieutenant."

Desperate to leave the engineers, he took a test for army intelligence. He passed and went to Fort Holabird, Maryland, to learn the duties of an intelligence officer.

One day as he lunched in a shop across the street from the installation, he heard some men speaking Russian. "They had sophisticated cameras and photographed everyone coming or going to Holabird," he recalled. Suspecting they were Soviet agents who sent their photos to Moscow, and that his image would be in a KGB dossier, Gostas shared his suspicions with a senior officer, who shrugged it off. The possible Soviet agents were not on government property, and taking pictures in public wasn't against any law.

From Holabird, Gostas went to the defense language school in Monterey. He became fluent in German.

His first duty station was Kaiserslautern, Germany, home to several large US Army units. Almost everyone in the civilian community spoke English.

Later he was transferred to a military intelligence company in the Third Armored Division, near Frankfurt. "One day a train from the Czechoslovakian town where my mother grew up was hit by a US M-60 Patton tank that had skidded on an icy road and came to a stop with its 105mm gun barrel stuck under a rail," Gostas recalled.

The crew jumped out of the tank, the locomotive flew three feet in the air over the tank, and twenty-five freight cars of industrial equipment derailed and were strewn over the top of the locomotive.

Gostas was in an armored personnel carrier behind the tank. He remained there, shivering under a blanket until a helicopter with two stars on its underside landed nearby. By then the battalion commander had arrived. The general hopped out of his bird, turned to the battalion commander, and said, "Colonel, clean up this mess!"

Salutes were exchanged, the general got back in his helicopter and flew away. The battalion commander turned to the tank company commander, Capt. Gordon Sullivan, and said, "Captain, clean up this mess." He then left in a jeep.

Gostas was standing with a few other onlookers. "Gordie turned around and looked at me and the others. 'Does anybody speak German?' he asked.

"My frozen hand shot up straight in the air. 'I speak fluent German,' I said.

"Sullivan said, 'Lieutenant, you're the solution to our problem. You're gonna talk to the railroad people so they can get out here and unscramble this mess.'"

They found a phone in a nearby village, and with Gostas translating, arranged for a ninety-seven-ton railroad crane to come from Dusseldorf. "To light that crane's furnace took twenty men holding a long pole with a kerosene-soaked rag burning on the far end," Gostas recalled. "They stuck it in there and *whoosh!* it lit up the afterburner. They pulled that fifty-ton tank out of the track as if it were a butterfly.

"By the time the track was cleared, I was almost exhausted. A mess cook brought me a tray of food. Up until then the troops never spoke to me. When they saw me coming, they'd go the other way, because they knew I was a spook and they were kind of afraid. Now they made me an honorary member of the Third Armored Division, the same division Elvis Presley had served in."

In 1967, Ted Gostas arrived at Cam Ranh Bay, South Vietnam, as a replacement. He was not happy to see his name in the *Army Times* under the heading "Army Intelligence" with the announcement, "Capt. Theodore Gostas assigned to Vietnam."

His next stop in-country was Saigon. After going to sleep one night, he was awakened by North Vietnamese rockets. When his commanding officer gave him a choice of remaining in Saigon or going north to Hue, where he'd be nearer the action, he decided to go to Hue. He didn't want to stay and do menial tasks.

His commanding officer pulled out a manila folder with pictures of Gostas's wife and kids. "Still want to go north?"

Gostas replied, "I love my family, but a lot of guys love their families and they go north, sir."

In April 1967, using a cover name in a clandestine unit that was part of the 135th MI Battalion, Gostas set up shop in Hue with a small crew.

On the last day of January 1968, Gostas was writing to his wife when he heard the unmistakable sound of an AC-47 Spooky gunship firing its mini-guns. One round in five is a tracer. "It looked like one solid stream of red, so I knew the rate of fire was incredible," he said. "The sun was just going down. I saw the fire hitting an area to the southeast."

Gostas called headquarters. "I got a man on the phone and told him we were under attack. I said that we were in trouble. He said, 'Well, we are too. We're being hit—' And then the enemy cut the phone lines."

It was the beginning of the Tet Offensive.

Immediately, Gostas began burning his files—and accidentally set his house on fire. "I sent my men next door to a cement building. As we went out the front door, we passed North Vietnamese troops carrying supplies to set up a perimeter around the Military Assistance Command Vietnam (MACV) compound two blocks away.

"We hunkered down and watched thousands of NVA going toward the MACV compound. One of my men took a rifle and crawled outside and killed five NVA.

"They returned fire by shooting through a slit in the cement and hit him in the neck. He died soon after," Gostas said.

"That night I stood guard in that room and about a hundred rounds of rifle fire came through the slit. How they all missed me, I'll never know," he recalled. Then he went to look out the window. One of his men came to warn him against exposing himself and was killed by a sniper. "I've always wondered why it wasn't *me* the sniper killed. He had a bead on me for more than half an hour."

A few minutes later, a US Marine unit led by a jeep and followed by an M-48 tank came down Highway One. "We had no radio, but all of us tried to wave them off. They probably thought we were welcoming them, but we were trying to warn them that the enemy was everywhere. The NVA had an antitank weapon concealed near a street corner. Its first round blew the Jeep and everyone in it to smithereens," Gostas recalled. "The second round missed the tank, and the M-48 started backing up. With another man, I went to help what was left of the marines caught in the ambush.

"We got out to the sidewalk, and the tankers thought we were the enemy and fired off a round. It exploded just above our heads—we were both covered with plaster. We realized that they'd kill us before we had a chance to identify ourselves, so we ran back upstairs, and the tank fired again and blew off part of our building. The blast also destroyed the staircase. On the second or third day, the enemy realized that someone in our house had killed five of their troops. They fired a B-40 rocket, an RPG, at us at about 0600.

"I had my arm around a dying man. He was twenty-five years old and in a flak jacket, and he was on top of me, with my arms around him, when the B-40 came through the roof and exploded. He took most of the shrapnel in his back and I took some in my foot.

"We had been blown into the ceiling and it came down on our heads. I crawled out of the place and he crawled out behind me. The back of his flak jacket had been shredded by the B-40, and you could see part of his spine. He turned over and died.

"After a short firefight, we ran out of what little ammunition we had, and we knew our goose was cooked. We ran out of the building. I knew the Vietnamese stop signs said Dung Lai, so I yelled, 'Dung lai! Dung lai!'

"Then we worked our way down the twisted staircase. When we got downstairs, they tied our arms behind our backs with piano wire and took us across the street. We had to step over the bodies of five hundred dead marines."

Afterward, Gostas was held in solitary confinement for four and a half years in a room about the size of a fat man's coffin. His only friends were a praying mantis and a white rat. He was given perhaps four ounces of water a day and often had to drink his own urine. He was tortured and interrogated constantly. "I said, 'I'm a clerk typist. I don't have any idea of what you're asking,'" he recalled. "They treated me as though I was Nixon's right-hand man."

Almost until he was released, Gostas was subjected to endless varieties of such cruelly innovative tortures as would have inspired Tomás de Torquemada to quivering ecstasy. He was beaten daily, interrogated by Soviet officers, and trucked to China to be tortured and interrogated. Gostas found the only respite from his pain, fear, and loneliness was to abandon reason and take refuge in insanity.

Six months before the war ended, Gostas was moved to the Hanoi Hilton, where one of his fellow captives, Capt. Hal Kushner, a doctor, saved his life.

"He examined me and said, 'You'll die if I don't pull some of your eighteen abscessed teeth.'

"I said, 'I'm not gonna let you pull my teeth! I'll bite your fingers off. Just leave me alone. Didn't Socrates at least have hemlock?'

"He said, 'I save people. I don't kill them.'"

Four B-52 crewmen held Gostas down while Kushner wrapped a string he had made from threads of bamboo fiber around three teeth that had to come out.

"When they ripped them out of my mouth, a little bit of my jawbone came with them. I emptied about a half a cup of pus into Doctor Kushner's face," Gostas recalled. "He vomited and I vomited and all the other guys vomited. The whole place was full of vomit. Then I crawled off the bed and to the corner, and I sat there with my face swollen like a diseased chipmunk."

———◇———

Ted Gostas came home with other surviving POWs in early 1973. After emergency medical treatment in the Philippines, he went to Denver's Fitzsimons Army Hospital, where his gums were found to be so rotted they couldn't hold a needle for a lidocaine injection. A specialist in pediatric dentistry was flown in, and he carefully removed the rest of Gostas's abscessed teeth.

Doctors found Gostas was hosting some ten thousand hookworms in his intestines. These were purged with medication. Then shrapnel was removed from his foot.

Shortly thereafter Gostas's wife divorced him.

Though his body was on the mend, Gostas remained clinically insane. He was housed alone on the hospital grounds until, little by little, his mind healed. "They locked the door and I proceeded to destroy the room—mirrors, footlockers, everything. I destroyed my own bed. I destroyed everything in there. I don't know where I found the strength to do that, but when I looked over my handiwork, I was very happy with it.

"My mother came to see me while I was having dessert once. She said, 'My son,' and I punched her in the stomach. I didn't recognize her as my mother," he recalled. "I thought she was trying to take my dessert, and I hadn't had dessert for five years. No one was gonna take my dessert."

Asked by a general officer for advice for future POWs, Gostas suggested every combat soldier should be issued cyanide tablets. When he was released to go home, Gostas lived in his mother's basement. He drank heavily. "I would have drunk hair tonic if it had enough alcohol in it." Along with the drinking, he wrote a book titled *Prisoner*, which nobody wanted to publish.

"Later it was published by Golden Books for children, but I had to pay them for it," he recalled. He bought ten thousand copies and has sold or given away all but eight. He gave most of the books to Vietnam veterans who came to the 1992 dedication of the Vietnam Veterans Memorial. Because they were fellow veterans, he refused to accept payment.

For a brief time Gostas returned to active duty. Doctors finally discovered that his sometimes erratic behavior was caused because his brain was bleeding, undoubtedly the result of his many beatings. The medics suggested a very risky operation with a better-than-even chance he'd wind up in a vegetative state. Gostas refused the surgery. He was medically retired from the army with the rank of major.

In the forty-odd years since regaining his freedom and his mind, Ted Gostas has established himself as a painter. He explained, "I started painting to save myself from going into a loony bin."

With paint and canvas, and to critical acclaim, he tells the excruciating story of his years as a prisoner of war, producing some ten thousand sketches, more than three hundred acrylic paintings, and five metal sculptures. He has sold most of this work, not to support himself and his second wife but to help indigent veterans. Gostas has raised and donated over $35,000 for scholarships for the children of veterans.

He also spends much of his time speaking to active-duty servicemen and to students about his experiences as an intelligence officer and as a POW.

Now in his eighty-first year, Ted Gostas shows few signs of slowing down. He continues to paint and sketch, a burning example of the resiliency of the human spirit.

THINH "TIM" NGUYEN

The refugees from Vietnam's Communist government are among the most uplifting figures of a terrible war. Most came to America with nothing more than the determination to succeed and to prosper and serve their new home-land. They are the best new blood injected into America's veins in more than a century. And they have given their adopted nation far more than they have received.

On April 29, 1975, the North Vietnamese Army surrounded Saigon. Throughout the previous night, mortars, rockets, and heavy artillery fire landed throughout the city, but especially on Tan Son Nhut airport. The bulk of what remained of the South Vietnamese Air Force (VNAF) at Tan Son Nhut was a spotty collection of burning hulks. Of the airworthy aircraft with range enough to reach the nearest safe haven—Thailand—there was only one: a C-130 Hercules.

Twenty-four-year-old Lt. Thinh Nguyen, a maintenance officer, saw the C-130 taxi onto the runway, its rear loading ramp open, and made up his mind: he had to leave the land of his birth, the country where his family still lived. If he were captured by the communists, they would likely shoot him. Or worse.

Thinh sprinted onto the runway and gave chase to what he knew was his last chance at freedom. The aircraft slowed, then stopped, then bumped over a piece of debris, then started forward again, just as Thinh hopped onto the rear hatch.

Inside he found perhaps three hundred people—soldiers, civilians, women, children, infants—huddled on the floor of an aircraft designed to carry ninety paratroopers and their gear.

The runway was covered with debris. Each time the pilot, Major Phuong, slowed down or stopped, more people jumped aboard. Thinh sat by the left paratroop door, a prime location with a porthole.

As rockets and artillery shells fell on or near the runway, the loadmaster decided he couldn't take on any more people. He closed the cargo ramp, and the big plane lumbered forward with 452 passengers crammed inside.

Bumping down that runway, Thinh realized if the enemy fired an anti-aircraft missile when they were aloft, they were utterly defenseless. He didn't like the feeling.

On the flight deck were thirty-one additional passengers, none of them pilots. As the C-130, now moving very fast, passed the nine-thousand-foot marker on the runway, the pilot, Major Phuong, eased back on the stick, but nothing happened. The Hercules was burdened with ten tons more than it had been designed to carry.

Still slowly gathering speed, the aircraft passed the ten-thousand-foot marker and stubbornly refused to leave the ground.

There was still runway enough for Major Phuong to stop safely. Instead, he kept the throttles wide open, betting his life and those of his passengers on his aircraft.

At the end of the runway was an unpaved overrun area. "He couldn't get the nose up until we reached the end of the thousand-foot overrun," Thinh recalled.

Barely topping the trees, the C-130 rose on the cushion of air generated by its four propellers and bouncing back from the ground below (ground effect). It did not rise above the treetops until it had flown more than ten miles. Then it slowly climbed into the sky.

Those aboard didn't know it then, but they were on the last plane out of Tan Son Nhut before Saigon fell.

Major Phuong headed west toward Thailand. Only when he saw the dark waters of the South China Sea below did he realize he was heading east toward the vast Pacific Ocean. Another VNAF pilot pushed and shoved his way through the mass of passengers to the flight deck and slid into the copilot's chair. He normally flew the much smaller C-7 Caribou, but he had a map. On the Hercules instrument panel was an N-1 magnetic compass. With map and compass, he plotted a course for Thailand that took them back over Saigon.

Very much aware that the North Vietnamese had captured several VNAF aircraft at the Da Nang Air Base, including A-37 light bombers with high-speed miniguns as well as A-1E Skyraiders with 20mm cannons, Major Phuong flew low, hoping to avoid detection. After a three-and-a-half-hour flight, the grossly overloaded aircraft found the extra-long runways used by US B-52's at U-Tapao Royal Thai Navy Airfield and set down safely.

The next day, Thinh and most of the passengers from Tan Son Nhut left for Guam on several US C-141's. The Americans had established a refugee processing center there. Thinh Nguyen was surprised and saddened when he learned that South Vietnam had surrendered and the communists had taken over. "I realized then that I couldn't return to Vietnam, regroup, and fight again," he recalled.

During his brief stay on Guam, Thinh thought about his future. "I knew I couldn't just sit on the beach and daydream about going back to Vietnam," he said. "I knew I had to go to America."

Thanks to his VNAF training, Thinh knew enough about aircraft to realize that while luck had played a part in his escape, the C-130 that delivered him to safety had performed far beyond what anyone expected of it. He decided he would find a job at Lockheed, the company that built the C-130.

Thinh's next stop was a relocation camp at Eglin Air Force Base on Florida's western Gulf Coast. The camp was intended to help refugees learn English and to teach them the basic skills they needed to survive in America, such as handling money, using a bank, dressing appropriately, finding a job, and driving on American roads.

At Eglin, the refugees were issued such personal necessities as toothbrushes, towels, soap, and underwear. Shoes, however, were not issued. Most of the camp was paved and too hot for bare feet, so Thinh found a two-by-four plank, cut it into two pieces, and strapped the pieces to his feet.

A family in a nearby community agreed to sponsor him. They gave him a place to stay and helped point him on the road to a new life in a new country. He worked for a local newspaper during the day, making deliveries and doing odd jobs. By night he studied English. "I wanted a better job, but wherever I applied, they said I wasn't qualified because I didn't have a high school diploma," he recalled. Thinh bought a book to prepare for the General Educational Development test and passed it on his first try. He enrolled in Okaloosa Technical College and studied automobile mechanics, then found a job as an auto mechanic.

It was a very difficult time for him. He yearned to return to Vietnam, to see his family, and to take his place in a society he understood. He knew, however, that if he returned, the communists might shoot him or confine him to a so-called reeducation camp to break his spirit and force him to conform. News about such camps had begun to trickle out of Vietnam, and Thinh realized it would be foolish to return, no matter how unhappy he was in America.

"Should I go back to school and make myself somebody or should I become Joe Six-Pack?" he wondered. "Should I come home from work every night, drink beer, then sleep and the next day and the next do the same thing?" he asked.

"But now I'm here in the land of opportunity. If I don't take advantage of it, I'm foolish. I talked to myself a lot, and that's how I decided to go back to school and do something about making a better life for myself," he said.

He met his wife, an American volunteer named Cheri, at Eglin, and they were married at the base chapel. After their marriage, Thinh enrolled at the University of Alabama, where he studied electrical engineering and held down a full-time job at the university medical center. "We lived in Tuscaloosa, and the first time my wife and I went grocery shopping, we had to write a check to pay. They asked for my driver's license, and they wanted a second ID," he recalled. "The next time I had to pay with a check, they didn't ask to see any ID at all. I asked the checkout lady why. She said, 'This is a small town. There aren't many mixed marriages here. If your check bounces, we won't have any trouble finding you.'"

In 1981, Thinh graduated with a 3.7 GPA and a BS in electrical engineering.

He sent his résumé to what was then the Lockheed-Georgia Company. "Lockheed rejected me," Thinh recalled. "I was a little insulted."

He found a job in Savannah with Gulfstream Aerospace. Two years later he again applied to Lockheed. He was hired to work at the company's facility in Marietta, Georgia, just north of Atlanta.

Thinh's coworkers decided to call him Tim, a nickname that stuck.

Soon after joining Lockheed, Thinh's boss showed him a document relating to the C-130 that Lockheed continues to build and sell to the US Air Force and to friendly nations around the world. The document included an assessment of crew protection, which included the phrase "five-man crew considered expendable."

Thinh saw those words and flashed back to his time aboard a C-130. "If the crew is expendable, what about the ninety paratroopers?" he asked. Or the hundreds of refugees on his hegira from Vietnam?

From that conversation came a Lockheed proposal to the air force suggesting that equipment to protect both crew and aircraft be developed. The air force's Scientific Advisory Board responded with a report titled "The Enhancement of Airlift in Force Projection." Among its critical recommendations was that transports needed a suite of defensive equipment to counter infrared and radar-guided missile threats.

By fate or coincidence, Thinh's first tasks at Lockheed's "Possum Works" advanced projects group was to develop a prototype defensive system for transport aircraft. Survivability Augmentation for Transport Installation (SATIN) became Thinh's passion. "I really jumped at the chance to work on defensive systems," he said. "I saw so many aircraft shot down in Vietnam. That last morning, a VNAF AC-119 gunship was hit by a surface-to-air missile and crashed right in front of us. Although the crew bailed out, they were so low their chutes didn't open. I felt so helpless. I knew then I wanted to help protect flight crews so that never happened again."

SATIN was designed as a strap-on kit that required no permanent aircraft modifications. Antennas for a radar warning receiver and the missile warning radar that alerted the crew of incoming threats were screwed on the aircraft's exterior. The two standard paratroop doors were replaced with doors that each contained four chaff dispensers to launch clouds of tiny shards of spun aluminum or other materials to confuse radar-guided missiles or antiaircraft artillery. They also launched flares that burned at higher temperatures than the hottest parts of the aircraft, such as the engine exhausts. These served to decoy heat-seeking missiles away from the aircraft.

For two years Thinh's group tested SATIN against all kinds of infrared and radio frequency–guided missiles. Thinh often flew with the test crews. "It performed well. However, it was developed on the air force's nickel. When the time came to put the kit into production, the air force put the contract out for bids. We didn't win the production contract." But the air force came back and asked them to begin installing the necessary wiring and brackets for a defensive system on new-production C-130H3's. Every US-made large aircraft defensive system in service today is based on the work of Thinh's team.

In 1990, when Operation Desert Shield launched, the air force asked Thinh's group to develop a defensive system for the C-5 Galaxy strategic transport. He explained, "We crawled all over the aircraft, then developed a kit and tested it. Many at Lockheed didn't believe we could complete development in six months, but we did. We understood where the aircraft was headed when the fighting began." Thinh again worked with the aircraft maintenance team and went aloft to get the system installed and working.

Because SATIN didn't have any dispensers on the forward part of the aircraft, Thinh and his team knew they had to find a way to counter the advanced shoulder-fired missiles that were in Iraqi hands. "These missiles could lock on a target from any aspect," he explained, so they added forward dispensers. "Twenty years ago, you could almost fly straight and level, pop one flare out each side and defeat any threat," Thinh noted. "Today, an enemy doesn't need to aim at the hot spots on the aircraft. An advanced missile can lock anywhere on the aircraft. The target crew doesn't know where the missile is coming from, only that it's detected. They have to fire chaff and multiple flares to protect the area around the entire aircraft, not just specific areas."

As far back as the nineteenth century, German arms merchant Friedrich Krupp AG was busy selling the latest cannon to one country and their newly developed armor to their neighbors. Thus the cat-and-mouse game between advanced missiles and advanced defensive systems was nothing new. But it reached new heights during Operations Enduring Freedom and Iraqi Freedom. Crews must now use both defensive systems and a greater variety of flight tactics, such as rapid descents from altitude. Different threats call for specific patterns for releasing chaff and flares against them. "Because the threats are advancing, the defensive systems need to advance as well," Thinh explained.

In 1992, Thinh was selected as the Hercules program's employee of the year. He also volunteered with several community groups in his off-hours. "After I went to work at Lockheed, I had plenty of time, so I did a lot of volunteer work building houses for poor people," he said. On two occasions he joined Jimmy Carter on missions for the nonprofit Habitat for Humanity. Thinh worked as a carpenter alongside the former president, whom he describes as a "very nice human being."

By the turn of the twenty-first century, Thinh was widely recognized as a leading pioneer in the development and fielding of large aircraft defensive systems.

In 2000, with the approval of Lockheed security, Thinh returned to Vietnam. "On our approach to Ho Chi Minh City—everyone who lives there still calls it Saigon—I was very nervous. But the terrain looked the same. The runways looked the same and the revetments were still there. It brought back a lot of memories."

Returning to his birthplace in Nha Trang, Thinh found his father, brother, and sister. His father had survived years in a reeducation camp, but his mother had passed away. "My hometown had not changed much," Thinh opined. "The South Vietnamese Naval Academy and the Air Force Academy were both there, and they are still being used for the same purpose. The North just came in and changed the signs.

"After just a week in Vietnam, I missed being in America. I felt like an outsider."

———◇———

The latest versions of Lockheed's venerable C-130 feature a built-in defensive suite instead of the older strap-on equipment. Wiring and brackets are installed in every aircraft on the assembly line, and the software to operate the system is built into the aircraft's mission computer. Thinh played a leading role in testing these systems.

"We went down to White Sands Missile Range, where they had converted an F-4 Phantom into a remote-piloted drone. We equipped the Phantom with our latest antimissile system and watched while they fired one missile after another at it. The defensive systems worked perfectly; the Phantom landed safely.

"Three hours after we delivered the first C-130J to the Italian air force, we were in Italy installing the defensive system hardware," recalled Thinh. "We flew to a range in France, tested the system, wrote the report, and got clearance from the Italian government." Almost immediately after the aircraft arrived at the Pisa airfield in August 2000, Italian C-130J's began flying relief missions to Eritrea and the Balkan nations.

Thinh retired from Lockheed in 2016. He and Cheri moved to a small city in Alabama and spend much of their time traveling.

On a dangerous day in a hellish, frightful place, Thinh Nguyen made a decision that changed his life. Since then, his years of hard work and innovative thinking have made combat flying far safer for generations of American military flight crews.

"I have no regrets," he said. "I have been very lucky in many ways, and I am very proud to be an American, living in the greatest country on earth."

FREDERICK
W. SMITH

Ideas are a dime a dozen. Good ideas, two for a dollar. But a single world-changing idea in the hands of one determined to turn it into a new reality is priceless. This is the story of both a big idea and a rare man equipped with the courage, foresight, and intelligence to hatch that embryonic idea and nurture it through a rocky infancy into a genuinely astonishing productive adulthood. Make no mistake: this was not merely a big idea whose time had come. It took a man willing to risk his entire fortune and his reputation on an enterprise that many experts thought was at least a few decades away from practical.

All my relatives were World War II veterans," said Fred Smith. "My father was in the navy during World War II; he died when I was very young. My stepfather was a fighter pilot in China. My uncle Arthur was in the army and fought in New Guinea. My uncle Sam was in a tank destroyer unit in Europe. My uncle Bill ran away from home and became a gunner/radio operator on a navy torpedo bomber in the battle of the Coral Sea. My father-in-law was in the Marine Corps during World War II and Korea. So there wasn't any question in my mind, or for that matter in my mother's mind, that I was going to serve."

Smith was born into a well-to-do Mississippi family. His father founded Toddle House, a restaurant chain, and an interstate bus line, the Smith Motor Coach Company. The latter became the Dixie Greyhound Lines in 1931 when the Greyhound Corporation bought a controlling interest.

In his childhood, Smith was afflicted with a crippling bone disease, but he regained his health before he turned double digits. While in his teens, his family moved to Memphis, where he excelled at football. He also became a pilot at age fifteen, which launched a lifelong interest in aviation.

In 1962, Smith enrolled at Yale University, where he studied political science and economics. It's where he discovered his first entrepreneurial interest; he wrote a paper on the merits of an overnight delivery service. His professor was not impressed because he could not envision the business would be economically feasible.

At Yale, Smith befriended John Kerry, who would later become senator from Massachusetts and secretary of state and shared Smith's enthusiasm for aviation. They often flew together, and they became brothers in the Delta Kappa Epsilon (DKE) fraternity, where Smith was elected president. Both were also tapped for the collegiate secret society Skull and Bones. One of their fraternity brothers was George W. Bush, the forty-third president of the United States.

"Yale's class of 1966 was completely different from the class of '68," Smith opined. "By the time George W. Bush's class came along, the class of 1968 was completely antiwar. My class was much, much more traditional. I believe that a huge percentage of my class went into the military; the vast majority into the navy, including, most famously, John Kerry."

Instead of enrolling in Yale's excellent NROTC program, which required weekly classes and in summer sent its midshipmen to train on navy vessels, Smith chose the Marine Corps platoon leader's course because it had no weekly academic obligation. He trained in the summer, between academic semesters, with his eye on joining the marines after graduation.

Smith went to Vietnam in 1967 as a first lieutenant and served briefly as a platoon commander. By February 1968 he commanded Kilo Company, Third Battalion, Fifth Marines, First Marine Division. Before and during the 1968 Tet Offensive, his unit operated near the marine base at Da Nang.

He recalled, "The North Vietnamese never got into Da Nang or penetrated its air base. We set up a giant blocking formation, a classic L-shaped ambush, but on a huge scale—two battalions. Just as our intelligence predicted—we actually had the enemy's ops order—the Second NVA Division came up the railroad tracks that ran southwest to northeast into Da Nang. We had no idea this move was part of a coordinated, nationwide offensive.

"When the enemy entered the kill zone—I mean we put the hurt on those guys—we had eighteen artillery pieces zeroed in on them."

Because of American success in this battle, Da Nang was the only major city not penetrated during Tet. Neither was its air base, which was used by the South Vietnamese Air Force, the US Air Force, and the Third Marine Air Wing. It was the only major air base not penetrated during Tet.

About three months after Tet, while conducting a search-and-destroy operation in Quang Nam Province, Company K ran into a buzz saw on Goi Noi Island, a well-entrenched NVA battalion. As Smith's men assaulted the position, the North Vietnamese, supported by mortars, counterattacked Kilo Company's left flank. Smith ran through intense enemy fire to the point of heaviest contact. There he ignored his own safety to carry several wounded marines to safety. After directing his company's fire until the enemy withdrew, he ran across the fire-swept battlefield to an elevated area, where he ignored the danger while he adjusted artillery fire and air strikes as close as fifty meters from his position. Sensing the confusion this fire inflicted on the enemy, he raced back across the battlefield and led his troops to attack the NVA's weakest point. The North Vietnamese abandoned their positions and fell back. Kilo Company took two prisoners, collected valuable intelligence, and secured some of the enemy's most valuable equipment. For this action, Smith was awarded the Silver Star.

Smith served a second tour in Vietnam as a forward air controller (FAC). He flew more than two hundred missions in the back seat of an OV-10 Bronco (a twin-turboprop fixed-wing aircraft used for observation and light attack), directing marine, air force, and navy fighter-bombers to put their bombs, rockets, or napalm on targets he selected in response to requests from ground forces.

Capt. Fred Smith was honorably discharged in 1969. In addition to his Silver Star, he earned a Bronze Star and two Purple Hearts.

Back in civilian clothes, he returned to his love for aviation. He borrowed money to purchase a controlling interest in Ark Aviation Sales, an aircraft maintenance company. By 1971, he had refocused the business to buy and sell used jet aircraft. In June 1971, Smith raised $91 million in venture capital and also invested his inheritance to found a company he called Federal Express. It opened its doors for business in March 1973 with a fleet of fourteen Dassault Falcon 20 jets.

Initially offering small package and document delivery service to seven US cities, Federal Express expanded as Smith focused on developing an integrated air-ground system, which was an entirely new concept in the business world. He built an aircraft hub facility in Memphis, at the center of a virtual wheel that served as a clearinghouse for shipments from any city on the rim of the wheel.

This was a considerable refinement of the system he had conceived at Yale in the early 1960s. It incorporated what he had observed in action in Vietnam, specifically how USAF aircraft moved high-priority supplies, munitions, and machinery around the country. The central hub was at Saigon's Tan Son Nhut Air Base. Flights from there to major air bases north and south moved war matériel quickly around the war zone. But deliveries ended at these airports. Smith's genius was to integrate this air system with an elaborate ground-delivery system that in many ways mimicked the air portion of the network and expanded into hubs serviced by delivery trucks in each city. The business plan was based on, he said, "three separate and independent studies that confirmed the need for this new type of logistic system."

One of several things Smith applied to turn FedEx, as it is now known, into a profitable business is that things happen that cannot be planned for—exactly the lesson every combat commander learns in short order.

Smith explained the first unexpected hiccup Federal Express faced: "In October 1973, the Arabs turned off the oil spigot. That created complete chaos with our plan."

When members of the Organization of Petroleum Exporting Countries (OPEC), a cartel including Arab nations, Indonesia, and such South American countries as Venezuela, abruptly stopped selling oil, everything made from oil, including aviation fuels, became scarce. All across America, lines of cars at gasoline stations often stretched for blocks. Eventually, the federal government stepped in to regulate the available supply of all petroleum products.

"To get an allocation of the available product, you had to have had a history of using it," Smith recalled. "But we had never been in business before. We had no baseline usage on which to compute an allocation. I had to go to Washington and learn the whole scene up there. Finally, John Sawhill was put in charge of a new Federal Energy Office. I tried to make a case that we should get *x* amount of jet fuel a month. I couldn't do it; we had just launched the business. Eventually, we received an allocation; it cost us about eighteen months of profitability and created all sorts of other problems.

"In retrospect, had I known all the pitfalls, I might not have done it. Squaring the circle back to Vietnam, though, in building FedEx, I was trying to do something productive, in contrast to the completely nonproductive destruction I had been involved with—just a waste of people and resources. That was part of my motivation."

Smith proudly says he built his company by applying principles he learned as a marine. "We put great stock in our fundamental business strategy, in the fact that we fill a large and previously unmet need, in the key marketing decisions that we've made, and in the innovative operational concepts that we developed.

"Yet much of our success reflects what I learned as a marine. The basic principles of leading people are the bedrock of the corps. I can still recite them from memory, and they are firmly embedded in the FedEx culture. On a personal level, there are the little things. Even in a blue pinstriped suit, I make sure that the right edge of my belt buckle lines up with my shirt front and trouser fly. I shine my own shoes, and I'm uncomfortable if they aren't polished. I no longer sport a crewcut, but I keep my hair reasonably short. My kids would tell you I use some Marine Corps jargon, but that's another story.

"I've also incorporated Marine Corps tenets into FedEx. We tell our executives that the key to their success is to rely on their first-level managers, FedEx's counterparts to noncommissioned officers, to set the example for those under them and to publicly praise those who do a good job—all standard operating procedure in the marines, but rare in business and industry."

It doesn't stop there. Just as US Navy ships fly the Bravo and Zulu signal flags when their crews have done well, FedEx managers affix a sticker with BZ pennants to reports from subordinates that are particularly good. Workers who excel get to wear a lapel pin with tiny Bravo and Zulu flags. When an employee goes out of his way for a customer, he gets a "BZ check," a cash reward of up to a few hundred dollars. Apart from the bonuses, many of these practices are straight out of the Marine Corps Leadership Manual.

Today, Smith is the chairman of an enormous corporation, but he has remained humble. He won't cut the line in the company cafeteria. "From somewhere, a voice reminds me that a good officer lets his troops eat first," he said.

With upwards of 400,000 employees who handle more than 14 million shipments a day, in 2017, FedEx worldwide operations covered more than 220 nations and territories and earned more than $60 billion. With 664 aircraft, the company operates the world's largest commercial air fleet. FedEx is consistently rated near the pinnacle of the best companies to work for, is ranked among the most ethical of companies, and is unrivaled in brand recognition. It's also universally recognized as among the world's best corporate citizens. Smith's company aggressively seeks to hire military veterans. "They have experience in pressure situations, and they have leadership skills," Smith added.

As important as FedEx's success is on its own terms, it is now virtually impossible to think of an America without reliable and affordable overnight delivery to nearly every city, town, village, and hamlet. Without FedEx or the competitors who followed in its wake, there would be no Amazon, no Walmart, no rapid, reliable, affordable delivery of life-saving medical supplies or critical machine parts. And every package FedEx delivers contributes to the national economy.

Smith has served on the boards of many large public companies, as well as those of St. Jude Children's Research Hospital and the Mayo Foundation. A list of his professional and charitable associations would run to several pages.

Just for fun, in 2000, Smith appeared as himself in the Tom Hanks film *Cast Away*, filmed on location at FedEx's home facilities in Memphis.

Despite a long life of superlative accomplishments, Smith's days as a wartime leader are never far from his thoughts: "I think I have the same feelings as everybody who has been in something like Vietnam. You pay a big personal price. It never leaves you. I think about Vietnam probably every day . . . I think about all those guys and particularly the ones up on the Wall.[1] I am seventy-three and a grandfather; all those guys missed fifty years of life. While I owe so much to the upbringing that my mother gave me, the war was probably the biggest influence in my life. It has led me to dismiss some of the things a lot of other people think are very important. I have never been particularly motivated by money. I've experienced the dark side of humanity; an awful lot of what I think and believe is just recognizing how short life is.

"More in retrospect than at the time, my view of the world changed significantly during the war," Smith continued. "This might be because my perspective changed dramatically from the start of my tour in the Fifth Marines to the end of my second tour with Marine Observation Squadron 2 (VM02). The last month I was there, I controlled air strikes not far from where we operated when I joined the Fifth Marines in 1967. When I realized that we were fighting over the same ground over and over again, I began to question the strategy.

"My God, what a stupid way to prosecute the war," he said. "I'm still stunned by it. I get madder about it the older I get. I'm now running a company with almost five hundred thousand employees. Daily operations are integrally related to our overall strategy. Making sure they are all in tune with one another is my job description.

"Looking back at the war from the perspective of a CEO of an organization with almost as many employees as the US had in Vietnam at the apex of the war—God almighty, if I had a strategy as stupid as we had in Vietnam, we would be broke."

PART TWO

HEALERS

EILEEN MOORE

To most who served in Vietnam, nurses were flesh-and-blood examples of God's grace, angels of mercy who seemed to materialize when needed to minister to the wounded, to work endless shifts in blood-soaked emergency rooms helping surgeons save lives, offering comfort to the dying, or performing the messy, repugnant, but necessary tasks for men wounded so badly they couldn't bathe themselves or use a toilet. These nurses are shining examples of American selflessness who asked nothing more of their charges than they never give up on themselves. To others in that distant theater of war, they were defenseless sisters who had to be protected even at the cost of their own lives. And to a very few men, they were prey: attractive and available American women who would gratify their basest desires or be forced to submit.

A pilot came into the hospital," Eileen Moore recalled. "He still had one arm, but his other limbs were missing. He had an Irish name—I feel so guilty that I don't remember it. I sang Irish songs to him, 'Paddy McGinty's Goat' and 'When Irish Eyes Are Smiling,' whatever I could remember. It's strange, but I felt I was so connected to him I could somehow keep him alive just by willing it so.

"Someone in his unit dropped off two letters. One was from his wife, with her picture with their little boy. I read it to him, and although he wasn't speaking, I knew he understood because tears were running down his face. The other letter was from a friend. It was about what they'd done on R & R in Bangkok. Everything about it was gross, obscene, and disgusting. I'm sure this man would have been totally ashamed of it, especially after I showed him the picture of his wife and son. God gave me the presence of mind to change every word in that letter and let it be about what good friends they were and how important their friendship was. I just made it all up on the spot. I had to protect this man by not rubbing his infidelities in his face as he lay there without three of his limbs.

"I stayed with him for more than twelve hours—I had worked for several hours before I saw him—and finally I was so exhausted I couldn't stay any longer. Couldn't keep my eyes open. I just tumbled into bed without even brushing my teeth. He died twenty minutes after I left. I still feel that maybe, if I could just have stayed longer, I might have kept him alive. I know that doesn't make any sense, but that's how I feel about him. That was by far my worst day in Vietnam."

Eileen Moore grew up in Philadelphia. Both her parents were high school dropouts. She was one of six children, and her parents also supported her grandmother and her aunt. They all lived with just one bathroom.

Moore remembered, "My mother cried an awful lot. One day when I was about fourteen, I sat down at the kitchen table and said to her, 'Mother, did you ever want to be something?' It was a horrible thing to say to anybody."

Her mother explained she had wanted to be a librarian, but she came from a big family and had to drop out of school to work in a dime store.

It was then Moore decided she didn't want to be like her mother. Didn't want to cry all the time. She wanted to be *something*. At sixteen she told her father that even though no one in her family had gone to college, she thought she could do it. "My father said that my brothers needed to be educated; he couldn't afford to send me to college. He said I would get married anyway, so why not become a nurse? If my husband couldn't work for some reason, I could always help support the family."

After high school, Moore enrolled in a two-year nursing program at Philadelphia's Medical College School of Nursing. Upon graduation, she worked briefly in a local hospital before joining the army.

After stateside training, Moore was assigned to the Eighty-Fifth Evacuation Hospital in Qui Nhon, and she spent her first night in Vietnam in the transient nurses quarters. While it was dark, two officers attempted to break into the room she shared with two other nurses. The next morning, she reported this to the base executive officer. His response was to lament that he had missed out on the fun.

During the day, she helped an endless stream of wounded men who flowed through the hospital wards, most arriving directly from battlefields. The lightly wounded were patched up and returned to duty. Patients requiring extensive surgery or long-term treatment were evacuated to Japan, to the Philippines, or to the States.

Later, when she visited the enormous marine base at Da Nang, a hulking colonel snatched her off her feet and, despite her protest and to the amusement of his officers, forced his whiskey tongue down her throat while he fondled her. A chaplain belatedly came to her defense.

From those incidents, Moore realized when it came to sexual harassment, she was on her own, but she also knew that not all soldiers were beasts. When she hitched a ride to Saigon on an air force transport, it made intermediate stops. As it descended toward a runway, enemy small-arms fire pierced the ship's thin aluminum hull. Before the plane took off again, every member of the crew removed his flak jacket and swaddled Moore in them for head-to-toe protection.

In Saigon, Moore hailed a pedicab. It was raining, and the driver wrapped her in plastic. Ignoring her questions, he delivered her to a building on a narrow street where two Viet Cong grabbed her arms. Moore broke away and ran toward a lone GI in a jeep at the far end of the street. Responding to her shouts, he drew his gun and ran toward her. The kidnappers fled.

After Vietnam, Moore was assigned to Germany, where she completed her service.

When she returned to civilian status, she worked as a nurse in Chicago and then in Los Angeles, and she began to read, including Betty Friedan's *The Feminine Mystique*.[1] She explained, "It started working in my head. I wondered if it was possible that somebody like me, a nobody, the daughter of high school dropouts, could study at a university."

She enrolled first at a community college and then at the University of California, Irvine. There she came into contact with large numbers of Vietnam veterans and saw they were social lepers, loathed because of their service in an unpopular war. Many students took part in demonstrations against the war that still raged in Vietnam.

Moore graduated cum laude in 1975 and then started law school at Pepperdine University. Three years later, after passing the state bar exam, she entered private practice as a civil litigator. In 1989, Republican governor George Deukmejian appointed her to the Superior Court of California, County of Orange, as a trial judge, and eleven years later, Democrat governor Gray Davis appointed her to the Fourth District Court of Appeal, Division Three.

In 1997, while still a trial judge, Moore was asked to speak at the Richard Nixon Presidential Library and Museum by the Vietnam Veterans of America, Chapter 785. Also on the program was Medal of Honor recipient Col. William Barber.

"I told them about my first night in-country, about how two officers tried to break into the transient nurses quarters," Moore recalled. Colonel Barber seemed bothered by her choice of subject, but in the audience were three rows of men in tattered jungle fatigues. "It took me a few seconds to analyze and diagnose they were all self-medicated, homeless Vietnam veterans."

After her presentation, these men surrounded Moore. With evident respect, they gently touched her skin. Many had tears in their eyes. This made her realize "there was something important about nurses." Moore described, "Perhaps these men had no positive memories of Vietnam, except for the nurses who took care of them. I wondered if maybe they were still looking for us nurses to help them."

Until then, Moore had not involved herself with veterans' activities. But from that night forward, she became steadily more involved. She became a life member of Vietnam Veterans of America and took it upon herself to mentor veterans, among them women who had been sexually assaulted.

Justice Moore continues to take care of those whose war has not ended, the veterans whose hearts and minds have yet to heal.

In 2009, California was one of a few states with veterans' courts and the only one with a court exclusively for combat veterans. Veterans' courts begin by accepting guilty pleas for whatever a veteran is charged with. Under supervision, each veteran is followed through three phases of a recovery plan until the veteran demonstrates a capacity to succeed in society. Then his or her sentence is suspended.

As a mentor, Judge Moore attended a session of Orange County's combat veterans' court. "That day the judge called a case involving a Vietnam veteran," she recalled. "This was unusual because most of the vets in that court had served in Iraq or Afghanistan."

The Vietnam vet had been homeless and under the influence of some mind-altering substance for most of his adult life, but he was now sober and sublimely happy. He showed the judge a college paper with an A+ mark on it. He was thrilled at his own success and effusively thanked the judge.

Then a rattling sound issued from the side of the courtroom where in-custody defendants awaited their cases to be called. A man called out who "looked as if he'd lived in a gutter for forty years," Moore recalled. "What skin was visible was like broken concrete. He was absolutely filthy."

Yet the anticipation on his face was a beacon of hope after he saw a fellow Vietnam vet succeed. He wanted his chance. "He begged the judge to let him into veterans' court," Moore recalled. He had been rejected because the limited funding for this court meant only those most likely to succeed were allowed in. This inmate's years of being in and out of jail did not bode well for his chances of success.

But he continued to beg for another chance.

The judge relented. "There was consternation among members of a team of lawyers, probation officers, Veterans Affairs representatives, and mental health professionals who wanted someone with more promise to fill that spot," Moore recalled.

When the court recessed, Moore went to a holding cell and introduced herself to the veteran. "I told him I was a judge, but I had served as a nurse in Vietnam," she said. "He could not have cared less that I was a judge. He grabbed my hand and clutched it. He looked straight into my eyes and said, 'I would never let a nurse down. You were angels to us over there.'

"About eighteen months later, he came back to court looking like a college professor. Clean, sober, and scrubbed, he graduated from veterans' court.

He was asked to say a few words, and he turned to look at me. 'I told you that I would never let a nurse down,' he said."

That experience impacted her greatly.

—◇—

California has the world's largest court system, with approximately ten million court filings a year and almost six hundred courthouses. "There is a governing body called the Judicial Council," Moore explained. In 2008, she contacted the council's administrator. "I said, 'I'm afraid that the same thing that happened to Vietnam vets will happen to the returning vets from Afghanistan and Iraq, and I'd like the courts to be ready for them so that these veterans are not out in the cold again.'"

Thus was born the Veterans Working Group for California Courts. Moore has chaired it since the beginning. California now has thirty veterans' treatment courts. The first was in Orange County, where Moore lives and works. "I didn't start the court," she explained. "I gathered veterans to work as mentors to defendants in that court."

This working group tries to make it easier for veterans who are charged with lawbreaking to know that help is available and how to find it. An early task was the creation of a website for the California courts that spells out veterans' rights and provides forms to help them get into a veterans' court. It also lists the statutes that govern veterans. Moore's group devised a particularly useful form that courts are now required to provide to each veteran.

The first step in anyone's journey through the criminal courts is an arraignment, where a prosecutor describes the evidence against a defendant and the defendant is told of the charge(s) and must then plead guilty or not guilty. If a veteran enters a guilty plea, he or she is given the form that Moore's group devised. "At the bottom of the first page is a notation that a veteran service officer will be contacted by the court, and the veteran can get assistance through that officer without cost to the veteran," Moore explained.

The creation and manner of distribution of this form were critical to the success of the veterans' court because criminal defense lawyers were no longer involved in telling clients about the veterans' court. Not to impugn the motives of any criminal defense lawyer, but fees may be based on how much time and effort are expended in defense of a client. Those diverted to veterans' court have pleaded guilty to their offenses and their futures are in their own hands, guided by mentors and supervised by the court.

Although many states now have veterans' courts, Moore's work isn't finished.

"Most people, including many judges, are under the delusion that the statutes under which veterans' courts operate are only applicable in those courts," she explained. "But they may be used in any criminal court where a veteran is a defendant." Moore suspects that some judges are not aware of this and that many of those involved in the court system are reluctant to use them. "We have tried and continue to try to educate as much as we can," she said. "Sometimes you have to take baby steps," she added, in changing long-established attitudes.

Moore has widened her focus to family courts. "When somebody acts out violently, it's usually within the family," she explained. "I'm very concerned that veterans who have been subject to incredible explosions that toss their brains around inside their skulls—sometimes they act out violently and end up losing their children. They encounter all sorts of negative ramifications employment-wise. The courts have to be prepared to triage, to use a nursing term, to sort violent power and control freaks from veterans injured in combat who act out violently as a result. We didn't really know about brain damage until the Iraq War. But now that we do, the courts should respond."

Justice Moore's curriculum vitae lists thirty pages of awards and more pages of civic organizations to which she devotes time and effort. To answer the question Moore posed to herself so many years ago, yes, in America it's possible for a nobody to finish university and then law school and become an appellate justice *if* that nobody has the work ethic, guts, and brains of Eileen Moore.

HAL
KUSHNER

Prisoners of war are a distinct and highly deserving group of veterans. As much as combat troops suffered while fighting in the field, those taken prisoner by the enemy were forced to endure torture, starvation, and deprivation far beyond the bounds of human endurance. Most POWs did not survive their captivity. Those who did were never quite the same. Many of their spouses divorced them while they were in captivity. Others were so altered by years of pain and privation that their families could not live with them later. With only a few exceptions, however, former POWs went on to make significant contributions to their communities. Few have done more than Dr. Hal Kushner.

Hal Kushner does not care to talk about his years as a POW in Vietnam. He went to Vietnam in 1967 as a fit, strong twenty-six-year-old army flight surgeon. He returned home at age thirty-three an almost skeletal figure in the filthy rags of a prisoner of war, a loving husband and father who hadn't seen his family in six years, during which he endured unspeakable horrors and suffering. Tortured for his refusal to broadcast enemy propaganda, he focused on the lives of at least ten other American soldiers. But despite his valiant efforts to save them, without medication, surgical instruments, anesthesia, antibiotics, or even clean water, they died. Yet he and many other captives survived because Kushner used whatever he had, improvised, or stole from his captors. To this day, he credits his fellow captives for his survival: "If it hadn't been for *all* of us, none of us would be alive today."

Floyd Harold "Hal" Kushner was born in Hawaii's Tripler Army Hospital a few months before the Japanese attack on Pearl Harbor. His father, Robert, a first lieutenant in the Army Air Corps, was stationed at Hickam Field—very near the family's quarters—on December 7, 1941. He survived the attack. On Christmas Day, Kushner and his family, including his visiting maternal grandfather, were evacuated to the mainland.

Within weeks Robert Kushner was among the American aviators in the vanguard of the fight to drive the Japanese forces from the Pacific. He was wounded in action and returned to the States to recuperate, then he joined the fight against Nazi Germany.

Kushner spent the war years mostly at his grandfather's home in Danville, Virginia.

Through his mother, Kushner is a descendant of Philip Benjamin, father of Judah P. Benjamin, a Louisiana senator who resigned his seat at the start of the Civil War and served as the Confederacy's attorney general in 1861, secretary of war in 1861 and 1862, and secretary of state from 1862 to 1865.

After graduating high school in Danville in 1958, Kushner enrolled at the University of North Carolina at Chapel Hill and majored in chemistry. After a year of graduate work, he enrolled at Richmond's Medical College of Virginia. "I joined the army while I was a junior in medical school. Because of the war in Vietnam, just about every able-bodied doctor was drafted." Kushner joined the senior medical student program in his junior year and received a monthly salary of $222.30 as a second lieutenant. In his senior year he received a first lieutenant's salary. "I was on active duty and got credit toward retirement from the day I entered medical school. When I graduated from med school, I was commissioned a captain in the medical corps."

Kushner did his internship at Tripler Army Hospital, the same institution (but a more modern building) where he was born. Many of his patients were GIs wounded in Vietnam. "A large part of my internship was spent treating orthopedic injuries," he recalled.

Perhaps because of his father's wartime duty in the air corps, Kushner developed an early interest in aviation. He earned a private pilot's license, and while he was in medical school he bought a Piper Cub.

"I wanted to be a flight surgeon. I knew that flight surgeons would go to Vietnam, but I was all for going," he recalled. "I'd grown up in the fires of World War II, and I was very patriotic. I wanted to serve my country—a typical attitude in those days."

After his internship, Kushner attended flight surgeon school at Fort Rucker, Alabama. Aviation medicine deals with pressure-volume relationships, such as sinusitis, troubled hearing and vision, and psychiatry. "We were our aviators' family doctors," he explained. "Probably the most important thing we learned was Army Regulation 40-501, a document of about thirty pages that dealt with the criteria for who could fly and who should be grounded."

In August 1967 Kushner went to Vietnam. He was assigned to the justly famous First Squadron, Ninth Cavalry, the reconnaissance component of the First Cavalry Division (Airmobile). He replaced Capt. Claire Shenep, who had been killed in action the previous April.

Flying with his squadron commander, Lt. Col. Robert Nevins, Kushner was amused and amazed to see that Nevins wore a black Stetson hat instead of a flight helmet and, in the air, drank coffee from a cup with the division patch for a monogram. "He never said, 'I love the smell of napalm in the morning,'" Kushner explained, "but the Colonel Kilgore character in *Apocalypse Now* was modeled after Nevins."[1]

On December 2, 1967, the Huey helicopter in which Kushner was a passenger went off course at night in bad weather and crashed into a mountainside. Kushner, the copilot, and the crew chief were the only survivors. Kushner's medical supplies burned in the crash. The copilot died two days later, and the crew chief went to find help but was never seen again. Kushner waited three days for a rescue helicopter and then set off on his own. He was captured by the Viet Cong west of Tam Ky. Kushner suffered from many untreated wounds but was marched barefoot for more than thirty days to a POW camp. More than half of his fellow POWs died from starvation or related diseases during the forty-two months he spent there. "Most of the time we had nothing," he recalled. "No shoes, clothes, medicine, blankets, soap, or toothpaste. And very little food."

Along with his fellow captives, Kushner was shackled and frequently beaten. In 1971, he and the surviving prisoners were marched barefoot more than five hundred miles to Hanoi, where they joined other Americans in the infamous Hoa Lo Prison, known as the Hanoi Hilton.

While in captivity, Kushner used his medical skills as much as possible to alleviate the suffering of his fellow captives.

Kushner was released on March 16, 1973, during Operation Homecoming, when the Hanoi regime claimed to have liberated all the Americans and Allied prisoners in their custody.

Kushner was hospitalized at Valley Forge General Hospital in Pennsylvania for four months, during which he underwent four surgeries. He was discharged from the hospital in July and returned to active duty in August. "My next duty station was Brooke Army Hospital at San Antonio, Texas," he recalled. He took his family, including a son that had been born while he was in captivity, on a cross-country trip all the way to California and then back to San Antonio.

"The Army Medical Center tailored a one-year residency in internal medicine for me as a catch-up," Kushner related. Afterward, he spent three years as an ophthalmology resident.

"I had planned to stay in the army, but my wife very much wanted me to leave," he said. In the summer 1977, he received a call from an ophthalmologist in Daytona Beach, Florida, a man he knew well from vacations and other visits to that city, where his favorite uncle lived. "He asked me to join his practice as an associate. It was a difficult decision for me. I liked serving in the Army Medical Corps. I also liked living in Daytona Beach, where I knew all the ophthalmologists.

"I agonized over it for about a month before I decided to join him." Kushner went into the army reserve in 1977, having had more than fourteen years on active duty.

The move turned out to be good for the Kushners. "I was successful in my practice from day one," he said. "I treated my patients with medicines and with eye surgeries. I removed cataracts, transplanted corneas, repaired detached retinas. I did a lot of oculoplastic surgery of eyelids and tear ducts—things like that. I did just about every kind of operation you can imagine from the forehead to the base of the nose. Nothing was safe from me."

Although Kushner's wife, Valerie, had been very active in an organization dedicated to keeping the American public aware of the hundreds of American prisoners held by the North Vietnamese and pressuring the government to end the war and bring them home, their marriage did not survive. "It was just never the same between us after I came back," Kushner said. "We tried. Both of us tried."

"We have two wonderful children," he said. "My daughter has two grown boys, and my son, Michael, who was born while I was captured, is a film producer. His small production company is in Orlando, and he does mostly sport films—especially golf." Both of the Kushner's children are graduates of Kushner's alma mater, the University of North Carolina at Chapel Hill.

Kushner became one of the nation's best-known and most-respected ophthalmologists. His last surgical procedure took place at the end of June 2014.

Kushner was also active in medical politics. He was chosen to be the chief of the medical staff at a Daytona Beach hospital and chaired most of the hospital's major committees.

For many years he donated his time and expertise to visiting poorer countries, where he performed hundreds of eye surgeries at no cost to the patients. He has also donated his time and expertise to train doctors in third-world nations in state-of-the-art procedures.

"I've been to India three times, to Africa, Turkey, Haiti, and the Dominican Republic," he recounted. "I spent months in Peru as a fellow of the International Eye Foundation. When I was still in the army, I went on temporary duty to Peru, where I worked for the International Eye Foundation, which is affiliated with an arm of the United Nations. We did charity surgery. I have no idea how many procedures I performed. I also worked in a charity hospital for neurology patients and ophthalmology patients."

In 1985, Kushner joined Project Orbis. "It was conceived by a Houston ophthalmologist, David Paton. Our mission was not to do a lot of surgery but to educate ophthalmologists. We traveled in a DC-8 outfitted with a very sophisticated audiovisual suite and three operating rooms. We went to a hospital in Istanbul and picked up patients who needed surgery, took them to the airplane, and operated there. Meanwhile, anywhere from fifty to a hundred Turkish ophthalmologists sat in the airport and watched everything we did on closed-circuit TV. Performing the types of surgery that can only be done while viewing the patient's eye through a microscope, tiny cameras in the microscope allowed the Turkish doctors to see and hear everything we did."

Kushner remained in the army reserve, where he rose to the rank of colonel before retiring in 1986. In 2001, he was inducted into the Army Aviation Hall of Fame.

"I've tried to give back to my community," Kushner said. "I think it's my responsibility."

MIKE
HEPLER

The first Boys Club was founded in 1860 in Hartford, Connecticut, by Elizabeth Hammersley and sisters Mary and Alice Goodwin. In 1906, fifty-three independent Boys Clubs formed a national organization, the Federated Boys Clubs. In 1931, the organization renamed itself Boys Clubs of America. And in 1956, the Boys Clubs of America became a federally chartered nonprofit, championed by a pantheon of famous Americans, including former president Herbert Hoover, naval aviator and Medal of Honor recipient William E. Hall, Reader's Digest CEO Albert L. Cole, Postmaster Gen. James A. Farley, army chief of staff Albert C. Wedemeyer, Secretary of the Army Stanley Resor, AFL-CIO president James B. Carey, FBI director J. Edgar Hoover, Lewis L. Strauss (chairman of the Atomic Energy Commission), screenwriter Julius Epstein (Casablanca), and many other distinguished Americans. In 1990 the organization opened its doors to girls and became known as the Boys and Girls Clubs of America. It is safe to say that few men or women have done more for this organization than Mike Hepler, who believes the reverse is true. He believes he has received more than he has given.

Born Frank Joseph Hepler in 1948, he was given Michael as his Catholic confirmation name and thereafter called Mike by one and all. He was born and raised in McKees Rocks, a few miles northwest of Pittsburgh, Pennsylvania. Except for his army service, Hepler spent almost his entire life within a few miles of his birthplace.

"McKees Rocks is kind of a tough area," Hepler recalled. "My mom and dad divorced when I was very young, so I really never knew him. I saw him a couple of times later on in life. The last time was after he had a stroke, and shortly after that, he passed away."

Living in public housing with a single mom, Hepler had a tough childhood. "My mom was both our mother and father, a tough woman who made many sacrifices to keep her five children alive and well. But for a while I wasn't a very good kid," he recalled.

"Even though we were poor, my mother insisted that we go to church for mass and all that," Hepler said. "I no longer go to church every Sunday. But I carry my rosary beads with me to lower my stress level. And to not be an aggressive driver, I keep a Saint Therese prayer card in the car."

Hepler describes himself as a street kid. "I was in a gang. I was stabbed three times before I was fourteen. I hot-wired cars, and I was good at it. Some older gang members paid me fifteen bucks to hot-wire a car; then they stole it. I split that money with my mom. Then I started going to the Boys Club, and that's what pulled me off the street," he added.

After graduating from high school in 1966, Hepler enlisted in the army. He was trained as an armor crewman at Fort Hood, Texas. When he arrived in Vietnam, he took up the duties of a cavalry scout in D Troop, First Squadron, First Cavalry Regiment, part of the Twenty-Third Division (Americal Division).

"We operated out of Cam Ky, south of Da Nang," Hepler recalled. "Sometimes we were out west, other times east, toward the China Sea. And sometimes we were in the jungle." While he prayed often whenever he went into combat, he did not otherwise practice his religion in the combat zone. "I was not a good person in Vietnam," he said.

He was recognized early on as an exceptional warrior, so he was chosen to serve as the troop commander's radio operator in a mechanized infantry unit specializing in reconnaissance missions. "The captain was Bravo Six and I was Bravo Six Zulu," he recalled. "I was basically the captain's right arm and that was partly because of what I learned as I grew up in the Boys Club. I was a whiz with a map and compass. When we needed it, the captain called in air strikes and artillery. I could establish our position with pinpoint accuracy, and he did the rest. I was basically his bodyguard, and so my overall job was keeping him alive.

"I had two commanders, Capt. Walter Reed and Capt. Wayne Lewis," Hepler continued. "When I told Captain Reed not to get off the track,[1] he said that he wasn't going to listen to some nineteen-year-old nicknamed 'The Exterminator.' He left the track and that night we got hit pretty bad—probably because he was off the track. We hit a mine. He went back to check it out and was seriously wounded. His replacement, Lt. Mattaro, did not heed my advice on the placement of our armored personnel carrier during a night-time defensive situation. We became a primary target for mortars and RPG's and Mattaro was hit by shrapnel and died in my arms."

Hepler was later wounded in the neck by a ricochet from an AK-47, a serious wound. Before he went home, he was wounded twice more, but not as badly, and he was awarded the Silver Star and two Bronze Stars, one for valor and one for meritorious service. His contributions to the unit during a year of sustained combat were so exceptional that he was promoted several times in rapid succession, returning as a nineteen-year-old staff sergeant for a year of duty as a basic training drill instructor at Fort Knox, Kentucky. "It was fun," he recalled, though a lot of kids from the back hills of Kentucky "didn't even know what a toothbrush was."

Hepler thought about making the army his career. "I considered staying. I figured if I did, I would have retired at age thirty-seven," he recalled. Instead, he took an honorable discharge and followed his dream by going to college. He enrolled in Pittsburgh's Robert Morris University, majoring in business management.

While going to school, Hepler also worked for the local Boys Club as its aquatics director. "I had a water safety instructors rating and I was a scuba diver. I used to train lifeguards. So I was working full time and going to school full time, and it was tough. Then, in between, I got married."

———◇———

Some fifty years after accepting his first job with the organization, Mike Hepler still works for the Boys and Girls Clubs. "I worked at the Boys Club a year full time before I went into the army at age seventeen," he recalled. "Then twelve years in Pittsburgh as professional staff, including aquatic director, group club director, and program director." Then he took a job as executive director of the Boys and Girls Club in Jamestown, New York. Over seven years, he turned an underperforming operation into a Taj Mahal. "I built a big addition onto the building," he explained, by raising $4 million.

"I just kept moving up through the ranks," Hepler said, shyly proud of his service. His next job was vice president of the Boys and Girls Clubs of Western Pennsylvania (BGCWP). Two years later he became president and CEO of BGCWP, the job he has held for thirty years and counting.

The key to his continued success, Hepler explained, was his ability to raise money for the organization. "I've been doing that all my life," he said. "We don't have these huge fund-raising machines, so it's kinda grassroots. I write a lot of proposals for foundations, and I'm good at it. I write from the heart. God's the one that guides my hand; I just put it on paper. I'm old-school where I sit there and I write. It used to take me three weeks to write a proposal. Now I think about it for a day and then do it in three days."

The BGCWP serves 7,600 children in eight locations. They are supported by a staff of 150. "We see about a thousand of these kids every day. Over 70 percent are from single-parent households. We need over $4 million a year just to keep our buildings up and running and the staff paid."

Boys and Girls Clubs serve ages five through eighteen. "We do everything from workforce development to high-end educational programs," Hepler explained. "I partner with the Steelers, the Penguins, and the Pirates and run all their inner-city sports programs for them. When I was a kid, I was sitting on a fence—the streets pulling me one way and the Boys Club pulling me in the other. The club won. That was because of the people at the club, who were very caring. Ed Ferris, who was the director when I was a kid, saved thousands of street kids. He was a shepherd. He pulled me into a very caring environment, and he greatly enhanced my self-esteem. Made me feel this sense of belonging. Made me into a different person.

"He had a heart attack and passed away when I was in Vietnam," Hepler said. "I made a promise to pay him back. After fifty years, sometimes I think I should've just written a check.

"Over 70 percent of our kids are low income, and we're in many inner-city areas. The violence and the drugs and stuff over there—we're the safety net for those kids."

Hepler says that most kids who engage in club activities are initially attracted by sports. "Once we get them inside the doors, we can introduce them to after-school tutoring programs, and we have certified schoolteachers for that. We have social recreation and big game rooms, just for them to relax. We do STEM training—science, technology, engineering, and math. And employment. Last year I hired over a hundred teens. We run juvenile justice programs for first- and second-time offenders. We help them exit probation, and we provide employment and many other services for that special population."

During his long and storied career, Mike Hepler has earned a wall of awards, including the FBI's national Community Leadership Award, the US Marshal's Volunteer Award for Community Service, and the West Point General Matthew Ridgway Award, among many others. He was also inducted into the Soldiers and Sailors Hall of Valor for his service in Vietnam and the International Martial Arts Black Belt Hall of Fame.

"The clubs are kind of an oasis," Hepler said. "You could have a Boys and Girls Club in every community if the wherewithal is there. They are needed. Kids need that structure in their lives. They need that feeling of safety, and that's what we provide. Our buildings are safe and accommodating. But keeping eight buildings fully operational every minute of the day, that's a challenge."

Over his half century with the Boys and Girls Clubs, Hepler has raised well over $150 million. "Not bad for this rug rat from McKees Rocks," he said.

Hepler believes he isn't entirely responsible for these successes. "I pray nonstop. I believe that it's why my brain is still so fluid, so energetic, so vibrant, because I have cycles of prayer that I do throughout the day. From the time I get up to the time I go to bed.

"As soon as I got back from Vietnam, religion became a big part of my life. Maybe it was the feeling of guilt I had for what I had done over there. Religion was part of saving me throughout my life," he said.

Hepler rarely goes to confession in a church. "I confess to God," he explained. "Through my lifestyle, I try to limit the things I have to confess for. I try to be a good person, and God helps me do that every single day. I have over seven thousand kids to worry about every day in my profession. I pray for them every single day, and I believe that works."

DIANE CARLSON EVANS

Few have gone to war and returned alive and intact and have a monument in the nation's capital to show for it. Fewer still are female. Diane Carlson Evans, a farmer's daughter and a patriot to the core, has devoted much of her post-Vietnam life to ensuring that the sacrifices and achievements of the eleven thousand women servicemembers who served in Vietnam will never be forgotten.

I n 1863, just a year after Abraham Lincoln signed the Homestead Act into law, one of Diane Carlson Evans's ancestors, a Swedish immigrant, staked a claim to 160 acres of rich loess near Buffalo, in central Minnesota. He built a herd of dairy cows, and when he passed away, the farm went to his son. The farm was still in the Carlson family when Diane was born there during World War II.

"We were six kids and we all worked hard on the farm," she recalled. "My mother was a registered nurse, and five days a week I watched her put on her uniform and go off to work. As soon as I was old enough, I went to work after school as a nurse's aide at the hospital.

151

"In the midsixties, my two older brothers were in the army. The war in Vietnam was more and more on my personal radar. My oldest brother, who had enlisted, was in the 101st Airborne. My parents were devastated when my second brother was drafted; they were sure he'd go to Vietnam, but he went instead to South Korea.

"One weekend while I was in nursing school, I told my parents I had signed up to join the Army Nurse Corps and then go to Vietnam," Diane related. "I would stay in nursing school until graduation, and the army would pay for my tuition, books, uniforms, and so on. When I graduated, I'd be a second lieutenant in the Army Nurse Corps.

"My dad did not take this well. My mother understood and was very supportive. She had friends who served in World War II as army nurses, including her sister, who after the war used the GI Bill to get her doctorate and went on to become a college professor.

"Mom understood that I had a sense of duty," Diane continued. "The war was close to us. Farm boys weren't getting deferments—they were getting drafted. My brothers were in uniform, my 4-H buddy had died in Vietnam, and many of our community's farm boys had come back from the war in coffins.

"I'll never forget the day I left for Vietnam. It was about to rain. You can't let hay get wet; you have to get the hay in. My dad said, 'I won't be able to take you to the airport; come down to the barn and say goodbye before you drive out.' My dad was very undemonstrative—you might say a typical Scandinavian. But he hugged me as he had never hugged me before, and he started to shake, and then he started to cry. He said, 'I have four sons, and I send my daughter off to war.'

"That's when it struck me, what I had done to my parents. They would worry about me. They watched the evening news—and this was the peak of the war. Casualty rates were rising, and antiwar protests were taking place all around the country. It was visceral. Everybody felt the hostility toward the soldiers and toward the government. It wasn't popular for a young woman like me or any of the thousands of women who joined the military during the Vietnam era. Understand, we women did not need to join. But we wanted in some way to serve our country during that very turbulent time.

"People said to me, 'Why do you want to go there? What would you do that for?'

"I answered that they needed nurses. What would they do without nurses in a combat zone? I didn't know if I supported the war or not. I didn't know anything about the war, except that it was a war. But I *had* to go. We all had to go because we were nurses and our boys needed us."

She reflected on how little she knew about Vietnam—or war—before she left: "We didn't study Vietnam in high school or college. We heard it and saw it on the six o'clock news, the helicopters landing, picking up patients and body bags, villages burned, bombs dropping, soldiers crawling around rice paddies or moving through the jungle. It didn't terrify me. We were all naive. All of us young men and women who went to Vietnam or to any war zone, we did not know what we were getting into until we got there, because only war prepares you for war."

Diane Carlson Evans was twenty-one when she arrived in Vietnam on July 30, 1968.

"I felt like I was ready," she recalled. "I had good training. I was ready to practice nursing. I wasn't afraid to develop the skills to start IVs, hang blood, take care of chest tubes, put down nasogastric tubes, and take care of patients on ventilators with tracheotomies—observing and caring for all kinds of patients. But I wasn't prepared for the sheer numbers. For so many men my own age suffering and dying.

"It didn't take long for me to start asking questions," she continued. "Why are we here? What's our mission? What is the purpose of this? All these young men—who are they dying for? We heard their stories. Take a certain hill and then weeks later go back and take it again. And retake it again a month after that. Is that why we're there? To take hills? No. It was about body counts. For the senior officers, the government, the leadership, it was always about the body count.

"The truth was what we saw. But the truth was not getting back to America in the newspapers. Officers would tell me, 'You know, we tell our commander there were 18 dead bodies, and the commander would tell higher headquarters that there were 180, because it made the generals happier.'"

In 1969, Diane requested a transfer from the Thirty-Sixth Evacuation Hospital in the pleasant seaside city of Vung Tau. "I wanted to be closer to the fighting," she explained. She was sent to dusty, fly-blown Pleiku, in the Central Highlands, near the Cambodian border. That March, she remembered, "We were hit hard. We were getting four hundred casualties at a time, and so many came out of Cambodia. And yet the US government was telling the people of America that we were *not* in Cambodia. It was very frustrating to know that these truths were not being told to the American people."

Diane returned from Vietnam in August 1969, the year after the assassinations of Martin Luther King Jr. and Robert Kennedy and near the zenith of the antiwar protests. "Flags were burned and buildings bombed," she recalled. "Such a violent time. America was in terrible turmoil. I could see why people were angry at the politicians for their lies. I was angry too. But how could they be angry at *us*? At the people who served? We did just as our parents did during World War II and Korea and all of our wars. Isn't that what we were supposed to do? How could they take their anger out on *us*?"

Diane was also angry. "I wanted to know the whole truth about the war. Why were we killing Vietnamese civilians? I cared for hundreds of injured civilians, and so, so many children who were shot or burned. I can't ever forget them. I wanted to know why. What did we accomplish? What was our mission? How could our country now treat our young men so terribly, men who had suffered and died, and yet they were so, so brave, as brave as any soldier in any war. Why was our country turning its back on them?

"At first, I agonized over how our boys were treated, how their needs were ignored, how their courage and sacrifice were forgotten. And the tens of thousands who had been killed. But then, quite soon, I realized our leaders had turned their backs on us women, too, the thousands of American women who volunteered to go to war. I was just furious and so very disappointed in my country."

Diane served her last four years on active duty at Brooke Army Hospital in San Antonio. There she met Michael Evans, an army surgeon, whom she married. She left the army as a captain in 1973 and found work in a civilian hospital. As the years flew by she gave birth to four children. She concentrated on her work and on raising her children.

But she could not forget Vietnam. Year by year, her sadness and anger grew.

"Like many veterans, I didn't talk about the war. The few times I did, I was humiliated. Someone would say, 'Why did you go there in the first place?' and I'd leave the room. I just couldn't deal with responding to insults. I shut down. I didn't stand up for myself or anybody else. I told my husband that

I didn't want to talk about it and that he should never tell anybody I was in Vietnam, because when he did, it always ended badly.

"I didn't even know how many of us had been killed until the dedication of the Vietnam Wall in 1982, when they came out with the figures," she recalled. "More than fifty-eight thousand lost their lives. But the hundreds of thousands who were wounded were rarely mentioned. I was at times almost overcome with sadness. And then the betrayal—betrayal is the worst feeling a soldier can have. We had to come home and know that what we did was right, that what we did was good. As nurses, we all knew we saved lives. But thinking about what our men were asked to do, there had to be at the very least a sense that we had served for the right reasons, that we had accomplished something important, that we had contributed to our nation in some way that was tangible. Isn't that why we served? For freedom and liberty and all the things we were taught in school and what our flag stands for? When we took the oath, it was to support and defend the Constitution. What act is greater than that?

"But in Vietnam, we weren't fighting for God and country and the Constitution. We were fighting for each other, because all we had was each other. We couldn't depend on our senior officers, we couldn't depend on the generals, we couldn't depend on the Department of Defense, we couldn't depend on LBJ or Richard Nixon. We were there for our patients, for the guys in the field, and their mission became helping each other get home alive."

Living in rural Wisconsin with her husband and family, Diane and another Vietnam veteran started a vet center, a place for Vietnam veterans to gather and share their stories with those who would listen, a place where veterans struggling with the demons of post-traumatic stress disorder could seek solace.

"There were ten of us, and it was an amazing group. The stuff that poured out when everyone knew they were safe. One night there were only nine of us, and I asked, 'Where's Jim?' Someone said that he was coming, that he was late. A half hour went by and he's not there. This was a guy who had never missed a group meeting.

"I had a terrible feeling, a premonition of dread. I started to shake. Because the previous night our phone rang. Jim had said, 'Diane, you don't understand, but I can't live without her.'

"I knew that after years of struggling to know what was wrong with her husband, Jim's wife had threatened divorce. On the phone, he said, 'I could take what I took in Vietnam, but I can't take it here anymore. I can't take this anymore.' And he hung up.

"I fell asleep. I had four kids under the age of ten, and I was always tired. It didn't hit me what Jim meant until that moment when he didn't show.

"The entire group went to Jim's house. We found his body in the garage. Another casualty of Vietnam. He didn't die there, but the war killed him just the same. And that's just one story out of thousands. Thousands of Vietnam veterans committed suicide, including women," she continued.

"I knew I had to do something with my anger. It was going to kill me too. I was having suicidal thoughts, and I had four beautiful kids and a wonderful husband. I don't know what I would have done without Mike. He stood by me."

The Vietnam Veterans Memorial (the Wall) was dedicated in Washington, DC, on November 13, 1982. Diane told her husband, "I will crawl over broken glass to get to DC if I have to. I'm going."

Her husband offered to go with her.

"I said, 'Honey, I went to Vietnam alone. I came home alone. I've been trying to survive this alone. And I'm going out there alone.'"

On the Wall she found the name of a wounded patient who had asked her to write to him. It all came back in a flash; her first letter to him was returned unopened. With it was a note from his commanding officer. Her patient had been killed in action.

She also found the name of Sharon Lane, a nurse killed by shrapnel at Chu Lai in June 1969, and the names of seven other nurses who gave their lives in the war.

"I started to cry. The first tears I shed since Vietnam," she recalled. "When I went to my brother Chester's funeral, who died when he was thirty-eight, I had no tears. I was so shut down that my husband told me I was the strangest woman he'd ever known—I don't cry over anything. But at the Wall, I stood there and sobbed in front of those names. Then I went home and went into a depression. I didn't get out of bed for about two weeks. My mother came and stayed and helped with the kids."

After she returned home, Diane heard that some veterans didn't like the design of the memorial. The simple, stark monument inspired many but angered others. "They didn't like that it was black or that it was underground.

They didn't like that it wasn't heroic, and some didn't like that Maya Lin was Asian, that she was a 'gook.' That was horrible, but it was how many veterans thought."

A few weeks later, Diane saw a newspaper picture of the statue that was added to the memorial. Created by sculptor Frederick Hart, it depicted three men. Diane told her husband, "'Mike, they forgot the women. When that statue goes up, people will think that only men served in the war. They won't know that women were in Vietnam.' It bothered me. Soon I felt something burning inside me, talking to me. And finally I found my voice, the voice that had been silent since I returned from the war. I knew that I had to honor the women who served. Nobody else was doing it, so I would."

Diane went to the vet center and began talking to her fellow veterans about why she was depressed and angry. "I was getting all of this stuff out, talking about it, and to others admitting that, yes, I am a Vietnam veteran."

After the dedication of the Wall, America slowly began to realize that Vietnam veterans were not drug-crazed, glassy-eyed baby killers. Parades were held across the country, in New York, in Chicago, in Denver, in Los Angeles, and in many small cities and towns. In Minneapolis, where Diane marched, for the first time she was welcomed home. She met with other veterans and viewed several exhibits, including one by Minneapolis sculptor Rodger Brodin, a former marine, whose bronze of a platoon of infantrymen was on exhibit. "I stared at it, taken aback by how beautifully it was done," Diane recalled.

She took Brodin's card and phoned him the next day. She asked if he had ever considered sculpting a woman. A military woman. Brodin said that no one had ever asked him to do it. Diane made an appointment to see him and poured out her heart.

"Someone is working on a statue to the men who served in Vietnam," she said. "Next year it will be added to the Vietnam monument. I think we need one to honor the women. I don't know how to do this, except I think it has to be done."

Brodin replied, "First, let's do a statue." Five months later he finished the bronze. They took it to Minneapolis to an event sponsored by the Vietnam Veterans Leadership Program (VVLP), a nonprofit organization committed to helping unemployed and underemployed Vietnam veterans and those with lingering problems associated with their Vietnam experience.

Diane wrangled a meeting with the leader of the Minnesota VVLP and several other veterans. "We explained that Rodger and I had worked on a statue together, and we proposed it be placed in Washington, DC," she recalled. "Talk about being naive. That was a good thing, because had I known I would have to put up with ten years of animosity and mean-spirited, hate-filled people who threw obstacles in my way and did everything they could to stop me in my tracks, I never would have embarked on this.

"Before starting out, I talked to Mike. As an army surgeon, he spent five years at Brooke Army Medical Center, operating on soldiers just back from Vietnam. Mike has the highest respect for nurses, so when I told him what I wanted to do and that it would take about two years—that's how long it had taken the men to get their statue in place—he said, 'Go for it. Who could be against it? It's motherhood and apple pie.'"

Sure.

Getting the Vietnam Women's Memorial placed near the Wall required the approval of three federal commissions and two different bills that needed to pass both houses of Congress. It required thousands of volunteers who overcame controversy, rejection, and challenges by those who felt a woman's memorial was unnecessary.

It also required raising millions of dollars, mostly in small contributions from hundreds of thousands of people. Although she did not accomplish this alone, Diane Carlson Evans, the daughter of a Minnesota dairy farmer, was from the outset the movement's guiding light and energizing force.

In October 1987, after the men on the US Commission of Fine Arts voted down her statue four-to-one, a reporter asked Diane what it would take to get a statue of women nurses near the Wall. "An act of Congress and an act of God," she replied.

A few months later, Diane and some other nurses appeared on *60 Minutes*, the much-watched CBS news magazine. It reinvigorated the movement. Thousands of small donations poured in. Diane and her circle of helpers went back to work.

One of the first things she did was to ask New Mexico sculptor Glenna Goodacre to create a multifigure bronze featuring three nurses and a wounded male soldier in an eye-riveting tableau.

The Vietnam Women's Memorial, the first tangible symbol of honor for

American women and the capital's only statue of American military women, was dedicated on November 11, 1993, a few yards from the Vietnam Veterans Memorial. It is an enduring monument to the eleven thousand American women who served in Vietnam, mostly as nurses, but also as physicians, physical therapists, Medical Service Corps personnel, air traffic controllers, communications specialists, intelligence officers, clerks, and in other capacities in every branch of the armed services. All were volunteers.

Diane and Mike now live in Helena, Montana. She remains the chair of the Vietnam Women's Memorial Foundation.

PHILLIP
FULKERSON

Teachers are the underpinnings of a successful society. Equally essential are doctors. The very few who are both, who combine education with practical medical experience to teach others to become skilled physicians, offer a combination of heart and intellect that nurtures the growth of a nation.

When Phillip Fulkerson graduated from Ohio State in the spring of 1967, he had earned a doctor of medicine degree and immediately faced a fork in the road of life. "I could have done my internship and then started a residency somewhere while waiting for a draft notice, or I could have told Uncle Sam what year I wanted to start military service," he explained.

Only it wasn't that simple. His wife, Carolyn, a teacher, had left her job to care for their infant daughter. His internship paid only $5,000 a year; they were barely solvent. Fulkerson elected to enter active duty after completing his internship and one year of a residency in internal medicine. That decision brought him $10,000 a year until he entered active duty.

He went on active duty as a medical corps captain in October 1969. A brief course in how to be an army officer preceded an assignment to Vietnam. He left his home in Dayton, Ohio, on Thanksgiving morning and headed for the war.

Unlike most army doctors in Vietnam, Fulkerson divided his tour among four very different duty stations. "I reported to the Second Army Surgical Hospital in Lai Khe, a 1969 version of Hawkeye Pierce's beloved 4077th MASH," Fulkerson recalled. "The entire facility was three operating rooms, an ER, preop, several postop wards, a lab, an X-ray, and a pharmacy, plus supporting infrastructure. It was designed to be transportable by two CH-47 Chinook helicopters."

Fulkerson was assigned as the hospital internist. "I saw far more time in the OR as first assistant to the orthopedic surgeon and on one of the three general surgery teams," he recalled. He donned his stethoscope only to diagnose and treat a GI with leukemia, an elderly Vietnamese woman with heart failure, and an ARVN soldier with an advanced case of pneumococcal sepsis. "That was all I had to keep my brain from decaying," he said.

Not that working with severely wounded men was boring. "I came into the ER one day, and medics were putting a tube down this guy's throat to help him breathe, and there was a towel over his head," Fulkerson recalled. "I took the towel off and there was his brain—he had only half a skull. That image remained with me."

On another occasion, he worked on the driver of an armored personnel carrier who had struck a mine. "It blew his feet back up his legs a couple of inches. When you have long bone trauma—bone marrow is loaded with fat—that fat can get into the veins. If it migrates through the veins and it goes to the lungs, it causes a terrible mess. He had great trauma of the long bones of the ankle and lower leg. I was operating with an orthopedic surgeon. We couldn't fix much of his problem, but we could clean it up and stabilize it. Then he had a fat embolism and lost consciousness. His temperature soared and his oxygen fell. We transferred him to the evacuation hospital sooner than planned because he was on a ventilator and we only had one of those—we couldn't have it tied up. So we had to bag him and send him down to the Ninety-Third Evac in a helicopter."

Fulkerson and a medic accompanied the patient to the evacuation hospital on an air ambulance, then headed back to their own hospital on a helicopter gunship. "I noticed we were off course," he recalled. "Next thing I saw was a bunch of helicopters circling around us, including a couple of Cobras and a light observation helicopter. My medic suddenly put on his helmet and grabbed his rifle. Sitting there with my baseball cap and no weapon, I asked him what was going on."

The medic said a helicopter had gone down, and their bird was going to land and take care of the pilots. "So we went in, and there was a helicopter on its side and another that had landed near it," Fulkerson recalled. "The medic jumped off the helicopter before we landed, and I went with him. Then he jumped back on the helicopter and it took off. I was a little upset, but there I was, so I examined the downed pilots. Then we got them onto the other helicopter and took off. I thought that was pretty high drama," he said.

Fulkerson's next duty station was the Sixth Convalescent Hospital, which was near the beautiful white-sand beaches of Cam Ranh Bay. This facility cared for soldiers with injuries or illnesses that were expected to heal or significantly improve over several weeks, after which they could return to duty. Fulkerson provided postacute care to patients with malaria, infectious mononucleosis, hepatitis, and so forth. "It was a very nice job in a picturesque setting," he recalled.

Next, Fulkerson became the battalion surgeon of the Fifth Battalion, Seventh Cavalry, First Cavalry Division at Firebase Neal on a Cambodian hilltop surrounded by thick jungle. "I was the primary care doctor for about twelve hundred men, including about six hundred in active combat," he recalled. Fulkerson treated mostly malaria or hepatitis cases; wounded men were flown directly to a hospital.

When he wasn't at his aid station, Fulkerson hitched rides on Hueys flying resupply missions to make house calls to the troops in the jungle. He once also hiked to a Montagnard village and held sick call.

Fulkerson's final duty assignment was as the commanding officer of Alfa Medical Clearing Company at Bien Hoa, also a First Cavalry unit. "My duties were mostly administrative, with a little politics thrown in to keep things interesting," he said. Medical clearing companies were intended to provide secondary medical care for patients referred by battalion aid stations. "In fact, seriously ill or wounded patients were usually medevaced directly from the battlefield to evacuation hospitals."

When he returned to civilian life, Fulkerson completed his residency in internal medicine at Ohio State, and then he was granted a two-year fellow-ship in cardiology there. Until he retired in 2004, he was an associate professor of medicine, teaching cardiology to students, interns, and residents at medical schools in Ohio, Wisconsin, and Illinois. As he gained seniority, he also served in administrative positions.

But his passion was teaching. Between 1985 and 1988 he was a part-time student at Ohio State's College of Education, completing all the coursework for a master's but foregoing the thesis required for the degree.

"People like me do research, sometimes with another doctor," Fulkerson explained. "They think together and plot data and write papers together. But one of those people is primarily a researcher and the other is a clinician," he said.

"A medical school is a three-legged stool: research, teaching, and patient care. Most physicians do some of each, but the rock stars of medical schools, the full professors, are the researchers who bring in millions of dollars from research grants."

That's not Fulkerson's strength. He said, "In my heyday at Ohio State, I was on service four months a year. I was the doctor taking care of all the patients on one particular service. I had an intern, a resident, four medical students, and sometimes a pharmacy person or a cardiology fellow with us. We would make rounds. My job was to take the best possible and most humane care of the patients. At Ohio State, we often got the very sickest of the sick."

At the same time he was doing that, Fulkerson was teaching. "I taught students, interns, and residents. I took that very seriously. I devoted two hours a day to teaching. As we made the rounds, visiting each of my patients in turn, a student presented the case to the group, sometimes sitting in a classroom and at other times in the hallway. I would ask pertinent questions about, for example, the patient's family history.

"If we were presenting a case in the hall, I'd go see the patient with this group of five or six people. We'd walk in and I'd introduce myself. Often I had seen the patient the night before and completed his physical. I had to get it right for the patient. I had to take the patient's history and do a physical exam. Often it was written on the chart as well for the students to see.

"I educated interns and residents more in the afternoons. We would have our set of labs without students and we would talk about patient management issues," Fulkerson continued. "What drug? What dosage? What's the next care? What's the discharge date? Case management is a cutting-edge kind of thing that students don't need to be bothered with. They need to know the science of what's going on, because management will change by the time they get out of medical school and out of their training. But the basic science of a heart attack will not. So students must learn how to take a history and do a physical and relate that to the science of medicine. All that education was going on when I was on the ward.

"I spent a lot of time with patients; that was my primary responsibility. I couldn't screw that up. If patients don't trust me, then they won't tell me everything, stuff that may be critically important. So I spend a lot of time taking that history, talking to the patient, talking to the family. Every day I spoke to the family and the patient about what's going on, what we're learning, and what our treatment plans are."

When he was on that monthlong rotation, at any given time Fulkerson was responsible for the care of eight to twenty-four patients. To handle that caseload and spend adequate time with his students, interns, and residents, he was in the hospital by six o'clock every morning. Often he returned home as late as 11:00 p.m.

"If six patients came in overnight through the ER, that was six people I had to meet and do a complete history and physical that morning," he explained. His patients suffered from heart failure, heart attacks, and breathing troubles. Fulkerson is a pioneer in the use of echocardiography. "It was then brand new. So I had to learn it along with the rest of the world," he added.

The amount of time Fulkerson spent with students and patients was not the norm. "I spent more time with students teaching and more time with patients earning trust than most physicians in my situation," he said.

Fulkerson's approach to teaching medicine, if not unique, was at least highly innovative. Medical schools across the world have taught in much the same manner since at least the eighteenth century, placing great emphasis on lectures.

"I was big into curriculum, learning theory, and educational theory," he explained. "I don't believe teachers can impart things to students. They can only sequence and present things so students can learn. I believe most learning in medical school takes place between 8:00 p.m. and 2:00 a.m. when the student is home, reading their book, studying their lecture notes, and making the material concrete in their mind. They have to internalize the material and come up with understandings of what it means. And you can't do that in a lecture for 250 kids. Most of them are with you only 30 percent of the time. Their minds wander.

"I believe education has two parts," he added. "There's teaching and there's learning. Your job as a teacher is to provide appropriate learning activities so the student can actually get it done."

After giving a few lectures to sophomores, Fulkerson was put in charge of the sophomore cardiology unit. "Instead of lecturing in the afternoon, we had small group activities. I had them interpret chest X-rays with a teacher present to help them understand the principles of X-rays and what the X-ray means. We spent the afternoon reviewing six X-rays. Another day we reviewed EKGs," Fulkerson explained.

"One of the most fun and interesting things I did in sophomore cardiology was to buy sixty-five beef hearts, one for every three students," he recalled. "I wrote a manual on beef heart dissection, including both anatomy and pathology. Students had their anatomy dissection tools and a beef heart, which is the size of a football. A human heart is about the size of a softball. With greater scale, a student can actually see the smaller features of the heart. These hearts were fresh-frozen instead of embalmed in formalin, so they retain their color and flexibility, whereas an embalmed heart is blurry and stiff. They learned a great deal about cardiology from that exercise," he concluded.

Fulkerson was subsequently promoted to head the whole second year of the Ohio State medical school. "I did that for about eight years, and I made all those other units get out of the lecture hall in the afternoon and develop small group learning," he said. In that manner he revolutionized the second year of medical school toward learning instead of teaching.

Phillip Fulkerson retired from medicine in 2004, but he did not stop teaching. For the last fifteen years, he has spent much of his time tutoring elementary school students in the Rockford, Illinois, school system. He set up tutoring programs, involving members of his church to staff six half-hour morning tutoring sessions to provide ninety minutes of one-on-one instruction each week to twenty-four students in kindergarten and first and second grade. He describes these personalized one-on-one sessions as being particularly effective for students who start school with limited previous exposure to the learning process, often kids from homes that had no books. Each student's classroom teacher sets forth specific goals for each student.

In addition, Fulkerson's wife, Carolyn, and a few like-minded friends launched a scholarship endowment program, the Dayton Foundation, for graduates of Belmont High in Dayton, his hometown. They created two separate endowments. One offers $500 annual grants to students pursuing vocational or job skills training at a Dayton community college. The other offers an annual grant of $1,000 to students pursuing a degree in teaching, psychology, sociology, nursing, or another medical field. The Fulkersons intend to continue raising money to increase the number and value of these scholarships. Thus far the Dayton Foundation has dispensed $1.7 million for 2017, 2018, and 2019 and has accumulated an endowment of $70,000 for future scholarships.

PHILLIP
ROBY

The constant stimulation of war can be addictive. In a combat unit, something interesting—tragic or frightening—happens every day. Sometimes it's every hour. Even occasional periods of boredom are interesting for what they are not. Soldiers returning from a war zone, especially those who, thanks to air travel, are on the battlefield one day and home the next, often have a hard time adjusting, not to boredom, but to the loss of constant activity. Military pilots experience an even higher level of stimulation. There is something almost magical about flying an aircraft, a helicopter in particular. Rotary-wing aircraft require constant attention; there are no autopilots in combat helicopters. There is also the sheer novelty of rising straight up from the ground, seeing mountaintops up close and landscapes from above. Removed from war and daily flights, many helicopter pilots pine to return to the air. Combined with the almost indescribable feeling of having done something good, like saving a life, men like Phillip Roby never truly get old.

P hil Roby was born and raised in the tiny Mississippi delta town of Newellton, where his father and grandfather owned a store that sold clothes.

After high school, Roby went to Northeast University in Monroe, Louisiana, with the intention of becoming a dentist. His major field of study was premed. "I didn't apply myself," he recounted. "I let my grades slip."

During his junior and senior years, he accepted an ROTC scholarship. The program also offered flight training in fixed-wing aircraft. In his senior year, Roby earned a private pilot's license. "When I was commissioned and went on active duty, I was set to go to flight school," he explained.

He graduated in 1969 and was commissioned a second lieutenant in the Medical Service Corps. After officer basic training, he went to Fort Sam Houston, Texas, before starting flight school, where he transitioned to helicopters.

In 1971, Roby went to Vietnam and was stationed at Lane Army Airfield, near the port city of Qui Nhon. His duty assignment was to be a medical evacuation pilot in the 498th Medical Company (Air Ambulance). "About halfway through my tour, the 498th went home, and the 237th moved from the DMZ down to Lane. I joined them for the last half of my tour," Roby explained.

This was at a time when the largest US units—infantry divisions—were being pulled out of Vietnam and the Army of the Republic of Vietnam (ARVN) was taking over the brunt of the fighting. In the Central Highlands, where Roby flew, the ARVN fought alongside South Korea's White Horse Division.

"Each of our medevac helicopters had two pilots, a medic, and a crew chief. The latter were cross-trained," Roby explained. "The crew chief could do a medic's job and a medic could perform maintenance on the helicopter. The idea was that when we picked up a patient, we immediately started treating him with IV fluids, medication, and whatever we could do for him to expedite his care while we flew him to the closest hospital or field clinic that had the right kind of facilities for the care he needed. We did this for Americans, Vietnamese, Koreans, and sometimes the enemy."

As the US forces began to draw down, Roby's air ambulance unit dwindled to just six helicopters, almost exclusively serving Vietnamese and South Korean units.

Roby volunteered for this duty, and he was awarded the Air Medal with a V for valor for his actions on one particular mission. "Actually, we flew many missions that were far more dangerous than that one, but we received no mention for them.

"Many medevac units flew only in daylight, but we flew day and night.

We had no weapons on our helicopters," he explained. When they ran into trouble, they had to call for gunship support.

Possibly his hairiest mission occurred at night. "We flew with Vietnamese interpreters because sometimes there were no English-speakers to guide us in or tell us what was going on. One very dark night we were descending to a rice paddy, guided by a flashlight on the ground, to pick up a wounded Vietnamese soldier. As we hovered down to about 150 feet off the ground, we turned on our landing lights. At 50 feet, the enemy opened up with small arms from every direction. It was an ambush."

Roby was not at the controls when the ambush was sprung. The other pilot, Howard Modjeski, took a bullet through his neck. Roby immediately took the stick, killed the landing lights, dropped the helicopter's nose, and flew away at maximum speed.

"When we returned to LZ English, we got Modjeski into the aid station, and the doctors patched him up. Then I called in another medevac to take him to the field hospital in Qui Nhon." Fortunately, Modjeski's wound wasn't as serious as it appeared, but Roby didn't think their helicopter could be airworthy until he had a chance to inspect in daylight. "The next morning I found hardly any damage. One round had come up through the chin bubble between the pedals on Modjeski's side, went in and out of his neck, and out the top of the helicopter. There might have been one other round in the tail boom."

———◇———

Roby went home at the end of his yearlong tour in January 1972 with the intention of making a career as an army aviator. "I had a good tour," he said. "I lived through it. I think I did a lot of good. My mission was very purposeful and rewarding. I didn't kill anybody and I didn't get killed. The fact was that we had that war to fight. I think we should never have been there. We had no business being there and we had no plan to win the war. We only planned to be there and supposedly support the Vietnamese, which they never appreciated," he said. "It wasn't as good as my daddy's war, but it was the only war I had."

When he returned from Vietnam, Roby was posted to Fort Carson, Colorado, and a medical evacuation helicopter unit with a threefold mission:

training and support for Fort Carson troops in training and Project MAST. "The Military Assistance Safety and Traffic unit was designed to rescue and treat victims of accidents, including automobile accidents, mountain climbing, skiing, or anything else that occurred within a huge area," he explained. "That's what we did most of the time. Just like in Vietnam, we kept crews on ready status twenty-four hours a day. We didn't work many auto accidents. We picked up people injured in mountain climbing or skiing. We transported patients from hospitals in the smaller mountain communities to Denver or Colorado Springs; using ground transportation to get patients to a hospital from Aspen or Vail in the winter would have taken many hours in good weather and wouldn't have been possible in bad weather."

Roby's unit was also on call to respond to military training missions. "When they had night parachute jumps, we would stand by to pick up the broken-leg cases."

While he was at Fort Carson, Roby used most of his GI Bill funds to attend a civilian flight school. His aim was to get an instrument rating and log enough flight hours to find a job in aviation after his military service was over.

But it was not to be. When Roby left the army in 1974 and returned to Monroe, Louisiana, there were not many aviation jobs available. The airlines had their pick of thousands of recently discharged air force pilots. He didn't want to fly a crop duster, and he didn't want the days away from home that flying helicopters to the oil rigs in the Gulf of Mexico would have required.

For the next decades Roby tried a variety of professions. He sold life insurance. He was a stockbroker. And he tried to make a career from selling cars.

He made a living, but there was something missing from his life, and it took him a while to figure out what it was. "I decided to go back to school and start over," he said. "I started nursing school at the University of Arkansas in Monticello and earned a bachelor's in nursing. I was fifty years old when I graduated," he said.

What was missing from Roby's life was what had originally inclined him to be a dentist and then fly an aerial ambulance in a shooting war: a desire to be part of something bigger than himself and to help people.

"After a couple of years of nursing in Monroe, I became a traveling nurse, doing contracts of three months or six months at a time, mostly in Southern California."

In 2004, Roby took a full-time job at the West Los Angeles VA Medical Center. He found it rewarding. "I thought it would be cool helping my fellow vets," he said, with a note of pride in his voice. For ten years he worked the night shift in the emergency room until he burned out on that life and moved to the cardiac clinic.

Phil Roby retired in 2016, still missing flying but reconciled to the fact that his aviator days are over. He has three children. Continuing the family tradition, his only son joined the navy, served a tour in Afghanistan, then went to medical school before returning to the navy for a time.

GRACE LIEM LIM SUAN TZU GALLOWAY[1]

Not everyone who fought the Viet Cong was associated with the military. People of different backgrounds and skills came from all over the world to ease the suffering of Vietnam's civilians. At least one of these was a true volunteer. She came to the war zone on her own and found her calling. Her interactions with Americans, in uniform or not, opened her eyes to opportunities and to the humanitarian values expressed by American soldiers and civilians.

She was born Grace Lim into a large, wealthy, and greatly dispersed clan of the fabled Straits Chinese. Multilingual and mostly English-speaking, these ethnic Chinese are descendants of fifteenth-, sixteenth-, and seventeenth-century immigrants to the Malay Archipelago, Singapore, and the Dutch East Indies. Grace's family left China during the Communist revolution, which ended in 1949, and the cultural revolution of the decade after 1966.

"I grew up a Straits Chinese Catholic, mostly in Singapore and Southeast Asia, and I also spent some time in Europe," Grace explained. "I have family throughout the Straits of Malacca, from Sumatra and Singapore to Malaysia. We also have family in Thailand and all over Southeast Asia. And some are still in China. My family has the great distinction of having been kicked out of China twice and Indonesia twice."

In 1967, at the age of seventeen, "I began to get into trouble, political trouble, in Singapore," she said. Many shared Grace's problem. Singapore was then ruled by Lee Kuan Yew, and dissent from his iron-fisted rule was not tolerated. Grace left Singapore in 1967 for South Vietnam to live with relatives in Cholon, Saigon's Chinese district. The family had begun adopting street children, but as the war went on, there were so many abandoned and orphaned children roaming the streets that even their large house could no longer accommodate them.

"At that point, all they could do was feed them," Grace recalled. "Every day they fed hundreds of children whose sole nourishment came from that daily meal. My aunties taught me how to cook rice the old-fashioned way, by repeatedly washing it to get rid of weevils and dirt, adding just the right amount of water, and boiling it in a huge pot."

Grace's life changed abruptly after January 30, 1968. Just after midnight, at the start of Tet, the Lunar New Year, tens of thousands of Viet Cong and NVA troops attacked dozens of South Vietnamese cities. Although the Tet Offensive ended in defeat and the near annihilation of the Viet Cong's larger units, the fighting went on for months. Tens of thousands of civilians perished, including all of Grace's Cholon relatives. Their house burned to the ground before anyone could be saved.

Shocked and grieving, Grace returned to Singapore. "I thought, *You know what, I can't do this whole Vietnam thing. This whole war thing is just too much for me.*" But after only two weeks in Singapore, she decided to return to Vietnam. "I was dreaming about the children of the street. Who would care for them? The war changed how I thought about life and death."

In Saigon, Grace looked for volunteer work. "Since childhood, I had dreamed of becoming a nurse," she recalled. "That was all I ever aspired to. When I went looking for some kind of nursing work in Saigon, the nuns at Catholic Relief were the only people who would take me. I was a Catholic and I had a rosary."

She became a nurse's helper, assisting doctors and nurses to care for the flood of sick and wounded civilians. This brought Grace into contact with many Americans, mostly doctors and nurses with the US Army's Third Field Hospital.

"We were in constant need of medications, bandages, dressings—all the supplies needed by hospitals," she said. "But we were limited as to how much we could find, even on the black market. Every so often I would wander over to Third Field Hospital and talk to the young American soldier at reception and explain our situation as best I could. And not for one second did I ever think he wouldn't believe me. It never occurred to me that this young man would look at me and think, *You got to be out of your mind, lady, if you think I can believe that wack-a-doodle story.*

"Instead they took me to a nurse or a doctor. I would explain the situation again, and if they had it, they gave me whatever we needed. And they did this a lot. I certainly saw the worst part of Tet, but I also saw the best of the Americans, their compassion, their generosity."

One day Grace came across a particularly heartrending patient: a little girl no more than thirteen. "She had been living under a stairwell," Grace recalled. Raped repeatedly, she was pregnant and in excruciating pain. "She also had an STD. We couldn't find all the drugs she needed, and we couldn't save her—that was my worst day in Vietnam. I'll never forget her."

That was a turning point in Grace's young life. "If you think about what shapes you, what defines who you are and how you live," she explained, "Vietnam made me sit back and think, *Boy, I got it good. I really have it good. I have a roof over my head. I'm not worried about where my next meal is coming from. I've got nothing to worry about.*"

This was also when Grace began to truly appreciate her patrimony and her upbringing. "My family was wealthy. We have a grand history of not just philanthropy, of sharing our wealth with the needy, but also of truly caring about less fortunate people. That's my heritage," she said. "In Singapore, my grandfather was adored and venerated. Anytime there was a crisis—if a monsoon or a fire wiped out a village—he was always there to help with funds or with people to help rebuild. I grew up thinking that this was normal and that it was my obligation as well."

Grace learned more about noblesse oblige from her teachers: Father Gerard Kelly and Sisters Elizabeth, Sabine, and Hillary. "They informed my thinking with the notion that prayer alone is not enough; you must also take action. We are not placed on this earth to acquire fame and riches or to be recognized for earthly accomplishments. We're here for a reason, and each of us must find that reason. Even now, I often feel as though I am in constant pursuit of what more I need to do."

As the months passed and Grace learned basic nursing skills in the crucible of war, her social circle expanded, with friends among the volunteers of other nongovernmental organizations and the international press corps. Among these was freelance photojournalist Sean Flynn, son of film star Errol Flynn, with whom she began a serious relationship.

In April 1970, as North Vietnamese troops advanced into Cambodia, Flynn and colleague Dana Stone were abducted by Khmer Rouge guerrillas and disappeared. Rumors of sightings abounded, but none proved true. Many of Flynn's colleagues headed to Cambodia to look for him. Others queried contacts in the military for any relevant information. For eight months Grace roamed Laos and Cambodia, often alone, seeking information on Flynn and Stone. But the American journalists were never found; their fate remains a mystery.

"Those eight months nearly destroyed me emotionally," Grace recalled. "I had to leave Southeast Asia."

In 1971, Grace settled in Richmond, Virginia, where her mother had lived for several years. Based entirely on her experience with orphans and abandoned children in Vietnam, the YWCA hired her in 1972 to develop and run a shelter program for battered women and their children, one of the first three such shelters in the United States.

Grace knew these people often had wounds not visible to the naked eye, that healing minds was as important as healing bodies. But such shelters were very new. There were no established policies and procedures. There was only a burgeoning need for safe places for battered women and children.

"We had no protocol, for example, to deal with a batterer who comes to the shelter," Grace recalled. "But I knew that under no circumstances could we acknowledge that any particular woman was in our shelter. That, and a Louisville Slugger, was our initial protocol. For the first year or so, we had to make it up as we went along."

An offshoot of her shelter was SCAN (Stop Child Abuse Now). "This came about as we saw that battered women often had abused children," she explained. "It took me four to five years to get SCAN" established. SCAN, the women's shelter, and its successor programs continue to this day. "I am very proud that the Richmond YWCA was the first place in the region to develop such programs," Grace said.

Once her programs were rooted in the community, Grace decided it was time to pursue her childhood dream. She enrolled in a community college that offered a two-year registered nurse degree. "I wanted to get into the workforce quickly," she explained. "The other degrees would come later. But I felt compelled to take what I knew and utilize it better by getting a nursing degree."

For the next several decades Grace worked in hospitals, frequently in emergency rooms, including several years at the Richmond veterans hospital. Although each shift with veterans triggered flashbacks, unexplained anger, nightmares, sleepless nights, and sudden weeping bouts, she continued to do what she thought was her duty.

Meanwhile, she continued her formal education.

"I decided I not only could but *should* do more in my professional life. I trained to become a nurse practitioner, and after a while I saw I could do much more, that I was still not doing enough."

Grace returned to academia for a second master's and then went on to finish a doctorate in public health. Meanwhile, she married and became a mother to a daughter, Li Mei. After a subsequent divorce, she spent a year or so with the Ringling Brothers and Barnum & Bailey Circus, initially as a nurse and then as a performer, a trapezist. That was followed by a decade traveling the world with her daughter as a performer with Club Med.

This break from the stress of nursing, Grace believed, went a long way to alleviate her own post-traumatic stress disorder. "My wartime experiences in Vietnam taught me that peace is always the answer, that dissidence does not equal disloyalty to the country and in fact is patriotic," she said. "It also taught me how fleeting life is. It taught me how precious children are. I learned to appreciate the simple things in life. I learned I had an obligation to do something to right the wrongs I saw. Hindsight tells me that I made a ton of mistakes, but it was important that I tried."

In 2012, Grace married a friend of forty-five years, Joseph Galloway, an author of this book. They live in Concord, North Carolina.

Now well past retirement age, as she has since 2008, Grace continues to serve her community as a volunteer. Three days and one evening a week, "Doc Gracie" sees patients at the Concord Free Clinic, which offers free and low-cost care to those too poor to afford health care yet not poor enough to qualify for the state's bare-bones Medicaid program.

DERYLE
PERRYMAN

War often requires young men to do things that, had they been blessed with the wisdom and maturity to understand the ramifications of their actions, they would have refused to do. That rarely happens in the middle of a shooting war, but as time goes by and young men reach their middle years, some begin to regret what they have done. A few seek ways to atone for their younger selves, and some of those dedicate their remaining years to doing something that actually makes a difference.

In his senior year at Stephens High School in his hometown of Florence, Alabama, Deryle Perryman and two of his buddies were offered baseball scholarships at Florence State University (now the University of North Alabama). But instead they spent the summer after graduation goofing off.

"The college semester had started while we were drinking beer up in Tennessee when one of my buddies said, 'Hey, classes have already started, dude. What are you gonna do?' I was nineteen and I had a sixteen-ounce can of beer in my hand, and I realized this particular question had never occurred to me. I took a swig of the beer and looked over at him and said, 'Well, I'm joining the army.'

"Two of my buddies, Scotty and Bubba, said, 'Well, we'll go with you.'"

"'Man, y'all not even out of high school,'" Perryman replied.

They nevertheless enlisted on the buddy plan. "That lasted about thirty minutes after we got to Fort Benning," he recalled.

"When we got to the induction station, I'd forgotten to bring my glasses, so they sent me for an eye test. Next time I saw those two was six weeks later in the Fort Benning PX."

Before he signed his enlistment papers on Halloween 1966, Perryman sought his father's advice. His dad had served in World War II with the Thirty-First Infantry Division, a National Guard unit dubbed the Dixie Division, which fought in the Pacific.

"My daddy said, 'Boy, you don't have to be in the infantry. I've already done that. In the artillery, they make a lot of rank.'"

At the recruiting station, he was handed a contract and told that he could have his pick of training for any of 168 noncombatant jobs in exchange for a three-year enlistment.

Perryman said, "Can I be in the artillery?" The recruiter said, "There are 168 jobs that you can get that have nothing to do with combat arms." He pointed at one on the list that said motion picture camera operator. And Perryman asked again, "Can I be in the artillery?"

The recruiter asked if he knew that the combat arms were infantry, artillery, armor, and engineers. Again Perryman asked to be in the artillery.

"He took that clipboard and *slam!* threw it down, looked to his buddy, and said, 'Can he get in the artillery? Can he get *in the artillery?*' Then he took another clipboard and spun it over to me and said, 'Sign your name right there.'"

Perryman joined the artillery.

His father was right. Perryman made corporal in nine months. He made sergeant soon afterward and would have become a staff sergeant less than a year later. Then he learned that his unit was preparing to deploy to Vietnam, and if he accepted the promotion, he'd have to transfer out. This series of rapid promotions was, of course, less about the availability of opportunities in his unit and more about Perryman's work ethic, leadership qualities, and his unforced, down-home charm.

Perryman's battalion of M-107 self-propelled guns shipped out on the

USNS *Upshur*. They sailed from San Francisco and arrived in Vietnam near the end of 1967.

An M-107 weighs thirty-one tons and fires a 175mm projectile weighing ninety-five pounds through a sixty-foot-long barrel to ranges up to twenty-two miles. Because of road conditions in the Central Highlands—many bridges and culverts had been destroyed by the Viet Cong—each gun and its crew of fifteen was accompanied by a bulldozer to speed their passage.

"When we got off the boat in Qui Nhon, I was a buck sergeant and the gun crew chief," Perryman recalled. "They put us on trucks and we headed toward An Khe in a convoy. Two hours later, still on the trucks, one of my guys riding in the back called to me, 'Hey, we just crossed a creek. The bridge was blown up.' I began to notice the little kids along the road flipping us off, making obscene gestures. Another one of my guys asked, 'Did they give us any ammunition?'

"Just about then we pulled over to the side of the road and stopped. We were issued C rations and rifle ammunition. . . . When we put loaded magazines in our M-16's, somebody said, 'Are we in the enemy zone or are we not?'

"I was standing next to the truck while we were divvying up the C rations when an old woman came out onto the road from between two hoochies. This was our first day and it was a totally alien world. This woman walked alongside the road, never taking her eyes off me. That made me pay attention. We had already been told that civilians sometimes sabotaged our vehicles by putting Gatorade and rubber bands in the gas tank. Women put razor blades in their vaginas and, oh, my God. So I was really worried. This woman, she was just like Ms. Grisbee, who lives down the street from my grandma. I knew I couldn't shoot her.

"Then she squatted down and pulled up her dress—never took her eye off me—and relieved herself on the road. Whoa! All of us, eighteen-, nineteen-, and twenty-year-olds—we're not hardly believing our eyes."

From An Khe, Perryman's crew made their way west to Pleiku and then north to Kon Tum Province. "When we got up to Dak To, there were Montagnards everywhere. Men wearing loincloths with a machete stuck in it and carrying a crossbow. Women carrying baskets and wearing no blouses. And I'm seeing these people were no threat to America. Were they gonna take San Francisco with machetes and crossbows?

"I think I've been had. Knew it for a fact. And there ain't a goshdarn thing I can do. Zero. Zilch. I was a patriotic young American, a southerner. My country called, so I said, 'Let's go.' I was young and dumb and full of testosterone. I signed up and took my buddies, and I put myself in a spot," he said, not exactly bitter, but still feeling what he felt fifty years back.

In July 1969 his unit was notified that most of its members would be transferred to other units and that new men would replace them. "That was because they didn't want to replace the whole unit at once. I couldn't believe it."

To Perryman, this was yet another betrayal. He had trained with this crew. They knew and trusted each other. And now they would be leaving, one by one, and they'd probably never be together again.

Perryman's unit was part of I Field Force Artillery (I Field Force was a headquarters with tactical control over several US and Allied divisions and separate brigades). The I Field Force Artillery, manned on any given day with from eleven to twenty artillery battalions, assigned battalions to support each Allied unit. The battalions were a mixed lot, ranging from Perryman's long-range 175mm guns to battalions with eight-inch guns or howitzers, 155mm and 105mm howitzers, and track-mounted quad 40mm cannon and .50-caliber machine gun "dusters" for close support.

In Kon Tum and later farther north in Dak To, Perryman's unit completed fire missions against targets around the Central Highlands. Almost always their fire was controlled by a forward observer, either airborne or on the ground, and they had only a general idea what their target was. One mission he recalls vividly was firing several rounds of white phosphorus at targets too distant to be seen. When exposed to air, white phosphorous burns fiercely. It was used in marking rounds to adjust the big guns' fire and for antipersonnel missions. "We knew that stuff was what we fired, but we never had cause to think about what happened after that," Perryman recalled.

"One day after we fired some white phosphorous, for some weird reason a chopper landed near our battery on the side of a hill next to the Dak To airstrip. Aboard were three enemy soldiers who had been hit with our white phosphorus. They were marched right through our battery area so we could see what our rounds did—those men were all horribly burned. We could smell their charred flesh. At that very moment I swore I'd never fire a WP round again, except as a marking round. I realized we were blowing up grass hoochies with the most sophisticated weapon we had at the time, blowing up people who had no way to defend themselves and who maybe didn't have anything to do with the VC or the NVA.

"Later in my tour, I was in a 155mm unit. Twice I refused to fire a WP round. The action officer came out of the bunker with his telephone and said, 'I'm giving you a direct order.' I held the firing lanyard up and said, 'If you want to shoot it, here it is.' And I dropped the lanyard."

Perryman left Vietnam on December 19, 1968. He completed his service at Fort Carson, Colorado. After his discharge, he went back home to Alabama and immediately enrolled at Florence State, where he became a star pitcher on the varsity baseball squad.

After graduation from college, he was hired as the chief probation officer for the juvenile court in Tuscumbia, a little town south of Florence where Helen Keller was born. "I was a hotshot and I was curious and I was interested and I was really involved," Perryman recalled. "One year I ran the Alabama Chief Probation Officers' Association's annual conference, and the keynote speaker heard me speak. He'd just received a $3.5 million grant to do something about the treatment of little kids in jails and children who were victims of institutional abuse," he explained. "He asked me if I would come and work for the National Coalition for Children's Justice in Washington, DC. Our board of directors included Ralph Nader, Shirley Chisholm, Roosevelt Grier, and NFL referee Jim Tunney.

"I had an office in the National Press Building. We also had an office in Princeton. And from that time, I've been a youth advocate and a youth worker," Perryman said.

Very likely as a result of Perryman's exposure to the herbicide Agent Orange, his first son was born with hydrocephalus and died after six and a half years. "I'm convinced and I'm trying to prove it that his birth defect was the result of my exposure—and Kon Tum Province was a heavily sprayed area," he said.

Perryman founded the Cornstalk Institute in Florence, an experiential education center that mentors schoolchildren to become the leaders of tomorrow. "I ran that as a spiritual education program for twenty years. At first, these were street kids, but then I got them out of the thugs and woods thing to do some prevention work. We took kids from poor families on bike trips to places like Norway and Argentina. We took them hiking, biking, climbing. We did art projects. We built three houses. We had a vegetable garden," he explained.

"Then I moved to northern New Mexico to help start a nondenominational spiritual retreat, which is still going. I did a lot of youth work in Albuquerque. I helped start the New Mexico Youth Conservation Corps. I've been on the board of a lot of youth organizations.

"When I turned sixty-three, I made a decision. I've been dealing with youth since 1972, so I really needed to do something else for a while."

In 1995, Perryman returned to Vietnam, his first visit since the war. "I went to Kon Tum. There weren't many foreigners up there. Actually, foreigners were specifically banned from going there; the Hanoi government considered it a frontier zone," he explained. "When I went through there the first time, in January 1967, I thought it was one of the most beautiful places I'd ever seen. I didn't know until I returned that, between our troops and the North Vietnamese, during the 1972 Easter Offensive, we essentially destroyed most of what we knew as the city of Kon Tum. There was nothing there but some French colonial buildings and the Montagnard's stilt houses. When I came back in 1995, I didn't recognize the place."

Since 1995, Perryman has returned to Vietnam twenty-one times. "I went to Kon Tum every single time. I've gone to some other places, but I kept going on to Kon Tum. Because of the fact that I'd killed innocent children in the war, I felt I needed to do something about that. I wanted to heal myself."

After the war, Vietnam's Communist government began a systematic program to take land from the Montagnards and resettle Vietnamese on it.

"I remembered how immobile these people were when I first met them. And now their lands had been taken. Their kids wanted to go to school, but there were few schools," Perryman recalled. "I saw this wasn't right and that these people needed some help, especially their kids."

Perryman continued to visit the area. "Finally I met a couple of young community organizer men of the Bahnar people. And I saw they were losing their culture. Their kids just want to play rock 'n' roll and hang with their friends. But the Bahnar are beautiful people. I thought that at least their culture ought to be preserved. Over the years I've made enough contacts and

I've raised some money and brought them some musical instruments. I met a young man of twenty-seven whose mission is to preserve the Bahnar's music. This kid is a superstar. He could leave Vietnam and be a world-class musician, but he's staying with his people and working to save his nation's music.

"We started a music school and expanded into a media center, teaching video and audio production so the kids can learn good skills," Perryman continued. "This was kind of a backdoor way to get these youngsters to see the preciousness of their traditions. We want to preserve, promote, protect, and archive the music of the Central Highlands, starting specifically with the Bahnar of Kon Tum and then some other tribes as well."

Perryman is also building a library in Kon Tum. "We just delivered our first load of books and showed them to Vietnam's minister of cultural affairs," he explained. "I told him that I'd get a thousand books at a time, but first I've got to make space for them. And I'll have to raise more money."

Perryman is also concerned about the future of the Bahnar children. Vietnam is modernizing. English is being taught in the lowland schools to prepare its people to deal with the international community. "But the Bahnar have nobody to teach them English. They're being left out. I know some Bahnar, enough to speak to people, but not enough to be able to teach them English."

Perryman has assigned himself still another mission: to educate Americans, especially those who fought in Vietnam, about the realities of the war. He speaks of a conversation he had with Chuck Searcy, who has lived in Vietnam, off and on, for some twenty years. He once ran a very successful Vietnam Veterans of America program in Quang Tri Province to safely remove some of the millions of explosive devices that dot the countryside: mines, unexploded rockets, mortar and artillery shells, and aerial bombs, including the brightly colored bomblets scattered by cluster bombs.

"Chuck said, 'I don't believe those boys have recalibrated their thinking since they were over there, do you? A lot of people are still trying to make some sense out of their wartime experiences, and I understand that. They want it to count. They want it to matter. I understand that. But there are some vets who go, "We coulda, shoulda, woulda won it." I tell them, "Hey, they kept us from winning that war."'

"'What? The politicians?' I asked.

"'No,' he said.

"'The Hippies?'

"'No.'

"'Who?'

"'The Vietnamese people,' Chuck said. 'The Vietnamese people refused to allow us to have our way with them.'"

These days Perryman, still living in Albuquerque, is making short documentary films about Vietnam. He lives modestly from the proceeds of some property that he sold, and he continues to raise money for his library and multimedia studio in Kon Tum. "I've visited Vietnam many times," Perryman said, "and I learned that we all need to make peace. To forgive and to be forgiven by our former enemies. It's the only way to move forward."

JEFF
FREDRICK

A trait long associated with Americans, and with American fighting men in particular, is their indomitable spirit, their dogged refusal to give up or quit, even in the face of the most desperate circumstances. There are very few better examples of this spirit than Jeff Fredrick, who had every reason to quit, to accept defeat and live the rest of his life as a powerless victim. But that is something Fredrick will never do.

While serving with the 101st Airborne in Vietnam in 1968, Jeff Fredrick attended a three-day combat leadership course at Bien Hoa, an enormous US base just north of Saigon. "If you're respectful, and they were going to make you a three-stripe sergeant, they'd send you to this course," he recalled. It was mostly three days crawling on the ground and learning to use field explosives. Fredrick was nineteen. His impression of the twenty-year-old sergeants teaching this course was that they didn't care much what their students learned.

When he returned to his unit, Company B, Second Battalion, 506th Parachute Infantry, no one would speak to him. "I felt like a pariah," he said.

"I was no longer one of them. Because none of the guys I knew were still alive." Over the next four or five days, he got bits and pieces of what had happened. On July 22, Bravo Company lost seventeen dead and about twenty-four wounded. "One of the first to die was Spec. Allan F. Hamsmith," Fredrick explained. "We were always together in the field. I knew fifty years ago and I know today that he was where *I* would have been had I remained with the company. As he entered a wood line, he encountered a VC spider hole concealing a sniper and two machine gunners. They pinned Bravo Company down. Hamsmith was shot in the groin and in the throat. He bled to death. And the rest of my squad was killed too."

A year earlier, just out of high school in Winter Park, Florida, Fredrick had learned he could volunteer for the draft and then volunteer for airborne. "That's what I wanted. I was interested in Special Forces, and I planned to reenlist or ask to be reassigned," he recalled. "After a few months in Vietnam, I put in for an in-country transfer to Fifth Special Forces."

On July 27, however, while on combat patrol, Fredrick triggered a booby trap that blew off his right leg. Two days later, still fighting for his life in a Cu Chi army hospital, he received a letter encouraging him to submit a transfer request to Fifth Special Forces.

When he returned stateside, Fredrick was assigned to the amputee center at Fort Gordon, Georgia. "When I got back, there was no physical therapy," he explained. "There was no anything. They just said, 'Here's your discharge papers,' and you walk out the door with an artificial leg.

"I never had any problem with anybody spitting on me because I'd fought in Vietnam. I'd have killed them. You could sense my attitude a mile away. I limped and I had a bad attitude. I wasn't sick or in great pain. I just wouldn't have taken any crap from anybody. But people treated us as though we were crippled and made me feel humiliated. I was embarrassed in front of women.

"I got a leg blown off," Fredrick said. "These days, people often say to me, 'Oh, look what you've done with your life.' I want to tell them, 'I was nineteen, dude. What was I supposed to do? Let my life be ruined?' I wanted to try to leave something behind for the next generation. To be someone who says, 'Okay, I lost a leg, and this is what I learned,' instead of, 'I'm broken, I'm all screwed up. Look what happened to me.'"

Fredrick enrolled at the University of Central Florida in Orlando, where he earned a bachelor's in political science and a master's in special education. "I wanted to do something to help kids," he explained. "I wanted to change the world."

Many traumatic amputees suffer from post-traumatic stress disorder. "I didn't go through that," he insisted. "Instead, I made 608 parachute jumps. Skydiving was a big deal back then. That's what rehabbed me. Making those jumps brought me back to feeling like a man again, to feeling strong again, to feeling like a whole person again. I was the one-legged guy at the drop zone that did everything everyone else did. I ended up becoming a jumpmaster. And then I was one of the senior guys. And that gave me back my dignity.

"Last year, just to prove I could, I made five more skydives. It damn near killed me, because I was sixty-seven. It's not like when I was thirty."

After college, Fredrick worked in a company that manufactured prosthetic devices. In 1981, he completed the orthotic certification program at Shelby State Community College in Memphis and received prosthetic certification from Northwestern University.

Then he borrowed some money and opened his own business. "One of the problems we have, as I see from the inside, is that money has replaced much in medicine. When I was a kid, doctors were great. The prestige of being a physician far outweighed what they made. They cared about people. Now, much of the medical profession is corporate. I've worked for a large company. And when it was sold and went on the New York Stock Exchange, instead of the patient being the main constituent, the stockholder became the main constituent. It has a tremendous negative effect on the quality of care in our culture. When I started my company, I knew I could have a medical-type business to make money. Or I could have a medical-type business out of compassion and caring," he explained.

Fredrick chose the second option. "I have three constituents: the patients, my employees, and the bills. I wanted to be independent and set up my own programs, and that's what I did."

Rehabilitation Engineering's business model was centered on delivering affordable, individualized patient care, and it was the engine that built a thriving practice serving Tallahassee in Florida and Thomasville and Valdosta in Georgia. He merged Rehabilitation Engineering with the Hanger Orthopedic Group in 1998. In 2006, Fredrick started a new company, Rehab Engineering, through which he and his staff continued to deliver quality patient care to their community.

During all those years and through three different companies, Jeff Fredrick also delivered free or nearly free care and prosthetic devices to the poor and underserved in the Tallahassee area. Not bad for a guy who lost a leg and launched a career based almost entirely on a burning desire to change the world.

But there is much more to Jeff Fredrick's boundless compassion. In 1994, before diplomatic relations between Hanoi and Washington were established, he wrote a grant proposal that was accepted by the Vietnam Veterans of America Foundation. The funds came from a war victims' appropriation bill ramrodded through Congress by Vermont senator Patrick Leahy.

The grant funded the establishment and operation of a center to provide artificial limbs and braces to treat children in Vietnam. Many had lost limbs to unexploded ordnance. Fredrick administered the grant, which required him to visit Vietnam nine times.

But before he could start helping Vietnam's maimed children, he had to convince the Hanoi government to allow him to do so. "I went to see the deputy foreign minister," he related. "Through his window, I could see Ho Chi Minh's tomb. The man I spoke with was movie-star handsome, with perfect white teeth. Trying to be deferential, I began our conversation with, 'You know, you guys won the war.'"

The official shook his head. "No, we didn't," he said. "As a child, I was in Hanoi during the bombing. They showed us movies of all the demonstrations in America. McNamara, Johnson, and Nixon wanted the war. The American people went into the streets, and they made their government stop fighting. America is the greatest democracy in the history of the world."

"I love the Vietnamese," Fredrick declared, but he might say the same about many nationalities. "I think the Vietnamese are the Americans of Asia. We have the same sense of humor. We really have a lot in common. Looking back, it was almost like brothers fighting. It's very strange."

Fredrick's view of the war has evolved considerably since he fought in it. "I love America," he declared. "I don't regret a minute having served in Vietnam. But I was raised by a mom who said, 'When you're right, I'll stand with you. When you're wrong, I won't.' So you better be right if you want

Mom on your side. And that's how I feel. I love America, but it isn't 'love it or leave it.' It's a love it that believes if America is wrong, I'm gonna kick its butt. That's my generation: let's fix it, quit crying about it, fix it. Get off our butts and fix it."

Before leaving Hanoi, Fredrick was granted an audience with Vietnam's military hero, Gen. Vo Nguyen Giap, who was responsible for the French defeat at Dien Bien Phu and for the conduct of the war against the American and Allied forces.

Two days later, in the former Saigon, now Ho Chi Minh City, Fredrick was interviewed by CBS reporter Bob Simon. "I repeated what the deputy foreign minister told me," he said. "And then I added, 'For crying out loud, don't let them cut that part out.' But they did cut it."

To ensure the success of his artificial limb and brace project, Fredrick trained two men at his company in Tallahassee, among the first Vietnamese to come to America for any sort of training after the war. Afterward, they returned to Vietnam.

But providing limbs to Vietnamese children was only part of his humanitarian efforts. Including his nine working visits to Vietnam, Fredrick has thus far made twenty-six overseas journeys, bringing basic medical care and prostheses to Columbia and to Haiti, where he set up an entire program. "Often the reason people need artificial limbs and braces stems from poor medical care and a lack of access to pharmaceuticals," he explained. "In 1986, I developed a program called Adopt a Village Missions. With volunteer doctors, we opened a full-range medical and rehabilitative services clinic in the village of Dumay, Haiti."

In 1997, Fredrick cofounded the Collection of Surgical, Health, and Rehabilitation Equipment (COSHARE), which has shipped medical supplies to Ukraine, Vietnam, Cambodia, Jamaica, Haiti, and Bosnia.

"I think our generation, the Vietnam generation," Fredrick said, "if there's any grand distinction between us and the generation of World War II, it is that ours was a tragedy instead of a drama. The previous generation came back victorious, went to work, made a lot of money, had a life. They came out of the war to celebrate their lives, and God bless them.

"*We* came out of *our* war to see that a big mistake had been made. We came out seeing how terrible and costly and useless our war was, and how strange were the politics of our parents that encouraged our soldiers to kill all the Japanese one minute and buy their cars the next. Our parents' generation should have set their minds to ending war once and for all. Where our generation has so far failed was to not take that candle and run with that light and try to make a better world. So that's what *I'm* trying to do."

KAREN
OFFUTT

Until 2016, women were not permitted to serve in combat units. According to the Vietnam Women's Memorial Foundation, about eleven thousand women, all volunteers, served in the Vietnam War. The vast majority were nurses. The rest served in a small number of other jobs available to women: physicians, air traffic controllers, translators, intelligence analysts, clerks, typists, and other headquarters noncombat jobs. Because the foe in Vietnam included both North Vietnamese regular troops, Viet Cong guerrillas, and innumerable VC sympathizers and agents, no American soldier anywhere in Vietnam was truly safe. Billets in Saigon were occasionally bombed. Soldiers in several cities were kidnapped, stabbed, shot, or garroted. Grenades were sometimes thrown through windows. And, of course, there was always the chance of a sniper. Getting around the country was safest by air, but because Agent Orange had been so widely dispersed throughout the country, it was tracked into helicopters and buildings on boots and clothing.

In 1970, Spec/5 Karen Offutt, a stenographer who worked for general officers in a big Saigon headquarters complex, looked out the window of her room in a hotel taken over by the US Army as an enlisted billet. Next to her building was a hamlet occupied by hundreds of Vietnamese civilians, mostly the families of men who were off to war. Fire billowed from one of those buildings.

Barefoot, Offutt ran downstairs and entered an alley between thatched huts; the thatch was afire. She grabbed up small children and took them outside, returning again and again. Offutt returned to the building several more times, risking her life to help elderly and infirm people remove some of their possessions and lead livestock to safety.

Offutt's heroism did not go unnoticed. The hamlet chief wrote to the commander of US forces in Vietnam. A senior officer wrote up a recommendation for the Soldier's Medal, reserved for army personnel who risk their lives to save others in a noncombat situation.

A few weeks later, Offutt was awarded not the Soldier's Medal but a certificate of appreciation. A senior officer told her the Soldier's Medal was reserved for men.

Offutt was born in Arkansas but lived in several states as she grew to adulthood. "We lived in Arizona, Oregon, and California," she recalled. "I went to so many schools that I can't remember them all. But that taught me a lot of things about getting along with people and making friends easily, so it was okay.

"I graduated high school at seventeen and went to Europe that summer as an exchange student. We went to England, Italy, Switzerland, and France," she recalled. "Several of us had decided that when we graduated we wanted to be nurses and go to Vietnam."

At age seventeen she enrolled at the California Hospital School of Nursing in Los Angeles.

"I left nursing school after a few months," she recalled. "I was one of the youngest in the whole school and I had no college or any other of the usual prerequisites, so I was taking nineteen and a half class units and working in a hospital."

It was just too much for her. Go back home? "My father basically said there were no free meals at home. He took me to an employment agency. When we left, I spotted a little red, white, and blue trailer. I crossed the street, and I signed up for the army.

"The recruiter told me I should go to stenography school. I didn't know how to type or take shorthand or anything, but I said okay. After basic training, I was supposed to go to Fort Benjamin Harrison, Indiana," Offutt recalled.

"In basic, I turned into *Private Benjamin*. I did everything but ask for a different color uniform. Somehow I got through it. When I got my orders, they didn't say Fort Benjamin Harrison, Indiana. They said Fort Benning, Georgia. And I was then at Fort McClellan, Alabama, which was hot and humid and horrible.

"Because I played the clarinet, after basic training I was invited to join the Women's Army Corps Band and remain at Fort McClellan. I didn't want to stay there. It was just too humid and awful. I didn't know what to do. My orders were obviously in error. Finally, I got the nerve up to go to my sergeant's room and knock on her door. I said, 'Sergeant, there's been a mistake, a terrible mistake, I have the wrong orders.' She said, 'Write your congressman,' and slammed the door shut.

"I went back to my barracks and sat there thinking, I didn't know who my congressman was, so I couldn't write to him. There was no internet, nowhere to look anything up, so I had to go back. Oh, it was horrible. I had to go back and knock on the sergeant's door again.

"And she said, 'What is it now?'

"I said, 'I'm sorry, Sergeant, but I don't know who my congressman is.' I won't use the language she did, but it was something like, 'Then write the effing president.'

"So I went back to my barracks and wrote President Johnson a long letter, in longhand, of course, telling him that my father didn't serve and my brother had asthma and my first brother died and I was very patriotic and all this stuff.

"I sent the letter. Nothing happened until a couple of weeks before I had to go to Fort Benning. Then my name was called on the company loudspeaker. I was to report to the orderly room.

"There I was handed a phone. Someone said it was the Pentagon, but I didn't know what the Pentagon was. I took the call, and a woman said, 'President Johnson has read your letter, and he's very upset. We will cut immediate orders for you to go to Fort Benjamin Harrison, Indiana. And we're sorry for this.'

"My sergeant called me in and said, 'What the hell were you thinking? Don't you know better than to jump the chain of command?'

"I said, '*You* told me to write the president!' She was furious. Then a major came and sat with me in a room. She said, 'You've caused a lot of problems by not going through the chain of command, and you're gonna sit here until you can type—I think it was thirty-five words a minute or something—to get into this school. And you damn well better do good because of all the problems you've caused. There will be repercussions if you don't do well in school.'

"I went to Fort Harrison, and I was so scared that I graduated second in my class. I took shorthand at 140 words a minute—I'd never even seen shorthand before that school—and I forget how fast I could type, but it was very fast.

"Because I was an honor graduate, they sent me to work in the Pentagon, which was just hilarious to me. I was working at the Pentagon, and I was seeing all this stuff on the news, stuff about Vietnam. I had a room at Fort Myer, Virginia. I rode a bus over to the Pentagon every day. So every day I looked out my window and saw men of the Third Infantry Regiment, the ones who guard the Tomb of the Unknown Soldier and perform ceremonial duties at Arlington National Cemetery, the Pentagon, and the White House.

"And every day or so they're escorting horse-drawn carriages, burying people, and I'm thinking, *Oh, God, why are there so many people dying?* I didn't understand it. I didn't equate those funerals to Vietnam or anything like that. But on the news, I heard about the protests going on and I kept wondering why it was only the men—they were boys really—how come only the boys are risking their lives and dying? How come women aren't?"

Offutt began asking her superiors if she could go to Vietnam. "I wanted to see the truth about the whole thing," she said. "I kept bugging them, and finally they said there would be an opening to work for Maj. Gen. Raymond Conroy, and later I was to work for Gen. Creighton Abrams, commander of all US forces in Vietnam; his stenographer was getting out in October. So I went to Vietnam," she said.

"We landed at Bien Hoa and they put us on a bus. It had chicken wire on the windows, so I asked the man next to me what it was for. 'To deflect grenades,' he said.

"I glanced back to see if the plane was still there and if I could maybe get back on it."

Offutt expected the bus would take her to Headquarters Military Assistance Command Vietnam, in Saigon. Instead, she was taken to Long Binh. "It was a really desolate place," she recalled. "I didn't have a fatigue uniform. I didn't have anything really." Offutt spent her first night in a room with several other women.

"We had pots and pans all over the floor to catch the rain because it was monsoon season and the roof leaked," she recalled. Desperate for sleep after the long flight, she was awakened when her bed began to shake and she heard a succession of nearby explosions. "Somebody said, 'We're getting hit—but don't worry. The VC are really lousy at aiming.' That didn't seem like much to write home about. I figured I would die on my first night," she recalled.

No one needed a stenographer at Long Binh, so Offutt found herself on work details. "They had a small pool full of insects and slime and stuff, and they had me out there, wading in there, getting the bugs out," she recalled. Her protests that she was supposed to be in Saigon working for Major General Conroy fell on deaf ears. "One day I left the base and found a tall building—maybe the finance building or something—and I went in." She begged the use of a telephone, and someone told her how to call MACV HQ in Saigon. Eventually, she reached someone in Conroy's office.

Later that day or the next—Offutt can't remember—a black sedan pulled up in front of Offutt's barracks. A sergeant major asked to see Offutt.

"I came downstairs, and there were several older women—lifers—who ran the place, and they refused to turn me over. Something about me being too young to find a safe billet in Saigon. I was still only eighteen." There was some back and forth between the sergeant major and the women. Then the sergeant major said, "Get your gear." Offutt ran upstairs, packed her few belongings in a duffle bag, got in the car with the sergeant major, and drove away.

By road, the trip from Long Binh to Saigon was less than an hour. That brief journey was Offutt's initiation tour of South Vietnam's extremes of poverty and privilege. "I saw mind-blowing poverty, kids playing in mud and huts made out of crushed beer cans and cardboard boxes—a real eye-opener for me. But I felt horrible riding in that air-conditioned car as though I was the rich girl in town. All those poor people gawking at me made me feel really awkward, out of place, as though I was some sort of elitist."

In Saigon, Offutt was assigned to a room in Medford BEQ (bachelor enlisted quarters), an old four-floor hotel with a flat roof. Men lived on two floors and women on the other two. The hotel was very near Third Field Hospital.

"I shared a tiny room with a sweet girl who worked as the stenographer for General Abrams. But we were rarely there except to sleep. We worked twelve to fifteen hours a day and six and a half days a week," she recalled.

In October, Offutt's grandfather died, and she went home on emergency leave. She then came down with double pneumonia, for which she accepted treatment but refused hospitalization. She felt that she was needed in Vietnam. When she returned to Saigon, she had a new roommate, and due to her temporary absence, General Abrams had found a new stenographer. Offutt continued working for Major General Conroy, the assistant chief of staff for logistics. He often traveled by helicopter to distant parts of South Vietnam. Offutt sometimes went with him, but on a second chopper, taking dictation on the ground, so that a letter or several letters would be typed, proofed, and ready for his signature upon his return. She performed similar duties for other generals on Abrams's staff.

"I had an 'eyes only' clearance. If somebody from Washington flew in, say the secretary of defense or the secretary of state or whoever, then I would take their dictation in shorthand and type it out letter-perfect. And then that person would sign it and send it by courier to the president or whomever.

"And if we were gonna launch an air strike in the middle of the night, they called me in. I'd have to find a way to get to MACV in the middle of the night to take dictation and type up orders for that," she explained.

At the end of her tour, Offutt returned to the States, intending to make the army her career. And why not? She had rare skills, was valued and respected for her abilities by senior officers, and could look forward to a long and exciting career.

But then she fell in love. Twice.

"I was initially assigned to the Presidio of San Francisco, but I was engaged to a guy from Texas, and he wanted me to go to Fort Hood. So I had my orders changed. But when I returned from Vietnam, we broke up. I ended up going to Fort MacArthur in San Pedro, California.

"It wasn't a terrible duty assignment, but I dated a guy for about three and a half weeks and then married him. I wanted to stay in the service, but he insisted that I get out. There were very few women in the army then, so I was always around men. And my husband was jealous because they looked at me—back then, I wasn't bad-looking. So he made me get out of the army," she recalled.

Instead of seventeen years until she could retire from the army, "I had sixteen years of misery," Offutt said. "He wouldn't even let me tell anyone I had served in Vietnam, because he hadn't. He even destroyed most of my photos from Vietnam."

That was the beginning of many hard years for Offutt. Each of her three children was born with severe birth defects that Offutt believes are related to her exposure to Agent Orange. "My daughter was born with grand mal epilepsy," she explained. "One of my twin sons had Wilms' tumor, a cancer of the kidney, and the other had ADHD. They all had many other medical problems."

Through the years of this marriage, "I just kept on fighting to go to school. I'd take a class at a time until I finally got into nursing school and graduated in 1984—and then I left him."

Offutt worked several years as a medical-surgical nurse and as an oncology nurse in Southern California. She later moved to the San Joaquin Valley to work for the Tulare County Office of Education in Visalia, California, in Migrant Education. "I was a child and disability coordinator for the children of migrant farm workers. I was more like a health nurse in that I visited all the labor camps. It was very satisfying, but I felt a lot of sadness from seeing so many people living in poverty. The worst cases, other than when I was in oncology nursing, were the child abuse cases. Those have stayed with me a long time." She later worked in Modesto, at the Stanislaus County Office of Education, She first worked for Head Start as an RN, and then for Migrant Head Start as the health and disabilities coordinator.

Offutt regards her most important achievements in nursing as her years in Oregon as a nurse for the Cow Creek Band of the Umpqua Tribe, which is scattered over seven counties around Roseburg. "I was their only nurse, and they didn't have a doctor," she recalled. "I was basically a public health nurse."

Karen Offutt also worked several years in Tampa, Florida, as a private duty RN. She was involved in local veterans' organizations as well. In April 2001, she was asked to speak at an assembly marking the visit of the Moving Wall, a half-size replica of the Vietnam Veteran's Memorial in Washington, DC.

She spoke for several minutes about her experiences as a stenographer amid a shooting war. She also spoke, without apparent bitterness, about her children's health issues and those of her grandchildren—all, she thinks, because of her exposure to Agent Orange. When she finished, one of the event organizers, Linda "Scooter" Watson, approached her with a miniature dog-tag pin and a certificate of appreciation for her participation. She abruptly stopped, stared at the certificate, and ripped it in two. "Sorry, spelled your name wrong," she said.

The crowd, among them several television crews, gasped.

"Color guard!" shouted Watson.

Seemingly from nowhere, a color guard from Disabled American Veterans appeared and presented the colors. A uniformed Junior ROTC cadet came forward with a board bearing photos of Offutt from her army days. An aide to Congressman Gus Bilirakis appeared, carrying a small black case and a paper. The aide opened the case to show Offutt and read from the paper an order of the secretary of the army, awarding former Spec/5 Karen Offutt the Soldier's Medal.

This was the work of two Vietnam veterans, Mike Castle and Joe Oliver, neither of whom Offutt had previously met. Castle was on hand that day as a member of the color guard.

It took thirty-one years, but Karen Offutt finally received the medal she had earned. She is the only enlisted woman to be so honored and the only one who served in Vietnam.

JOHN PADGETT

Of the few good things to come out of the Vietnam War, one of the most important was the creation of a small corps of trained medical personnel with various specialties and a wide range of skills. With additional training to meet licensing requirements, these former military medics have helped to make up for the shortage of doctors and registered nurses in many of America's poorest communities. More than a few of these men and women have dedicated their lives to the healing arts, often at great personal sacrifice. Among the best known of this cadre are John and Vicki Padgett, husband and wife.

Since 1776 the men of John Padgett's family have volunteered to serve in the US military. His grandfather was one of Teddy Roosevelt's Rough Riders. Just before World War II, however, his father had to leave the Illinois National Guard after losing a lung in an industrial accident. During the war he worked in a defense plant.

Padgett grew up in Kankakee, Illinois, a small city in the fertile, rolling farmland south of Chicago. After high school, he attended a teacher's college at Illinois State until he realized he didn't want to be a teacher. In 1965, with draft calls rising, he dropped out to continue his family tradition. He enlisted in the army.

"I had heard and read a little about this American unit that did things like unconventional warfare and behind-the-lines operations and so forth, called the Special Forces," he recalled. "I thought, *That's for me*, and went down to the recruiters and asked to volunteer for Special Forces. The recruiter said, 'Son, you don't choose Special Forces. They choose you. I can get you as far as airborne training, but after that, you have to roll the dice.'"

Padgett rolled the dice. After eighteen months of training, he became a Special Forces medic and in 1967 went to Vietnam, where he served in a succession of small border camps staffed by an A-Team (a dozen highly trained Green Berets) and a few hundred Montagnard infantry. After the start of the Tet Offensive in 1968, he joined the elite Mike Force (mobile strike force), which was assigned the risky task of reinforcing Special Forces camps that were in danger of being overrun.

After a year in the mobile strike force, he went to Thailand for a year, where the Special Forces worked with the Royal Thai Army to deal with insurgent forces in remote parts of the country. When he returned to Vietnam, Padgett joined the legendary Studies and Observations Group, an innocuous name for troops tasked with the most secret, important, and riskiest missions.

"My duties included serving as what we called the chase medic," he recalled. He also ran the medical section of the Forward Operational Base's Command and Control Center. "When one of our teams was in trouble and had to be pulled out, the first helicopter in carried a medic so he could immediately administer life-saving actions on the most seriously wounded," he explained. As the helicopter left the battlefield and flew toward the nearest army trauma hospital, the flight medic treated the wounded until he was relieved by doctors on the ground.

That was how Padgett found himself immersed in the now-legendary Operation Tailwind, a covert penetration into Laos by a company-sized force of Special Forces and Montagnard commandos of the so-called Hatchet Force. The operation was intended to divert attention from a Royal Lao Army offensive and exert pressure on the North Vietnamese occupation forces in Laos.

"We had a Hatchet Force, or what we called an exploitation force, of about 110 men or so on the ground," Padgett explained. "Their mission was to block the Ho Chi Minh trail for twenty-four hours; it turned out to be four days. This was the deepest inside Laos any of our troops had ever been. When it was time to go get them, I was on the first helicopter, a big Marine Corps CH-53, to get the wounded out. As we flew toward the operation area, we ran through antiaircraft fire, puffs of black smoke from exploding 37mm shells. It was like something I remembered watching as a kid, *Twelve O'Clock High* and other World War II movies where our bombers flew through German flak. That's exactly what we were doing. I caught a piece of flak in my armored vest, but it didn't penetrate all the way through.

"We got to the landing zone, and the pilot—this was his crew's first combat mission—took us down to a low hover. I stood on the rear ramp while the assistant medic held me by the belt so I wouldn't fall out. Mike Rose, a medic who in 2018 received the Medal of Honor, was on the ground, trying to lift the casualties up to me. But the ground fire was so intense that before I could bring the first patient into the helicopter, the pilot decided to abort. He pulled up very sharply, and as he did so a B-40 rocket, fired from an RPG, came through the bottom of the helicopter and punched out through the gas tank and then the fuselage. For some reason, it didn't explode."[1]

As the chopper climbed out, fuel spewed from the tank, soaking the aircraft's interior. After about five kilometers, the pilot made a hard landing in the only open space available—an unoccupied North Vietnamese complex.

"I got the crew out and put them in a perimeter to rig the chopper for recovery and to fend off an attack. After about twenty minutes, which seemed like ten days, another CH-53 dropped a rope ladder from its tail ramp.

"I told my crew—the pilot, copilot, crew chief, door gunners, and assistant medic—to climb the rope ladder," he continued. "They just stood there looking at me. Meanwhile, I heard the helicopter taking hits from small arms. Finally, I yelled, 'Follow me,' and up the ladder I went. They came up after me.

"I was the one closest to the gate, and I carried D rings for just this purpose. I hooked myself onto the rope ladder. The crew chief yelled that they were not bringing us in because they had to leave before they got shot down. So everybody was dangling from the rope ladder, eight or nine of us, as we flew for another twenty or thirty kilometers across Laos.

"They set us down on a hilltop, and the big helicopter managed to limp away, unable to fly while carrying us. After about an hour or so, a couple of army Huey helicopters came to pick us up."

Padgett left active duty in September 1971.

The John Padgett who came home from Vietnam was not the one who had gone to war six years earlier. "I think I grew up a lot," he said. "I think many of us felt betrayed by what was going on in the United States—the anti-war movement, people in the streets waving the flag of the very people who were killing my friends," he continued, speaking for many of those whose stories appear in this book.

"It was ugly," he recalled. "I am the son of people who served in and lived through World War II when the entire nation was behind the soldiers. The civilian sector was involved in that war. There was rationing, paper drives, meatless Mondays, and all that. There was none of that while we were fighting in Vietnam. The war was sort of a peripheral thing. People could turn on the TV and see us, but they weren't actually supporting us."

Fast-forward to the wars in Iraq and Afghanistan. The civilian population was not asked to make any kind of sacrifice. President George W. Bush famously asked Americans to support the country by going shopping.

"But I noticed the We Support the Troops movement," Padgett said. "That became really big. Bumper stickers and yellow ribbons and what have you. When I was in Iraq, for example, we got packages from kids in grade school classes who wrote us letters and drew pictures and signed them. We got the feeling the people were behind us, and even if they weren't supporting the war, they supported the soldiers.

"When we came back from Vietnam, people were yelling 'Baby killer!' and spitting on us," he continued. "We were instructed not to wear our uniforms off-post, for traveling on public transportation. Put on civilian clothes, our officers told us, or else we'll get in trouble. And that's in our own country!

"It was all very disappointing. Plus, the fact that after all the treasure and blood we spent in Vietnam over ten years or so, Congress just decided, 'Well, that's enough.' They did not support the Vietnamese military after we left. There was an act of Congress that said, 'Nope. We're done. No more support.' That left the South Vietnamese trying to help themselves, trying to defend themselves, and they've got no more ammunition, no more medical supplies, no more fuel, no more nothing. The outcome was inevitable."

It was well known by Americans there was no love lost between the ethnic Vietnamese and the aboriginal Montagnards, whom they considered savages and often turned away from their medical facilities. That was why Pat Smith, an American physician, started a hospital in Kon Tum for Montagnards.

"On weekends, or when I had time, I would get in my jeep and go over to the hospital and help out where I could," Padgett related. "One of the hospital staff was a former Special Forces medic. I asked him if he was a doctor or a nurse. He said, 'I'm a physician assistant.' I'd never heard of a physician assistant. I didn't know what it was. He told me about the profession, that it was a brand-new category of medical caregiver. That sounded like something I could do when I got out, and I asked him what he thought. He said that, as an SF medic, I was exactly the kind of person the profession was looking for. He wrote me a letter of introduction to the University of Washington, from which he had graduated."

After a year and a half of schooling at Washington, Padgett became a physician assistant, the start of a long and satisfying career.

His first job out of school was working for one of his teachers. He moved to a start-up HMO and was shortly thereafter recruited by the University of Hawaii by the same former Special Forces medic who had written him the letter to UW. "The University of Hawaii hired me to go to Micronesia and teach what they called MdEx. This was the Micronesian brand of midlevel practitioner, not quite the same as a physician assistant, but trained in many of the same skills."

From Micronesia, Padgett moved to the Alaska pipeline, then under construction, where he treated patients with everything from pneumonia to gunshot wounds to injuries suffered from driving off an icy road. Once he had to rappel down an ice wall to retrieve a patient whose vehicle had gone over the side.

After Alaska, he moved from job to job, spending several years with his own practice in Southern California and along the way earning a PhD, before becoming the clinical coordinator of Oakland's Samuel Merritt College in 2000.

In 2003, Padgett, who had remained in the army reserve and had worked his way up to major, Medical Specialty Corps, was mobilized for Iraq. "I joined a civil affairs team and became Baghdad's de facto public health officer for a year," he related. Soon after he returned from Iraq, he retired from the reserve.

"When I came home, my wife, Vicki, said, 'Don't unpack, honey, we're going to Las Vegas.' We were recruited by Touro University to help set up a medical school in the Las Vegas suburb of Henderson. We started from the ground up. The university was housed initially in a warehouse that was previously the campus of a failed dot-com company."

The new university added modules to house each new specialty school as it was created: osteopathic medicine, physician assistant, nursing, physical therapy, and so forth. Padgett ran the physician assistant school, and his wife, who is also a physician assistant and a PhD, opened America's first clinical facility inside a women's shelter. Based on that success, the university started a mobile medical clinic for the homeless in Las Vegas, staffed by physician assistant students. "Vicki took the mobile clinic to Las Vegas's homeless corridor once a week, and I took it to the homeless veterans facility to hold weekly sick call. We retired in 2016, but the university has built on the success of the mobile clinic to open the second one," he said.

Among the many awards Padgett has collected during a long and illustrious career was his selection as 1994 national humanitarian of the year by the American Academy of Physician Assistants/National Professional Group. "What touches me most deeply was the suffering of the innocent," Padgett recalled.

About 1983 the Padgetts, along with several friends and colleagues—medical professionals all—created Refugee Relief International Inc. (RRII), which delivers humanitarian medical care around the world wherever other humanitarian agencies dare not go. Padgett serves as vice president and director of operations, while Vicki, a US Air Force veteran, is secretary-treasurer.

A typical relief mission sends a team of four to six medical professionals to a country. The teams travel by land, usually through very difficult terrain, to reach communities beyond the reach of local civilian medics. "We have used several means of transport to reach our operational areas: boot leather, pickup truck, dragon boat, banana truck, helicopter, C-47 aircraft, and elephant, but we haven't jumped in," Padgett explained. He has gone on some thirty-five missions. "Airborne operations require extensive logistic planning and paying for an aircraft, for drop-zone preparation, for parachutes, and qualified jumpmasters, and that is beyond our capability. We're a poor, all-volunteer charity."

The team is usually escorted by armed locals, familiar with the area, to provide security against bandits, soldiers, and other threats. In recent years these teams have broadened the scope of their missions to both treating patients and teaching local medical staff, whose training and skills range from almost nothing to sufficient to handle minor surgery, clean and dress wounds, dispense basic medication, and diagnose several types of disease.

The team works in a basic medical facility, often merely a converted hut. After assessing the situation, including available medical staff and patients, the team coordinates with local medical practitioners and improvises a surgical suite. They typically perform three to ten operations per day, from simple surgeries to amputations. They usually work without electricity or running water and with only the equipment they can backpack in. The team has developed special sterilization and anesthetic techniques that require minimal equipment and yet work well in a forest or jungle setting.

Although they are officially retired and now live in Corsicana, Texas, the Padgetts continue their pro bono work, lending their medical skills to underserved communities and continuing their work with RRII.

Both Padgett and Vicki serve on the boards of the Special Operations Association and the Special Operations Association Foundation. Padgett lectures around the nation on health-related topics and medical service in remote and denied environments to groups such as the Special Operations Association and the Joint Special Operations Medical Training Center. They both belong to their local volunteer fire department.

For John and Vicki Padgett, their war against pain, suffering, and needless death goes on.

PART THREE

OFFICEHOLDERS

BARRY
MCCAFFREY

The Vietnam War offered opportunities for military careers. A rapidly expanding army, for example, allowed many midcareer officers to step up to command of larger units, with promotion to follow. It was a different paradigm for junior officers—the lieutenants and captains who saw the war up close and personal. Army and marine captains and first lieutenants suffered the highest mortality rates of all ranks. It was close to miraculous for a junior officer in a command position to serve two combat tours and return to the States alive and intact. One of the few who did went on to join the pantheon of America's greatest military leaders. His success in battle and personal heroism are virtually unmatched. From his first day in combat, Barry McCaffrey, son of a general and a West Pointer, led from the front.

Barry McCaffrey grew up on army posts but wanted to be a doctor. "As a kid, I lived at West Point for three years, played youth hockey, and hung around the cadets," he recalled. "I was in Paris as a high school junior with early admission to Johns Hopkins University. I was going to be a doctor. Then my dad said, 'You look like you're twelve years old. You're not going to

Johns Hopkins. You're going to a prep school.' I got into a very special place, the Phillips Academy in Andover, Massachusetts, for my senior year of high school.

"I went there as the smartest boy in the history of the world. I was a scholarship boy, which was another great thing. I worked in the dining facility many hours a week, punching a time clock," he continued. "I'd been a straight A student. President of my junior class. A letterman. When I got to Phillips, the first thing I learned was that I wasn't as smart as I thought. I was in over my head. They were so far beyond me, it was just unbelievable. In mathematics I was lost from day one, so they placed me in a math class of one. In the evenings I went to see the math professor at his house.

"In the middle of that year, I realized I missed the army, the military posts, and my friends. By then my friends were getting into the Naval Academy and West Point. I applied to West Point, was accepted, and never looked back."

In April 1965, civil war broke out in the Dominican Republic. With thirty-five hundred US civilians in the country and reports of Communist Cuba backing the rebels, President Johnson ordered marines and elements of the Eighty-Second Airborne Division to intervene.

Among the paratroopers of the Eighty-Second Airborne was Lieutenant McCaffrey, West Point '64, who earned a Bronze Star for his leadership. "We were down there maybe eight months," he recalled. "A lot of shooting, a lot of complexity. It went from an active combat mission to a peacekeeping role.

"Then a marine regiment and the 173rd Airborne went to Vietnam," he recalled. "When we returned from Santo Domingo, we were scared we'd miss the war in Vietnam because, with the marines and an airborne brigade there, it would be over in six months. So three or four of us lieutenants raced up to the Pentagon in a car. I spoke with a major who said, 'Lieutenant, you've already got the combat infantry badge. Would you rather be a platoon leader again or a battalion commander?'"

McCaffrey said, "A battalion commander."

The major said, "Then you want to be an advisor in the Vietnamese airborne division."

"When I went home, my dad said, 'You stupid bastard,'" McCaffrey recalled.

He became an advisor to the ARVN Second Parachute Infantry Battalion.

"These were elite soldiers, with combat-hardened NCOs and officers. Some had fought with the French airborne in their Indochina War," he recalled. "Our role was to coordinate US artillery, air strikes, armed helicopters, medevac, logistics, and intelligence. Most of the division was stationed in Saigon. When not in the field, we advisors lived in air-conditioned officers' quarters. We loved Saigon and thought we were the wealthiest people in the world. We got airborne pay, combat pay, and 'separation from US military support' pay. We sat around Saigon drinking and screwing around until we were activated and sent primarily as brigade combat teams into combat. We took horrendous casualties. Then it was back to Saigon, bury the dead, get clean uniforms, and return to our lives as rich Americans."

There was another side to McCaffrey's tour with the ARVN airborne. "First Corps was the most heavily contested combat area throughout the war," McCaffrey explained. "It was close to the demilitarized zone, so we fought North Vietnamese regulars. American units, the ARVN airborne, marines, and First Infantry Division tried to break up NVA battalions on their way south. In October 1966, we went up with two parachute infantry battalions, right on the Ben Hai River separating North and South Vietnam.

"Our two battalions landed at PK17, a marine outpost just north of Dong Ha. There was supposedly an NVA division crossing the river. We came in under fire. We pushed out from PK17 under increasing fire. We had some significant fights the first day and that night. We got right below the DMZ legal boundary and started digging in. They were ranging us with heavy artillery. Then an observation plane reported thousands of NVA soldiers crossing the river 'with wheeled heavy machine guns.'

"We thought we were cooked. Fortunately, we had a few reinforcements and a fifteen-man navy team to direct gunfire from a cruiser," he recalled. "They all wore fancy Australian bush hats. I grabbed the navy lieutenant in charge and said, 'There's a lot of enemy artillery around here. Make sure you dig deep tonight.'

"We began digging in. In the middle of the night came a series of massive artillery bombardments that went on throughout the night and much of the next day. We knew we were in trouble, so Maj. Keith Barlow, our brigade advisor, put out an emergency call. The whole system mobilized to save us. Although it was monsoon season and there were thick clouds, two B-57

Canberra bombers came down under the clouds. Both were shot down. Our medevac and armed helicopters were getting shot down, so they turned off medevac. Although we were barely in range of the marine four-deuce mortars, they did us a lot of good. Then marines started out from Dong Ha with tanks. They were stopped. By the morning of the third day, of our brigade's 1,400 troops, maybe 350 were killed or wounded. Capt. Bill Duell, my team's senior advisor, had been killed about two weeks earlier. The new senior battalion advisor, Capt. Brux, was mortally wounded during the night bombardment. Our senior advisor, Sgt. First Class Rudy Ortiz, was absolutely riddled by mortar fragments.

"When I crawled over to him, he said, 'Load my M-16. I want to die fighting with the rest of you.' I was hit twice and my left arm wasn't working, so I couldn't load an M-16. I took a .357 pistol from Captain Brux's dead body. We were not going to be taken prisoner.

"I called across to coordinate with a brigade advisor, 1st Lt. Bill Bannon, a tremendously brave, taciturn, handsome guy. We were both prone and talking about what was likely to happen. He said something like, 'We're never going to get out of here. We're all going to get killed.' Which I thought was believable.

"Then my Vietnamese battalion commander, Major Nguyen, was completely incapacitated. The battalion XO came to my foxhole, sat on his helmet, put on his red beret, and said, 'It's time to die now.'

"He rallied the remnants of the battalion, and with bugles blowing, we attacked. Our navy cruiser, maybe it was USS *Newport News*, had done incredible work all night long with its eight-inch guns. Then came word they had to withdraw to get ammo. We said, 'If you withdraw, we're all dead.' So they called for an emergency ammo resupply.

"Just as we started the attack, two incredibly brave pilots dropped their birds below the cloud cover at about a thousand feet, sitting ducks silhouetted against the low clouds. One was an AC-47 Spooky, which usually flies at night. It caught an entire battalion of NVA in the open just as they started their assault. The AC-47's miniguns hosed down their assault line from one end to the other.

"The other bird was an unarmed observation plane, which adjusted our artillery fire.

"The battle went on for the remainder of the day. Then this wonderful World War II veteran, Col. Jim Bartholomews, pulled in wearing a soft hat and smoking. He walked around the perimeter and talked to us all and sorted it out. Medevacs showed up and the cloud cover lifted, and lots of US aircraft started coming in. Marine air. Navy air. Replacement advisors came in, and there was another huge battle. I was medevaced on the third day. We blunted the NVA crossing for the day, but I don't think it had any long-term significance to the war."

It's a wonderful tale, but McCaffrey omits any mention of his own heroics. The following comes from his award of the Distinguished Service Cross:

At 0315 hours the camp received intense mortar fire which severely wounded McCaffrey in the shoulder. With complete disregard for his safety, he unhesitatingly ran through the intense automatic weapons and mortar fire to estimate the severity of the attack. He . . . discovered that the senior American advisor had been killed, and all but one of the company commanders were seriously wounded. After rendering aid to the casualties, McCaffrey took command and dauntlessly proceeded around the perimeter to direct the defense against . . . human wave assaults. Again he was wounded by mortar fragments, but ignored his own condition and quickly organized a counterattack which successfully repelled another . . . attack. During the remainder of the 12-hour battle, McCaffrey repeatedly exposed himself to hostile fire and directed artillery and air strikes against the insurgent forces. Through his unremitting courage and personal example, he inspired the besieged Vietnamese unit to defeat four determined attacks and inflict heavy casualties on a numerically superior hostile force. Only after assuring that all the wounded had been extracted and that a replacement advisor was with the battalion, did he permit himself to be evacuated.

McCaffrey was treated for his wounds and recovered on the USS *Repose*, a navy hospital ship. When he thought he was ready to fight again, he discharged himself and hitched rides to get back to Saigon. "I had heard there was a big parachute assault coming up, and I didn't want to miss it," he said.

But his wounds were badly infected, so McCaffrey was confined to a Saigon hospital. Weeks later he was discharged and returned to duty.

Altogether, McCaffrey was awarded three Purple Hearts for wounds suffered in Vietnam.

———◇———

After home leave and a promotion to captain, McCaffrey spent what he called a "glorious" year in Panama as an aide to Maj. Gen. Chet Johnson. "He treated me like his son," McCaffrey recalled. "I was with him constantly; we went to every Latin American country. We had extensive dealings with all Latin American militaries, the CIA, the State Department—a very educational tour. My wife and I had two little kids at the time, and they loved being in Panama and we loved Panamanians."

Then it was back to the meat grinder.

In mid-1968, McCaffrey took command of Bravo Company, Second Battalion, Seventh Cavalry. It was one of four companies in the 2/7 Cavalry and the unit that had been battered and bludgeoned at LZ Albany in 1965. He joined them at Camp Evans in I Corps.

Soon after that, the First Cavalry Division flew south to III Corps on an emergency basis to counter an expected attack out of Cambodia. "The division spread out along about 150 miles of frontier. We were the covering force with a reconnaissance-in-force mission to pick up NVA divisions as they crossed the frontier, then fall back ahead of them until we reached several other US divisions arrayed in an arc around Saigon."

For a few months Bravo Company was two or three kilometers from the Cambodian frontier. Then, using air assault tactics, they began falling back toward Saigon. "It was a series of running engagements," McCaffrey recalled. "Very bitter fights, heavy jungle, some scrub brush, open plains, and lots of casualties. My people got banged up or wounded, mostly from small-arms fire or grenades at very close ranges. We found logistics bases beneath triple-canopy jungle and corduroy roads made from logs twelve feet wide with woven overhead camouflage cover and giant bunkers every fifty feet. We did that for about five months until we hit the outskirts of Long Binh.

"The First Cavalry Division was an incredibly effective organization, optimized for that kind of combat. We had everything going in our favor, starting with the armed helicopters and the lift helicopters. The air force forward air controllers brought us incredible support from fighter-bombers. But the absolute key to our survival was our artillery. As a general rule, I would never be outside 105mm artillery range."

One day his radio operator asked McCaffrey why he seemed so serene as he went on each air assault. "It's simple," he replied. "There's nothing I can do about anything until we're on the ground—so when we fly, I'm saying an endless loop of Catholic prayers from grade school."

By this time, the 2/7 Cav was within ten kilometers of Long Binh, then the biggest military post on earth, a giant, sprawling logistics complex with a C-130 airstrip. "We were at the last line of defense," McCaffrey recalled. "Behind us was the Eleventh Armored Cavalry Regiment. Only one NVA battalion finally got through us and was killed almost to the last man on the outskirts of Long Binh by that regiment."

During this second Vietnam tour, McCaffrey was awarded two Silver Stars and a second Distinguished Service Cross for valor. One of his platoon sergeants recalled seeing him being evacuated in March 1969 with serious wounds. "I had most of my left arm shot off," McCaffrey recalled. The platoon sergeant said, "I wondered how we could get along without his leadership. It then occurred to me that he had done his job of preparing us to take care of ourselves."

Looking back on his years in Vietnam, McCaffrey said, "The combat we saw in the Vietnamese airborne was brutal. I didn't really expect that I would survive my next combat tour. After three combat tours at the infantry company level, I understood only too well the reality of combat."

Decades later, having retired with four stars on his collar, McCaffrey refined his perspective on the war in Vietnam. "By 1968, our military and political leaders had lost their way," he said. "They could not see a path to victory. They also could not bear the political costs of throwing in the towel. The war ended up on tragic autopilot. . . . The American people finally concluded that our national leaders had no strategy to succeed. The army and marines were bleeding to achieve no sensible purpose."

Already marked for greatness, McCaffrey's post-Vietnam career followed a path typical of the few officers whose outstanding performance under the harshest conditions of military service meant they were destined for stars. Instead of attending the ten-month Infantry Officer Career Course at Fort Benning, McCaffrey went to Fort Knox for the Armor Officer Career Course.

Between attending several military and civilian schools, McCaffrey served as a Military Academy instructor, assistant commandant of the Infantry School, deputy US representative to NATO, assistant to the chairman of the Joint Chiefs of Staff, and director of strategic plans and policy of the Joint Chiefs of Staff.[1]

In August 1990, the Iraqi army occupied Kuwait, intent on annexing the oil-rich country. This was met by international condemnation and economic sanctions against Iraq by the United Nations. Together with UK forces, US forces were deployed to Saudi Arabia. Several other nations joined the coalition, the largest military alliance since World War II. The great majority of coalition fighting forces were Americans, however.

Gen. Norman Schwarzkopf, a Vietnam veteran, was the overall commander of Operation Desert Storm. While air force and navy aircraft and missiles destroyed most of the Iraqi air force, Schwarzkopf had the navy station amphibious assault vessels and supporting ships off the Kuwait coast to give the Iraqis the impression that US Marines would be coming ashore in Kuwait. He sent marines into Kuwait from Saudi Arabia to probe Iraqi defenses and to reinforce that idea in Iraqi minds.

Meanwhile, he planned a massive attack through the Iraqi desert to strike the Iraqis from the rear. The coalition's goal was to force the Iraqis to move hundreds of thousands of deeply dug-in troops so they could be picked off by Allied air and ground fire. That assault began on February 24, 1991.

Schwarzkopf gave the most critical role to the Twenty-Fourth Mechanized Infantry Division, commanded by McCaffrey, then a major general. McCaffrey was to lead an army corps deep into Iraqi territory to seize control of some five thousand square miles. The other corps was arrayed around Kuwait to force the Iraqis to tie down most of their forces there. This was known as the "Two Corps" concept. No army in history had ever moved a force that size over three hundred miles on Schwarzkopf's schedule. If McCaffrey succeeded, he would flank the elite Republican Guard divisions in Kuwait and cut off all their avenues of retreat.

The briefing jolted McCaffrey. As he began to think over the complex logistics his attack would rely on, he realized with a little shock this was not the way our generals had fought in Vietnam. This was *not* to be a long, costly war of attrition. Schwarzkopf's army would put its strengths against Iraqi weaknesses. He was thrilled to realize that the US Army had learned from the Vietnam debacle. This time, things would be different.

But only if *he* could pull off his assigned role. "Iraq had the fourth-biggest army on the face of the earth," McCaffrey recalled. "A giant, modern air force. They had modern tanks, antitank missiles, obsolete but still deadly surface-to-surface missiles, poison gas, and perhaps a nuclear capability."

McCaffrey's command sergeant major, his chief of staff, and both assistant division commanders were Vietnam veterans. An hour before sundown and kickoff time, McCaffrey met with his command group in a circle. "I thought we would take light casualties, meaning two thousand killed and wounded, and there was a possibility I'd be among them," McCaffrey said. "I told them in normal, lighthearted infantry humor, 'Good luck to all of you. I guess this is the last time we'll all be together alive.'"

Between McCaffrey's men and their objective were hundreds of miles of presumably empty desert. But surely there were minefields. Perhaps there were Iraqis with shortwave radios scattered across the desert. How many tanks? How many personnel carriers? How many men would a few SCUD missiles with high explosive or nerve gas warheads kill?

There was the matter of fuel. McCaffrey brought along a fleet of armored tank trucks, but the trucks themselves burned a lot of fuel and were vulnerable. He ordered his men not to destroy enemy fuel dumps, tankers, or service stations.

Perhaps there was then another major general in the US Army who could have done what McCaffrey did over those next few days. Schwarzkopf was in charge. But the war, McCaffrey understood, was his to win or lose. He never considered losing.

Ever since February 27, 1991, McCaffrey's "left hook" maneuver across the Iraqi desert has been the subject of books and military college lectures. Suffice it to say that he succeeded in moving tens of thousands of men and thousands of vehicles across a rocky desert at an average speed of 30 mph to flank Iraq's best troops and destroy them. The Gulf War ended three days after McCaffrey's troops rolled into the desert.

His division's casualties: eight killed and thirty-six wounded.

Here is an account by Joseph L. Galloway, then a *US News* correspondent, who accompanied McCaffrey:

The 24th Infantry Division (Mechanized) was the heaviest division the USA ever fielded in wartime: over 30,000 troops. Thousands of M1A1 Abrams tanks and Bradley Fighting Vehicles and over a dozen battalions of howitzers and rocket launchers. McCaffrey commanded from his Bradley for the first 24-hour dash across the trackless Iraq desert with only two brief stops for refueling vehicles and a comfort break. Then we paused for a few hours' sleep before launching onto the main highway from Kuwait to Baghdad. McCaffrey switched from his Bradley to a Blackhawk helicopter loaded with communications gear. I joined him in the chopper and we dropped in on each of the three brigades for McCaffrey to receive reports and give orders for the next move. Then the brigade saddled up and moved out, sometimes leaving the Blackhawk sitting alone in a stretch of desert through which thousands of Iraqi troops waving white flags drifted.

On the final 18-hour drive to the gates of Basra, McCaffrey returned to his Bradley and I moved into another Bradley. We rejoined at his Blackhawk for a few hours' sleep before a scheduled 0300 hours attack down the last highway out of Kuwait. McCaffrey woke me around 0200 yelling "They called it off!!!" A ceasefire was scheduled for 0700 hours; our attack was canceled. McCaffrey ordered his artillery and rocket battalions to simultaneously fire one final barrage at 0330 hours. It lit up the desert sky for 180 degrees, the biggest lightning storm ever seen.[2]

———◇———

McCaffrey received his fourth star in 1994 to become the army's youngest and most-decorated full general. Many of his peers felt he was destined for the top army job: army chief of staff.

In 1996, while he was the commanding general of the US Southern Command, Secretary of Defense William Perry asked McCaffrey if he would like to be the director of national drug policy. It would mean leaving the army. "No," he replied. McCaffrey still harbored ambitions. He wasn't ready for civvies.

"So I wrote a policy paper and told them how to better organize the counter-drug effort," McCaffrey said. "I included the names of three people who would be appropriate drug policy directors and sent it to the White House. Perry, one of the best people I've met in a life in public service, called me in. 'Barry,' he said, 'when you wrote this paper for the president, you sealed your fate. I told the president that you ought to be his drug policy director.'

"When I told my dad how I got to see the president and told him who he ought to get for the job and how to organize it, my father said, 'The president asked you to do something. Shut up and do what you were told.'"

McCaffrey sacrificed the balance of his promising army career and retired from active duty. Confirmed unanimously by the Senate as director of the Office of National Drug Control Policy (ONDCP), McCaffrey came with experience from interdicting drug smugglers from South America as head of the Southern Command.

McCaffrey's policy paper was a surprise to civilian leadership, but he actually knew a lot about drug abuse. "During the Vietnam era, we had a military with zero drug use," he said. "By the war's end, it was a nightmare. After Vietnam, we launched a campaign to deal with drug issues. We had very expensive treatment programs at post and theater level, an active prevention program, interdiction, and law-enforcement operations."

McCaffrey came to the job with the conviction that any counterdrug strategy must be primarily prevention and education programs aimed at adolescents. "The centerpiece was dealing with children between the eighth and twelfth grade with a variety of tools to convince them to not become habitual drug and alcohol users," he said. A $1 billion budget went largely for prevention education and a national health campaign. An additional component was research into addiction.

The interdiction component was aimed at keeping drugs off the streets by intercepting them at ports of entry and on the high seas and by ending their manufacture. In 1999, McCaffrey led an initiative to begin eliminating coca farming in Colombia.

Another McCaffrey initiative was asking the entertainment industry to change the depiction of drug use in movies and television, including paying television producers to embed antidrug messages into programs.

The last component was treatment, largely paid for with individual health insurance. It was nevertheless costly, long-term, difficult, and poorly supported because of the stigma. "Nobody likes drug addicts," McCaffrey explained.

When he took office, about 7 percent of the population regularly abused drugs. Through interdiction, education, and long-term treatment programs, by the time he left office in 2001, the number of habitual users had fallen to 5 percent—a nationwide reduction of more than 25 percent.

"General McCaffrey made ONDCP a force to be reckoned with," said New York City police commissioner Raymond Kelly. "He brought a fierce intellect, compassion, and vision to the job. In short, he brought leadership."

CHARLES L. SILER

Sometimes the difference between good government and problematic government is one person. One man or woman who will do the hard work required to provide timely services to their constituents. In our long history of self-government, however, it is often the case that as the cream rises to the top, ambition trumps commitment. Too often the most effective elected officials spend much of their time and energy in pursuit of higher office, leaving the community that first elected them to struggle under a less-effective successor. It is a rare official, blessed with almost limitless talent and energy, who eschews higher office in favor of staying put for decades in order to help the people he knows best.

Colonel, it's my duty to tell you that the longer you try to sit on a mess, the more it will stink when you finally have to get up from it," said Maj. Charles L. Siler, the information officer of the famed First Cavalry Division (Airmobile). It was October 1965, and Siler was schooling his new boss, the division chief of staff, on the wisdom of dealing with the news media truthfully, immediately sharing as much as was then known about an incident.

A day earlier, one of the division's infantry platoons had evacuated the people and livestock from a tiny hamlet of thatched huts, then set it afire. A wire-service reporter was hoping to learn the reason.

The colonel's response was to deny it had even happened. "We don't burn down villages," he told the reporter.

Siler asked the reporter to step outside for a moment. With only Siler, the colonel, and a private on Siler's staff present, the public information officer explained that not only had this reporter witnessed the village being torched but so also had a network television crew. If the colonel insisted on denying his troops had burned the village, his denial would appear in newspapers nationwide on the same day the ABC network would air the footage. Even if this didn't trigger an official inquiry from the army's highest echelon, it would result in a series of news stories about what would be seen as a cover-up.

"The wisest course," Siler said, "is to tell the reporter what we know: this hamlet was sitting over an enormous cache of Viet Cong rice, several tons of grain the enemy had taxed from hundreds of tiny farms. Some of the top sacks were booby-trapped. Burning the houses would trigger these explosives and allow army engineers to safely remove the unburned rice and distribute it to refugees. It would also allow the platoon to proceed with its original mission: find and fight the Viet Cong.

"If we tell the truth, we're on page one for a day. If we try to cover it up, this story will be news for days, maybe even weeks," he concluded.

"Are you sure about this?" the colonel asked. "I don't like the idea of headlines about GIs burning villages."

"Colonel, I will not lie to a reporter," Siler replied. "If I lose their trust, if reporters can't rely on what I tell them, then you might as well send me to an infantry battalion where I can do some good."

The colonel reluctantly accepted Siler's advice. Two days later, when the wire service story appeared in the Pacific *Stars and Stripes*, the reporter revealed that a GI had borrowed his lighter to torch a villager's roof. He also quoted the colonel on the reason for the burning.

Siler's guidance to his boss was more than instinct. He had previously served as the PIO in eight other infantry and armored divisions around the world, as well as at major nondivisional commands, and for such high-profile events as the 1965 Selma to Montgomery March, led by Martin Luther King Jr., with US Army troops providing protection to the marchers. Siler had learned from bitter experience that when reporters believed anyone associated with the government lied to them, they would double down. They'd find new sources, dig up new details and previous incidents. They'd turn what could have been a few inches of copy buried on page five of a big-city paper into a week of front-page headlines.

On the eve of the Vietnam War, Siler produced an exhaustive staff study on issues related to dealing with the media at all levels of the military. This document found its way through command channels up to Army Chief of Staff Harold K. Johnson. Among its recommendations was a reconsideration of a long-standing policy that civilian journalists must be escorted by an officer. Siler knew his own division would go to war to prove that helicopters could be effective when used in large numbers on the battlefield. This alone was big news. The First Cav was making history. Siler expected to host dozens to hundreds of reporters, photographers, and broadcast crews. Putting escorts with the media would strip the division's fighting elements of its junior officers when they were most needed. "If we trust a company commander with the lives of his men," Siler wrote, "why can't we trust him to talk to a reporter?"

Johnson agreed. Siler's recommendations became official army and then Department of Defense doctrine, taught in the Defense Information School, along with the admonition it was also a public information officer's duty to educate his superiors. Did every PIO abide by the letter of these new regulations? Most did. Sadly, some at the highest echelons served commanders who distrusted the media and were unwilling to admit mistakes. But for the most part, Siler's wisdom prevailed, allowing US and third-country media to have unhindered access to the battlefield. The beneficiary was the American public, who were able to see what their fighting men were doing.

Siler's tour ended in August 1966 with an assignment to Fort Shafter, Hawaii, the so-called Pineapple Pentagon, as the public information officer. Promotion to lieutenant colonel followed soon after.

"My best day in Vietnam was the day I went home knowing that none of the troops directly under my supervision had been hurt or killed," Siler recalled. "My worst day was when I learned that more than a hundred of our men died in the Ia Drang valley."

The Battle of Ia Drang was the first clash between sizable numbers of NVA regulars and US Army conventional forces. A turning point in the war, the battle became the basis for a best-selling book by Lt. Gen. Harold G. Moore and UPI reporter Joseph L. Galloway, *We Were Soldiers Once . . . and Young*, and a film based on the book, *We Were Soldiers*, starring Mel Gibson.[1]

◇

The son of a coal miner, Charlie Siler was the sixth of eight children. Born in mid-1929 in Whitley County, Kentucky, then one of America's poorest communities, he grew up during the Great Depression and began working in his teens. In high school, he arrived each morning at six o'clock to light the fires in all thirteen classroom fireplaces. After school, he gathered kindling and distributed coal for the next day's heating. After basketball games, he swept the gymnasium floor. "I got a dollar a month for each of the fireplaces and fifteen dollars a month for sweeping the gym. Big money for that time," he recalled. Most of his earnings went to help feed his family.

The Silers lived on nearly a square mile of fields, streams, coal seams, and forest, the legacy of Siler's maternal great-great-grandfather, who homesteaded the southeastern Kentucky land after serving in the Union army during the Civil War. They heated their home with coal they dug from one of several coal seams on their land.

In high school, Siler took extra classes so he could finish six months early, among them two typing classes and one in shorthand. He graduated in December 1946 and took a job waiting tables. "I was making thirty-five dollars a week, but I couldn't save anything for college. I told my boss, 'If you can't raise me to fifty dollars a week, I can't stay on this job.' He said, 'I can hire two girls for that much.' So I said, 'You'd better start looking for them because I'm gone.'"

In March 1947, Siler enlisted in the army to take advantage of the Servicemen's Readjustment Act of 1944, also known as the GI Bill of Rights, which included a stipend and college or trade school tuition expenses.

When his basic training first sergeant learned Siler could type sixty-five words a minute, he made him the company clerk. He also was required to do all the physical training and to qualify on the rifle range. The rest of his time was spent in the orderly room, paddling in the endless stream of paper generated by company administration.

Upon graduation, Siler went to Camp Lee, Virginia, and the army administration school. In the first or second week, a colonel asked who knew Gregg shorthand. Siler and three others out of a class of 125 raised their hands. They went to another classroom with a female instructor. For eight weeks they worked exclusively on raising their speed and accuracy. The reason for this special training was not revealed. When it ended, Siler took a week's leave to visit his family and then took a train to San Francisco, from where he sailed for Japan.

Not until he arrived in Japan did Siler learn why he was there: he was to use shorthand to record courtroom proceedings at the International Military Tribunal of the Far East. This was the Pacific counterpart to the International Military Tribunal in Nuremberg, Germany, constituted to try Nazi war criminals. The Tokyo tribunal considered capital charges against twenty-eight Japanese military and political leaders. Another fifty-seven hundred lower-ranking leaders were charged with lesser war crimes in separate trials convened by the individual Allied nations: Australia, China, France, the Netherlands, the Philippines, the United Kingdom, and the United States.

Before turning his shorthand skills to work, Siler was dispatched to China to bring some eleven hundred minor criminals to Japan by ship. "I was sent to classify these men . . . in the time that it took to get them loaded and shipped back. I had to create a roster of who was who and what each prisoner's alleged crimes were. Then we could assign them to the proper cell in Sugamo Prison," Siler recalled.

This was a lot of responsibility for an eighteen-year-old with only half a year in uniform, but Siler encountered no problems he couldn't deal with. Once the trials began, Siler joined a team of court reporters who took shorthand in all the languages used during the trials. When daily proceedings ended in the late afternoon, he translated his shorthand into English on a typewriter, made copies on a mimeograph machine, and distributed the copies to the officers of the court before the next session.

The tribunal's work concluded on December 23, 1948, with seven hangings at Sugamo. Siler was required to be present and record the medical officer's findings at the time of each death. It was a gruesome experience.

None of the condemned men died immediately; one lingered for twenty-seven minutes.

Afterward, "I just couldn't get the executions out of my mind. It was several days before I could eat anything without vomiting, except one egg in the morning," Siler recalled.

When the tribunal concluded, Siler's enlistment was up. He returned to Williamsburg, married his high school sweetheart, Dorthalene, and enrolled at Cumberland College.

In June 1950, less than a year after his return to civilian life, fighting began in Korea. Siler's enlistment included an additional three-year army reserve obligation. "I was called back to active duty almost immediately," he said. He reported to the recruiting station in Corbin, twenty miles north of Williamsburg. The same sergeant who had recruited him four years earlier was in charge of the station.

"Sgt. Paul Haynes knew me well. He knew all about my clerical experience. He said, 'We can stop you right here if you want to work for us,'" Siler recalled. Nominally a recruiter, Siler served as the station's acting administrative officer, in charge of the Niagara of paperwork associated with processing enlistees and forty draftees a day, the latter selected by the local draft boards. He also administered written tests and arranged draftees' transportation to a doctor's office for the necessary physical exams.

By the spring of 1952 Siler had been promoted twice and was now a technical sergeant. "I told Sergeant Haynes I knew that I was going to Korea, but I'd rather go as an officer."

Siler was accepted for officer candidate school and went to Fort Benning to start Infantry OCS, a challenging six-month course.

"I was a little overweight when I reported to OCS. I'm short and I had chevrons all the way down to my elbow," Siler recalled. "My tactical officer, a second lieutenant and recent OCS grad, said, 'I'll give you eight weeks. At the eight-week board, you're gone.'"

Siler finished first in his class in academics and fourth on the physical proficiency test. "The thing is," Siler explained, "my legs are short and I can't run" as well as some of the taller men.

After graduating OCS, Siler went to jump school, the army's three-week paratroop training course, and then to jumpmaster school, which qualified him to supervise the paratroopers who would be jumping from an aircraft.

Then Siler went to Korea and joined Bravo Company, First Battalion, Seventeenth Infantry in the waning months of the shooting war, but just in time to take a bullet through his left forearm. After some sixty days in combat, the battalion surgeon and the battalion executive officer decided that Siler's company commander, a reservist, was suffering from what was then called "battle shock." Siler took command of the company for the remainder of his time in Korea. Before the end of his thirteen-month tour, an armistice between the warring parties went into effect.

Siler returned to Fort Benning to attend the Infantry Officer Career Course, a ten-month school designed to prepare captains for duties higher in the chain of command. He was promoted to captain before the end of that course. Then it was back to Japan and his first job as a public information officer.

"The Eighth Cavalry Regiment was sent from Korea to Hokkaido island because the Russians were threatening to invade Japan's northern islands," Siler recalled. "I went as their information officer."

In the years that followed, Siler became the father of two sons and a daughter and served in a succession of division-level units as a public information officer. He held that position in the 11th, 101st, and 82nd Airborne Divisions, the 2nd Infantry Division, and the 4th Armored Division, as well as the John F. Kennedy Special Warfare Center and School and the US Army Combat Capabilities Development Command.

Siler spent most of 1957 and 1958 in Thule, Greenland, in command of a paratroop rifle company whose mission was to protect the radar stations on the DEW Line, facilities emplaced to give "distant early warning" if the Soviets launched missiles or bombers over the North Pole. His company was prepared to parachute into any radar site to protect it from a ground attack that might be launched from Siberia.

———◇———

Promotions were slow for reserve officers in the Cold War years between the Korean and Vietnam War. Siler spent eight years as a captain before he was promoted in 1963 to major. When his promotion list was published, he noted with satisfaction that he was one name ahead of the tactical officer who had predicted Siler wouldn't last more than eight weeks in OCS.

Siler's last army public affairs assignment was at Fort Bragg, North Carolina, handling media inquiries about the Jeffrey MacDonald case, the infamous triple murders of February 17, 1970. MacDonald was a Green Beret, a captain, and a doctor. He was arrested by the Fayetteville police and charged with the murder of his wife and two small daughters.

Siler was sent to deal with the media circus surrounding the murders. When the army ceded jurisdiction to the civilian authorities, that ended Siler's involvement. Shortly after this assignment, Siler retired from the army and returned to his farm in Williamsburg.

Not long after that, one of Siler's neighbors hired men and machinery to strip mine a seam of coal on his property. "Elmer Patrick got a permit to strip a top seam. He sold the coal, pulled his machinery out, but he didn't reclaim the land," Siler recalled. "I tried to get him to clean up his mess, but he was our representative in the Kentucky General Assembly, plus he operated the coal-stripping outfit. He just ignored me."

For months, Siler tried to get the state or the federal government, the agencies charged with enforcement of both state and federal laws that mandated Patrick clean up his land, to enforce the law. He struck out. Nobody took any action to force Patrick to follow the law.

Then Siler's wife, Dorthalene, said, "The only way you're going to get any action against Elmer is to get him out of office."

Before he filed to run for office himself, Siler checked the records of the previous elections. There were about thirty-eight thousand people in the district, which includes Whitley and Laurel Counties, but only about four thousand who voted. "Patrick ran and won against some people that were more highly qualified and better situated in life than I was," Siler recalled. "I couldn't understand that, so I tried to figure out how he did it. And finally, I learned that the 'clan daddy' was the solution."

In Siler's part of Kentucky there are many extended families that, through intermarriage, extend to three and four generations. There's a lot of distant cousins, all or most of whom live within a mile or two of each other. The patriarch of these clans is commonly referred to as the clan daddy. His influence throughout his extended family is pervasive. Few women would marry a man their clan daddy disapproved of, and few couples would sell their houses without offering it first to a member of their clan. This influence extends to voting. Most or all members of the clan look to the clan daddy to decide which candidate they should vote for.

"You don't waste your time going to every house in the county," Siler realized. "If you know that Johnny Rose is the guy who votes for the Rose family, you approach Johnny. And I did that. But first I had to spend a lot of time in a lot of country stores asking enough questions to identify the clan daddies in that part of the county.

"I was going up a valley, and I'd stop at every house and talk to them. They'd say, 'Well, you sound like a good candidate, but how's Otto going to vote?' About three times that happened to me. I didn't know Otto, so I turned to the escort I had for that region. He said, 'Otto lives in that big white house up there.' So we drove there, and his wife came to the door. I said, 'I'm Charlie Siler and I'm running for state representative.'

"She said, 'You look just like your picture. You look like an honest man.'

"I thanked her and asked if I could see Otto. And she said he was hanging cabinets in a kitchen for someone. So I went there and found Otto trying to put a screw in the top of a cabinet above a sink. I came in and told him who I was, and then I held the bottom of the cabinet. That freed him up a little and he drove the screw in and turned around and sat down on the counter," Siler recounted.

After answering Otto's many questions, Otto said, "Well, I found me a candidate. I'm behind you." Siler asked if he needed to visit the people down the hill and tell them Otto was supporting him. "Oh, no," Otto replied. "They'll vote as I tell them." And then he gave Siler the name of another clan daddy. "You go see this fella and talk to him," he said.

After a few conversations with the other clan daddies, Siler understood they didn't believe their community was getting as much from the state of Kentucky as other districts did. So Siler traveled the length and breadth of the district. He looked through the eyes of a man who had spent more than half his life in other nations and other states, and he saw that the Eighty-Second Legislative District hadn't changed much since his childhood. It was poor back then and even poorer now.

And he won the seat in the assembly.

Whitley and Laurel Counties needed more jobs, especially jobs that paid well. Their roads needed fixing, and they needed new roads if they hoped to attract new employers. They needed clean drinking water. They needed to improve educational standards so the next generation of job seekers would be ready to fill those new jobs. Whitley County's public schools were academically next to last among the fifty states. And they needed a dozen other things that most parts of America had but they didn't.

"I drove to Frankfort a couple of days before the start of the next session," Siler recalled. "I contacted the Legislative Research Commission and asked for the name and contact information for each of the cabinet officers. They prepared a list and I got on the phone. I called each secretary and said, 'I'm newly elected from Whitley County, and I'd like an appointment. If you don't have time, give me someone from your staff who I can meet with.'

"I did that with every member of the governor's cabinet. I asked each one, 'What projects do you have that pertain to my district? What's in your file?' Invariably I received the same answer: 'We don't have anything slated.'"

Siler told them, "Get an empty folder started, because I'm going to fill it up."

He began with transportation. "I told the transportation secretary that we didn't have a reliable east-west corridor in either county. Almost everything is north-south. Highway 92 does run east-west all the way across, but few will take it because it's in terrible condition. There are accidents all the time. Then there's Highway 90. It goes halfway across the district and then peters out. There needs to be a pickup on 90 to take it on to Barbourville."

This east-west corridor became a project that lasted during Siler's entire time in office. "I put in for it during my first year and got it finished, a $26 million job, in my last year. But that first year, the one big thing I could get was $1 million worth of guardrail along Highway 92 to make it safer."

Early in this first legislative session, Siler felt a familiar tug on his conscience. Kentucky's legislature is part time. He wasn't going to go to Frankfort for sixty days one year and thirty days the next, with a few special sessions thrown in at the governor's request, and make any kind of dent in the problems of his district.

Siler knew he would have to run for reelection many times before his community could catch up with the rest of the state and the rest of the country. He understood over the next decade or two, over and above the work he had to do to make his own farm successful, he was going to have to work harder on his neighbors' problems. That was a lot to ask of a man who had spent twenty-six often lonely years of danger, hardship, and privation in service to his country.

He decided it was his duty because it didn't look like anybody else could or would even try. Between 1984 and 2010, as his seniority and influence in the legislature grew, he served on the labor and industry, veterans affairs, education, and judicial committees and was the vice chair of the appropriations and revenue committee. He also served as the volunteer finance chair of the Veterans Nursing Homes of Kentucky and other civic organizations.

Working with like-minded neighbors and accessing the levers of power in state government, Siler brought new and better roads to his district, shortening the journey from Williamsburg to several nearby communities and allowing trucks to bring goods to the new stores that opened in these previously underserved communities.

His farm was reached by a rutted, winding, twisting, unpaved road. Over several years he had that road paved a little at a time. The last stretch of road to be paved ran past his own property. "In the army, I dug my own foxholes. When I got in a chow line in the field, I got at the end, so that if we ran out of food and anyone in my outfit had to go hungry, it wouldn't be one of my men," Siler recalled. "You have to lead from the front, and you must always look after your people before you look after yourself."

One of the biggest projects Siler addressed was bringing safe water to every home. "The well water here is contaminated," he explained. "Because of the amount of coal and aluminum ore and other naturally occurring minerals in the soil, our groundwater has a lot of iron and at least seventeen trace minerals." And that was the only water the people in Siler's district had until the late 1980s.

Before the Great Depression and the creation of the Tennessee Valley Authority, the lands adjacent to the upper Tennessee River were often flooded. The TVA put dams on the Powell, Clinch, and Tennessee Rivers, creating dozens of freshwater lakes and generating an enormous amount of electricity. But until Siler's time in the assembly, little of that fresh water was getting to Laurel and Whitley Counties.

"Today, way over in Jellico, Tennessee, thirty-five miles from my home, is a pickup point. The water that comes out of a faucet here comes from that pickup point or from a connection line that connects Jellico to Williamsburg, where we get water from the Cumberland River Basin. They can swap water in either direction.

"I put that fresh water into every section of Whitley County—and the last house to hook up to that water system was *my* house, not because I couldn't have done it sooner, but because it wasn't right that I would put water in my house when my neighbors didn't have it in theirs."

The cities of Corbin (twenty miles north of Williamsburg) and Barbourville (several miles east of Corbin) also had water issues. There was plenty of fresh water in nearby Laurel Lake, but it was not high enough to provide sufficient water pressure. Siler was able to get Corbin $600,000 in state funds to build a water tank that's filled with treated lake water, providing clean water to both cities.

Siler also helped Williamsburg build its first citywide sewer system.

But the most visible improvement Siler brought to his district was a general-purpose airport, a $21 million project. "I convinced the transportation powers in Frankfort that an airport big enough to accommodate the largest jets was needed for emergency landings between Louisville and Knoxville."

Not long after the Williamsburg–Whitley County Airport was built, a helicopter ambulance company moved in to offer emergency patients swift delivery to the regional trauma centers. Then a twenty-four-hour fueling center was built, which soon proved its worth by accommodating cross-country fliers, including military aircraft.

Siler arranged for state funding that enabled Corbin to build a ten-thousand-seat arena, a venue that attracts nationally known performers as well as product exhibitions and such rodeo events as bull riding.

Siler also found state money to build a technology center in Corbin that's used by students from a dozen high schools, two community colleges, and Eastern Kentucky University. "It has computers for all grades, a wide variety of labs, and a team of expert teachers," he said.

In 2017, the Williamsburg school system's test scores placed well above the state average in reading and math. "The students were good students and they had good teachers. The problem all along was the administration," Siler recounted. "So we fixed that."

But whatever happened to the coal seam that had been strip-mined next to Siler's farm? "Not only did I get that one cleaned up, I had another one on Patrick's farm cleaned up too. One of Elmer Patrick's brothers acquired the property. He said, 'I don't know how you feel about Elmer, but he doesn't have anything to do with this strip-mined land. We need to get this cleaned up.'"

During the years Siler served in the legislature, the state official in charge of coal land reclamation services had previously served in the Third Brigade of Siler's Vietnam War unit, the First Cavalry Division. He told Siler, "I'll do anything in the world for you that's legal." So Siler said to him, "Bad as I feel about Elmer Patrick, his brother's farm needs to be cleaned up." He called in a team right away, and they restored the strip-mined land to pasture land.

Dorthalene died in March 2014, at age eighty-one. Now eighty-eight, Charles Siler still lives on his ancestral land in a modest brick home. While he's no longer an elected official, he remains active in civic affairs. And although there are still pockets of rural poverty in the Eighty-Second District, Williamsburg is now a prosperous community with rising land values and a bustling business community.

CHARLES
"CHUCK"
HAGEL

The most important thing every combat veteran learns is the necessity of cooperation and teamwork for successful mission completion; lone wolves rarely survive the experience. Throughout his long career in public life, cooperation and enlightened compromise have been Chuck Hagel's path to uncommon success.

The oldest of four brothers, Chuck Hagel was born in North Platte, Nebraska, but he grew up in nine small western Nebraska towns. His father, Charles Dean Hagel, worked for a large lumber company and was transferred from town to town to manage and make profitable a succession of failing lumber yards.

During World War II, Charles Sr. served in the Pacific theater as a radio operator and tail gunner on a B-25 Mitchell medium bomber. When Chuck was sixteen, his thirty-nine-year-old father died suddenly.

Two years later, Chuck graduated from St. Bonaventure High School in Columbus, Nebraska, and then enrolled in the Brown Institute for Radio and Television.

In 1966, he volunteered for the draft. After basic training at Fort Bliss, Texas, and infantry training at Fort Ord, California, he was one of ten chosen to learn to fire the army's newest and then secret weapon: the FIM-43 Redeye shoulder-fired antiaircraft missile. But when he received orders to ship out to Germany, Chuck volunteered for Vietnam.

He landed at Tan Son Nhut on December 4, 1967, at a time when most of the major units in Vietnam had been engaged for months or years, and those arriving in the war zone were individual replacements for casualties or those who had completed their year of duty.

"I wound up in a rifle squad of the Ninth Infantry Division's Second Battalion, Forty-Seventh Infantry. Our base camp in the Mekong delta was at Dong Tam, the southernmost base camp in Vietnam," he recalled. It was a mechanized battalion, with dozens of armored personnel carriers, but the delta region is swampy lowlands intercut with hundreds of rivers and canals. "We didn't do a lot of mechanized work," Chuck said. "We did most everything on foot, in the jungle. In addition to reconnaissance missions, we did a lot of air assaults, riding helicopters in and out."

Chuck saw his first sustained combat in the early morning of January 30, 1968, at the start of the Tet Offensive. When the headquarters of US Army Vietnam—Gen. William Westmoreland's HQ at Long Binh—came under attack, the 2/47 was ordered to hurry north in their armored personnel carriers and engage the enemy at Widow's Village, a hamlet across a dirt road from the huge Long Binh complex.

As they approached, Chuck's battalion came under fire. During that day, this battalion lost many of its officers and noncoms, killed or wounded.

Chuck told a reporter, "On that day . . . I learned about uncommon valor and unselfish, heroic acts. I learned much about myself. . . . I learned all I would ever need to know about bravery to anchor me the rest of my life. . . . Those who survive wars are either embittered or inspired to help make a better world. Vietnam veterans chose the latter course, as America's veterans have always done."

Chuck's brother Tom enlisted a month after his older brother, and after basic and infantry training, he received orders for Germany. Instead, Tom volunteered for Vietnam. His initial assignment was the Third Squadron, Fifth Cavalry, a unit attached to the Eleventh Armored Cavalry Regiment, commanded by Col. George S. Patton IV. Tom soon requested reassignment to the Ninth Infantry Division to be closer to Chuck.

His request was approved, and for reasons unknown, he was assigned to Company B, Second Battalion, Forty-Seventh Infantry. About a month after Chuck had arrived in Dong Tam, he saw Tom walk into the base camp. They served side by side for the remainder of Chuck's tour, the only brothers to serve in the same unit—much less the same squad—during the Vietnam War.

Until Chuck was promoted to sergeant and took over as squad leader, the brothers often alternated at walking point, which, despite their fatigue, the oppressive heat, legions of flying insects, and the jungle floor's perpetual gloom, required hypervigilance.

Walking point in the jungle is probably an infantryman's most dangerous job. A good point man often spares his squad, his platoon, or even his company many casualties. *Great* point men like Chuck and Tom sensed the sound of an AK-47's safety clicking off and shot the opposing rifleman before he could fire. Great point men found trip wires and booby traps before they caused trouble.

Chuck was wounded twice. Tom was wounded three times.

Chuck finished his tour in December 1968 and, with only 140 days left on his two-year commitment, he was granted an early discharge.

"I think I learned a lot," he said. "I came out of that experience, I hope, a better person. Everybody who goes through those situations sees a lot, goes through a lot. You can't just leave that behind. You never do. But I think, overall, it helped me in a lot of ways. As I saw the world and reality and different points of view, serving with different kinds of people from different places, relying on each other, I was not the same man who went to Vietnam. I was changed, of course, like everybody else. I was more confident in myself."

The Hagel brothers returned home to Nebraska, "which was somewhat insulated from what was happening on the two coasts," Chuck recalled. "The anti–Vietnam War stuff and so on. Tom and I never felt the kind of scorn a lot of the veterans did who were farther east or farther west than us. We were aware of it, of course. We saw some. But it was never a real problem for us."

In the summer of 1969, both brothers enrolled in the University of Nebraska, Omaha. To supplement his GI Bill stipend, Chuck worked nights as a bartender, at a liquor store, and then as an announcer, newscaster, and talk show host for different radio stations. He graduated in May 1971.

"I'd always had an interest in history, in politics, in Washington. As a little kid I used to read *Time* and *Newsweek*," he explained.

In 1970, Nebraskans of the Second District elected John Y. McCollister to Congress. "I got to know the congressman; I interviewed him on my talk show a few times," Chuck recalled. "He said, 'If you come to Washington, stop in my office. I'll help you if I can.'"

In an era when Vietnam veterans were rarely welcomed, Chuck went to Washington to look for a job. "I went from office to office and left résumés. At the end of the week, I had no offers."

He returned to Omaha and resumed his broadcasting job. A week later, "McCollister returned to Omaha. When he learned I hadn't found a job, he offered me a temporary position. He needed somebody to help his staff reply to hundreds of constituent letters. He offered me two hundred dollars a month to work half days in his office. He'd let me sleep in the basement of his Washington home, and I could use the rest of the time to look for a full-time job."

A year later Chuck became McCollister's chief of staff. Four years later, McCollister gave up his seat to run for the Senate—and lost.

Chuck became a lobbyist for Firestone. In 1980, he worked as an organizer in Ronald Reagan's presidential campaign. In February 1981, he was appointed deputy administrator of the Veterans Administration. He quit the next year when his boss, intent on cutting VA program funding, referred to veterans' groups as "greedy" and said Agent Orange was not much worse than a "little teenage acne."

"The Reagan administration began cutting funds for all Agent Orange programs and especially epidemiological surveys," Chuck recalled. "They wanted to dismantle all vet centers. I was opposed to all that. I tried to convince the White House and Bob Nimmo, the administrator, a World War II veteran, that it was the wrong thing to do. I went to the president's chief of staff, Jim Baker, and told him that if this continued, I couldn't stay. I told the president too."

Chuck subsequently submitted his resignation.

"I was warned by everybody in Washington I'd never get another job, that my name would be zero, no one would talk to me and so on," Chuck related. "I began looking for another job, and for a few months, I didn't get many return calls. Some offers came in. Then a couple of guys who I got to know while working for McCollister, and who were involved in cable television franchises, came to me."

In 1983, Chuck was offered a partnership in a new firm that focused on getting franchises on AT&T's new emerging technology: cellular telephones. "I had no idea what they were talking about," he recalled. "They gave me information on the technology and so on. I read everything I could read. I went up to New York and visited with some friends who ran a telecommunications business at Merrill Lynch and Lehman Brothers. I came to believe this technology would go somewhere and agreed to partner with Bill Collins and Dave Smith. We started a company called Collins, Hagel, and Clarke. Dave Smith left to pursue another opportunity.

"Everybody had to put up some money," he recalled. "I didn't have any, so I sold my car, a 1979 Buick, and cashed in two life insurance policies I'd had since I graduated from high school and came up with five thousand dollars cash. My partners gave me more equity because I was going to work harder, and that's how it all started."

Renamed Vanguard Cellular, this mobile phone service carrier made Chuck a multimillionaire. While serving as Vanguard's president, he found time to serve as president and CEO of United Service Organizations (USO) and the Private Sector Council, as deputy director and chief operating officer of the 1990 G7 Summit, and on the board of directors or advisory committee of the American Red Cross, the Eisenhower World Affairs Institute, Bread for the World, and the Ripon Society. He also served as chairman of the Agent Orange Settlement Fund and on the Council on Foreign Relations.

In 1992, Chuck returned to Nebraska to become president of the McCarthy Group LLC, an investment banking firm. He also served as chairman and was CEO of American Information Systems Inc. (AIS), later known as Election Systems and Software, a computerized voting machine manufacturer jointly owned by the McCarthy Group and the *Omaha World-Herald*.

In March 1995, Chuck resigned from the board of AIS and prepared a run for the Senate, although he retained millions in stock in the McCarthy Group. Chuck pledged he would serve no more than two terms. "I've always believed these jobs require new energy and new thinking and new vitality," he said. A Republican, Chuck won a seat in the Senate in 1996 and was reelected in a 2002 landslide. He chose not to run for a third term in 2008.

"In the Senate, you don't do anything alone. But you can help lead. I'm very proud of my leadership in setting up the China Executive Commission in 2000," Chuck said. "This is members of the House, the Senate, and high-level Executive Department officials, such as the secretary of the treasury and the trade ambassador." This twelve-member commission explores the relationship with China and trade and all facets of that relationship. In 2000, this was a new approach to binational cooperation.

Chuck served as the commission's first chairman. "China was just emerging as a trading partner and a partner in other ways. We had no organization that could apply both the expertise of the Congress and the Executive, working in coordination with our Chinese counterparts, rather than just approaching each issue by itself," he explained. "I think it facilitated a better understanding between our two countries and helped resolve our differences instead of magnifying them."

Chuck chaired congressional climate-change delegations to the first UN protocol in 1997 at Kyoto, Japan, and to subsequent meetings across the world over the next several years. "I am very proud to have been involved in many climate change issues, trying to promote understanding on all sides," he said. "What is going on? What do we know? What do we not know? Let's rely not on politics but on science, trying to get the best information we can."

Chuck was foremost among those in Congress working to secure funding to improve veterans' facilities. He was a principal cosponsor for the Post-9/11 Veterans Educational Assistance Act of 2008, expanding education assistance to veterans who served after September 11, 2001.

"I had a great twelve years as a senator," he said. "I saw an awful lot, did an awful lot. It was a great privilege. But I'm the kind of guy who has a lot of different jobs, and I was ready for something new."

In February 2009, Chuck became a distinguished professor in national governance at the Walsh School of Foreign Service at Georgetown University. Among his many other activities were serving as chairman of the Atlantic Council (a foreign policy think tank), as cochairman of President Barack Obama's Intelligence Advisory Board, as a member of the Public Broadcasting

Service's board of directors, and sitting on several private sector boards of directors. In October 2012, Defense Secretary Leon Panetta asked Chuck to chair an advisory committee for the Vietnam War fiftieth anniversary commemoration.

But Chuck was not done with public office. After Obama won a second term, the president asked Chuck to be his secretary of defense. Many of his former colleagues in the Senate were unhappy about that.

"I was a pretty outspoken opponent of the Iraq War," Chuck said. "It was a terrible, dumb war that started the entire unraveling of the Middle East. I said so during those days and went against a Republican president, my Republican colleagues, and Republican leaders. Also, they never forgave me when Senator Barack Obama got the Democratic nomination for president and asked Senator Jack Reed and me to go to the Middle East with him in the summer of 2008 to help him understand what was going on.

"I said, 'Guys, if Obama becomes president, wouldn't you want some of us, some Republicans, to have some influence with him on foreign policy?'"

Chuck said several Republican senators told him he would get enough votes to be confirmed secretary of defense and they wanted to work with him, to be in his "kitchen cabinet." But they added, first, they would have to rough him up a little during his confirmation hearing. It wasn't personal, merely political. "I didn't particularly enjoy it, but I understood it," Chuck said.

When he took office in February 2013, nearly everyone in the uniformed services had been on a war footing since 2001. "Not only were we now in the two longest wars America had ever fought, but for the first time ever, we were fighting them with an all-volunteer force," Chuck said. "Which meant the same people went back to fight over and over, serving five, six, even seven combat tours. That was taking a tremendous toll on the families, our facilities, on everything. I ordered a worldwide review of all medical facilities and our family support programs. As we were looking at this, at deployments and reenlistment bonuses and so on, the sexual assault scandal hit. I initiated a new approach to sexual assault prevention. I brought in outside experts and put a huge emphasis on stopping sexual assaults, including changing the curricula at the service academies and making prevention part of all training.

"We haven't stopped sexual assault; it's a societal problem as much as anything else. Nonetheless, I told our troops, 'When you take an oath of office for this country, when you wear the uniform, you're saying to America, "You've given me the privilege to be something special and America has higher expectations for my conduct." So we're not going to allow this kind of behavior in our ranks,'" Chuck said.

During Chuck's time in office, it became public that officers assigned to nuclear missile silos were systematically cheating on the tests required to demonstrate their readiness and fitness for such vital jobs. "I'm particularly proud of the work we did to restructure, revitalize, and revamp our entire nuclear operation," Chuck said. "We had paid little attention to the land-based missile element of our deterrent and its capabilities. When these smart young men and women who come out of the Air Force Academy were asked for their assignment preferences, none wanted to go into land-based missiles because they saw it as a dead end. Also, we kept cutting maintenance budgets.

"I went into every one of those silos in Wyoming, Montana, Nebraska, and North Dakota. They had communications equipment that didn't work, missile doors that didn't open—it was incredible. We revamped the entire thing. Air Force Secretary Deborah James, my pick for that job, was in charge of that. We got $10 billion for renovations and training and changed all the testing curriculum."

Chuck's last initiative was named the Third Way. "We began to call on outside assistance, not only from defense contractors to build better bombers and ships but for research in concert with the Defense Advanced Research Projects Agency (DARPA)." He sought ways to tap into Silicon Valley companies to give the Pentagon a sharper cutting edge on technology.

During his tenure, Chuck worried about Russia's intervention in Ukraine, a satellite of the former Soviet Union. He telephoned the Ukrainian minister of defense and warned him against using his armed forces against the civilian population.

At the start of the Crimean crisis in February 2014, Chuck warned his Russian counterpart against military maneuvers that could lead to miscalculations. Deeply suspicious of Russian motives, in May 2014, Chuck called for renewed financial commitments from all NATO members and warned that NATO "should expect Russia to test our alliance's purpose, stamina, and commitment."

Frustrated with the White House decision-making process and with its micromanagement of his department, Chuck resigned in 2014 from the Department of Defense, a mutual decision between him and President Obama.

"I'm the kind of person who never looks back. You try to learn from your mistakes and maybe some things you did right and appreciate all the opportunities you had, but I don't go back and replay anything," he said. Chuck now spends his time teaching, speaking to various groups, and looking after his business interests.

Chuck Hagel was the first former enlisted soldier to serve as secretary of defense. But who would know more about what troops need in battle, about combat leadership and personal courage, than a soldier who led an infantry squad in combat and, to keep his men safe, walked point in a dim, dank, deadly jungle?

DWIGHT LIVINGSTON

If the Mississippi is America's river, the city at the juncture of the North and South Platte Rivers is surely the beating heart of American patriotic hospitality. North Platte, Nebraska, is a railroad town. The Bailey Yard, the Union Pacific Railroad's marshaling center and the largest rail yard in the world, lies within the city limits. But it's been decades since passenger trains stopped in North Platte; the Bailey Yard is full of freight cars. During World War II, however, millions of fighting men rode trains from the training camps to troop ships on both coasts, ships bound for either the war in the Pacific or the war in Europe. And most of these trains stopped in North Platte for a few minutes to take on water for their steam engines. In 1941, soon after the first troop train stopped in North Platte, inspired by the efforts of Rae Wilson, a twenty-six-year-old drugstore cashier, the city fathers and mothers, the Boy and Girl Scouts, softball teams, quilting circles, book clubs, 4-H clubs, and virtually every organized group in the town (and soon those of more than a hundred nearby communities) established the Canteen. From December 1941 until the war's end, volunteers met every train, as many as twenty-three a day, between 5:00 a.m. and midnight—three thousand to five thousand soldiers a day. The Canteen provided sandwiches, pie, cake, cookies, and small gifts such as stationery, sewing kits, pens and pencils, etc. They played music and danced with soldiers, even baked them birthday cakes. Every day of the war there were volunteers at the depot. They never missed a train. Six million American soldiers ate those sandwiches and enjoyed North Platte's hospitality. And it cost the government nothing. Aside from a five-dollar bill sent by President Roosevelt, all the funds were raised by the citizens of North Platte and its neighboring communities. And then the war ended, and no more troop trains came to town. But North Platte never forgot the Canteen. Tales of that patriotic enterprise were passed from parent to child to grandchild. It was told to newcomers and to visitors. It is a big part of what made this small city on the Nebraska plains special.

Dwight Livingston grew up in Lincoln, Nebraska, 225 miles east of North Platte, a bigger and, by most standards, more important city. After high school, Livingston tried college and didn't like it. He worked on a sod crew in Lincoln and then moved to Des Moines, Iowa, to work for a printing company. In 1969, he was told to report for a draft physical. When the next draft call came, however, his name wasn't on it.

"I didn't want to be drafted," he explained. "My dad was in the navy during World War II. I thought I should follow that tradition and join the navy, but they were full up just then, and I figured I'd probably get a draft notice before they took me."

An air force recruiter grabbed him. Livingston thought maybe he could be an air traffic controller and use his training to get a good job afterward. He was two inches over six feet tall. The air force decided to make him a cop.

After basic, he took air police training at Cannon Air Force Base, New Mexico. He remained there for almost a year afterward. It was not a happy time for him. "I didn't have a car, so when I had a pass, I had to hitchhike into town. As I stood by the side of the road, waiting for someone to offer me a ride, people in cars would slow down, roll down the windows, and then holler and scream and swear at me as they drove on by."

Livingston landed at Da Nang Air Base in May 1970. As a military policeman, he was among the force that oversaw base security and maintained perimeter defenses. From time to time he left the comparative safety of the base for duty on Monkey (Son Tra) Mountain and Marble Mountain.

One of the events that haunts Livingston occurred while he was on guard in a bunker. "It was pitch black. I was lying on top of the bunker. And stupid me, I lit a cigarette. Thank God I don't smoke today. I might as well have put a beacon on my head. I don't know where the shot came from, but it hit the sandbag just beneath me," he recalled.

"Then all hell broke loose. We came under a serious attack, including 122mm rockets. But beyond that night, my tour wasn't bad," he added. While none of Livingston's buddies were killed in action, a few tried but failed to kill themselves.

"The most miserable time of my life, probably, was when I came back from Vietnam," he recalled. After landing at an air force base about an hour outside of Los Angeles, returning troops encountered war protesters. "They were throwing rocks, screaming and hollering at us, and calling us baby killers," Livingston recalled.

Along with several others, he took a cab to Los Angeles International Airport, where they encountered more protesters. "It started when we landed, and it was the same at all the airports that we went to. People stared at us and called us names. I was thankful to get out of California. I flew into Kansas City, and it was the same thing. People were not friendly to men in uniform.

"In Vietnam, we had friends, and we took care of each other. That's why it hurt so much, the way we were treated. I did nothing wrong. I did what the air force told me to do. I served my country, and I'm still proud of that," he said.

Livingston's final duty assignment was at the North American Aerospace Defense Command (NORAD), near Colorado Springs. "Things were much better because there are so many military people there."

Near the end of his enlistment, the air force allowed Livingston to attend a civilian police academy in Colorado Springs while remaining on active duty. "That was pretty awesome," Livingston recalled. "It was a twelve-week program at a community college with instructors from local police departments." Livingston finished first in his class. He turned down an offer to go to New Jersey, expenses paid, and interview with police departments there. "I got calls from eight or ten Nebraska departments, including North Platte. They asked me to come and speak with them. I took North Platte's test, and several weeks later they offered me a job," he said.

He became a North Platte police officer a few days after his air force discharge. "I liked North Platte. I'd never lived in a town that size—then it was maybe fifteen thousand to eighteen thousand—but it looked pretty cool. It was quiet compared to Omaha and Colorado Springs, but we had our share of problems. We have ironworkers, and sometimes they'd get to hooking and jabbing with the cowboys. There was a murder here the week I hired on, a shooting."

Livingston admitted, "I truly had no intention of staying in North Platte. I just wanted to get my feet wet, see if I liked the town and the job, or not, and move on from there." But it didn't work out that way. Over the first few years of his police career, the department recognized Livingston was something special. In 1975, he was selected to attend the FBI Academy. He worked his way up through the ranks, holding every rank through deputy chief. He used his GI Bill benefits to attend night school, and in 1992 he earned a BS in business administration, with a minor in psychology, at the University of Nebraska, Kearney.

It wasn't an easy thirty-eight years. "I saw some pretty horrific things," he said. "A cop who hit his partner in the head with a hammer. When I got there, the end of the hammer was sticking out of this dude's head.

"We had a guy on the second floor of a house with a grenade in his hand. I could see that the pin wasn't pulled. On TV, maybe a guy could stick it in his mouth and pull that pin, but in real life, he'd probably pull his teeth out before the pin would come out. I talked him down."

Livingston solved a few murders. And one dark night he found himself creeping up on a man who had been firing into a house with a shotgun. Then an officer in a squad car turned a spotlight on Livingston, who backed slowly away, talking all the while, until he reached safety. The spotlight winked out. The man turned around, and Livingston, now forty feet away, streaked up behind him and knocked him down. "There was a shell in the chamber of his gun. If he'd turned back . . . ," Livingston said.

There were many other close calls, where things might have gone differently in the blink of an eye. But they didn't. "My wife says I had an entire league of angels watching over me," Livingston said.

Beyond the travails of policing, some of Vietnam's horrific sights remained with him. For years, Livingston had nightmares and fits of anger. He self-medicated with alcohol. He went through two wives. Rhonda, his third, has helped keep him on track.

In 2018, Livingston was elected president of the Police Officers' Association of Nebraska. He's in the Nebraska Police Officers' Association Hall of Fame.

"I retired in June 2011, and I got to tell you, I was pretty good at that," Livingston said. His wife kept her job as an administrative secretary at the police department.

Several months before he retired, a few people asked Livingston if he was interested in running for mayor. "That's not what I had in mind," he recalled.

"Four or five months later, happily retired, my wife handed me a business card belonging to the fire chief," he said. "She told me he and a few others wanted to talk to me about running for mayor."

"I've never thought much about it," he said and put it out of his mind. Several weeks went by before Rhonda convinced him to at least talk to these folks.

Many in North Platte were unhappy with the current mayor, and the group wanted Livingston to run for office. He spoke with his family, and they thought it would be a great thing for the town and them. Half an hour before the filing deadline, he went to the county courthouse to file. He was sent to city hall to pay filing fees and barely returned to the courthouse in time. "Saturday morning the newspaper's front page had a photo of me in my uniform: 'Retired Police Chief Files for Mayor.'"

He won in a landslide.

"I believe my most important job, and the one I enjoy the most, is talking with the young people in our community, speaking at schools, D.A.R.E. (Drug Abuse Resistance Education) graduations, to county academic all-stars, reading books to elementary kids, attending kids' club activities, and serving as a mentor for the Community Connections organization," he explained. "These kids and young adults are our future, and I love having the opportunity to help mold them into future leaders."

Livingston also speaks to veteran organizations and at Memorial Day ceremonies, Veterans Day ceremonies, law-enforcement memorial services, Vietnam veterans' reunions, and the Spirit of the Canteen. Yes, *that* Canteen.

"This gives me the honor of thanking our veterans for their service and for their sacrifices for our country."

Dwight Livingston no longer thinks about the glories of retirement. He's got his hands full, and he loves it. "My goal is to get everybody together for a common cause. I've worked hard at changing the culture," he said. "We've always worried about property taxes and bringing in new businesses. We're working to reduce the property tax, and we've done that every year since I came on. I'm pretty proud of that. We need more housing, so I created a housing task force to work on that."

Livingston is also president of the League of Nebraska Municipalities. "There are probably six hundred members from all across the state," he explained. "We work to preserve local control and empower municipal officials to improve their citizens' quality of life."

In June 2018 came a call to the North Platte Hospitality Center from a bus company that was carrying seven hundred men of the Arkansas Army National Guard's 142nd Field Artillery Brigade from Wyoming to Arkansas. Over the previous three weeks, the 142nd had conducted an emergency deployment readiness exercise at Camp Guernsey, Wyoming. As they would in combat, they deployed their self-propelled guns in various locations around the camp. They set up local security to protect their guns. They fired at distant targets. At night they slept in tents or on the ground. And they ate field rations.

After the exercise, the brigade's guns and other heavy equipment were loaded on railroad cars for shipment back to Arkansas. The brigade's men would return to Arkansas in chartered buses, an eighteen-hour trip, including rest stops and a stop for snacks. The bus company determined the snack stop would be in North Platte. They called the city's visitors bureau. "Could the town handle twenty-one buses arriving one after another and get seven hundred soldiers in and out for a quick snack?"

Could they ever! When the people of North Platte heard the soldiers were coming, hundreds called the visitors bureau and offered to help.

The troops arrived over a two-day period. As each bus emptied, the soldiers were greeted by lines of cheering people holding thank-you signs. They were welcomed to the Events Center, decorated especially for them, and served sandwiches (steak, turkey, or ham), deviled eggs, salads, and fruit. Local churches baked pies, brownies, and cookies.

As the last bus was loading, an army paymaster appeared. Funds had been budgeted for this snack stop. He was there to settle up. "Keep your money," he was told. "This is how North Platte welcomes our troops."

"We were overwhelmed," said Lt. Col. Nick Jaskolski, the brigade commander. "I don't have words to describe how surprised and moved we all were."

Mayor Livingston, who clearly remembered the treatment he received on his return from Vietnam, stood at the door for two days and shook every soldier's hand. "I don't know whether those moments were more important for them or for me. I knew I had to be there," he said.

NASIF
MAJEED

The B-52 Stratofortress is a monster airplane. Its 185-foot wingspan is almost twice the length of the B-29 that dropped the first atomic bomb. The B-52 is 159 feet long, and its cockpit is almost 40 feet above its belly. It can take off with almost half a million pounds of aircraft, fuel, and payload. The first B-52's were designed to carry a few hydrogen bombs as part of America's three complementary nuclear delivery systems. The H models flown during the Vietnam era, however, were modified internally to carry more than thirty tons of conventional TNT bombs.

Nasif Majeed was born Bruce Lightner in 1945 to a prominent family in Raleigh, North Carolina. In 1911, his grandfather Calvin, then among the 1.7 percent of African Americans with a college degree, opened a funeral home with an associated cemetery in the city. (It remains in business and is still owned by the family.) Majeed's father, Clarence E. Lightner, was Raleigh's first popularly elected mayor in 1973 and later served in the North Carolina senate.

In 1968, Majeed graduated from North Carolina A&T State University in

Greensboro with a BS in business administration and a second lieutenant's commission in the US Air Force. After basic officer training at Lackland Air Force Base in San Antonio, Texas, he went on to flight school, then graduated to multiengine training on A-37 Dragonfly light attack bombers and was selected for the elite B-52 program, which drew few volunteers. B-52's are difficult to fly, often uncomfortable for the crews, and require tremendous concentration.

"Flying a subsonic aircraft, you have time to think about what to do, which switch to toggle, which instrument to consult, and so forth," Majeed explained. "Everything happens much faster in a B-52. You have to speed up your thinking so your mind is moving a little faster than the airplane. I would tell myself, 'I'm the pilot of this beast. It will do what I want it to do and nothing else.' Otherwise, things tend to get away from you, and that's always bad."

From 1971 to 1973, Majeed served three tours flying B-52H's from Guam and U-Tapao Royal Thai Navy Airfield to bomb North Vietnam. The Guam missions were long and grueling. During the Vietnam War, Andersen Air Force Base on Guam had the world's longest runways. Made chiefly of crushed coral, they were slippery when wet. On each takeoff, the thought of sitting in a B-52 cockpit as it slipped sideways with sixty thousand pounds of TNT in its belly was a nightmare.

Even with those long runways, a loaded B-52H needed every foot of the gently sloping downhill airstrip, which ended with an eighty-foot cliff. "It was weird and scary watching the ship ahead of us roll over the end of the runway, disappear over the cliff, and then a few seconds later emerge and climb into the sky," Majeed recalled.

Because it took so much fuel to get airborne, each B-52 bound for North or South Vietnam refueled over the Philippines. "Flying while hooked to a hose at 400 knots, the controls get sloppy," Majeed said. This is partly because transferring fuel shifts thousands of pounds from the tanker to the bomber. The B-52 flies only a few feet behind and below the tanker through the turbulence left by the tanker's passage. "And refueling while flying into a setting sun requires almost superhuman concentration," he added.

Between the flight from Guam to the refueling point, the B-52 is on autopilot. Crewmen nap, read, listen to music, or chat. The same was true for the shorter flight to Vietnam. As they near their target—identified only as a number—the radar navigator takes control of the aircraft then releases the bombs at the precise moment his onboard computer indicates they will find their targets.

"While all this is going on, the sky is filled with aircraft, missiles, and antiaircraft flak," Majeed recalled. "F-105 Thunderchiefs attacked the radar sites, while F-100F Super Sabre "Wild Weasels" equipped with radar homing and warning receivers located the signals emitted by enemy missile radar and monitored heat sensors to detect missile launches. Our tail gunner was watching for North Vietnamese MiG-21's. There were also MiG's based across the border in China. They would approach at high speed, fire their whole load of rockets at our formation, then skootch back over the border where our F-4 Phantom fighters couldn't follow them."

Both authors of this work have observed B-52 strikes on North Vietnamese troop formations or headquarters in South Vietnam. From their vantage point in helicopters a mile up and five miles from the target, they knew the big bombers were seven miles above them, though they could not hear or even see them. Several seconds after the bombers opened their bomb bays, a brown zipper half a mile wide would open in the green jungle below and run for a mile or more. Amid great clouds of smoke and billowing dust, they saw the flashes of the exploding bombs. Shock waves were visible in this dust, radiating out from each bomb at supersonic speed. These shock waves were capable of rocking an aircraft miles away.

On the ground were scenes worthy of Dante's Inferno or the paintings of Hieronymus Bosch. Enormous craters were surrounded by huge trees blown flat or into kindling. Small fires burned in the damp foliage. Parts of human and animal bodies were everywhere underfoot, hanging from trees and bushes, plastered to tree trunks. The stench of death mingled with the acrid odor of TNT. The jungle was utterly silent, save for the footfalls of troops exploring this terrestrial Gehenna as they sought survivors.

The B-52 was a powerful weapon, but it was only as effective as the intelligence that selected its targets, and this was as often wrong as right. Further, the North Vietnamese and the Viet Cong were world-class diggers. With only picks and shovels, they built hundreds of underground bunkers and enormous tunnel complexes, many of them deep enough to survive a bombing mostly intact.

B-52 targets over the North were most often structures. It is difficult to imagine the results of even one five-hundred-pound bomb exploding on a headquarters roof.

Majeed survived physically unscathed 139 missions over North Vietnam. By then he was a captain, and he was pressed to remain in the air force and promised rapid promotion.

"I'd had enough," he recalled. "More than enough."

That was how, a week later, he found himself walking down a street in Raleigh with no idea of what to do next, no home of his own, and what would over a few months build into a paralyzing case of post-traumatic stress disorder.

Majeed was angry and irritable and didn't know why. He had nightmares and flashbacks. He began to drink, and when he was drunk, he would drink more. After months of this sort of behavior, he was admitted to a hospital, where his alcoholism was treated. Along the way to dealing with this and PTSD, Majeed encountered other African Americans who had found a spiritual path to controlling their war trauma and their substance abuse.

"I was raised a Christian, and I was always certain there was a God, a higher power," Majeed related. "But as time went on, I felt less comfortable calling myself a Christian. The concept of a blue-eyed, fair-skinned, light-haired Jesus who looked nothing like me was something I couldn't relate to."

In the hospital, Majeed was introduced to another pathway to holiness, another way to worship God. He changed his name and adopted a different manner of dress as he sought the comfort of belief in a different prophet of God.

When his father died, Majeed founded the Clarence E. Lightner Youth Foundation, dedicated to teaching middle school students the importance of civic participation and community service. Speaking of his father's legacy, he said, "Helping young people to aspire to be as successful as they can in school and life. That would be his legacy."

When he was fit and sober, Majeed accepted an offer to fly for Piedmont Airlines. During the 1973 Arab-Israeli War, however, Arab members of the Organization of Petroleum Exporting Countries (OPEC) imposed an embargo against the United States to retaliate for the US resupply of the Israeli military. This caused a nationwide shortage of gasoline, diesel oil, and jet fuel. Airlines curtailed schedules and laid off staff, including pilots.

Majeed was approached by an old friend who held a senior government post in Guyana. He asked him to move to the South American nation and work as an agricultural advisor there. Majeed knew little about agriculture and less about Guyana, which had once been a British colony. Intrigued by the idea, he reenrolled in North Carolina A&T State University and, by 1979, earned an MS in agricultural education. Before he graduated, however, he had second thoughts. While English is the official language of Guyana, the people's native language is Guyanese Creole. Majeed wasn't sure how successful he would be in that environment.

Then another friend approached him with a business proposition. As partners, they would buy a Burger King franchise and open a restaurant in Charlotte. But by then, Majeed's Guyanese friend was prime minister, and he offered Majeed the post of secretary of agriculture.

Majeed thought about his missions over North Vietnam and the dozens of B-52's that had been shot down by missiles, MiG's, or antiaircraft fire. He thought about what his life might be like as a high official in a third-world country. He knew he could get fabulously rich without lifting a finger. And he knew that when rich men accept bribes, the poor ultimately suffer. He didn't need a burning bush or a visit with an archangel to tell him that the God who had saved him from death over North Vietnam didn't want him to become another corrupt third-world official.

On the other hand, opening a fast-food emporium in Charlotte was an opportunity to provide something the African American community needed more than fast food: jobs for young people, entry-level and first-line supervisory positions that would introduce teens to the world of work, keep them out of gangs, and perhaps lay a financial foundation for postsecondary education.

But Majeed knew nothing about running a restaurant, and neither did his partner. So he enrolled in the University of Florida and earned an associate degree in restaurant management. His Burger King opened in 1981.

Managing a restaurant with a partner left Majeed free for other activities. For the next fourteen years, he served the North Carolina Department of Corrections as a clinical chaplain, working with incarcerated men and their families. He also found time to join Metro-Meck Land Development Company as a managing partner.

In 1991, after serving as president of the West Charlotte Merchants

Association, Majeed ran for a seat on the Charlotte city council. He served eight years on the council, during which he obtained more than $200 million in infrastructure improvements in his district. He spearheaded a successful effort to build East Charlotte's first regional recreational center, a $40 million state-of-the-art facility. He also worked to establish and chaired the board of directors for the West Charlotte Business Incubator, a successful effort to increase job opportunities through the development of new businesses.

He served on the Governor's Commission on Education for Economic Growth, working to set policies to better prepare North Carolina's workforce for twenty-first-century jobs through improving educational opportunities.

In 2014 and again in 2016, Majeed was a Democratic candidate for the North Carolina senate in a heavily gerrymandered district. He lost both times.

In 2018, after state and federal courts compelled the Republican-dominated legislature to redraw certain district lines, Majeed won the Democratic nomination for a House of Representatives seat, and then, in the general election, he won the seat.

Why would a Muslim candidate run for office in overwhelmingly Christian Charlotte? "All religion guides us in addressing the needs of people and ensuring that people are served properly," Majeed explained. "On the city council, we made sure that people had safe communities and that services were provided in a fair manner. I hope to do the same in the North Carolina Assembly."

COLIN POWELL

What more is there to say about Colin Powell, long a public figure and one of the first African Americans to rise to national prominence? As it happens, plenty. Powell's public persona is authentic, yet within this complex man is a long-suppressed desire for social justice for all Americans, along with the hard-won knowledge that social justice for minorities is rarely bestowed through benevolence. It is won by an educated populace who possess the tools to demand and work for that justice.

The son of Jamaican immigrants, Colin Powell was born in 1937 in the New York City neighborhood of Harlem. His father, Luther, worked as a shipping clerk, and his mother, Maud, was a seamstress. Powell grew up in the South Bronx and attended Morris High School. After school and on weekends he worked in a furniture store, where he learned Yiddish from his Jewish employers and customers. On Saturday, the Jewish Sabbath, he served as a "Shabbos goy," performing small but necessary tasks that Jewish families could not do for themselves because of their religious obligation to do no work on the Sabbath.

After graduating high school in 1954, he enrolled in the City College of

New York, where he majored in geology and studied military science in the reserve officer's training corps. He has more than once described himself as a C student. Powell graduated in 1958 with a BS and a second lieutenant's commission in the reserve. Before he began training at Fort Benning, Georgia, his reserve commission was upgraded to regular army. After training, he was sent to West Germany to command an infantry platoon.

Powell's thirty-five-year career as a professional soldier is among the most distinguished in American history. He served two tours in Vietnam, the first as an advisor to an ARVN infantry battalion. That first tour ended prematurely when he was severely injured by a punji stake. On his subsequent tour, Major Powell was the operations officer of the Twenty-Third Infantry Division. On a routine flight, his helicopter crashed and burst into flame. Despite his own injuries, Powell rescued the other passengers and crew from the fire, which earned him the Soldier's Medal.

Powell recalled setting off for Vietnam in 1962 and feeling that his mission was a noble one: to halt the spread of communism. At the end of his tour, in 1963, he went home feeling that he and his fellow advisors, no less than the ARVN units they had advised, had been running around the jungle trying to catch people—the Viet Cong—who mostly could not be caught. Frustrated, the ARVN had resorted to burning villages and their fields of rice and manioc, later spraying defoliant on their crops. Powell realized that rebuilding a thatched hut doesn't take long and crops could be replanted. After his second tour he concluded the war was not merely a struggle between communism and capitalism but something vastly more complex—namely, a war against the aspirations of a nation that rejected foreign interference, a war there was no way to win short of pouring millions of American troops in to occupy the entire country, a war that American voters would not support—hence, an unwinnable war.

Among the lessons he drew out of the Vietnam War was that it was vital to avoid a war with a nation that had a greater investment or a greater cause than we did and to understand the commitment of troops, funds, and political support that are required to win any potential war *before committing* them to combat. He concluded it was unwise to enter any conflict without knowing precisely what its military and political objectives were. When those objectives were clear, then one should immediately commit all the people and resources required to win decisively and quickly, in accordance with the ancient military doctrine of mass. From this came the Powell Doctrine, a set of criteria to determine when military force should be used—namely, as a last resort, with strong public support, and only if there is a well-defined national interest at stake. When troops are to be committed under those conditions, all operations should be executed with overwhelming force *and* with a clear exit strategy.

In 1971, after his second tour in Vietnam, Powell earned an MBA at George Washington University. During his long career, he progressed steadily through the ranks while serving in both command and staff positions. In 1973, he served as a battalion commander in South Korea. This was a difficult period for commanders at every level. Desperate to fill its ranks, the new all-volunteer army accepted some recruits who formerly would have been rejected. Many were undisciplined, comparatively poorly educated, or habitual drug users. Powell came up with ways to remedy his men's educational deficiencies, imposed tough but fair disciplinary policies, and refused to tolerate drug use.

From 1987 to 1989, Powell served as national security advisor to President Ronald Reagan. Nearing the end of his army career, he was promoted to four-star general. From October 1, 1989, to September 30, 1993, he served as chairman of the Joint Chiefs of Staff, the army's highest position. This assignment included advising the commander in chief on the conduct of Operation Desert Storm in the 1991 Persian Gulf War.

Before leaving the army, Powell planned a second career by earning fees for speaking engagements. Journalist and humorist Art Buchwald, a World War II marine who served in the Pacific with the marine air wing, was Powell's friend and a much-in-demand speaker. Buchwald offered to suggest which lecture agencies would best serve his friend, so one of Powell's staff telephoned to invite Buchwald to lunch at the Pentagon. Buchwald joked, "Lunch? Don't I get a parade? I was in the Marine Corps three and a half years and I never had a parade."

By the time he became a public figure, Buchwald was well past his youth, a balding, comical, roly-poly figure. Few believed he had served in the marines. Nevertheless, Buchwald was very proud of his wartime service.

When he came to the Pentagon, Buchwald was escorted to the general's office, where Powell, skipping all the usual pleasantries, said, "Follow me," and led his visitor into a very large room. Fifty of Powell's staff, a group of senior officers, came to attention, saluted, and paraded by, each stopping to shake Buchwald's hand. Buchwald had his parade.

When he actually retired from the army, Powell embarked on a speaking career. He also wrote several books, including a best-selling autobiography, *My American Journey.*[1] Soon after that, he became chairman of America's Promise, the Alliance for Youth, a national nonprofit dedicated to mobilizing people from every sector of American life to build the character and competence of young people. In 2001, he was unanimously confirmed as secretary of state under President George W. Bush, the first African American to serve in that position.

Soon after taking office he faced the national crisis that followed the disastrous events of September 11, 2001, when terrorists commandeered American civilian airliners and crashed them into Manhattan's World Trade Center, the Pentagon, and a Pennsylvania field.

Seeking to use the respect and admiration accorded Powell, President Bush and Vice President Dick Cheney used cooked intelligence reports from what turned out to be a single, dubious source: an Iraqi, code-name "Curveball," seeking permanent residence in Germany, who told German intelligence officers whatever he believed they wanted him to say. Powell was persuaded to go before the United Nations and accuse Iraq's Saddam Hussein of possessing and building weapons of mass destruction, a pretext for invading Iraq. No evidence of such weapons was found by the American and Allied forces who occupied Iraq. While Powell has not publicly addressed this, many, including the authors, believe that Powell was tricked into presenting a canard before the UN to justify Bush and Cheney's desire to invade Iraq. Powell resigned his office and left the Bush administration in 2005.

For reasons still unclear, the commander in chief, acting on ambiguous and faulty intelligence, chose to ignore the Powell Doctrine. US troops were sent into Afghanistan and then Iraq without clear public support, an exit strategy, or sufficient strength to pacify either country.

After leaving office, Powell focused his attention and energies on what had become his passion: education, especially for children from poor families like his own. Specifically, he put time and energy into what is now called the City University of New York.

"In the late nineties, some very generous friends, the Rudin family, decided it would be a good thing to name a small center in CUNY after me," Powell explained. "They called it the Colin Powell Center for Policy Studies." Powell was unable to pay much attention to it until after he had completed his term as secretary of state. "Then I went up to CUNY to see what was being done in my name," Powell recalled. "I found a small center and met with some of the students. I was so inspired by these students. They were mostly minorities, including many immigrants. They went around the table, telling their individual stories of how they came to this country, or that they were born here with immigrant parents. Each had a story to tell of why they were now in college and what they intended to do in the future. When they got back around to me, I was crying. I said, 'My God. This is *me* fifty years ago.'" He decided he wanted to get more involved with the center.

In 2013, the president of the City University decided to expand this small center into an entire school of the university. It became the Colin Powell School for Civic and Global Leadership. Powell said, "Notice that both 'civic' and 'global' are in there. As a result, all of the social science departments are now under the Powell School, as well as several smaller activities that were folded into it. I also wanted to focus on the leadership capability of these young people as much as their service. To connect what they learn in school with services they would do in the community or elsewhere in the country. And that became the motif of the Powell Center."

Because the school bearing his name fills a vital need, the Powell Center is now a major element of the CUNY. "Roughly 25 to 30 percent of the entire student body take classes in the Powell School," explained the former secretary of state. "Consequently, I spend much more time involved with it than I might have years ago. It touches something deeply personal. Ninety percent of our students are one kind of minority or another. Upwards of 80 percent identify themselves as either being born in another country or as the first in their family to attend college. This resonates with me. My parents were immigrants who came to the United States on a banana boat, and they did not go to college."

Although Powell lives in Virginia, he spends much of his time at CUNY. He chairs the board of visitors and raises a lot of money for the university.

He is also very proud that nine other US elementary and middle schools bear his name. "I have visited all nine and have a pretty good idea of what they're about," Powell continued. "These are all new schools, and none are for the children of wealthy families. They are for kids like I was, with hardworking parents who want their children to have better lives than they themselves had."

In 1997, Powell became the founding chairman of America's Promise

Alliance, a national coalition of organizations devoted to improving the lives of children. His wife, Alma, an audiologist, now chairs it. "There are five things a child needs to be successful in life," Powell explained. "Five promises that we must make to every child.

"The first is having responsible, caring, loving adults in their lives. If not their family, then their coaches, ministers, rabbis, friends, and teachers. Adults that live good lives. We must have some in the lives of children early, or else the child doesn't know how to behave. The child doesn't know what is possible. We have too many children who are being brought up without that kind of adult presence in their life," Powell explained. In a chapter of his book *It Worked for Me*, titled "We're Mammals," he described how a tiger raises its cub and how an elephant raises its calf.[2] "Read it and you'll see how we're supposed to be raising our children," he added.

"The second promise is to provide safe places for our kids to learn and grow, such as after-school programs or programs from the Salvation Army, Big Brothers Big Sisters, the Boys and Girls Clubs—there are hundreds of them across the country. But still not enough. We spend much of our time encouraging communities to have more and more of these kinds of programs. And hardly a day goes by that I don't run into somebody who has started such a program.

"The third promise is a healthy start for every kid. It's disgraceful that we don't have universal health care.

"The fourth promise is a marketable education, that is, an education that will prepare each child for a job. My own parents continuously pushed me on that idea, and that was to help keep me in school," Powell explained.

His fifth and last promise is to require that early in their lives, all young people must find ways to give back to their communities, to their country, to the world. "I believe in service," he said. "I don't think it should be mandatory in civilian life, but I think we should start encouraging kids to serve others in school systems. There you *can* make it mandatory. More and more high schools are making service programs mandatory in their curriculum. A number of colleges are doing likewise. For example, each student must get so many hours or so many credits in a service capacity before they can graduate.

"In recent years, America's Promise has focused on the high school graduation rate," Powell continued. "That is now roughly 83 percent—the highest ever. My wife, Alma, is pushing to get that up to 90 percent by 2020. That last 7 percent is very tough to achieve because it encompasses kids living in very distressed neighborhoods and in very difficult life circumstances. Nevertheless, we're going after that 90 percent. We think it's achievable."

In retirement, most of Powell's time is split between America's Promise, CUNY, and the speaking circuit, which is his principal income source. "I love it," he declared. "Not so much for the income, which is nice, but because it gets me around the country to talk to different groups of people. I learn so much about the different industries, the companies and associations, and every sort of thing that's taking place in the country. The speaking circuit is also the principal source of my continuing education. I study every organization I'm going to speak to."

Powell also speaks without taking a fee at any of the schools bearing his name, whenever he finds himself in their vicinity. "I'll call and ask to come to the school. I love doing that," he said. The one closest to his home is in Centreville, Virginia, some forty minutes from the Powell residence, and he's been there several times.

In war or peace, in uniform or civilian garb, few Americans of any generation have contributed to their nation and their communities as much or as long as Colin Powell, son of hardworking immigrants, a warrior for peace and education, an elder statesman of those who served in the Vietnam War.

Colin Powell's Thirteen Rules of Leadership[3]

1. It ain't as bad as you think. It will look better in the morning.
2. Get mad, then get over it.
3. Avoid having your ego so close to your position that when your position falls, your ego goes with it.
4. It can be done!
5. Be careful what you choose.
6. Don't let adverse facts stand in the way of a good decision.
7. You can't make someone else's choices.
8. Check small things.
9. Share the credit.
10. Remain calm. Be kind.
11. Have a vision.
12. Don't take counsel of your fears or naysayers.
13. Perpetual optimism is a force multiplier.

LEWIS MERLETTI

World War II was fought across half the planet. Except for a relative few who had vital jobs in the civilian sector, almost every able-bodied American man under forty-five saw military service during the war. They served for the duration of the war plus the months afterward necessary to demobilize millions in an orderly fashion. Men often remained with a single unit for the entire war. But Vietnam was a different kind of war. Its operations were almost entirely restricted to Southeast Asia, and its fighters typically served just one year in the war zone. Career servicemen might serve a second or third tour in Vietnam, but often in a markedly different type of job.

From Pearl Harbor to the unconditional surrender of first Germany and then Japan, close to 100 percent of Americans, civilian and military, supported the war and its goals. Not so Vietnam. When the first American combat troops deployed to the war zone in the summer of 1965, their efforts were largely supported by a citizenry whose overwhelming majority believed that international communism must be stopped before it swallowed all Asia. By 1968, however, the nation was divided between those who still believed communism had to be contained and the war could be won and those who believed the war was unwinnable and it was not America's business to intervene in a civil war.

The Vietnam War was fought by a mixture of draftees and volunteers, but it's hard to place many soldiers in either category. This is because many waited to get a draft notice before they enlisted while others asked to be drafted so as to minimize their service time and get their obligation over with as soon as possible.

Physicians, nurses, paramedics, shamans, medicine men—healers of every stripe—have held a place of honor in every culture throughout recorded history. So, too, combat medics since the Civil War have accompanied US units into combat. They are a storied group that, generation after generation, war after war, have distinguished themselves with conspicuous valor on the battlefield. Within that worthy group is a small, separate breed: the highly trained medics of the Special Forces.

Americans have fought in unconventional ways since the French and Indian Wars, when Maj. Robert Rogers, a New Hampshire farmer, led small bands of rangers, trained in the stealthy tactics of the first Americans, against France and its Native American allies. But unconventional warfare didn't come into its own until the Vietnam War, when Green Berets recruited tens of thousands of indigenous fighters to carry the war to the North Vietnamese Army and to the Viet Cong guerrillas. In Vietnam, Special Forces medics, trained not only as healers but as warriors, linguists, and diplomats, served under fire, in torrential rain and baking heat, in conditions so challenging that few would have even attempted what they accomplished so masterfully. Their success both individually and collectively is a testament to the indomitable spirit that has sustained Americans since the Revolution. More than a few Special Forces medics gave their lives in service to their country. Among those who survived the war, few contributed more to the nation than Lewis Merletti.

Twenty-one-year-old Special Forces medic Lewis Merletti was in a mountain range eight miles west of Nha Trang and prone behind a tree beneath a sliver of moonlight struggling against the midnight darkness. He was with a patrol of Nung, Cambodian, and Montagnard mercenaries, and they were waiting to ambush the Viet Cong guerrillas who regularly used the nearby trail.

"*Bac si!* [Doctor!] This man is bite by two-step," one of the Montagnards whispered.

A two-step was what GIs called the krait, a cousin to the cobra, and one of the deadliest creatures on earth. If you were bitten by a krait, the saying goes, you'd be dead before you could take two steps.

Merletti laid his rifle against the tree while two men laid the victim on the ground in front of him. The medic covered himself and his patient with his poncho, then took out a flashlight with a red filter over its lens. He fumbled in his medical bag, hunting for a scalpel. He had none. With no time to lose, he pulled a Buck knife from his belt. He kept its 3.75-inch blade razor sharp and used it for everything from slicing meat to cleaning his fingernails.

"I had no alcohol, no way to sterilize the blade," Merletti explained. "I couldn't even light a match and sterilize the blade with the flame, because that would be the end of my night vision. Also, I'd seen a poncho catch fire from a single match, and I couldn't risk that."

The patient was a Montagnard. The bite was on his thumb, now swollen to more than twice its size, as were his hand and arm. Merletti made a tourniquet of the man's belt and tied it above the biceps, trying to keep the deadly venom from reaching the patient's heart, where it would pump poison throughout his body. With his knife, Merletti made an incision across each of the two puncture holes, then attempted to suck the poison out, all the while hoping his mouth had no open cut where the poison could enter his system. But the thumb was so swollen that almost nothing came out.

A Special Forces medic is more than a dispenser of Band-Aids and aspirin; his training is the equivalent of an emergency medical technician. Merletti thought back to his classes at Fort Bragg. *Why* was the arm swollen? Because of a compound the body produces when it encounters poison or suffers trauma, a chemical cocktail of histamines. Merletti realized the man was gasping for air. Histamines had swollen and constricted his trachea, and little air was getting to his lungs.

Only antivenin could save this man, but that was at the other end of a fifteen-minute helicopter hop. Merletti knew he had to do something immediately or the man would suffocate.

The only antihistamine he had was Ornade, a combination of

chlorpheniramine and phenylpropanolamine. It was an over-the-counter capsule sold under a dozen brand names all over the world to alleviate cold symptoms.

Merletti began giving his patient Ornade capsules one after another. By the time the man had swallowed the last one in his medical bag, Merletti had counted twenty and the man's labored breathing had eased. He tore the patient's shirt off, found a grease pencil, and wrote "20 Ornade" in big letters across the man's chest.

The medic was under no illusion this would save a life; he had merely bought him some time. "I got on the radio and called for an emergency medevac," Merletti recalled. "They asked the guy's name. Apparently, they thought he was important enough to save, so ten or fifteen minutes later, we heard a chopper approaching."

Team leader Sgt. John Deschamps ran into a jungle clearing barely big enough for a helicopter and turned on a battery-powered infrared beacon. The chopper pilot headed toward the beacon, then eased his craft through the trees amid the hurricane of its rotor wash. A dozen feet above the ground, the pilot switched on his landing lights, and for a few seconds an eye-stabbing radiance bathed the landing zone. The patient was carried to the helicopter, which then lifted off immediately.

"Even if the field hospital had the right antivenin, and even if he got there soon enough, that guy didn't have much of a chance. But I knew I did everything I could have done to save him," Merletti recalled.

———◇———

Lewis Merletti was born in Pittsburgh in 1948. His father, Felix, was a plumber who had been drafted at age thirty-two to serve in World War II. Felix Merletti wound up in a searchlight unit; their powerful beams helped antiaircraft gunners find targets at night. "Dad's unit didn't go overseas," Merletti explained. Instead, it was deployed to protect American cities from enemy air attack. In his later years, the elder Merletti served as commander of an American Legion chapter.

The grandson of Italian immigrants, Lew Merletti and his older sister, Karen, grew up in a modest three-bedroom home in Penn Hills, an eastern suburb of Pittsburgh. They lived in a solid, middle-class neighborhood in a city that had long been America's arsenal. Pittsburgh steel built the tanks and ships and planes that won World War II. Pittsburgh steel built the gigantic locks of the Panama Canal and the railroads that linked North America coast-to-coast-to-coast. It built the millions of cars and trucks swarming the nation's roads and the skeletons of its cities' towering skylines.

Growing up in this lunch-bucket community, Merletti learned at an early age that success rested on hard work. When he was old enough, he spent summers working for his dad's company or hauling plaster for his uncle.

Merletti attended all-boys Central Catholic High School. On November 22, 1963, a special assembly was called to announce that President Kennedy had been shot. It would be several hours before the nation was told he had not survived, but Merletti was pretty sure that Kennedy's Secret Service detail knew if he was still alive. "That's when it hit me that I'd love to be a Secret Service agent," said Merletti.

A few years later, on a warm June day in 1965, Merletti learned a new word: Vietnam. His sophomore history teacher had served in the marines during World War II, and he was the Jesuit school's prefect of discipline as well as the football coach.

Merletti said, "He came into the classroom and pounded his fist on the blackboard hard enough to throw off a cloud of chalk dust. This was the day after newspapers and television reported the president was sending combat troops to South Vietnam.

"Mr. Wheeler turned to us and said, 'Gentlemen, this is *your* war,'" Merletti recalled. "I thought to myself, *No, uh-uh. I have junior year, senior year, and four years of college. Six years. That war is* not *my war.*"

Nevertheless, the presidency of John Kennedy and his subsequent assassination had imbued Merletti with a strong desire to serve his country. "When Kennedy said, 'Ask not what your country can do for you—ask what you can do for your country,' I felt he was speaking to me."

Merletti had long considered he might serve his country with a career in law enforcement. Not with a local police force, but with the FBI or another federal agency.

In the autumn of 1966, after high school graduation, Merletti enrolled at Pittsburgh's Duquesne University. His first semester courses included ROTC, which he enjoyed. When the spring semester rolled around, he added two accounting classes to his schedule; he knew the FBI often hired accountants. But Merletti found accounting dull and uninteresting. He dropped both courses. That made him a part-time student—and vulnerable to the draft.

Then he came across the March 10, 1967, issue of *Life* magazine. The cover story, featuring spectacular photos by Dutch photojournalist Co Rentmeester, described Operation Junction City, which involved thirty thousand US troops. A battalion from the 173rd Airborne Brigade had parachuted into War Zone C to find and fight the enemy.

"That's what I wanted to do," Merletti decided. He had never been in an airplane, but he wanted to be an army paratrooper. When his draft notice arrived, Merletti made a beeline for the army recruiter. After basic combat and advanced infantry training, he volunteered for jump school. "The instructors included some World War II paratroopers who had made combat jumps," Merletti recalled. "They pushed us beyond what we believed were our limits so that we knew what was expected of us if we wanted to wear silver jump wings." After completing five jumps, he stood on the drop zone and proudly accepted his wings.

Merletti then volunteered and was accepted into the Special Forces training group at Fort Bragg, North Carolina. This was probably the toughest, most demanding school in the US Army, with a washout rate of around 85 percent. Merletti was selected to cross train as a medic, and after earning the army's most coveted insignia, the Green Beret, he was selected for Vietnamese language training. In this total-immersion course, he spoke and heard only Vietnamese virtually around the clock for four months.

By the time Merletti completed all this training and spent additional months in a Special Forces A-Team at Fort Bragg, almost two years had passed since his enlistment—and he still had no orders for Vietnam. Merletti decided he couldn't wait idly any longer. "I did some networking and got the names of the two people who worked on the Special Forces assignment desk in the Pentagon. I called them. I was told to submit my request for Vietnam duty in writing. I fired off a letter the same day."

Weeks ticked by, and Merletti called the Pentagon again and was told he would get orders soon. When they didn't come, he hitchhiked from Fort Bragg to the Pentagon and presented himself at the assignment desk. He left with orders in his pocket.

After home leave in Pittsburgh, Merletti reported to Fort Lewis, Washington, where he expected to board a plane for Vietnam immediately. Instead, an aircraft scheduling snafu left him and a dozen other Green Berets in a transient barracks, doing busy work for days. Impatient to get into the war, Merletti found the enlisted man who made up the flight manifests and convinced him to jump him and his buddies to the head of the line.

Merletti arrived in Vietnam in August 1969 and was assigned to Detachment A-502, the biggest A-Team in the world. Most A-Teams have two officers and ten enlisted men. When Merletti arrived, A-502 had almost three times that many Green Berets. His first day there was almost his last: a supply clerk accidentally discharged a pistol, and the bullet barely missed Merletti's left ear.

In Vietnam, the Green Berets were employed as a force multiplier. A dozen Special Forces soldiers could—and often did—recruit, train, arm, and lead five hundred indigenous fighters of the Civilian Irregular Defense Force (CIDG) against the enemy. Rather than deploy in mass, pairs of Green Berets led twenty to fifty CIDG men on raids, reconnaissance and ambush patrols, and other counterinsurgency tactics aimed mostly at denying Viet Cong guerrillas and North Vietnamese regulars the ability to move freely at night. Special Forces–led CIDG units also protected fire support bases, and they screened and patrolled hundreds of miles of thickly jungled and vaguely defined borders.

———◇———

On the night Merletti treated the Montagnard for the snakebite, intelligence sources suggested a small Viet Cong unit would be returning from R & R. With another Special Forces sergeant, he set up an ambush along a trail often used by the Viet Cong. After the medevac chopper departed with his patient, Merletti's men resumed their ambush positions, resigned to the fact the helicopter had probably given away their position and spoiled any chance of an ambush.

Not so. About two hours later, a Viet Cong guerrilla triggered one of the patrol's M-18 Claymore antipersonnel mines. A brief but intense firefight ensued. At first light, Merletti and his men found many blood trails, indicating wounded Viet Cong who had been carried away, along with a few bodies and their weapons. The ambush was a success.

At the end of 1969, A-502's base was turned over to the South Vietnamese.

Merletti moved to B-33, where he provided support to A-334 at Tong Le Chon, farther south and closer to the Cambodian border.

A few weeks later, while doing paperwork in the B-33 dispensary, a Montagnard of the camp's CIDG appeared and called to him. Merletti greeted the man and asked what he needed. Smiling, the man extended his right thumb, displaying two still-healing scars. *"Bac si*, you save my life," said the snakebite victim.

—◇—

Merletti's enlistment and Vietnam tour both ended in July 1970. He had intended to resume his studies at Kent State University, Ohio, but the shooting of unarmed students protesting the war there made him decide to return to Duquesne, which offered automatic admission to veterans upon presentation of their discharge papers.

"One of the first university people I met was my counselor, who helped me select classes," Merletti recalled. The counselor explained that Duquesne would waive its foreign-language requirement if he could prove he had studied a foreign language at a certified institution for a minimum of 100 hours. "I showed her my graduation certificate from the US Army Language School, where I studied Vietnamese for 360 hours and had a proficiency rating of limited fluency. She said, 'I don't recognize Vietnamese as a foreign language.'"

Merletti appealed her decision, and the school ruled in his favor. Although he was not required to learn a foreign language, he nevertheless opted to study Chinese.

This and other experiences made Merletti guarded about sharing his status as a Vietnam veteran. "I heard an occasional negative remark about my Vietnam service from other students, but nothing overwhelming," he recalled. "Some students expressed a real interest in my Vietnam experiences."

Nevertheless, the fact of his service was sometimes an issue. "I was on the GI Bill and money was tight," Merletti recalled. "I lived off campus. When I learned the university offered a free room to resident assistants, I decided to apply. Each dormitory floor had an RA responsible for monitoring student behavior on their floor and offering assistance when needed. A panel of three RAs, two women and one man, reviewed my application. One of the women said, 'I don't want Vietnam veterans in our dorms. I'll never approve one as an RA.'"

Merletti graduated in 1973 with a degree in political science. During his senior year, he was recruited by the National Security Agency. "They wanted me to do the same kinds of things I did in Vietnam with Special Forces, but for their agency." Merletti declined.

Just before graduation, Merletti applied to the Secret Service. He was interviewed by the special agent in charge (SAIC) of the Pittsburgh office, Jerry Bechtel, a rising star who would go on to become deputy director. Bechtel offered him a job, but before he could be hired, President Nixon instituted a freeze on federal hiring.

Merletti found work selling Xerox copiers. Personable, highly intelligent, and handsome, within a few months he was earning good money. But he wanted more out of life than a comfortable income.

"The freeze was lifted in 1974. I went back to the Pittsburgh office and met the new SAIC, Jim D'Amelio," Merletti explained. After a second interview, he was hired and sent to Philadelphia to begin as a trainee field agent. His salary was a third of what he had earned with Xerox.

In 1983, after working on counterfeiting details, Merletti joined the presidential protection detail, whose duties include protecting the president, first lady, their family, and visiting heads of state, along with accompanying officials.

The normal tour of duty with this detail is four to five years. Merletti served for fifteen, protecting Presidents Reagan, Bush, and Clinton.

In February 1993, agents of the Treasury Department's Bureau of Alcohol, Tobacco, and Firearms (ATF) were investigating suspected firearms violations by members of the Branch Davidian, an apocalyptic cult based near Waco, Texas. Led by Vernon Howell, aka David Koresh, the secretive cult had stockpiled large numbers of weapons. After a fifty-one-day siege by the ATF, FBI, and Texas National Guard, government agents raided the compound, resulting in the deaths of Koresh, eighty-two of his followers, including women and children, and four ATF agents.

Merletti was chosen to select and lead a Treasury Department team to investigate these events. His only charter was to find the truth. The report his team produced exonerated the four ATF agents who perished in the raid but revealed mistakes and flawed decisions by a few supervisory agents. The book-length report was made public and earned high praise from news organizations for its depth, its unsparing honesty, and its rigorous completeness.

———◇———

In 1994, Merletti became the twenty-second person to hold the position of special agent in charge of the presidential protection detail. He began his new responsibilities on a bright, beautiful day in Washington, DC. President Clinton was scheduled to speak at a Washington hotel. Merletti escorted him from the Oval Office to his limousine, a distance of some thirty yards. Merletti said, "I was focused, feeling a touch of pride. I had been assigned to this detail for about twelve years and I had held every position on the detail. And now, finally, at what I considered the apex of my career, I was the special agent in charge. The one person totally responsible for protecting the president at any cost.

"The president and I walked to the limo, where the special agent of the first shift held the rear passenger door open. He looked me in the eye and said, 'You're the SAIC now. The president is all yours.' I thought to myself, *Yes! He is!*

"President Clinton got in and I closed the door. I opened the right front door. And found a thick telephone book on the seat. On it was a yellow Post-it note that read, 'Sit on this phone book, it should help you see over the dashboard.'"

In October 1996, the Secret Service began preparing for President Clinton's visit to Manila to attend the Asia Pacific Economic Cooperation Forum. The Philippines presented many security challenges: criminal gangs ran much of Manila, official corruption was rampant, and long-festering insurrections by both communist and Muslim guerrillas simmered on several islands of the Philippine archipelago.

On November 23, 1996, *Air Force One* landed in Manila. Clinton was scheduled to meet with Philippines president Fidel V. Ramos at 4:00 p.m. The planned motorcade route from the president's hotel to that meeting would take fifteen minutes.

"Keeping the president on his schedule was of the utmost importance to his staff and to the Secret Service," Merletti explained. "At 3:15 p.m. I went to the president's suite and reminded his staff that in order to arrive on schedule the motorcade must depart at 3:45 p.m.

"At 3:45 the motorcade was ready—but President Clinton was on a phone call with the White House. At about 4:00, the president and several staff members came out of his suite, walking quickly. One shouted, 'We're late; we have to move fast.'

"We took the elevator and descended to the ground floor. As we left the elevator, I received a radio call: Philippines intelligence had intercepted a radio transmission on a rarely used frequency. The transmission was one sentence: 'The wedding is across the bridge.'"

Merletti recalled reading an intelligence report three or four years earlier in which a terrorist had used the word *wedding* as code word for "assassination." He couldn't recall which terrorist or even which country was involved, and that single interception was far from conclusive, but Merletti knew the presidential motorcade's primary route would cross a bridge in central Manila.

Meaningless coincidence or actionable intelligence? He had less than a minute to decide. "There wasn't time to consult with anyone, but I had a gut feeling that something was wrong. When I climbed into the limo, the president said, 'We're late! We have to get going.'"

In Vietnam, Merletti had learned to trust his instincts. A bridge, he realized, was a perfect place for an ambush, because there was no way to maneuver left or right or even to turn around. For an instant, his mind raced back to a high school auditorium and then to Dallas, Texas, exactly thirty-three years earlier. (It was November 23 in Manila, but due to the International Dateline, still November 22 in the States.) He made up his mind: Merletti was willing to lose his job, but he wasn't going to lose his president.

Turning in his seat, he looked at the president and said, "I'm changing to the alternate route. That will add an additional twenty minutes to our drive."

"Lew, don't do that. I can't be *that* late," replied Clinton. "What's wrong with the primary?"

Merletti replied that fresh intelligence led him to believe it would be best to avoid the bridge on the primary route. The president was upset about being behind schedule. As the motorcade raced away from the hotel, Merletti radioed an intelligence team and told them to check the bridge.

The president's unhappiness with the route change made the

thirty-five-minute ride seem even longer. "I knew this was not over," Merletti recalled. "I would have to explain myself to the president's staff, tell them why I disrupted the schedule by switching to the alternate route."

About halfway to their destination, the intelligence team reported they had found a bomb on the bridge. Merletti had mixed emotions. On the one hand, he had certainly made the right decision to change the route. On the other, somebody was trying to kill the president of the United States of America, the leader of the Free World.

Secret Service agents disarmed the bomb. Every resource of the US intelligence community was focused on determining who had put the bomb on the bridge. After three weeks, Merletti learned the man behind the plot was a new breed of terrorist: a tall, wealthy, mysterious Saudi named Osama bin Laden.

On June 6, 1997, Lewis C. Merletti became the nineteenth director of the US Secret Service. "It was a great honor," he said. "But, tell the truth, I was not cut out to be an administrator. I spent my time testifying before Congress about budgets, briefing the treasury secretary about ongoing investigations, and pushing paper. I missed being in the field, with a badge in my pocket and a gun on my hip, trying to do right by my country."

Merletti retired from government service in 1999 and accepted an offer from the Cleveland Browns NFL team to serve as head of security and stadium operations.

Merletti's marriage of twenty-five years ended in 2002. It produced two sons, Michael and Matt, who in many ways have emulated their father in their career choices. In 2011, Merletti remarried. He now lives with his second wife, Josette, a nurse, in Naples, Florida.

"Overall, my Vietnam experience had more of a positive impact than any other life experience," Merletti said. "Vietnam changed my outlook on life. I came to realize that all of us are the product of our training and experiences. I learned many things: I learned that courage changes the face of everything and that in valor there is hope. I learned that some things happen in a flash, but their memories last forever. I learned that you must always be prepared, you must never stop trying, and that you never stop learning. I came to accept that Vietnam was a place where many good young men came to die. Most importantly, I came to fully respect my brothers in arms who answered our country's call to service. God bless them!"

GEORGE
FORREST

An underappreciated resource, retired career military officers return to civilian life with leadership skills, management expertise, demonstrated integrity, and a worldview rarely matched by their peers without similar service. Some join large business enterprises. Many become college or high school teachers, coaches, or government officials. And a few do it all to the great benefit of their respective communities.

Growing up in a small Maryland town during the early part of the civil rights era, George Forrest decided he wanted to become a civil rights lawyer. His father, among the few African Americans of his generation with a college education, was born in 1911 and had graduated from the Hampton Institute (later Hampton University). "My father was probably the smartest and greatest man I've ever known," Forrest opined.

After high school, Forrest, one of five children, enrolled at Morgan State College (now Morgan State University). According to the rules of all land-grant colleges, male students were required to take two years of ROTC. "I still wanted to be a lawyer," Forrest recalled. His grades, however, were not good enough for law school. "My father advised me to take two more years of ROTC and, after commissioning, take the six-month option," he recalled. In that time between the Korean War and the Vietnam War, when the US Army was far below wartime strength, ROTC graduates were allowed to serve six months on active duty and complete their six-year service obligations as reserve officers.

Forrest graduated in 1960 and was commissioned a second lieutenant. The following year he reported to Fort Benning, Georgia, for the infantry officer basic course. "Most of my classmates were West Pointers," he recalled. "Class of 1961."

At Fort Ord, California, his first duty assignment, a senior officer recommended he apply for a coveted regular army commission. "I applied, got lucky, then was sent to Germany during the Berlin Crisis, after the Soviets built the wall between East and West Berlin."

Next, Forrest reported to the Third Infantry Regiment, the "Old Guard," at Fort Meyer, Virginia. The Third was responsible for all military honors at Arlington National Cemetery and supplied the guards for the Tomb of the Unknown Soldier, honor guards for official funerals and visiting dignitaries, and other ceremonial duties in Washington, DC.

"At that time there was exactly one billet for an African American officer in the Old Guard," Forrest explained. "I was six feet, two inches tall and good-looking, so I was a one-for-one replacement for the tall, good-looking African American officer who was leaving."

Forrest took command of the platoon that guarded the Tomb of the Unknown Soldier. "I served in the Old Guard from late 1963 to early 1965. I was there for President Kennedy's funeral and for Douglas MacArthur's. I was also there for the 1963 March on Washington," he recalled.

From his first duty at Fort Ord, Forrest had acquired a mentor, Ken Pond, a senior officer who saw his potential and helped guide his career. While Forrest was in the Old Guard, Pond was in the Pentagon office that managed the careers of infantry officers by ensuring each received the right assignments at the right times in their careers.

"Pond said, 'There's a war coming. There's an experimental unit at Fort Benning, the Eleventh Air Assault. They're going to be committed to that war at some point, and you need command time.'"

So Forrest went to Benning and initially served as a staff officer in the Eleventh Air Assault. This unit was inventing helicopter-borne warfare, experimenting with equipment for a very mobile infantry division, devising and refining tactics, teaching helicopter pilots and crews to quickly and efficiently move combat infantryman great distances by air and put them into small landing zones, and teaching infantrymen how to work with helicopters and their crews.

In June 1965, the men and equipment of the Eleventh Air Assault were merged with the Second Infantry Division at Fort Benning. The Second lost all men and equipment incompatible with air assault concepts and doctrine. No tanks, self-propelled artillery, or heavy trucks. Fewer jeeps. The division's 105mm howitzers were replaced with newer, lighter models. Big trucks jammed with communications equipment were replaced with jeeps with miniaturized radios. Every M-14 7.62mm rifle in the division was replaced with the new M-16 5.56mm rifle. Every man in the division qualified with the M-16 and learned to rappel from a hovering helicopter.

As described earlier, the Second Infantry Division and the First Cavalry Division, then in South Korea, exchanged colors and assumed each other's designation. In August 1965, the First Cavalry Airmobile—it's 437 helicopters and other aircraft, vehicles, weapons, and equipment and its 15,000 men— were loaded on ships and sailed to South Vietnam.

An advance party of 1,030 men flew from Georgia to South Vietnam. Their mission was to turn a nine-hundred-foot long strip of packed red clay—an airstrip abandoned by the French in 1954 and surrounded by hundreds of acres of old-growth, triple-canopy jungle—into a cantonment to disperse all the division's men and helicopters.

This deployment was the result of an urgent request by South Vietnamese prime minister Nguyen Cao Ky.

Of the First Cavalry's fifteen thousand men, only a handful of officers and a few dozen senior noncoms had seen combat in World War II or Korea. The great bulk of the men were draftees and enlistees, unblooded and untested in battle.

Shortly before the division deployed, Capt. George Forrest took command of Company A, First Battalion, Fifth Cavalry.

On November 14, 1965, in response to intelligence reports of NVA troops in the valley of the Ia River (in Vietnamese, Ia Drang), leading elements of Lt. Col. Harold Moore's First Battalion, Seventh Cavalry (1/7) air assaulted into LZ X-Ray. They took fire going in. The remainder of the battalion landed under heavier fire. Fierce fighting ensued, and the famed Battle of Ia Drang was on. Much has been written about this battle, most definitively by Moore and Joseph L. Galloway in *We Were Soldiers Once*.[1]

The details of what followed at LZ X-Ray are best read there. For George Forrest, it is enough to say that he and his company entered the fray as reinforcements during a pause on the second day. Two days later, victorious but exhausted and depleted by heavy casualties, Moore's 1/7 flew out to rest, recuperate, and mourn their many dead.

After four days and nights fighting off the NVA's attacks, LZ X-Ray was evacuated. The Second Battalion Fifth Cavalry (2/5) and the Second of the Seventh (2/7), which came late to the battle and were less battered and bloody, withdrew on foot. A B-52 strike was ordered for X-Ray and the area toward nearby Chu Pong Massif, where the NVA's reserve battalions waited in tunnels and bunkers. "By walking out, we hoped the NVA remaining near X-Ray wouldn't realize they would be in the strike area," Forrest explained.

The 1/5, under Lt. Col. Robert Tully, reached LZ Columbus safely. Meanwhile, the 2/7, under Lt. Col. Robert McDade, proceeded in a column toward LZ Albany. At that time the battalion was without its Company A, which had reinforced the 1/7 at the beginning of the battle and was still with the 1/7. In its place was Forrest's A/1/5, bringing up the rear.

"We were the red-headed stepchild," Forrest recalled. "The order of march, I think, was B company, C Company, D Company, Headquarters Company, and then us. Perhaps McDade assumed, because of the battle just concluded, we had pretty much annihilated the NVA or at least the regiments in the area. And so the march was kind of loosey-goosey.

"I had very good NCOs, and they told me we were not on a stroll through the woods. They said, 'We are in bad-guy country, and we need to make sure we have combat integrity,' meaning that as we moved, we had to be prepared to defend ourselves from attack.

"So we moved out. After some effort, I finally established radio communication on 2/7's command net. I was able to talk to their operations guys."

As McDade's unit approached LZ Albany, troopers in the recon platoon captured two NVA soldiers. McDade halted the column, which was then about a hundred meters from LZ Albany, and with his radio operators, he moved back up the column to interrogate the prisoners.

It was a fatal mistake.

While McDade was occupied, the column—except for Forrest's company—was strung out over some 550 meters. Flank guards were posted, but the tall grass made visibility difficult. McDade then called all the company commanders forward. As most of the men, exhausted after more than two days without sleep, sat down and relaxed, the company commanders, accompanied by their radio operators, made their way toward McDade.

Some seventy minutes after the two NVA were captured, Alpha Company and McDade's command group reached LZ Albany, a clearing in the woods with a copse of trees. The remainder of the battalion remained strung out east of the landing zone.

At the end of that column was Forrest's unit. "We had limited radio communication," he recalled. "I kept one radio on my own battalion's, the 1/5's command net, because I never knew when I was going to have to call my boss. I kept the other one on McDade's command net."

To communicate with his platoons, he said, "My radio operators, Henry Smith and Robert Hirst, were so efficient, they could switch back and forth conveniently." Hirst, from Philadelphia, wanted to go to medical school after he completed his tour in Vietnam.

When McDade called all the company commanders forward, "I assumed this was so he could position us around LZ Albany," Forest recalled. "I thought that was unusual, but I was a young captain and I didn't question it."

Accompanied by his radio operators, Forrest started for Albany. "There were some trees and some anthills," he recalled. "It kind of reminded me of an arid jungle with limited visibility."

Forrest's first sergeant was on emergency leave. His acting replacement and his executive officer, Lt. Don Adams, remained with the company.

As Forrest headed up the trail, he began to feel something was wrong. "There were men all along the trail as I went forward," he recalled. "I'm seeing guys sitting on packs, smoking and joking. I'm thinking, *What the hell is going on here?* I knew the other company commanders had gone forward, but where were the NCOs? But I can't be a Monday-morning quarterback about this."

Just as he reached McDade and the meeting, he heard incoming mortar fire. "My first thought was to get back down this trail, because the only guys I knew and the safest place for me was back with my men.

"As I started back, I saw that my radio operators were with me," he recalled. "No matter what, whenever I turned around, they were there, like my shadow. But when I got back to the safety of my company, they were gone. I assume they had been killed along the trail."

In the time it took Forrest to run 550 meters, A Company's junior leaders had formed the company into a perimeter, ready to repel the attack. Meanwhile, more than five hundred North Vietnamese of the NVA Sixth Company, Eighth Battalion, Sixty-Sixth Regiment had come boiling out of the tall grass to fall on the column south of LZ Albany.

McDade's command group ran into a clump of trees between the two clearings of LZ Albany. The trees and termite mounds provided some cover from rifle and mortar fire. McDade's recon platoon and the First Platoon of 2/7's Alpha Company took charge of the defense. Within a few minutes, this small group was cut off from the rest of the column, which was now full of NVA soldiers. Waiting for air support, the Americans holding LZ Albany drove off a few NVA assaults and sniped at any exposed enemy soldiers wandering around the perimeter.

The soldiers in the rest of the long column were not as fortunate. The column had dissolved into small clumps of GIs, who were ineffectively trying to defend themselves from much larger groups of NVA soldiers coming at them from every direction.

Even before darkness fell, the NVA began to hunt for wounded Americans who had taken cover in the tall grass, killing each one they found.

In addition to his radio operators, Forrest's company lost several men who had been along the trail when the enemy seemed to materialize out of the tall grass. "Adams was wounded along the trail. Larry Hess, my first platoon leader, was killed. I lost Rodgers, the first platoon's platoon sergeant, and Sergeant Wang, a decorated Korean War veteran. Altogether, I lost seventeen men in that initial ambush, and their names are indelibly etched in my mind."

Meanwhile, just up the trail, a massacre was going on. As sobering as A company's 17 dead were, they paled in comparison with the other companies' losses: 138 men killed or missing and 124 wounded.

Safely inside his company's hastily assembled perimeter, Forrest called his battalion commander at the 1/5 Cav. "I said that we were under attack. We needed a medevac." Lacking a tactical map and given the chaotic situation, he also needed to locate himself on the ground.

"The medevac had already gotten the word that a battle was in progress and headed for us to evacuate the wounded. I was able to get most of my wounded from the trail into our perimeter and then fly them out," he recalled. "I called for artillery because my forward observer had come with us. He was able to provide a map and brought in fire from a 105mm howitzer battery at Plei Me Special Forces Camp, a few miles away.

"We established a strong perimeter and hunkered down. But during the night we began getting calls from Ghost 4-6. He said they had been ambushed, and there were several wounded, but he couldn't give us a count of the men he had there. These were not my men. All but one of mine were accounted for. Although this might have been an NVA trick, I decided we needed to get these guys. Ghost 4-6 said he could hear the enemy executing our wounded.

"By then, all of my wounded were medevaced out. My remaining officers were my weapons platoon leader, the second platoon leader, and the acting first sergeant. I decided I was going to take a detail and go to the ambush site and evacuate these guys. Then the acting first platoon leader, the platoon sergeant who had taken command, said, 'You can't go. You need to be here to command what's left of our company.' So we organized a rescue effort with my medic, Daniel Torres. They went out into the ambush site with three or four stretchers and enough men to carry them back. Maybe a squad plus. But when they got there and found the wounded men, the sergeant in charge radioed there were more wounded than stretchers, and some were so badly wounded they couldn't be moved.

"I told them to bring out as many as they could, and we would try to get the rest at first light. Torres, the medic, volunteered to remain with the wounded. He was armed only with a pistol. The stretcher-bearers brought back five or six men, and we provided whatever medical assistance we could to the others.

"In the meantime, my battalion commander sent Bravo Company from my battalion, commanded by Capt. Buse Tully, a cousin of the commander of 2/5 Cav. His men reinforced our perimeter, and we hunkered down for the night. The next day we retrieved the wounded, and shortly after that we were flown back to LZ Columbus."

When Forrest returned from Vietnam, he went back to Fort Benning, and for the next ten months attended the Infantry Officer Career Course. Then he was assigned to teach at the ROTC program at St. Norbert College in De Pere, Wisconsin. "I didn't want to go to an ROTC unit, but I took the assignment because Green Bay was about forty miles from De Pere, and with the assignment came a pair of Green Bay Packers season tickets.

"I was there during the glory years of the Packers. The first Super Bowl, the Ice Bowl where they beat Dallas in subfreezing weather—I was at that game. My family and I were the only African Americans north of Milwaukee. And being as big as I am, everybody I met in Green Bay assumed I played for the Packers. Every February, after the Super Bowl, all of the African Americans on the team went south. But I remained in Green Bay, and people would come up to me in grocery stores and ask, 'What are you still doing here?'

"My next assignment was back at the Old Guard as operations officer. Then I came out on the command list. I went to Leavenworth for the Command and General Staff College. I was promoted to lieutenant colonel. Then I went to Germany, where I commanded an infantry battalion. I was on a promotion list for O-6, a full colonel. But by then my mentor had left the army, and I was fed up with the military. In 1981, after twenty years of service, I retired.

"I'd had enough. I had four children. I had a son at Virginia Tech who was a good football player. I'd never seen him play high school ball because I was chasing the pipe dream of becoming the first African American chief of staff of the army."

Forrest was offered a position in Baltimore at his alma mater, Morgan State, as an academic advisor for the football team. In years past, Morgan State had been a football powerhouse, winning consistently and sending many of its star players to the NFL. "My old football coach was the athletic director. He offered me the academic advisor job; they were failing miserably at graduating. They also needed a defensive coordinator. I had some football experience, so I took the job," he said.

Forrest remained at Morgan State for nine years. "I established a mandatory study hall, and I developed a curriculum where players had mandatory hard classes. If you didn't go to class, you didn't play for me," he recalled. "We improved the graduation rate from 45 percent to about 90 percent. One of my success stories is Scott Dingle, one of my defensive backs. He's now a two-star general in the Army Medical Service Corps. He is only one of the many success stories I can tell about kids that I recognized had potential but, like me when I was growing up, were lazy and did not apply themselves."

Forrest lost his job because, despite his academic successes, "in nine years I think we won five games," he recalled. "In the overall scheme of things, I consider my nine years at Morgan State one of my most successful jobs.

"I retreated to the safest place I knew, and it kind of flashes back to Vietnam, the familiar surroundings. I went home to Leonardtown. Because of my father's name, I got a job teaching at a Catholic high school and coached basketball there. We had such an outstanding program at that school that one day the Leonardtown superintendent of schools called and said, 'How would you like to get a bump in salary and move to a job where you can impact African American kids in the public school system?' I took that job," he recalled.

"My father was an education pioneer. In Maryland's St. Mary's County, he was the first African American appointed superintendent of schools. He received an honorary doctorate from St. Mary's College of Maryland. His name got me a job. I was hired as principal of the school that was later named after him: Dr. James A. Forrest High School."

A few years later, one of Forrest's closest friends was elected county commissioner. "He asked if I wanted to help modernize the county government," Forrest recalled. "I became the deputy county administrator for St. Mary's County, the mother county of the State of Maryland and the state's smallest. The county administrator is the chief executive officer. He runs public safety, housing, highways, permits, anything that has to do with government. Two days after I took office as deputy administrator, the county administrator was fired. This was long before the #MeToo movement, but he got caught in that kind of inappropriate behavior.

"I became the county administrator. I held that job for nine years," Forrest continued, "under Democratic administrations. In 2007 the Republicans took over, and I was asked to leave.

"Being an active person, I wasn't ready to retire. I went to work for a defense contractor, ManTech International, specializing in training, with the title of executive management trainer. I trained the trainers in all the things

I learned at the Benning School for Boys. I began as a second lieutenant on up to a county administrator: marksmanship, leadership, strategic planning. I just translated it into a language civilians could understand."

It's been more than fifty years since Forrest led his company through the ambush at LZ Albany, but to him it's as fresh in his mind as yesterday. He still mourns the deaths of the seventeen men entrusted to his care who died that day, men whose names and hometowns he still remembers, men he loved almost as his own sons.

"I'm a spiritual man," Forrest explained. "I should be dead. My radio operators were killed, so how could they miss *me*? I'm over six feet tall, there are a bunch of antennas running behind me, we hadn't yet learned that we needed to take off our rank and insignia, and I'm sure the enemy had good marksmen, and so my revelation was that whoever the deity is, it had something better planned for me.

"I think all that came to fruition. I had the opportunity to impact the futures of a number of young men, most but not all of them African Americans. Guys whose lives would have gone another way had I not been there to guide them. At one of our veterans reunions, a kid came up to say that his father had been in my unit and that because of my actions, *his* father did *not* die. That kid is alive today only because of what I did. And this lightened the burden that all good commanders feel when they're responsible for deaths that are beyond their control."

MARSHALL
CARTER

Like the military, business organizations are usually hierarchical in structure.
Most businesses, however, exist to make a profit, while military organizations
have different goals. Many business executives define success by the size of their
salaries and their proximities to the summit of their organizations, while the
organization itself defines success by profits or the value of its stock. Military
organizations define success as mission accomplishment, whether the mission
is to seize terrain, evacuate civilians from a flood zone, erect a bridge across a
river, or destroy an enemy formation. The successful accomplishment of a mis-
sion validates the organization's existence. When a successful military officer
becomes a corporate executive, he or she will usually conform to their organi-
zation's goals and practices. Sometimes, however, the right military officer can
show a profit-driven organization how to prosper by adopting military mores.

His father was Marshall S. Carter, a West Pointer who rose to three-star
general after serving in the field artillery and subsequently became
deputy director of the CIA. Later he headed the National Security Agency.
His grandfather was Brig. Gen. Clifton C. Carter, also a West Pointer, who

retired from the army and then returned to teach at West Point for decades. So it was pretty much foreordained that Marshall N. Carter—Marsh to friends and colleagues—would also go to West Point.

But he wouldn't become an army officer.

"I didn't want to go in the family business," Carter explained. "I'd seen worthless lieutenants who people sort of carried along because their old man was a general." Whatever came Carter's way, he wanted to earn it, and he wanted it known that he had done so. "The Marine Corps didn't know or care where you came from," he said.

When he graduated in 1962, Carter ignored his father's advice about limited career prospects and took a commission in the Marine Corps. Four years later, after peacetime duty as an infantry platoon leader and company executive officer, Carter took command of a rifle company in Vietnam. His combat experiences were in many ways typical of his corps peers at that time. "In January 1967, I was a twenty-six-year-old captain commanding the 224 men of Company C, First Battalion, First Regiment, First Marine Division. We were near Da Nang. I had been in the field for four months and was relatively experienced in small-unit combat operations. In a rifle company—clearly the pointed end of the spear of American policy—there isn't a lot of strategic thinking. Our day-to-day tactical responsibilities, designed to achieve our military objectives, dictated our activities.

"Daily life was focused on continuous small patrols of fifteen to forty-five men with the mission of finding, killing, or capturing Viet Cong guerrillas. We would establish a base camp that could be defended by a third of our company, and the rest of the men would go on patrols. Or if it was rice harvest season, we would provide security for the farmers. We bathed from our helmets and ate combat rations that needed no cooking or heating. Every few days armored vehicles would resupply us with food, clothing, mail, ammunition, grenades, land mines, barbed wire, sandbags, and replacement parts for broken or damaged weapons.

"We were responsible for security in a roughly ten-square-mile district. We carried out all sorts of tasks, including providing medical care to villagers and backing up the local Vietnamese militia, police, and regular military forces. But our primary job was seeking out the Viet Cong. One key to our operations was mobility: we carried everything we needed on our backs.

"At the outset of 1967, it seemed to me the war was entering a dangerous new phase. We had begun encountering hardened NVA soldiers who had come down the Ho Chi Minh Trail. . . . Our challenge was multiplied. We faced local Viet Cong guerrillas who posed a substantial threat to civilians while remaining ready to engage in conventional infantry combat alongside North Vietnamese regular units. Ho Chi Minh's objective had always been to reunify his country, and he needed his regular army in South Vietnam to counter the aggressive tactics of the US and South Vietnamese forces.

"The escalation of the war became clear . . . when my company was assigned a mission outside our normal operating area—a raid on an enemy village and safe area that was to host a meeting of more than a hundred Viet Cong leaders. A few days before, an enemy courier had been killed in an ambush; his documents revealed the meeting was set for noon on January 14 in the village of Ban Lanh in Quang Nam Province.

"At noon on January 14, 176 of us loaded into twelve helicopters and headed for the designated area. All our helicopters received fire as we prepared to land and off-load troops. They remained under fire until they took off again."

While air strikes, helicopter gunships, and a smoke screen kept the enemy contained, "we fought our way into . . . a fortified village; each house had fighting positions and bunkers, and the village was protected by bamboo groves that restricted our movements.

"Even during the French Indochina War (1946–54), this area had been considered a communist stronghold. As we attacked and started taking casualties, it became apparent the enemy force was much larger than we expected; we needed to accomplish the mission and then be extracted rapidly. I recall observing mountains to the southwest; I knew the enemy had reinforcements there . . . outside of areas that had been marked . . . for pacification.

"All of us were impressed with the discipline, intensity, and aggressiveness of the enemy. A few weeks later we learned the area was defended not only by Viet Cong but also by large NVA units who, once they saw that only twelve helicopters had dropped troops off, began to reinforce the village. It was here that our marine training and precombat planning paid off—as junior leaders were wounded their corporals and sergeants took over without skipping a beat.

"Under heavy fire, around 4:00 p.m. we reached the meeting area, a Buddhist pagoda. Nearly all the Viet Cong leaders had fled. We knew we couldn't stay overnight, as we were short of ammunition and not in an area where we could be reinforced by other marine units. There was nothing to do but to regroup for extraction. We had suffered many casualties. . . . It took time to recover them. At one point, some of us had to crawl under enemy fire to recover a wounded marine.

"In the end, we killed more than fifty North Vietnamese fighters and captured one senior cadre member. As we called for helicopters to evacuate our thirty-two wounded and five dead marines, we needed air strikes to break contact with the enemy and to protect the helicopters.

"We still felt confident we could defeat the guerrillas and the North Vietnamese Army units. But it was also apparent not enough was being done by the government of South Vietnam to remove the causes of the insurgency or the conditions that had driven so many Vietnamese to want to live under communism. When I found time to think strategically, the nagging thought arose: *Yes, we can win on the battlefield, but is that enough to win the war?*"

For his heroism on that raid, Carter was awarded the Navy Cross, second only to the Medal of Honor as a measure of individual heroism.

"My best day in Vietnam," he recalled, "was a couple of weeks after the raid when somebody said to me, 'Do you know that your artillery forward observer, a second lieutenant, along with a lance corporal and a PFC, went to see your battalion commander and told him that since you were not going to tell him what happened out there, they would?'" This was a surprise to Carter. "I saw their statements perhaps ten years later, and I thought that they were probably as good a recommendation as you could ever have."

It was an open secret in Vietnam during much of the war that more than a few senior commanders had been decorated only because they ordered a staff officer to recommend them for a medal, when the commander's only accomplishment was to spend half an hour hovering over the battlefield while micromanaging a company commander below. Even more egregious examples of this were not unknown: a battalion commander was relieved after it was discovered he had colluded with one of his company commanders to shoot up his own jeep while on a quick trip to pick up laundry. The two then put each other in for medals.

That was *not* how Marsh Carter earned his Navy Cross. His citation reads as follows:

The President of the United States of America takes pleasure in presenting the Navy Cross to Captain Marshall Nichols Carter (MCSN: 0-85375),
United States Marine Corps, for extraordinary heroism while serving as
Commanding Officer, Company C, First Battalion, First Marines . . . during a heliborne raid against insurgent Viet Cong forces . . . on 14 January
1967. . . . During the withdrawal to the landing zone for re-embarkation,
one platoon was pinned down by rapidly increasing Viet Cong forces. . . .
Captain Carter moved immediately to the point of crisis. Efforts to evacuate the body of a fallen comrade under intense enemy fire prevented the
platoon from being withdrawn. With complete disregard for his personal
safety, Captain Carter exposed himself to the heavy volume of enemy fire
by crawling forward and bringing the fallen Marine to a point where he
could be further evacuated. Captain Carter then covered the withdrawal of
the platoon to the re-embarkation site by single-handedly hurling grenades
at the Viet Cong in close combat. Upon returning to the landing zone he
supervised the loading of his entire company into helicopters before he
himself would leave. Captain Carter's personal valor and professional excel-
lence assured the success of the operation. By his conspicuous gallantry
and heroic action in the face of great personal risk, Captain Carter reflected
great credit upon himself and upheld the highest traditions of the Marine
Corps and of the United States Naval Service.[1]

Upon completion of his Vietnam tour, Carter attended the navy postgraduate
school in Monterey, California. He served a second Vietnam tour as an advisor
to Vietnamese marines.

When the war ended in 1975, Major Carter requested a transfer to the
reserves. "I'd been overseas about fifty-five months of my first seven years of
marriage," he explained. "And I found it increasingly difficult dealing with
some of the higher-ups. The Marine Corps did not go through the classes
that the army did, led by General Schwarzkopf. They didn't go through an
internal catharsis and change themselves. But the corps didn't believe that
they had done anything wrong in Vietnam. I think that what hit the army in
the seventies (a thorough reexamination of their failures in Vietnam) didn't
hit the Marine Corps until the eighties. Both performed exceptionally well in
the 1991 Gulf War."

Fresh out of uniform and caught in the wave of anger and disrespect for the men and women who had served in Vietnam, Carter found it impossible to find a decent job in the private sector. He had a BS degree in civil engineering, an MS degree in systems analysis and operations research, and an MS degree in science, technology, and public policy. He spent a year on a State Department internship, and he sent out eighty-five résumés.

He received one response, which came from Chase Manhattan Bank. They offered him a job in the international financial planning and budgeting division. "I had no banking background," Carter recalled. "I had to ask someone the difference between a merchant bank, an investment bank, a commercial bank, and so forth. Coming right out of the military, Chase was a great company that gave me a chance to develop and grow."

The transition from marine to banker was not seamless. Carter was always older than his bosses. And some weren't sure what to make of an infantryman turned banker. "At staff meetings, a couple of my bosses seemed to act as though they were worried I might have a combat flashback and jump on the table," he said.

"Everything was okay until the Vietnam War movies started coming out. In 1978 there was *The Deer Hunter*, which had a scene about troops playing Russian roulette. I was asked if I'd ever seen anything like that. I wasn't sure how to respond, so I tried humor. I'd reply that we could never get revolvers and with a Colt .45 automatic, the odds against surviving go way, way up. And then I'd walk away and leave them scratching their heads.

"Even now, all these years later, people ask me about the war. 'How was that? Did you see this or that?' I answer truthfully. Yes, I carried an eighteen-year-old marine whose leg was blown off across a rice paddy. Yes, we had to keep some badly wounded guys overnight because two medevac helicopters were shot down, and over the long hours of darkness I had to watch their conditions deteriorate, but there was nothing we could do for them. Most people don't want to hear an answer like that. So it was quite a cultural change. I had lived in a foxhole or in the jungle for months at a time in Vietnam, and now I was in a place where second vice presidents worried about having a desk by the window. But there were quite a few at Chase who mentored me, taught me the big picture and also what I needed to focus on to do my job."

Two years after joining Chase, Carter became corporate budget director.

Three years after that, in 1981, he was promoted to product manager and then put in charge of the letter of credit division. In 1984, climbing the corporate ladder at a rapid pace, he was named corporate risk management executive. A year later he transferred to a new Chase acquisition, Lincoln First Bank in Rochester, New York, as the information and systems group executive. It was a culture shock.

"When I joined Chase there were not a lot of Vietnam veterans in the financial services industry on Wall Street. In New York City, many young people hadn't served in Vietnam. Many of them went to college, and it seemed like most of them had deferments. The Vietnam War was unpleasant for the American population. Many people seemed to blame the servicemen for it; we couldn't even get an interview. But Rochester felt more like the Midwest than the East. Heck, everybody was a veteran."

Carter now teaches a course on the Vietnam War at the Naval War College twice a year. "My students are all navy four-stripers or army and marine colonels. Most are between fifty and fifty-four years old—they were children during the war. When I tell them how the draft worked, they roll on the floor in laughter. I said, 'If your draft number came up and you took the armed forces qualification test, you only needed fifteen points to pass. Part of that test was pictures: a claw hammer and then a railroad spike, a thumbtack, and a nail. And then a picture of a submarine with a glacier, a fishbowl, and the ocean. You had to match them up. This was the test that MIT and Harvard students were flunking on purpose."

Carter was at Chase for fifteen years. In 1991, he was invited to become the president and COO of State Street Bank and Trust in Boston. Within months he rose to CEO and chairman of the board. "I think what helped me in the corporate world was that, while I was at Chase, I spent a lot of time training the people below me and making sure they were competent in their jobs," he recalled. "That was fairly unusual at big corporations. The corporate world is mostly about individual achievement; the military is mostly about unit achievement. Where I served at the company level and a little above that, people supported each other. You don't necessarily have that in the corporate world. I always tried to avoid playing the politics of the corporation and focused on having my organization accomplish its mission. And that meant ensuring everyone knew how to do their job."

At Chase, Carter acquired a reputation for acting decisively. On his way up the Chase ladder, he was three times assigned to lead corporate units that were underperforming or failing in their particular missions. The executive in charge was fired and Carter took over the unit. He didn't come into each new job understanding its intricacies and nuances, but he understood how to get the most out of his employees.

"On the seventeenth floor of Chase Plaza, the carpet was about four inches thick," he recalled. "It was deathly quiet. Everybody had their own little office with their own little bathroom, and they believed what they told each other. When I became CEO of State Street, I emptied out the executive floor. The only people who remained were me and my secretary. Everybody from the CFO, with his accounting and numbers nerds, and down the line moved his office downstairs with their units. Then they and I would go out and visit them. Walk around and let the troops see us. Ask us questions. Share their problems. Until then, the supervisors had been isolated from what their units were doing. They were out of touch with the markets they served."

Marsh Carter remained with State Street Bank until he retired almost ten years later. In an industry often plagued by self-interest and public distrust, he had maintained the values instilled in him as a young West Point cadet and subsequently in the Marine Corps. He left State Street with a sterling reputation as an honest, fair, and ethical leader.

In 2003, an ethical crisis emerged at the New York Stock Exchange when it was revealed the longtime chairman of the exchange had been paid over $140 million, all of it from the companies he was charged with supervising: the brokerage houses and banks that traded securities on the big board.

Carter was one of six experienced banking executives called out of retirement to form a new board of directors. In 2005, he was unanimously elected chairman, a position he held until his final retirement in 2013. Today, he lectures at MIT and Harvard as well as at the Naval War College and relaxes by flying a seaplane.

"I was proud to serve in the marines in Vietnam, and I believed in our mission," he said. "I went on to a thirty-five-year career in the financial sector, including positions as the chief executive of a Fortune 500 company and the chair of the New York Stock Exchange Group. But I never felt I had as much responsibility as being the commander of the 224 marines of C Company, who put their faith in my leadership abilities and entrusted me with their lives."

MARY
STOUT

Army wives are the nation's unsung heroines, the glue that holds military families together through constant relocation from one duty station to another. They look after family finances and the education of their children while maintaining a comfortable home, despite decades of the hardships imposed by military service. The result is that when their spouses retire from military service, these women have developed a remarkable and useful skill set: the ability to adapt to constant change.

Mary Stout had a cousin named Sharon. "She was a couple of years older than me. In high school, she took secretarial courses, so after graduation, she got a job right away. Within about six months she moved into an apartment with some girlfriends. I was a sophomore or junior in high school and one night, during dinner, I mentioned Sharon was living on her own. My father almost exploded with anger at his brother Johnny for allowing her to go. He looked at me and said, 'Don't you ever think you're leaving this house until you get married.'"

Mary loved her parents and her two older brothers, but she was almost desperate to get out from under her father's roof, get out of Columbus, Ohio, and see what the world held for her. Her ticket out was Mount Carmel College of Nursing, only a few miles from home, but with a mandatory campus residence. She began classes there in 1962, when Vietnam was still a blip on the edge of the national radar screen. Her next move, over her father's strenuous objections, was to join the Army Nurse Corps. She graduated from nursing school in 1965 with a diploma and a second lieutenant's commission.

After officer training at Fort Sam Houston in San Antonio, Texas, Mary signed in at Fort Ord, California, a basic training center. She was assigned to the pediatric ward in the base hospital. After work, she hung out with Carl, a recent Artillery OCS graduate, who was serving as a training officer. The attraction was immediate and mutual. They made plans to marry. Then Carl received orders for Vietnam. Although she had less than a year of her service commitment remaining, Mary volunteered for Vietnam.

She was at An Khe and Chu Lai while he was at Pleiku and points north. They stayed in touch over hoot-and-holler tactical phone circuits and saw each other a few times. At the Second Surgical Hospital, she worked in several departments, including the intensive care unit. She also performed the heartrending duty of a triage nurse, deciding which men would not survive even with the doctors' best efforts, which could wait for treatment, and which needed immediate attention.

One of her ICU patients was Steve. "He was in pretty bad shape," Mary recalled. "I came on at 7:00 p.m. and the nurse coming off shift reported he was doing poorly and said, 'We've called his doctor up here twice. The last time, he said don't call me again.'

"A little later Major Natcher, the hospital commander, came in. It seemed almost every time Natcher was in intensive care, some patient's condition became worse. And that night, when I was worried about Steve, Natcher came to the ICU and walked up to Steve's bed. Soon his condition took a turn for the worse. He'd had a tracheotomy to help his breathing and suffered from an aggressive infection. We were giving him medication, but shortly after Natcher arrived, Steve went into cardiac arrest. We tried CPR and everything else we could do, but he died. Before he left the unit, Natcher turned to me and said, 'This is your fault,' and left.

"The next morning, I got up at seven. I was off until the following day. I had a bottle of whiskey I was going to take to Carl the next time I saw him. I decided to drink the whole bottle at once. I knew it might kill me, but I didn't care. But before I could open the bottle, there was a knock on the door." It was Joey Myers, Carl's battery commander.

"I just wanted to stop by and introduce myself," he said, "and let you know that anytime you can come out to the battery, you're certainly welcome."

"When are you going back?" Mary asked.

"I have to catch a helicopter now."

"I'm coming with you," she said, grabbed her wet gear and steel helmet, and went to see Carl.

"I didn't tell him about Steve. I didn't tell him about Natcher. I just spent the few hours we could be together being together," Mary recalled.

"When I returned to the hospital, I went to the club. I didn't start work until seven o'clock the next morning, and I had found that a few boilermakers helped to dial back the adrenaline," she said. "I sat alone at the officer's club bar, sipping my boilermaker, when Major Natcher walked up. 'It's nice to see that you can have a good time after you killed somebody last night,' he said."

The Second Surgical Hospital was then at Chu Lai, on a coastal height above a beach. "I left my drink and walked out of the club and down the road straight into the ocean," she recalled. "To this day I don't know who it was. If I said it was Steve, you'd say I was crazy, but that was my thought at the time. Whoever it was pulled me out and held me while I cried for I don't know how long. I sat on the sand, and this soldier held me and let me cry, didn't say anything until I stopped, walked back up the hill, and went to my hooch.

"Many years later, I concluded for each of us who served in Vietnam, there was one person I call the epitome of the tragedy. One person who sticks with you. That one person you just can't really ever get over. I've talked to other people and they've usually agreed. For my husband, it was a radiotelephone operator who was killed. For me, it was Steve."

Mary's last day in the army was a nightmare. She reported to Fort Lewis for discharge processing and like everyone else was required to take a physical. "We arrived on a cold, rainy November morning. I wore my summer green uniform. My raincoat had rotted away in Vietnam, so I was wet and freezing," she recalled. "They set us up with several appointments: dental, eye, ear, nose and throat, ortho. Everything. I was also required to have a gynecology appointment. The clerk said I would have to wait three days before a doctor could see me.

"But I had a plane to catch that evening. I just lost it. What do you mean *three* days? All the *men* will leave *today*. Why do I have to wait three days?"

The clerk called a sympathetic officer in the inspector general's office, and after a short while, a gynecologist agreed to see her immediately. The clinic's waiting room overflowed with pregnant military dependents. A colonel appeared and angrily told her that he had decreed she would have to wait three days. He disappeared in search of an answer to why she had presented herself in his clinic. "Then another doctor arrived and had me follow him down a very long hallway to an exam room as far from the office as we could get," she recalled. "He examined me, signed my paperwork, and sent me out the back door to finish my discharge processing."

A civilian again, Mary flew back to Ohio and her family. But the war had changed her. "My God, I didn't even want to see my friends," she lamented. "I felt like I was twenty years older than them. The things they cared about and talked about were absolutely not mine. I no longer fit in. I couldn't wait to get back in the army, because I thought I'd fit in there. I'd feel okay. I'd be with people who know what this is about. I didn't even recognize myself. I couldn't wait to get back with Carl and to be back on an army base."

Mary joined Carl in San Pedro, a Los Angeles suburb next to Fort MacArthur, where he commanded a company whose mission was processing and discharging troops returning from Vietnam. They married at Fort MacArthur. In their first two years of marriage, Mary bore first a daughter and then twin daughters, three little girls in the span of a year and a day. "We decided three was enough," she recalled.

Mary Stout put her nursing career behind her and gladly joined the hard-scrabble sorority of army wives. Over the years of Carl's career, she took on volunteer projects, taught health classes in military clinics, headed a community childcare center, and taught skiing in army winter-survival courses.

During Carl's twenty-three years in uniform, the Stouts reported for duty all over the world, including Germany, Oklahoma, Kansas, South Korea, California, Maryland, the Pentagon, and West Point, where Carl taught cadets.

Early in their marriage, they spent two years in Kansas, where Carl completed his bachelor's at Wichita State. It was a time when military units were targeted by antiwar protesters. "I was really afraid," Mary said. "I heard stories about people having their houses firebombed." Before his first class, Mary told Carl, "Don't you dare tell anybody you're in the army."

At first, Mary watched the children in the morning while he was in class, and he came home to be with them while she took afternoon classes. "After about two months, Carl said he couldn't handle the double duty," Mary recalled. She dropped out of school. Years later, when Carl was attending the Command and General Staff College at Fort Leavenworth and their children were all in school, she attended St. Mary's College in Lansing for a year.

A few years later, they were posted to Columbus, Ohio, where Carl studied for his master's. Mary enrolled in Ohio Dominican, which accepted her nursing school credits. She earned a bachelor's in social welfare in eighteen months. Then, with a little free time each day, Mary looked for something to do. She found a part-time position with the USO. Then Carl graduated, and they went to West Point, where Carl taught for three years.

"While we were at West Point, the Iran hostages came there," Mary recalled. "That was a difficult time for many Vietnam veterans, because of all the hoopla about the hostages coming home. There was nothing like that when we Vietnam veterans came home.

"On the day the hostages left West Point, the post was closed so that reporters couldn't get in," she continued. "The hostages were bused to Stewart Air Force Base to be flown to Washington, DC. Almost the entire community lined the road out of the Academy to honor those people and to let them know they hadn't been forgotten and that people cared about them.

"But it was also a pain in my heart for me and my forgotten comrades in arms. We never saw anything like that. I hid my Vietnam service for years. I told Carl not to tell anyone that I had been in the army or served in Vietnam. I didn't want to deal with that. When we went to parties, and guys who served in Vietnam sat around telling war stories, I'd listen and never say a word."

While Carl was in Korea for a year, Mary and the children returned to Columbus. "Here I was, alone," she recalled. "I was faced with the full responsibility of a house, a car, kids—and all I could think about was Vietnam.

"I wasn't sleeping well. I had strange dreams. One of the things we now know about PTSD is that it kind of mounts you. I developed sensitivities about the war: missions and memories. I found myself sitting at the kitchen table, trying to write checks for our bills, but thinking about Vietnam.

"I was taking a psychology course then. I told my instructor what was happening to me. He had not a clue. Not a clue."

One afternoon Mary went to the movies and watched *Patton*, a biopic about Gen. George S. Patton. There is a scene where the general walks into a field hospital. Suddenly Mary was back in the Second Surgical Hospital. "It was the most incredible thing," she recalled. "I can't explain it, but I was no longer in a movie theater. For just an instant, I was in that hospital in Vietnam with all the sights and sounds and smells. I burst into tears, just sobbing in a darkened theater."

Around that time, Mary got back in touch with the USO. The executive director remembered her and asked her to rejoin the board. "I had a great time when I worked with them before," she recalled.

Every Memorial Day, the USO sold tickets to one of the city's minor league baseball games. The USO received a portion of the ticket price and distributed a program recognizing USO people at the ballpark. They also sold advertising for the program.

"We went to talk to some of the veterans' services organization and asked them to sell tickets for the USO and get some of their people to come out to the ballpark so their organizations could be recognized." Her pitch to leaders of the local VFW and American Legion chapters was well received. They suggested perhaps the AmVets and the Disabled American Veterans would be interested as well. Then Mary asked if anyone knew someone in a Vietnam veterans' organization.

"I asked the VFW guy about that because the group might help the USO sell tickets. But I also wanted to see if there were Vietnam veterans around to help me deal with whatever this stuff was that I was going through.

"The VFW post commander said, 'No, they're a bunch of radicals. We don't want them involved.' The hair on the back of my neck stood up. I was taken aback. The USO director, Jim, was a Vietnam veteran, and he asked, 'What do you mean a bunch of radicals?' The VFW leader replied, 'They had a state meeting, and they came here and borrowed our tables.' I thought, *Gee, real radicals*.

"Jim had a number for the Vietnam veterans," Mary continued. She called the Vietnam Veterans of Columbus and spoke to Parker Lee Hargrove. "I explained who I was and what the USO was doing, and he said, 'When did you serve in Vietnam?' I have no idea how he knew. Sitting on my kitchen floor, I was stunned, because nobody had ever asked me that. Even when I came home from Vietnam and saw friends, people I had grown up with, they asked, 'What have you been doing?' The people who did know, particularly guys, asked questions like, 'Do you think we ought to be there?' I'd been back only a week, and I was just stunned."

Less than an hour after speaking to Hargrove, she walked into his office in what had been a car showroom in one of the city's poorest neighborhoods. On the wall was a big map of Vietnam. "People put pins in the map to mark where they had served. On the walls were pictures of people in Vietnam," she recalled.

From this office the VVA ran a jobs program. A meeting was in progress. "Members wore orange T-shirts because they were working with a state legislator to get an Agent Orange study in Ohio. The shirts said 'Vietnam Veteran, a Right to Be Proud.' I realized instantly this was what I'd been missing: I'd never been able to take pride in my service, to say that I did something good. I never talked about it. I didn't think about it in that way. But here was an organization that told me I have the right to be proud."

From these men, Mary learned about PTSD and that what she was experiencing was a normal reaction. "If you've gone through traumatic situations and you don't have some kind of reaction, some painful memories—things like that—then you're probably not normal. How do you start working through that? The VVA was maybe a lifesaver. It was a place I wanted to be. I wanted to be with those people because I felt at home again. I didn't have to talk about what I did in Vietnam or where I served. And they were thrilled to have a woman Vietnam vet. I was the first in the chapter. Carl was still in Korea. I wasn't working, and my girls were in school. I joined the VVA and asked what I could do to help out."

Mary worked in the office and got her hands dirty. She saved the chapter a little money by putting their mailing lists in zip code order. She pitched in wherever needed. For the first time in years, she was feeling good about herself and her service.

This was a critical time for the VVA in Ohio. The several chapters around the state collectively lobbied the legislature to be recognized as a veterans' service organization that helped veterans navigate the VA red-tape labyrinth and get their deserved benefits. That brought state funding and an office in the state office building. "They were looking for someone to run the office," Mary recalled. "So I applied for the job.

"I went to the state council meeting, and they were discussing this. There were several applicants. The Columbus guys were kind of talking me up, and many on the state council liked my résumé. One said, 'I think she's very qualified to do this, but don't you think we ought to have a Vietnam veteran?' About fifteen people jumped down his throat. My DD-214 [military discharge document] was part of my résumé, and it showed I had served in Vietnam."

Mary got the job and held it until Carl returned from Korea. After a six-month course at Fort Ord, they went on to their next duty station at Aberdeen Proving Ground in Maryland.

For a long time after she got back from the war, Mary had defended America's involvement in Vietnam. "It *had* to be right for us to be there, because I was there and my husband was there," she reasoned. Gradually her views changed. She began reading about Vietnam, especially about its history and politics. She spoke with her VVA brothers and sisters. Today, she believes "we had all those wonderful military and diplomatic minds, and they blew it." This conclusion is not in conflict with the mainstream of the only federally chartered organization devoted exclusively to the issues of Vietnam veterans.

By the late seventies and early eighties, no issue was as important to Vietnam Veterans and the VVA's national leadership as the host of serious medical issues arising from the effects of exposure to Agent Orange, a defoliant that had been sprayed over millions of acres of South Vietnam. Within a few years after the war ended in 1975, veterans began seeking VA health-care treatment for diseases that were rare in relatively young adults, such as Hodgkin's disease, malignant lymphoma, ischemic heart disease, multiple myeloma, non-Hodgkin's lymphoma, Parkinson's disease, early onset peripheral neuropathy, porphyria cutanea tarda, and children born with birth defects. The Veterans Administration (now Veterans Affairs) did not recognize any of these conditions as service connected.

Four years after joining VVA, Mary Stout was elected national secretary. Among her projects was doing something about Agent Orange. Two years after becoming national secretary, on August 2, 1987, Mary Stout, then forty-three and living in Arlington, Virginia (Carl was stationed at the Pentagon), was elected president of the Vietnam Veterans of America.

Mary Stout's election to VVA national president inspired widespread press interest. She did countless radio, television, and print interviews. "I had lots of opportunities to talk about Agent Orange and other issues facing Vietnam veterans," she recalled. This was a time when other veterans groups offered no support for Agent Orange legislation, and the VA refused to accept veterans' questions about it. VA doctors would not even discuss the possibility that any of the conditions a veteran suffered were associated with exposure to Agent Orange.

"Before we began working on this, Vietnam veterans had been stonewalled by the federal government," Mary recalled. "Congress would not allow our scientists to testify about their findings at congressional hearings or at committee meetings. It seemed to most of us in the Vietnam veteran community that the US government was ready to wait until the whole army that served their nation in Vietnam had died."

The VVA worked with scientists to determine that the cause of all these conditions was exposure to dioxin, a carcinogen created as a by-product of the manufacture of Agent Orange. In 1983, they learned the town of Times Beach, Missouri, population two thousand, had been thoroughly contaminated with dioxin. The federal and state governments bought all the property and evacuated the residents. If dioxin was too dangerous for the residents of a small Missouri town to come into contact with, why wasn't it too dangerous for the troops who had served in Vietnam?

Even after science proved that exposure to dioxin was linked to birth defects and many unusual forms of cancer, the VA refused to acknowledge that Agent Orange was responsible for any of the diseases suffered by thousands of Vietnam veterans. Many of these afflictions were ultimately fatal. Others caused the afflicted to be unable to work and support themselves and led to early deaths. The only step the VA took was to record each rejected claim.

The VA was part of the executive branch, led by the president. But its funds came from Congress. Many in Congress seemed unwilling to recognize the effects of Agent Orange exposure simply because they didn't want to spend the billions required to compensate and treat the hundreds of thousands who had served in an unpopular war.

The long and complicated story of how Mary Stout and the VVA leadership, over several years, were able to convince key members of the VA and Congress that Agent Orange and its horrific effect on Vietnam veterans required both monetary compensation and urgent medical attention in VA hospitals is a tortured tale that has been told in detail elsewhere. In summary, it was only through years of selfless efforts by Mary and a handful of her VVA colleagues that key figures in the Washington establishment came to understand the depth of the agonies that huge numbers of Vietnam veterans suffered as a result of exposure to Agent Orange and that the VA must do whatever possible to help these men and women.

Nearly a million Agent Orange veterans have so far entered the VA health system for care. Many receive disability compensation. Each should be grateful that a stubborn army wife, defiantly proud of her Vietnam service, refused to give up the fight until all her brothers and sisters—a now ailing army once sent to win an unwinnable war—found justice for their exposure to a nightmarish chemical.

MAX CLELAND

Losing a limb, whether in a peacetime accident or a wartime event, is a trau-matic event, one that goes beyond the obvious difficulties arising from having only one leg or one arm. The challenge of daily functioning can seem over-whelming. But Max Cleland is not an ordinary man. Possessed of an indom-itable will, he found ways to continue to serve his country with only one arm and no legs, setting an example for both the disabled and everyone else.

I had what General Patton used to call the valor of ignorance," Max Cleland said. "I volunteered to go into Khe Sanh. I thought that would be the quin-tessential battle of the war. And I thought that if we won, the war would be shut down. If we lost, the war would continue."

In March 1968, thousands of US Marines at Khe Sanh were besieged by a far larger, well-armed, and aggressive North Vietnamese Army force. The NVA suffered horrendous losses from repeated B-52 strikes but held on nevertheless.

"I thought Khe Sanh would be either an American Dien Bien Phu [the climactic battle that defeated French forces during their Indochina War] or else we would prevail," Cleland continued. "I wanted to be part of the rescue force, and so I wanted to prevail.

"I volunteered to leave the division signal battalion and go down to an infantry battalion, the Second of the Twelfth Cav, commanded by Lt. Col. Dick Sweet," he said. "On April 1, the entire division, led by its Third Brigade, lifted off from its base camp at Camp Evans, just north of Hue, for Operation Pegasus. The division moved to LZ Stud, north of Ca Lu in Quang Tri Province.

"There was more than a horse's patootie hanging out there in reinforcing the marines at Khe Sanh. It was the whole reputation of the United States," Cleland continued. "President Johnson had said, 'I don't want no damn Dien Bien Phu at Khe Sanh.' So all heaven and earth were moved to save Khe Sanh. I mean, B-52 strikes were part of our tactical air support. We lifted off on the second day of April; the third night was spent at LZ Stud; and then we landed at Khe Sanh on the night of April 4, which was the same day when Martin Luther King Jr. was assassinated. But *we* were the story." The cream of the Vietnam press corps had rushed to Khe Sanh. "Even Maj. Gen. John J. Tolson, the First Cavalry Division commander, was there.

"On or about April 6 or 7, our battalion was ordered to move into the Khe Sanh perimeter," Cleland related. Almost immediately, "That's where I damn near got killed," he continued. "One of those 122mm rockets landed directly on a bunker with four guys in it, and they all got killed. Had one of them landed on me, I'd be dead. Overall, we lost about two hundred people in the entire relief of the siege of Khe Sanh."

When the battalion command post came under heavy enemy rocket and mortar fire, Cleland left his covered position, exposing himself to the horrific barrage to administer first aid to some wounded cavalrymen. He then helped to move these men to safety. Still under fire, Cleland organized his men into a work party to repair the communications equipment damaged by enemy fire. For this, he was awarded the Silver Star.

"On April 8, a significant day in my life," Cleland said, "the sun came up, as the poet Kipling wrote, 'like thunder out of China 'cross the bay.'" That day, Maj. Maury Cralle, the battalion operations officer, told Cleland he needed a radio relay site at LZ Stud to connect the battalion headquarters at Khe Sanh with the First Cavalry Division's logistical base at Camp Evans. "I was the battalion signal officer," Cleland explained. "I thought it was my responsibility, so I volunteered to get on the chopper with a small group of men and some radio gear and fly back to LZ Stud."

Cleland had less than a month left on his tour in Vietnam. The trip to LZ Stud took a few minutes. "When I got off the helicopter at Stud, I turned around and saw a grenade on the ground." Clutching his M-16 rifle in his left hand, he reached for the grenade with his right. And the grenade exploded.

"I should be dead," Cleland opined. "It was an American grenade, and they have a killing radius of five meters. I was medevaced within a few minutes to the division aid station, and then helicoptered over to the South China Sea, to the Thirty-Eighth Medical Battalion, to a surgery, where five doctors operated on me and gave me fifty-three pints of blood over a five-hour period and saved my life."

Cleland lost his right arm just below the elbow and both legs below the knee.

Max Cleland had been born in Atlanta in 1942 into a family whose Georgia roots run back a century or more. His father was a navy enlisted man stationed at Pearl Harbor after the December 1941 attack. After high school, Cleland enrolled in Stetson University in DeLand, Florida. "We were all subject to the draft, and for those of us who were young in the fall of 1960, if you were in college, the choice was to go in the military as a draftee and probably remain an enlisted man or go to officer training while in college. I joined Stetson's ROTC program and completed a four-year program. I was commissioned on June 1, 1964, the day I graduated.

"Then I received a deferment to go to graduate school for one year and get my master's in American history," he continued. "I went on active duty on October 18, 1965. I went into the Signal Corps, and while I was at Fort Gordon, Georgia, in the Signal Corps basic course, the Battle of Ia Drang was going on. Led by the First Air Cavalry's Hal Moore, the Seventh Cavalry was making history. Foolish young man that I was, I thought, *Damn, I need to be over there.*"

Cleland completed airborne training and volunteered for Vietnam in 1966. "But then I went to microwave radio school at Fort Monmouth, New

Jersey, and was selected to be a general's aide," he explained. It is the sort of assignment that can't be refused. "The general canceled my orders to go to Vietnam," Cleland continued, "and I remained at Fort Monmouth for a year."

In the spring of 1967, Cleland volunteered for the First Air Cavalry division and went to Vietnam. Then a first lieutenant, he was assigned to the First Cavalry's Thirteenth Signal Battalion. The battalion supported the First Cav's many infantry, artillery, aviation, and engineer units in the field. "I worked for the division signal officer. I ran a platoon that had teams scattered all over South Vietnam," he recalled.

In late 1967 the enemy began to reinforce the northern part of South Vietnam. "I knew our division would ultimately be going north, so when we did, I thought this would be the end of the war. We got up there and got our butts kicked by NVA divisions that came south from the DMZ," he explained. "The Cav was set as a blocking force, north of Hue, and then moved to Camp Evans, a marine base. We did without supplies, we did without JP4 jet fuel, and we got our butts kicked again.

"Although we liberated and took over Khe Sanh, much to my chagrin, it was plowed up by the American military within a week," Cleland recalled. "It was like it didn't matter at all. All those lives lost. It just didn't matter. That has fed my cynicism about Vietnam and ultimately my conclusion that it was just all a waste."

—◇—

Cleland was treated at Walter Reed National Military Medical Center for eight months. "Classified as a long-term case, I was shipped off to the Washington, DC, VA hospital," he remembered. "I thought the Washington, DC, hospital would be first-class, because it was near Washington. I was sadly mistaken.

"I kept fighting for a set of limbs. I came out of Walter Reed with stubbies—World War II technology made from balsa wood," he recounted. He remained in the Veterans Administration system for a year until he was sent to the VA prosthetic center in New York, where he finally received a set of artificial limbs.

Afterward, Cleland went home to Lithonia, Georgia. "There was nobody willing to hire me. In early 1970, I sat in my parents' living room and took stock," he recalled. "I thought, *Well, Cleland, you got no girlfriend, no money, no car, no job, and no future. Now's a great time to run for the state senate.*"

He won that first race and became the youngest member of the Georgia State Senate. He campaigned while using his artificial limbs, but he found them so heavy and cumbersome that before midday he was almost totally exhausted. With mixed feelings, he moved to a motorized wheelchair.

The election that brought Cleland to the Georgia Senate propelled Jimmy Carter into the governor's mansion. "We became dear, close friends," Cleland remembered. He ran for lieutenant governor in 1974 and lost. California senator Alan Cranston hired him as a staffer on the Senate Committee on Veterans Affairs in Washington.

In 1976, Carter was elected president. "I got this call from White House chief of staff Hamilton Jordan, who said Carter wanted a Vietnam veteran to head the Veterans Administration." On March 2, 1977, Cleland was sworn in to that position. "The biggest thing I had ever run up to that point was a platoon," he recalled. "The VA was the second-largest agency in the entire federal government; I think it had 230,000 employees. It was unbelievable."

Cleland spent his first few months trying to grasp what the VA was doing, what its focus was, what it did well, and where it needed to improve. "It had no focus on Vietnam veterans at all," he recalled. "It was 1978 before VA psychiatrists agreed there was something called post-traumatic stress disorder," he continued, still peeved. "VA doctors did not agree that Agent Orange was a problem. Nevertheless, I created an Agent Orange registry so that if exposure to Agent Orange was later found to be responsible for damage to veterans' health, individual veteran's claims could be backdated to when they were reported.

"I'm most proud of becoming the first administrator to support the Vet Center Program," he said. Senator Cranston pushed through the legislation and President Carter supported the Veterans' Readjustment Counseling Program. It established places where veterans could go without being diagnosed as a psychiatric case, without the associated stigma. It was for those who suffered from PTSD, the aftermath of war, both for veterans and their families. "Veterans were so angry at the VA in the late seventies that we had to disguise our vet centers. There was nothing that said the VA in these storefront centers, but it was all paid for by the VA.

"We began in California. By 1980, we had fifteen vet centers around the nation," he continued. "Now we have three hundred centers and sixteen hundred counselors; 40 percent of them served in the Afghanistan and Iraq Wars—a new generation of counselors and team leaders who help deal with the trauma of more recent wars."

Despite these accomplishments, Cleland is disappointed it took him so long to move the legislation to set up the vet centers. "I couldn't get the focus on the Vietnam veterans fast enough. I just couldn't move this huge agency fast enough."

In 1946, Gen. Omar Bradley, one of the great heroes of World War II, took over the VA. "Bradley did a hell of a job," Cleland said, "but the people he hired, who stayed after he left, became known as the Class of '46." These men became the upper crust of the VA. Their departments, hospitals, and other organizations became ossified bureaucracies whose primary objective was protecting their individual fiefdoms from anything that could threaten their existence. "You couldn't hardly get anything new past them," Cleland recalled.

Throughout Cleland's tenure, the VA was severely underfunded. "About 1970 *Life* magazine ran an article that showed the Bronx VA hospital with rats running around it. There was such a hue and cry that Senator William Proxmire of Wisconsin pushed legislation through to get forty thousand more staff in the VA health-care system. I get there in time to implement that, to upgrade the VA health-care system dramatically and to focus on the Vietnam veterans. The VA is still in my heart," Cleland concluded. "I wish them well."

After his term at the VA expired, Cleland went home to Georgia and ran for secretary of state. He served three consecutive terms in that office, and in 1997 he was elected to the US Senate. He ran for reelection in 2003, just two years after Georgia had changed its state flag to remove the Confederate Battle Flag that had been added in 1956. A 2000 Georgia Senate report described the adoption of the 1956 flag as a symbol of racist protest, citing legislation passed in 1956 that rejected the landmark *Brown v. Board of Education* Supreme Court decision that held segregated schools unconstitutional, along with pro-segregation comments by Georgia governor Marvin Griffin.

In 2003, Georgia Republicans stirred new opposition to the 2001 flag by rural whites who competed with black Georgians for jobs, causing them to vote in record numbers. But by this time, national politics had become a blood sport. Cleland was leading in the polls when his opponent, Saxby Chambliss, scion of a family long instrumental in Georgia politics, began running ads and making speeches impugning Cleland's patriotism. Chambliss had never served in the military.

In 2001, Cleland had voted for the original Patriot Act that followed the attacks on the World Trade Center. He later voted against amendments that allowed the government to spy on American citizens without obtaining a court order. Cleland angered Republicans by criticizing President George W. Bush and Vice President Richard Cheney because neither had served in Vietnam, but after the terrorist attacks of September 11, both sought to invade Iraq for what Cleland saw as specious reasons.

Chambliss's campaign ran television ads that implied that Cleland had deliberately injured himself in order to leave Vietnam before the end of his tour. It also cited his votes against reauthorizing components of the Patriot Act as the basis of other ads that equated him with Saddam Hussein and Osama bin Laden. Republican Senator John McCain, himself a Vietnam veteran and POW, called the ads "worse than disgraceful" and "reprehensible."

Cleland lost his seat. He plunged into a depression far more severe than he had suffered after losing his limbs. He returned to Walter Reed Hospital, where he was diagnosed with post-traumatic stress disorder.

"It was the worst period in my life," Cleland said. "When I went back to Walter Reed thirty-five years after the war, I realized that this time I had to repair my mind and my soul and my psyche. Walter Reed is really the best in the business. Their doctors understand post-traumatic stress disorder and the things that can follow: the depression, the extent to which life can go black."

After his long, slow recovery, Cleland wrote a memoir titled *Heart of a Patriot*.[1] "It was a form of therapy. I wrote the book for myself, and if anybody coming from Iraq and Afghanistan reads it and it helps save their life, then it will be worthwhile. It was therapeutic to go back over and over and over all of this stuff and try to make sense of it. Ultimately, I came to believe that life itself is an act of faith. A book written by Hal Moore's driver Toby Warren, titled *A General's Spiritual Journey*, quotes Patrick Overton: 'When you come to the edge of all the light you have and must take a step into the darkness of the unknown, believe that one of two things will happen. Either there will be something solid for you to stand on or you will be taught how to fly.' That's the most powerful statement of faith I've ever heard."[2]

In June 2009, Max Cleland was alongside President Barack Obama in Normandy, France, to commemorate the sixty-fifth anniversary of D-day. A few days earlier, the president had appointed Cleland as the secretary of the American Battle Monuments Commission, charged with overseeing the cemeteries and memorials around the world that honor the US soldiers who died in battle.

Thirty years after Cleland lost three limbs, David Lloyd, a marine who had witnessed the incident and used his web belt for a tourniquet on Cleland's leg, told Cleland the grenade he had picked up "had been dropped by a soldier new to the combat zone who did not know how to handle grenades. He did not know to tape the handles down or bend the fuse pins to keep them from falling out. He was a walking time bomb who had pulled all the pins on the grenades hanging from his web gear. One dropped off as he got off the chopper." Lloyd reported the unnamed soldier was crying. "It was mine," he said. "It was my grenade."

Despite a life of hard knocks, Cleland has swallowed his bitterness. "I have this mission to make sure the twenty-four US military cemeteries worldwide properly memorialize our troops. That job pays the bills. Second, it gives me a sense of place and purpose I didn't have before. I'm not born to be a consultant. I'm not born to be a lobbyist. I'm not born to be in the private sector. With public service comes a lot of good things. Memorializing those who gave everything they had touches me deeply."

RICHARD ARMITAGE

Among the legions of Americans who served as advisors to the South Vietnamese military, none went further to blend in with his hosts than Richard Armitage. None was more dedicated to helping the Vietnamese succeed. And surely none was more disappointed, more angry, more embarrassed when America threw in the towel and left its former ally to fend for itself without even fuel for its vehicles or ammunition. Unlike his nation, however, Dick Armitage never gave up.

Dick Armitage was captain of the football team at Atlanta's St. Pius X Catholic High School, and during his senior year he was starting to think about college. He wasn't much concerned about military service. This was the peacetime year of 1962, and college students with satisfactory grades were granted automatic deferments. "I was looking around to see what the hell I was going to do for college. And I was looking for scholarships. I had a couple of schools that were interested in me," he recalled.

One day his father was in Annapolis, Maryland, on a business trip and stopped in a bar. The man on the next stool was the freshman football coach at the US Naval Academy. "Dad started singing my praises," Armitage explained. "The Annapolis coach said to have my coach send him some films."

Armitage's coach sent the films. "Next thing I know, the Naval Academy offered me a place," Armitage said. He made the team as a reserve linebacker. His classmate and quarterback was Roger Staubach, who would go on to an NFL-Hall-of-Fame career with the Dallas Cowboys. Above Armitage's locker was a framed photograph of Don Whitmire, a 1940s all-American tackle at both the University of Alabama and the Naval Academy. Before practices and games, Armitage dressed for the gridiron under this photo.

· In 1967, Armitage graduated from Annapolis and was commissioned a navy ensign, just as the war in Vietnam was approaching its peak. He took counterinsurgency training at Coronado, California, which included a six-week total-immersion Vietnamese language class as it was spoken in South Vietnam. Two weeks before the end of that class, the man Armitage was slotted to replace in Vietnam was killed. Armitage's training was cut short and he immediately embarked for Vietnam.

When he arrived, however, he was posted to USS *Buck* (DD-761), a Sumner-class destroyer. But before he could proceed to his duty station, he had to qualify as a surface warfare officer. Once that was out of the way, Armitage joined the South Vietnamese Navy as an advisor. Vietnam has a long, ragged coastline, and its vast Mekong delta holds dozens of big rivers and thousands of canals connecting them to each other or to a population center. While South Vietnam's blue-water navy worked with the US Navy to patrol the coast and its myriad bays, inlets, and beaches, the brown-water navy patrolled the rivers and canals, intercepting Viet Cong infiltrators and arms shipments.

By all reports, Armitage took to his work like an alligator to a swamp. He spoke fluent Vietnamese, and although he was taller and bulkier than most Vietnamese sailors, he dressed as they did, ate their food, slept on the ground as they did, told bawdy jokes in the local idiom, called himself Tran Phu, and quickly acquired his counterparts' trust and admiration.

According to Vietnam navy Capt. Kiem Do, who served with Armitage, the advisor "seemed drawn like a moth to a flame to the hotspots of the naval war." Several Americans who fought alongside Armitage suspected he was part of the CIA's clandestine Phoenix Program, which Armitage denied. From time to time, however, he admitted that CIA officers asked him to provide them with intelligence reports.

"I loved being an advisor," he recalled. "I liked the immersion. I liked the culture. I liked learning the different language. I liked the idea of being helpful. We didn't need to teach the Vietnamese how to fight; they've been fighting a long time. I was the guy who had a radio. So if we got into trouble, I could call in the army or call for air support or medevac."

He spent the year of his second tour on a river patrol boat (PBR), advising the commander of a unit with twenty PBRs on the Cambodian border, patrolling the Van Co Dong River, trying to interdict the flow of arms and fighters coming in from Cambodia. "We patrolled southward from the border of Cambodia down to a place called Go Dau Ha, halfway between Tay Ninh and Saigon.

"Most of my days were good days. I respected my Vietnamese counterparts. I was never let down by them. I know a lot of people who were, but I wasn't. It made sense to stay with them 24/7, so they had to trust me and I had to trust them. It worked for me," he added.

Most of his days and nights on patrol were quiet, but now and then they were engaged in heavy fighting. "I wouldn't say it was a lot compared to someone in an infantry unit, but at the time it was enough for me," he said.

Armitage compares his time in Vietnam to the war in Afghanistan. "Afghans know how to fight. They know how to shoot. Can we train them again? We can do that. Can we outfit them? Yes, we can. But just like in Vietnam, we can't put into their stomachs and into their hearts the willingness to die for a corrupt government."

Armitage recalled one particularly difficult day with the brown-water navy. "It was in Tay Ninh, and our PBR pulled into the bank to set up an ambush. But there was a booby trap in a tree that overhung the bank. It blew the arms off a Vietnamese sailor, blew off both his eyes and his nose, and left a big hole in his chest. So we rushed the PBR back to the base, and I threw him in my Jeep.

"I had a second-class petty officer driving. I was in the back with this sailor, and I gave him three syrettes of morphine. This was not to save him. It was to kill him in the nicest, most painless way. His arms were off, his eyes were out, his nose was gone, a huge gash in his chest. I didn't think he'd live, and if he did, he wouldn't have much of a life. We were not supposed to give morphine for those kinds of wounds. I put the used syrettes into what was left of his shirt so it would be obvious to the hospital staff. They would get the message. The US doctors at the hospital triaged him. Put him in a corner while they worked on men they thought they could save, because this guy was certainly not gonna make it. By the time they got around to him, I was back at the base," he recalled.

"I always felt bad about that man, because he was in so much pain. But then, three or four months later, he came up to our base with his wife. He was blind, of course. Yet he thanked me for saving his life. I was thinking to myself, *I was trying to put you out.* That showed me how indomitable is the human spirit," Armitage concluded.

Armitage returned to America from his third tour in Vietnam somewhat changed. "I was very interested in cross-cultural things, in foreign things, in foreign policy, and it made me feel, being in Vietnam, that I was going to try not to be the business end of the screwdriver, but the handle. I was gonna try to take part in the great events of our time. It made me drive toward that. I wasn't a superpatriot. I only went to Vietnam because I thought it was expected of me."

Nixon signed the Paris Peace Accords in January 1973, and shortly there-after, the last American troops left Vietnam and the advisory command folded its tents. Upon reading the text of that agreement, Armitage resigned his commission. He felt these agreements guaranteed a North Vietnamese victory, and they were a betrayal of everything the American and South Vietnamese troops had fought for.

As a civilian, he joined the office of the US defense attaché in Saigon. Then he returned to the States and his wife in San Diego. In 1975, the North Vietnamese Army advanced toward Saigon, and Armitage was increasingly alarmed. Near the end of April, he called the only people he still knew in the Department of Defense. "I told them I hoped they realized the war was lost."

Erich Von Marbod, the assistant secretary of defense, ran something called the Southeast Asia Program. He called Armitage and told him to get to Washington as fast as he could. "When I got there, he gave me a passport and a visa for South Vietnam, and I was sent back there," he recalled. Armitage returned to Saigon on April 24. Four days later, Marbod sent him to Bien Hoa

Air Base with two Americans from the US Air Force. "Our mission was to recover or destroy some classified electronic equipment we didn't want to fall into North Vietnamese hands.

"We landed about 9:30 a.m. at Bien Hoa. This had once been the busiest airport in the world, and there was no one there! Nobody. Nothing. It was the eeriest feeling you can ever imagine. No sound but the wind coming down the runway.

"We located the equipment, and one of the guys fired up a forklift. We put it in a central location in a warehouse and were hoping to have a C-130 come and pick us up," he explained. "The morning passed. In the early afternoon, stragglers from the South Vietnamese Army began showing up in ones and twos. When they found us, they realized we were their only chance to get out of Vietnam alive. I spoke to them in Vietnamese, and we struck a deal: they would provide security for us, and I would figure out how to get them out of there."

Then the North Vietnamese began shelling the airfield with 130mm heavy artillery. "By late afternoon NVA troops began to come down the runway," Armitage explained. "The South Vietnamese were in the culvert, protecting the warehouse, and we hoped they could keep the NVA away. Then Erich called on the radio and said he was sending a helicopter for us. 'You gotta get out of there, I can't tell you why,' he said."

Armitage replied that a helicopter wouldn't work because of the thirty South Vietnamese soldiers who were protecting them. Marbod was not amused. By then the US Seventh Air Force was otherwise engaged, evacuating tens of thousands of South Vietnamese military and civilians, and had no aircraft to spare.

"So Erich arranged for Bird Air, a CIA proprietary company out of Thailand, to pick us up. When their plane landed, there was Erich. He showed me what he couldn't tell me on the air: a radio intercept of the North Vietnamese that said, 'We have surrounded the enemy in Bien Hoa, kill it.' At that moment, four captured A-37 light bombers bombed us."

Marbod, Armitage, and all his men escaped with their equipment. The South Vietnamese soldiers were dropped at Saigon's Tan Son Nhut Air Base, where the evacuation was in full swing. When Armitage returned to the Saigon embassy, he realized this was it. The long overdue embassy evacuation was underway. Armitage found his way to the Republic of Vietnam Navy (VNN) headquarters and Capt. Do Kiem, who was deputy chief of naval operations and an old friend. "I told him we were gonna leave the next day. And he and I, only the two of us, had been talking about this. Do said, 'You know the Vietnamese. I can't get my people out if they have to leave their families.'"

Armitage understood. He also understood that saving the sailors and their families would be an enormous and complex task. "I was asking him to commit treason against his government," Armitage added. "The president of South Vietnam, Duong Van Minh, had yet to surrender. So asking Do to steal most of the navy was an act of treason."

On the night of April 29, 1975, Armitage realized he had another big problem: "I had told no one in the States what we were gonna do. Nobody. They thought I was destroying the VNN ships. I took the position that by saving those ships, I was denying them to the enemy. The fact that these ships had thousands of Vietnamese on them was subtext. I had to figure out a way to get the US to accept this."

Late that night, a US Marines helicopter took Armitage to the spacious flight deck of USS *Blue Ridge*, command ship for the entire Seventh Fleet. At that moment, more than a dozen US Navy vessels were positioned in international waters in rows, waiting to accept what would be tens of thousands of refugees. By then, the first of hundreds of helicopters crammed with South Vietnamese aviators, soldiers, and their families had landed on US vessels, and hundreds of small boats likewise jammed with refugees had discharged them to those ships. Many more would come the next day and the next.

Armitage was dropped on the ship, and the helicopter returned to the US embassy. He spotted a flag lieutenant, a US Navy officer with the distinctive gold braid of an admiral's aide circling the right shoulder of his khaki uniform. The task force commander was Rear Adm. Don Whitmire, long ago a two-time all-American football player.

Armitage was thirty and a civilian contractor. He carried no Department of Defense identification, no wallet, no identification of any kind. He had lost his Naval Academy ring. He was dressed in slacks and a sweat-stained shirt, and a pistol was jammed between his belt and his trousers.

"Lieutenant," began Armitage, "I know this will sound far-fetched, but you need to get Admiral Whitmire and tell him I'm here on a special mission from Secretary of Defense James R. Schlesinger. And that I dressed under his picture at Navy for three years." That was a sly way of saying he was a Naval Academy football player.

"The flag lieutenant looked at me kinda cross-eyed and went upstairs to see the admiral. The admiral said, 'Bring him up.'"

Armitage told Admiral Whitmire about his mission and that Whitmire needed to send a flash message to the Pentagon for confirmation. "He was not real happy about hearing that, but he sent the message." In about twenty minutes, which was flash message time in those days, he got an answer confirming Armitage's claims and telling the admiral to do what he said.

Armitage was bundled into a small boat for a journey of about twenty minutes to USS Kirk, a destroyer escort. He climbed the Jacob's ladder onto the ship. "I went into the wardroom and found Adm. Donald Roane, commodore of the Kirk's flotilla; Comdr. Paul Jacobson, the Kirk's skipper; and his executive officer. Admiral Roane said, 'I'm not used to strange armed civilians coming aboard my ship in the middle of the night.'" Armitage told him they had a job to do.

The Kirk sailed for Con Son island, some fifty miles off South Vietnam. From the air the shape of the island resembles a running dog. The space between its outstretched legs is a huge harbor, which was filled with hundreds of vessels, including thirty-one VNN ships. The others were freighters, fishing boats, colliers, ferry boats—almost anything that could float. Many were sinking, and others had lost propulsion. The Kirk's sailors examined the smaller vessels and made repairs, transferred refugees from one ship to another, rendered first aid, and did everything they could to get the odd flotilla ready for a long sea voyage.

Meanwhile, Kirk's antiaircraft batteries were trained on the sky, ready to shoot down any North Vietnamese aircraft that might attack the clouds of helicopters flying out to the US fleet. The destroyer escort radioed some of the South Vietnamese helicopters and invited them to land on their stern chopper pad. When any did, and after they had disgorged their human cargo, they were pushed over the side to make room for the next. A CH-47 Chinook, however, was too big to land. It hovered over the flight deck while its passengers leaped into the arms of the sailors. Then the Chinook flew a short distance away, and its pilot ditched in the sea. The seamen from the Kirk rescued him.

Armitage believed it was his duty to lead this ragtag flotilla across a thousand miles of open sea to the Philippines. Other US destroyers would join the small fleet. One cooked tons of rice to feed the refugees; another distilled fresh water for them.

Neither the US nor the Philippine governments was glad to learn of what Armitage had pulled off. The Philippines wanted to maintain good relations with the victorious North Vietnamese and refused to allow the VNN ships into Subic Bay. Armitage rolled with the punch. He found enough US flags from the accompanying destroyers to flag all the South Vietnamese ships. By treaty, the Philippines had to accept US ships into the base.

But the Philippine government would not allow the refugees to disembark. "I was on house arrest aboard a vessel for two days," Armitage recalled. Then huge Military Sea Transportation Service ships arrived to take the refugees to Guam for processing before sending them to the US mainland. Most of the former VNN ships, all American-built, were turned over to the Philippine Navy.

In 1978, Armitage served as foreign policy advisor to presidential candidate Bob Dole. After Ronald Reagan won the presidency in 1980, Armitage became a foreign policy advisor to the president-elect. After Reagan took office, Armitage became a deputy assistant secretary of defense for East Asia and Pacific Affairs from 1981 to 1983. In June 1983, he was promoted to assistant secretary of defense for international security policy, where he represented the Department of Defense in developing political-military relationships and initiatives around the world. He helped to spearhead US Pacific security policy, including the US-Japan and US-China security relationships, managed all defense security assistance programs, and provided oversight of policies related to the law of the sea, US special operations, and counterterrorism.

Following those assignments, in 1989, Armitage served as a special negotiator for the president on military bases in the Philippines and as a mediator on water issues in the Middle East. He was formally nominated for assistant secretary of state for East Asian and Pacific affairs by George H. W. Bush on February 27, 1989. Before the Senate could take up his nomination, though, he was nominated for secretary of the army on April 25, 1989. Armitage asked that his nominations be withdrawn so he could spend more time with his wife and their eight children.

In 1991, he was appointed special emissary to King Hussein of Jordan. Then, with the rank and title of ambassador, he went to Europe to direct US foreign aid to the countries that were formed out of the former Soviet Union. In 1993, he returned briefly to the private sector.

During the George W. Bush administration, Armitage was named deputy secretary of state under Colin Powell. "Secretary Powell empowered me to act with the same authority as a secretary of state," Armitage recalled. "I was the guy who decided anything that didn't need to go to the secretary. When he traveled abroad, I participated in meetings with the president or other Cabinet-level officials and arranged meetings at the level at which the secretary would normally attend. I also had responsibilities for getting appropriations and distributing them to the department," he continued. In short, Armitage ran day-to-day operations and sat in for Secretary Powell when he was traveling overseas.

Armitage regarded his most significant accomplishment as deputy secretary of state as "lowering the temperature and stopping a war between Pakistan and India in 2002, when it seemed they were about to launch nuclear weapons at each other. I went to Islamabad to talk to President Pervez Musharraf, whom I knew, and I persuaded him to say that he would stop acting across the border with India.

"Then I spoke with top Indian officials. I didn't put any words into Musharraf's mouth that he hadn't uttered. And then I gave a press conference, which I was not supposed to do, to kind of make both sides pregnant[1] with the notion that both had agreed to negotiate peace. And that ended talk of war."

Armitage left the State Department on February 22, 2005. He now sits on the board of several international corporations and runs Armitage Associates, a consulting firm. "We're *not* foreign agents. We don't do foreign nation advocacy. We don't lobby. But if a US company has a problem overseas, other than a legal problem, we're glad to help them out," he explained.

During a lifetime of public service, Armitage has accumulated dozens of awards. He is an honorary Knight Commander of the Order of St. Michael and St. George. He was appointed an Honorary Companion of the Order of Australia. The Queen of England appointed him an Honorary Companion of the New Zealand Order of Merit. He was also awarded the Department of State Distinguished Service Award, the Department of Defense Medal for

Distinguished Public Service (four awards), the Secretary of Defense Medal for Outstanding Public Service, the Chairman of the Joint Chiefs Award for Outstanding Public Service, the Presidential Citizens Medal, and the Department of State Distinguished Honor Award.

The president of Romania conferred upon Armitage the Order of the Star of Romania with the rank of commander. On March 22, 2013, he was given the Naval Academy distinguished alumni award.

But the one thing he is most proud of, the thing he talks about, is stealing the South Vietnamese Navy.

SILVESTRE REYES

In an era when the majority of those in the US House of Representatives are attorneys, career politicians, wealthy businessmen, or all three, Silvestre Reyes stood out as a man of the people. He is the grandson of a Mexican immigrant farmer, an army combat veteran, a retired law-enforcement officer, and a true representative of his electorate. Reyes's often hair-raising experiences in Vietnam left him certain that war rarely solves anything.

The eldest of ten children, Silvestre Reyes was born in 1944 and grew up on his grandfather's 384-acre farm just west of El Paso, Texas. "My father and grandfather raised cotton, alfalfa, and milo [grain sorghum]," he recalled. They also raised hogs. The farm was started in the 1920s by his grandfather, who had ridden with Pancho Villa before immigrating to Texas, by paying a thirty-five-cent head tax.

At any time during the planting or harvesting seasons, about half the farm's four hundred workers were undocumented. Reyes recalled he, as a small child, had the job of sitting in a two-ton truck with an air horn and watching for an Immigration Service car. If he saw one approach, he blew the air horn to warn the undocumented workers to hide. "You could hear that horn all over the farm," he said.

After graduating from high school, Reyes earned an associate degree at El Paso Community College. He then enrolled in the University of Texas at Austin but dropped out. Soon thereafter he received a draft notice and entered the army in 1966. After basic training, Reyes was selected for helicopter maintenance training at Fort Rucker, Alabama.

His first duty was in West Germany. Based at a small town near Munich, he flew recon missions along the Czech border. After seven months of training there, his company was deployed to Vietnam. Half the company accompanied the helicopters and heavy equipment. Reyes was with the other half. After two weeks' home leave, he flew to Vietnam and was assigned to a different unit as crew chief on an unarmed Huey in a helicopter company based near Da Nang. "We flew all sorts of missions: air assaults, logistical flights, medevac, and recovering the bodies of our soldiers killed in action," he said. Reyes was wounded three times, once in the head, and was aboard three aircraft that were shot down but autorotated to safe landings. "I said my Hail Marys aloud as we flew into danger," he recalled. "I also said a weekly rosary, because I knew my mother and grandmother were doing the same back home."

When his base camp was attacked, Reyes manned a bunker. A mortar shell landed nearby, and the blast destroyed the hearing in his right ear.

Reyes arrived in Vietnam weighing 240 pounds. "I went home 90 pounds lighter," he recalled. "I hated the noise, the poor food, the constant danger."

Reyes was at Fort Stewart, Georgia, when his father died. While he was home in El Paso, seeing to the funeral arrangements and consoling his mother, he was notified he had received a compassionate discharge.

In June 1969, Reyes was hired by the US Border Patrol, then part of the Department of Justice. On July 1, he reported to the Border Patrol Academy in Brownsville, Texas. A newlywed, Reyes and his wife, Carolina, rented a converted garage, which was now a one-room apartment with a kitchenette.

On September 1, halfway through the academy's four-month initial training course, President Richard Nixon ordered the Border Patrol to commence Operation Intercept. Reyes and other trainees left for dozens of locations along the US-Mexico border.

Paired with a senior agent, Reyes was posted to Del Rio, Texas, where they patrolled the southern bank of the Rio Grande. On the first day there, they observed a few people swimming across from Mexico and apprehended them.

One was a pregnant woman in labor; the birth was imminent. The senior agent ordered Reyes to help deliver the baby. Growing up on a farm, he had witnessed the births of cows, pigs, dogs, cats, and horses. But this was the first human birth he witnessed. With Reyes's help, the woman delivered a healthy baby girl on the riverbank. The mother named her infant daughter "America."

After two months on the river, Reyes returned to the Border Patrol Academy and completed his training. Then he went back to Del Rio, where he and his wife had their first child and eventually bought a 720-square-foot mobile home and later a small house. After five years in Del Rio, Reyes was transferred to El Paso. During his four years there, he worked on each of the five bridges connecting El Paso with Ciudad Juarez, Mexico.

In 1978, the Border Patrol INS Training Academy was moved from Brownsville to Glynco, Georgia. Reyes served as an instructor there for three years. "Then I was offered the position of deputy regional chief and returned to El Paso. The southern region encompassed thirteen states from New Mexico to Florida and from South Carolina to Colorado," he explained.

Five years later he became the chief of the McAllen Border Patrol sector, encompassing the coastal border from Brownsville to Houston, the entire eastern side of Texas. After nine years in that job, Reyes returned to El Paso to take over the El Paso sector, which covered the state of New Mexico and two counties in West Texas.

Shortly before he retired from the Border Patrol, Reyes dealt with complaints from El Paso businesses and local law enforcement that undocumented immigrants were flooding the city and causing trouble. Acting on his own authority, he launched Operation Hold the Line, which drew national and international attention and brought Reyes to local prominence.

On September 19, 1993, a Sunday morning, dozens of Border Patrol vehicles and hundreds of agents took up positions along the border between El Paso and Ciudad Juarez. On the US side of the free bridge, some fifty agents occupied the crest, blocking entry to those without appropriate documents. People on the Mexico side of the bridge began throwing rocks and bottles at the agents.

Simultaneously, hundreds of agents were deployed along the twenty miles of the border between Anapra and the Ysleta Border Patrol headquarters in east El Paso, long a popular crossing area. This altered immigration patterns along the entire border. Would-be immigrants began avoiding heavily policed areas and sought entry at more remote areas, a pattern that continues to this day.

After Reyes retired from the Border Patrol, he was approached by several members of the El Paso business community, who encouraged him to run for Congress. Reyes ran for the Democratic nomination in a heavily Democratic district and won. He spent the next sixteen years in Congress.

Reyes is very proud of his ability to work with his Republican peers in Congress. His friend Duncan Hunter Sr., a California Republican, helped get Reyes on the Military Construction Committee. "Hunter was instrumental in helping me work to save Fort Bliss," Reyes explained. "I was already on the Armed Services Committee, and Hunter was either the ranking member or the chairman of the committee. He helped me get on the Military Construction Subcommittee and used his influence to get others on that committee to vote to save Fort Bliss."

He considers saving Fort Bliss from closure as his most significant accomplishment. "Fort Bliss's main cantonment and headquarters are in Texas," Reyes explained. "The rest of the 1.12 million acres, or 88 percent of the base, is in New Mexico. It's six-hundred-thousand-acre McGregor Range Complex and the contiguous US Army White Sands Missile Range comprise the largest military installation in the United States."

In 2002, Reyes was one of only twelve Vietnam veterans in Congress, and he voted against giving President George W. Bush authorization to go to war with Iraq. "I voted against that because I'd been through the experience of combat," he explained. "I knew we hadn't exhausted all diplomatic means to bring Iraq around. Also, by that time I was chairman of the House Intelligence Committee. Contrary to the administration's claims, I knew our intelligence sources were not sure that Saddam Hussein had the capability to use weapons of mass destruction, chemical, biological, or nuclear."

After the real estate bubble burst in 2008, Reyes served as the chairman of the committee that passed the bill authorizing an infusion of billions of dollars into the economy, principally for local infrastructure projects. "Since I was at the table, and I was the only one who represented a border district, I was able to put in millions of dollars to help border districts like mine. We put in transportation money and levied rehabilitation funds for the Rio Grande."

After eight terms in Congress, Reyes was defeated in the 2012 election. He returned to El Paso and a comfortable retirement with his wife and three children. Shortly before he retired, he told his constituents:

I have often wondered how different my life would have been if, in 1966, I had not joined the US Army. I was born and raised on a farm. . . . I believe that had I not served in the army, I might still be on that farm today instead of serving in the United States Congress.

Today, when I speak to students about decisions they will make that can dramatically change their lives, I stress to them what I learned long ago as a young soldier: "Freedom is not free."

We live in the greatest democracy in the world and in a country that gives every one of us the opportunity to work hard and succeed. This democracy and opportunity are possible because of the dedication and commitment of our men and women in uniform. These men and women stand ready today, as they did in the past, to sacrifice their lives for their country.

But as a soldier, you also learn that no one will be left behind, even at times risking all for the sake of saving one. There are those who wonder what motivates the vigil to account for our MIA/POW comrades. Understanding may be answered by simply saying, "You had to be there to understand."[1]

PART FOUR

GOVERNMENT SERVICE

HAROLD "BEN" GAY

In some American families, and especially in the South, the tradition of service to country—through military duty or any of a multitude of law-enforcement agencies or elective offices—runs deep through numerous generations. It persists despite hardship, danger, and limited financial prospects. To these patriots, nothing is quite so satisfying as serving their communities, their states, and their country.

A few minutes into Ben Gay's first flight as a cadet, "Two training helicopters collided right in front of us and exploded. One of the gas tanks twirled as it fell with other debris. My instructor pilot called the tower, reported the midair collision, and asked for a medevac with a few body bags," he recalled. "He was so calm I wondered if midair collisions were common occurrences. I was in shock, but I kept my mouth shut and soldiered on."

Welcome to army aviation, Cadet Gay.

The oldest of seven children, Harold "Ben" Gay grew up in Norfolk, in Virginia's Tidewater, home to the largest concentration of military bases in the United States. His father enlisted in the navy after Pearl Harbor, and over the next thirty years he rose in rating to senior chief boatswain's mate. He fought in the Pacific during World War II and later in the waters off Korea.

"I was raised in navy housing on naval bases, and the service treated our family very well," Gay explained. "I enjoyed that structured environment. I think that had a lot to do with wanting to serve in the military."

Gay enlisted in August 1967, and after basic training at Fort Polk, Louisiana, he went to Fort Wolters, Texas, for preflight training. Like officer candidate school, flight school is demanding. Students were expected to solo after ten to twelve hours of instruction. "If we couldn't take off, fly three patterns, and land safely, we were out," he explained.

On October 21, 1968, he pinned on aviator's wings and warrant officer's bars. Twelve days later he was part of the 155th Assault Helicopter Company in the Central Highlands city of Buon Ma Thuot. The 155th's troop-carrying Hueys ("slicks") and heavily armed Hueys ("guns") flew in support of US, ARVN, and Allied infantry and artillery.

Gay flew every day. About once a week he took part in an air assault, usually inserting South Vietnamese soldiers. His aircraft often returned to base with bullet holes.

Flying the Central Highlands was challenging. The dry season brought fine dust that got into everything and caused severe visibility problems during landings. In the rainy season, the dust became mud. The region's saving grace was daytime temperatures in the nineties, compared with triple digits at sea-level elevations.

Despite these handicaps, Gay took to combat flying like a barracuda to a coral lagoon. "The mountain scenery was breathtaking," he recalled. November in the Highlands is cold at night but warm and pleasant during the day. "We built little wooden hooches and dug underground bunkers. We came under mortar or rocket attack maybe once or twice a week."

Soon he was flying twenty-five to thirty hours a week. In April 1969, Gay was transferred to the Forty-Eighth Assault Helicopter Company, based at Ninh Hoa, just north of the seaside resort city of Vung Tau. He qualified as an aircraft commander and two months later was promoted to a gunship platoon known by the call sign Jokers. Flying a gunship is more challenging than a slick, and Gay's missions were far more demanding.

Soon after Gay became Joker 73, the Forty-Eighth traded in their UH-1B gunships for newer, faster, and more rugged UH-1C's. Gay decided to extend his tour in Vietnam. "I was twenty years old, single, and an aircraft commander. I had great friends. It was a very exciting time."

His duty became even more dangerous. In his first year in combat, Gay lost several friends, mostly through accidents while flying in bad weather or at night. "We had no navigational aids as we did in the States. There was no one to call who could find you on radar and vector you to an airfield," he explained. "We were on our own and we had poor maps, which was a bad combination that took several lives. We also lost some men in combat."

Gay was twice shot down, "as in the aircraft was coming out of the sky because pieces and parts were coming off," he explained. The first time he autorotated his slick into an open field and was extracted. His aircraft was recovered. The second was a far more harrowing experience. He autorotated a gunship into the dense jungle near the Duc Lap Special Forces Camp. He and his crew left the ship in a tree and evaded the enemy to reach the camp.

His worst day in Vietnam came on October 30, 1969. Three NVA regiments, supported by an antiaircraft battalion, had besieged Firebase Kate, a steep hill with a bald top. For five days and nights, swarms of enemy soldiers assaulted Kate's tiny garrison.

Joker gunships protected medevac helicopters that hauled Kate's wounded to safe hospitals. Gay led a two-ship fireteam with wingmen Nolan Black and Maury Hearn. With Black and Hearn following him, Gay made several passes over Kate to fire rockets at an enemy heavy machine gun. "As I turned in behind Blackie, I observed fire from a second heavy gun hidden about ninety degrees from the first one," Gay recalled.

It was a flak trap. The second gun had remained hidden until the first had lured a gunship into range. "I saw Black's ship hit," Gay said. "His bottom fuel cell burst into flames." Moments later, the stricken Huey's tail boom separated from its fuselage, and the ship flipped upside down, plunging fifty feet into the jungle and exploding.

"I was in shock as I circled over the spot where Blackie and Hearn crashed. I wasn't aware of what I was doing. Green tracers were flying everywhere. Someone was calling me on the radio, but my mind was elsewhere and I didn't respond," he recalled. "It wasn't until I'd left that area and climbed to a safe altitude that I asked another aircraft to check my ship to see if anything was leaking. I'll never get over losing those friends, but a day or two later I was back flying again."

One night in May 1970, after about eighteen months in Vietnam, Gay's fireteam was on alert. "I lay in my bunk, thinking. I considered myself a Christian, but I wasn't devout. I didn't go to church or study the Bible as I should have. That night I somehow got to wondering about God. Is there really a God? For the last year and a half, I've been out here killing people, and they've been trying to kill me. My friends are dying. It was really grinding on me that I couldn't decide if God was real or not."

In the midst of this meditation, Gay's fireteam received a mission: a Special Forces base twenty-five miles to the north had been attacked. A medevac was en route; Gay's gunship would fly cover. Fifteen minutes later he circled the camp on the shore of the South China Sea.

"We had a nice moon, almost full, and the sea was very calm. When the medevac chopper arrived, we spoke on the radio; I said that we were circling at about eight hundred feet between the camp and the end of the beach. The medevac approached from the sea, but his first approach was too low and fast, so he decided to go around and try again.

"I watched him through my right door, and when he got about a quarter mile out, he turned back over the water and flew right into the sea. His last radio transmission sounded like 'Jokerbalup.' I was certain the whole crew was gone."

Gay radioed for another medevac. While waiting, he flew out to look for the helicopter in the water. "It was on the bottom and inverted; the landing lights were still on. Then I saw a little red flare shoot into the air." Four men were floating on the gentle waves.

Gay radioed for another slick, which pulled the downed crewmen from the sea. "Those guys hit the water at around ninety miles an hour. They were dressed like me in a heavy, fire-resistant flight suit, boots, flight helmet, a pistol, and a twenty-five-pound steel plate on their chests. They were strapped into their seats. It's dark and when they hit the water the aircraft flipped over. Yet somehow all four survived. I spoke to one of them the next day and asked how he got out. He said, 'All I know is that we hit the water. The next thing I knew was that all four of us were bobbing around on the sea.'"

Gay realized he had an answer to his question if there is a God. "It was kind of, 'Yes, there is, and I am here.'"

—◇—

Gay went to Vietnam a typical American teenager. "I thought the world owed me something, that everything would be easy, with no problems. Vietnam was a great big ol' bite of a reality sandwich. Instead of being in a fraternity and drinking beer and having a good time and nothing bad happening, I joined a military fraternity. We drank a little beer, of course, but seeing death, losing friends, it was a period of experiencing and adjusting to and accepting things. When I got home, as the saying goes, I had a young face but old eyes. Serving in Vietnam gave me a grip on reality and what life was really about. I was able to prioritize what I wanted to be, what I wanted to do, where I wanted to go."

After Vietnam, Gay was assigned to Fort Eustice, not far from his home in Norfolk. He left active duty in 1971, and less than a week later he joined the Virginia Army National Guard, where he flew a gunship. "I never came off of flight status," he recalled. In January 1972, he enrolled in college. By taking extra courses and going to summer school, he earned degrees in police science and government in just over three years.

A few months later, Gay was accepted by the Naval Investigative Service (now Naval Criminal Investigative Service). His four years there included one aboard USS *Forrestal*, a nuclear-powered aircraft carrier with a crew of about fifty-five hundred men. "It was like being the sheriff of a small town. I was the only agent aboard and answered only to the captain," he recalled. While most of his work involved narcotics, he also investigated several cases of sabotage by crewmen attempting to delay the ship's deployment.

In 1979, Gay joined the Defense Criminal Investigative Service. "Our major job was investigating fraud against the Defense Department," he explained. Among his most significant cases was a North Carolina company that provided aluminum chaff. This is a countermeasure device carried on ships, aircraft, and helicopters to foil radar-guided weapons. Metal strips or wire are used to confuse the enemy's radar frequency by providing a large number of echoes that obscure the target.

Gay's nine-month solo investigation proved the company had intentionally manufactured chaff in a manner designed to save them money, but it did not function as required. "Eventually they pled guilty, reimbursed the government millions of dollars, and corrected every issue," he explained. While several people were convicted, Gay found it frustrating that none went to prison, "especially because this was an item that could actually kill our troops."

Another investigation revealed a serious manufacturing flaw in ballistic helmets, and yet another looked into faulty aircraft ejection seats. Gay found the evidence to convict the manufacturers of fraud.

In 1983, Gay joined the Customs Service, then a part of the Treasury Department, as an investigator. "We investigated illegal imports and exports," he explained. "I handled the illegal export of US currency, the import of narcotics and other restricted items, and the illegal export of munitions technology." Among his most important cases was the clandestine export of gyroscopes used in tactical missiles. "They were sent to South America but eventually would have gone to the Middle East," he said. This ten-month investigation employed undercover operatives. "It culminated in the delivery of gyroscopes to suspects. But these items had been doctored so that even if they escaped, the gyros were of no value. We thought this gang would fly out of DC. Instead they drove north toward Rhode Island, which caught us off guard." Gay and his colleagues chased them down and arrested them. His actions were recognized with a ceremony and a plaque from the US attorney general.

During all his years with NIS, the Defense Investigative Service, and Customs, Gay remained in the National Guard. In August 1990, his unit, by then a medevac company, was mobilized for Operation Desert Storm. He spent five months in Saudi Arabia, much of it aloft under dangerous flight conditions.

Gay retired from Customs in July 2000, with twenty-five years of federal service. By then, he and his wife, Janet, had built a home in Lanexa, on the Virginia Peninsula. He could have retired on his federal pension to relax, travel, and spend time with their two sons and two grandchildren. But that was not for Ben Gay.

Since 1997 he had been working for the New Kent Sheriff's Department as an unarmed auxiliary deputy, "just to see if it was something I wanted to do," he recalled. Following his federal retirement, Gay struck a deal with the sheriff. He didn't want to sit behind a desk or work in a courtroom. He wanted to be on patrol, with a gun on his hip, justice in his heart, and each day a little different from those before or yet to come. For more than seventeen years,

Gay worked fifty- to sixty-hour weeks on traffic enforcement or marine patrol on the Pamunkey, York, and Chickahominy Rivers.

"I don't know that I could give a good answer as to why I do this," Gay said. "It's not monetary. It's not for fame or glory. When I went to work for the sheriff, who is a very good friend and a fine man, we agreed that whenever I wanted to be off, I would be off. The other agreement was that if he promoted me, I'd quit. I want no other responsibility than doing my job and enjoying myself as I try to keep the people of this county a little safer."

BRUCE
BEARDSLEY

How is it that in Tunisia, Algeria, and Morocco, we now find natives with fair skin and blue eyes? In Ireland, and especially along its west coast, we find people with dark hair and dark eyes, the so-called Black Irish? In North African countries, this is largely due to the slave-trading efforts of the Barbary pirates, who, mostly during the seventeenth century, abducted more than a million hostages from both northern Mediterranean nations and from seaside towns and villages in England and Denmark. Few of these hostages were ransomed. Most were sold into slavery, including sexual slavery. In Ireland, generations of Portuguese, Spanish, and North African traders sold their produce, including wine, to local merchants. Some intermarriage occurred. In Vietnam, the story is similar but darker. Over a decade, nearly three million American soldiers contributed to what had been a highly homogeneous gene pool. And the children carrying these foreign genes were rarely welcomed into their communities.

The son of a World War II naval officer who went on to a career with the Internal Revenue Service, Bruce Beardsley was born in 1942 and grew up mostly in Reno, Nevada. As a child, he lived in Thailand while his father served as an advisor to the minister of finance and in Japan during the Occupation after World War II.

In 1964, Beardsley graduated from the University of Nevada, Reno, with a degree in history and an ROTC commission as a second lieutenant in the army's new military intelligence branch.

After infantry training at Fort Benning and a few months of stateside duty, Beardsley went to South Vietnam, where he and a team interrogated POWs, moving from unit to unit throughout the country, wherever their services were needed.

"We were never violent, but when you're talking to soldiers who've just been picked up on the battlefield, they're often sick or wounded. They're thinking that every breath will be their last. We had a huge psychological advantage over them. Just treating them like human beings was a great relief to them," Beardsley recalled. "That's when they're most likely to share useful information."

He was awarded the Bronze Star for his service in Vietnam. When Beardsley left the army in 1966, he used his veterans benefits for graduate school. He also took the foreign service exam, and then he joined the Foreign Service in 1969 and entered language school to learn Vietnamese.

In Vietnam, many Foreign Service officers served in Civil Operations and Revolutionary Development Support (CORDS), a joint pacification program of the US and South Vietnamese governments, with military and civilian components. Its objective was to build support for the unpopular government of South Vietnam among the rural population that was largely under the influence of or controlled by the Viet Cong and/or the People's Army of North Vietnam (PAVN). And this meant that CORDS assignments were often risky.

"I started off as the deputy district senior advisor in a district in Tay Ninh Province," Beardsley said. "I was in charge of civic action projects, such things as village development, irrigation projects, agricultural issues, and related matters." Then the US government began to shrink both military and Foreign Service force levels as the first step in an exit policy. After a few months, Khiem Hanh and Hieu Thien districts were combined under a single CORDS team.

"By then I knew something about both districts, so I was put in charge of the military advisors in both," he remembered. "My Vietnamese was pretty fluent. On a typical day, I might go to a village, walk out into a field and talk to a guy behind a plow, or chat with a shopkeeper. I was trying to get the pulse of the place. Find out what was really happening as opposed to what the district chief might choose to tell me.

"I noticed how some fields were dry when they needed water, and others were flooded when they didn't need to be. I discussed it with an engineer, who confirmed my suspicion that water did, indeed, flow downhill. I had access to small sums of discretionary funds, basically a few dollars here and there, whatever I could scrounge from various budgets. Our engineers explained that the secret to digging and emplacing a culvert beneath a road was to ensure it was buried deep enough and that the road atop the culvert was smooth. Otherwise, traffic would soon destroy it."

Beardsley spoke with villagers about building culverts. "I would provide a few bags of cement if they supplied the people to do the labor. I inspected the excavation to make sure the culvert was buried deep enough. I was kind of proud of myself, that I had learned something practical and that these villagers were involved and that I was making a difference here.

"But sometimes I'd go back to a village and find they'd dug up some of the road but never finished the culvert. Or some of the cement was diverted to build a fortification. Or something else," Beardsley recalled. "I was always kind of pushing and shoving. This program was funded to build something useful to the whole community, such as a classroom, and not something that looked an awful lot like somebody's house. But often it went for a house for the village headman."

Beardsley's Hieu Thien district was along the border where Highway One crosses into Cambodia. It's a major commercial hub, and "also a likely place for things like smuggling," he explained. "The district chief was reputedly quite wealthy from his position astride this smuggling route. He was sharing what he collected with those up the chain of command, of course."

Beardsley grew frustrated with the corruption that interfered with CORDS programs. "Before I became district senior advisor, I often walked around to look at whatever was going on and see what people had to say about it. One day I found a gas station under construction and stopped to talk to a lady who said that she owned it. I noticed the equipment being used to bury fuel tanks was all military. And all the workmen were soldiers. It was a military engineering project. This woman said she paid 25,000 dong [about

$70 US] for the use of the soldiers and their equipment. She had made an arrangement with the soldiers' commanding officer."

Beardsley jotted down vehicle markings and learned it was a unit supposedly in Cambodia. He wrote a report. "I was told, 'That's a very nice report, Bruce, but don't waste your time with this sort of stuff. Nothing useful will come of this.'" From this he saw that official corruption by his Vietnamese counterparts ran from top to bottom. And CORDS wasn't configured to deal with it.

"As I moved on to other nations in the Foreign Service, I began to recognize that actions that are criminal offenses for Americans are considered very modest self-enrichment in other countries," he said. "So then it's, How do we play the system so that, if corruption is bound to happen, we can prevent it from seeping into our own offices? How can we sometimes turn corrupt officials to our advantage?"

In 1972, Beardsley was posted to Beirut, Lebanon, and then, in 1974, to Kabul, Afghanistan. In 1975, he was dispatched to Wake Island for several months to serve as civil coordinator for twelve thousand Vietnamese who were evacuated during the fall of Saigon. When they had been sorted out, vetted, and then admitted to the US mainland, Beardsley returned to Kabul.

In 1977, he was chief of the consular section of the US Embassy in Copenhagen. Early in this assignment, he was again tapped to deal with Vietnamese refugees—the thousands who had fled Vietnam in tiny boats that wind and currents had brought to Malaysia. Beardsley supervised the processing and resettlement of these people to the United States.

In 1980 and 1981, Beardsley returned to academia and earned a master's at Harvard's Kennedy School of Government. Then he went back to the Far East, to Seoul, Korea, to become deputy consul general. Between 1981 and 1985, he dismissed a dozen employees for malfeasance and instituted more stringent internal controls to prevent future occurrences. Beardsley's star turn came in 1988, while serving in Bangkok, Thailand, as the US Embassy's counselor for refugee and migration.

———◇———

There is no reliable count of the number of children fathered by US soldiers and civilians in Vietnam during the war years. But thousands of American

Vietnamese children were left behind when their GI fathers went home. Vietnam's traditional society valued premarital chastity and prized ethnic homogeneity. For these reasons and others, few births of those born of liaisons with foreigners were officially recorded.

They were called *bui doi*, "children of the dust," and were often abandoned at birth. Those who survived were treated as unwanted interlopers. After the war, the communists who occupied the South closed many orphanages and left children to fend for themselves. Amerasian children were packed off to brutal reeducation camps or to work farms. The communists confiscated the wealth and property of those who had supported the US-backed government of South Vietnam; evidence of any American connection, including letters, photos, and official documents in the possession of women who had an Amerasian child, was destroyed or hidden.

The bui doi were taunted as half-breed dogs and often denied ration cards with which to buy food. Most could not attend school. Few ever attempted to find their American fathers, mostly because they didn't know where to start. Many of the birth mothers didn't know the full names or hometowns of the fathers.

Few Americans knew or cared about these children until 1980, when Representative Stewart B. McKinney of Connecticut called their abandonment a national embarrassment and urged Americans to take responsibility for them. Protracted negotiations ensued between the two countries over the issue of the mixed-race children. This was during a time when there were no formal diplomatic relations between the United States and Vietnam. In the early eighties, Congress passed the Amerasians Resettlement Act, which included Korea, Japan, and Vietnam. Then came the matter of who could leave Vietnam and enter the United States. "If one was a fifteen-year-old kid and he has a mother, then the mother could come along with the child," Beardsley explained. "But what about the mother's other children? What about her current husband? There were very stringent requirements about who could go and which family members they could bring back. Very few people actually benefited from it."

With the help of a few US attorneys trying to find specific children, a slow procession of Amerasian children were reunited with their fathers. Then came 1987. The Vietnamese economy teetered on the edge of collapse, the product of the same corruption that had dogged the Saigon government in the sixties and seventies and a Marxist-Leninist command economy that eliminated the profit motive from every enterprise. In return for economic aid, Hanoi agreed to allow the bui doi to leave.

Bruce Beardsley was the principal American negotiator for the departure of these children. The children chosen for resettlement were those who looked like they might be the child of a Caucasian (light eyes and fair hair) or an African American (very dark skin and Afro-textured hair). Sometimes a child's mother had evidence that the father was an American, such as a photograph or a letter.

Then, Long Island congressman Robert Mrazek became involved. He had been severely injured while in naval officer candidate school during the Vietnam War and medically discharged without seeing overseas duty. In 1982, he was elected to Congress. In 1987, in response to a magazine's picture story about a particular Amerasian child, high school students in his district wrote to the Vietnamese mission in New York City and asked Vietnam to let its Amerasian children come to America. Mrazek went to Vietnam and brought back Le Van Minh, an American Vietnamese child who had survived by begging on the streets. Mrazek also met dozens of other Amerasian children who begged to "go to the land of their father."

Mrazek contacted Beardsley and a few of his Foreign Service colleagues. They drafted a proposal permitting the resettlement of Vietnam's Amerasian children, along with certain relatives. "We gave our draft to Congressman Mrazek outside official channels. Since he was on the Appropriations Committee, as soon as it came out of committee, the Asian Homecoming Act was voted into law." Beardsley was proud of this law and asked Mrazek for a signed copy of the actual legislation.

The new law empowered Beardsley's office to admit any and all Vietnamese Amerasians they chose to the United States. "And then, of course, as in a lot of other things in life, once you get moving along, purity evaporates. It dawned on me there's a difference between efficient and inefficient corruption, reasonable corruption and unreasonable extortion. Because suddenly these despised children became golden children. They could bring their families; they were a ticket out of Vietnam. People began buying and selling them. Often a group of unrelated people who had never known a kid until a few months earlier was magically transformed into his loving adopted mother, his stepfather, and all of his stepsiblings. We interviewed all the kids. Sometimes we found they had been threatened. Someone paid a bribe for a family exit permit; the child was told he or she must pretend to have lived with these people for some time—or else. We had a lot of issues with that type of thing. It was a real can of worms," Beardsley continued. "We finally got the Vietnamese to cooperate with family unification. By the time I was finished with it, we had all the pieces in place for a very robust program."

Altogether, about twenty-one thousand Amerasian children and fifty-five thousand relatives came to the States through Beardsley's efforts. Less than 5 percent of these children were reunited with their biological fathers. According to Dennis Rockstroh of the San Jose *Mercury News*, most of these new Americans, often after years of struggle, found lives of dignity. After finishing college, many enjoyed considerable success as teachers, entrepreneurs, and businesspeople.

According to the Migration Policy Institute, a Washington, DC–based think tank, a 2014 survey of Vietnamese immigrants found their median household income was $59,933. (Median income for all immigrant households was $49,487 and $54,565 for US-born households.)

Despite Beardsley's efforts, hundreds of Amerasians remained in Vietnam. In recent years, privately funded efforts have sought to match their DNA with that of former American soldiers who belatedly sought their children. This process continues today.

Beardsley's Foreign Service career continued through 2000. In that time, he served as consul general in Manila, minister counselor in Mexico City, as the University of California–Los Angeles's diplomat in residence, and as the refugee coordinator in Kosovo.

Since retiring from the Foreign Service, he has served as an election supervisor in Kosovo, taught university classes in Florida, and for a dozen years served as a trainer and "subject matter expert" to prepare US Army brigades for deployment to Kosovo, Iraq, and Afghanistan. He is writing a book about his experiences managing the Orderly Departure Program.

EUGENE "GENE" DEATRICK

No military service can be truly professional without a cadre of careerists, officers, and enlisted ranks who can and do pass on the fruits of bitter experience to succeeding generations. Among career officers, much of the glory, often deservedly so, goes to famous generals, yet the colonels and lieutenant colonels provide the command framework on the dirty end of the stick. They are the commanders of battalions, squadrons, flotillas, brigades, and other combat commands. Colonels and lieutenant colonels and their naval counterparts run most of their service's senior staff departments, schools, research-and-development projects, and the organs of command and control. America might be able to get along without most of its generals but never without its colonels.

L t. Col. Eugene Deatrick, USAF, pushed his A-1E Skyraider along at 250 knots and 100 feet over a mountain river in Laos. Then the river made a sharp left turn. Deatrick, commander of the First Air Commando Squadron, dropped his left wing, stood on his left rudder pedal, and as his aircraft banked sharply, a flash of white from below caught his eye.

He came around for a second look, wing still down, but he could not see directly below the plane. (The Skyraider is a low-wing monoplane, the biggest single-engine propeller-driven aircraft ever built for the American military.) As he flashed by, he thought he saw a man on a rock in the middle of the river waving something white.

Deatrick radioed his wingman, who was circling above from where he could stay in radio contact with their base at Pleiku, South Vietnam. "Come down here and see if you can tell better what I saw," Deatrick said. "Maybe you can see what it is. It went by so quickly."

The other Skyraider dropped down and made a low pass over the river. The wingman said, "Looks like he's trying to write an SOS on the rock."

Both aircraft ascended, and then radioed a search-and-rescue unit in Saigon. For the next hour, they circled the river, all the while wondering if the man on a rock might be a trap. But the man on the rock was a US Navy lieutenant, Dieter Dengler.

Dengler was born and raised in Germany's Black Forest region. His father, a soldier, was killed during World War II on the eastern front when Dengler was a child. One day he saw an Allied fighter plane fly by, and from that moment, Dengler wanted to be a pilot.

He grew up in extreme poverty, sometimes subsisting on the wheat-based paste his mother boiled from wallpaper that his brothers recovered from bombed-out buildings and from scraps left by the men who slaughtered sheep near his town. Apprenticed at age fourteen to a blacksmith, he was regularly beaten. An ad in an old American magazine seeking pilots made him decide to go to the United States. To pay for his passage, he salvaged brass and other metals. At age eighteen, Dengler bought his passage to America. For days he lived on the streets of New York, scavenging food from garbage cans, before he found a US Air Force recruiter.

Trained as a mechanic and a gunsmith, Dengler applied for flight training, only to learn that air force pilots required a college degree. After he was honorably discharged, Dengler lived with his brother in San Francisco for two years, working in a bakery and going to college. Finally, he was accepted into the navy's aviation cadet program.

In 1965, he learned to fly the navy version of the Skyraider. On February 1, 1966, Dengler took off from the USS *Ranger* to attack a North Vietnamese truck convoy on the Ho Chi Minh Trail in Laos. According to Bruce Henderson, best-selling author of *Hero Found*[1] and one of the "Airedale" crew who maintained and armed Dengler's aircraft, Dengler wore civilian clothes under his flight suit and carried his German passport.

Heavy antiaircraft fire brought Dengler down. Despite the loss of a wing, he was able to land his battered Skyraider in a small clearing, but he was captured by the communist Pathet Lao. He was tortured and all but starved to death before he was turned over to the Viet Cong. After more torture and starvation, he escaped with several other prisoners, but only Dengler was ever seen again. By the time he was spotted on the rock in the river, Dengler was almost skeletal after weeks with almost no food.

"It took about an hour before authorities in Saigon approved a rescue mission," Deatrick recalled. Finally, with Deatrick and his wingman still circling overhead, a helicopter swooped in and brought Dengler out. He was the only American military aviator to survive captivity by the Viet Cong and find his way to freedom.

Gene Deatrick was the son of two West Virginia college professors. "My mother taught chemistry at West Virginia University, and when I was younger, she often said, 'My son will never go to war. He'll go to Leavenworth first,'" he recalled. Then his father, who taught agriculture at WVU, took a job in Washington, DC. "When I started high school, mother decided it was time for me to be with him," he said.

When Deatrick returned to Morgantown in 1942, just after the start of World War II, his mother, perhaps wanting to keep him out of the war, asked if he wanted to go to West Point. "I said, 'Everything I know about West Point is that they beat navy every year at football,'" Deatrick said with a chuckle.

Then and now, cadets are appointed to the military academies by their senator or congressman or, after enlistment in the uniformed services, by the president, based on a competitive exam. His parents had no political connections, so Deatrick enrolled at West Virginia University and joined the Air Corps Reserve. Among his mother's friends, however, was the editor of the *Dominion News*, Morgantown's daily newspaper, and he knew Senator Jennings Randolph. In 1943, the senator appointed Deatrick to West Point.

During his first year at the academy, an Air Corps AT-6 trainer made a simulated strafing run over Deatrick's company during field training. Deatrick decided he would rather be strafing than be strafed. The Air Corps was then part of the army. As a second-year cadet, Deatrick applied for an aviation program that upon graduation awarded him both an Army Air Corps commission as a second lieutenant and aviator's wings. On June 1, 1946, almost a year after the war ended, Deatrick's wings were pinned on him by Gen. Carl Spaatz, commanding general of the army air forces.

His first assignment was flying the B-25 Mitchell medium bomber at Enid, Oklahoma. He then moved up to the much larger B-29 Superfortress at MacDill Field, Florida. Then he volunteered for search-and-rescue duty at Adak Island in the Aleutians, where he learned to fly the PBY Catalina flying boat and an SB-17G Flying Fortress rigged with a boat below its fuselage, which was dropped in the water near survivors to await rescue.

Deatrick's reputation as a quick study with new types of aircraft caught the eye of the air force brass, who saw in him the makings of a test pilot. In 1949, he was assigned to the 3759th Electronics Test Squadron, devoted to the development of new radars as a path to increased bombing accuracy. In 1950, the squadron moved to Eglin Air Force Base, Florida, and Deatrick became the bomber engineering test pilot. He also flew the T-33 Shooting Star jet trainer, the legendary P-51 Mustang fighter that helped the Allied air forces break the back of Nazi Germany's air power, and the F-84 Thunderjet fighter-bomber, an aircraft with a troubled development history.

With so much experience with so many different aircraft types, Deatrick was a natural for selection in 1951 to the first class of the air force's experimental test pilot school at Edwards Air Force Base, California. Creation of this school was recognition that new aircraft development would be an ongoing requirement and that the newer the aircraft, the more complex its various systems were. Test pilots had to cope with emerging technologies as they affected aircraft performance and to anticipate and adjust to each new machine's performance quirks. Those who failed crashed and died.

After training at Edwards, Deatrick served five years in the bomber flight test division at Wright-Patterson Air Force Base, Ohio. There he flew development tests on B-47 Stratojet and B-52 Stratofortress strategic bombers, among several other aircraft.

In his most dangerous peacetime assignment, Deatrick participated in Operation Castle at the Pacific Proving Grounds in the Marshall Islands. "We were trying to learn how the radiation, heat, and shock wave that follow an atomic blast affected an airplane in flight." On one bomb run, Deatrick flew the chase plane. "There was a strong tailwind and the bomber's pilot made a mistake: he dropped his bomb about thirty seconds early," Deatrick recalled. "I still have a tape that says, 'Bomb down, so let's get the hell out of here.'"

In preparation for Operation Redwing the next year, Deatrick took an accelerated course on the B-52A at Boeing Field near Seattle, Washington, then flew the first B-52B. This huge aircraft was packed with instruments to measure the effects of a nuclear explosion. In March 1956, flying as copilot, he participated in eight test runs over detonating nuclear blasts, including the first airdrop of a thermonuclear bomb and the first test of a three-stage thermonuclear bomb.

After these nuclear tests, Deatrick became the executive officer to Maj. Gen. Howell Estes Jr., deputy commander for aerospace systems, Air Force Systems Command (AFSC), and later vice commander of AFSC. By then a lieutenant colonel, Deatrick followed Estes on a series of high-level assignments throughout the world.

Deatrick had spent the years of the Korean War in test pilot assignments. When 1965 rolled around and he came up for reassignment, he was within a year of twenty years' active duty and might have requested a terminal assignment close to where he wanted to retire. But that was not the way Deatrick flew. He had yet to command and to fly in combat. He told his friend Col. Pete Everest that he planned to volunteer for Vietnam. "I asked if he could help me get an assignment where I'd fly an F-100 Super Sabre, then the fastest fighter-bomber in Vietnam. Pete gave me the best advice I ever took, which was that if I were assigned to an F-100 unit, I'd probably spend most of my time in Saigon flying a desk. 'You want to volunteer for A-1's. No respectable fighter pilot would be caught dead in one,' Pete said. If I could get through a year in that, maybe I could get back to test flying."

The A-1E Skyraider had been designed and tested during World War II, but it was not ready for service until after the war. It saw extensive service as a carrier-based attack aircraft during the Korean War. It was the same aircraft Dengler flew on his ill-fated first mission over Laos. In Vietnam, the Skyraider became the infantry's best friend. It carried as much ordnance—rockets, bombs, napalm—as a World War II–era B-17 Flying Fortress heavy bomber, as well as four 20mm cannon. Despite what happened to Dengler, the A-1 was built to survive a lot of ground fire. It could also fly farther than most fuel-hungry jet fighters and linger over the battlefield for hours, providing both support and deterrence against enemy infantry. In addition to close air support missions, some Skyraiders flew air cover for long-range helicopters on search-and-rescue missions.

After a brief indoctrination course in the A-1E Skyraider at Hurlburt Field, Florida, in March 1966, Deatrick took command of the First Air Commando Squadron, based at Pleiku in the Central Highlands. One of his innovations as squadron commander was to encourage his pilots to get acquainted with the infantrymen they would be protecting by inviting them to orientation flights over the battlefield. His pilots thus provided better close air support through improved communications, and by following the infantryman's advice on selecting munitions best suited for their missions.

On November 10, 1966, Deatrick's West Point classmate Eleazar Parmly IV, commanding Task Force Prong, was ambushed by a larger enemy force. Parmly's troops were three Montagnard companies supported by Special Forces advisors; their mission was to screen the battlefield near the Cambodian border for elements of the US Fourteenth Infantry.

Sensing that his men were in peril, Parmly radioed a nearby forward air controller and asked if he knew Gene Deatrick of the First Air Commando Squadron and said, "Give him word that his old classmate is in deep sh*t." Elements of Deatrick's squadron, already airborne, arrived less than ten minutes later. Their well-placed bombs and rockets allowed Parmly's troops to break contact and move to a safer location.

If finding Dieter Dengler was Deatrick's principal claim to fame, it was by no means typical of his combat year in Vietnam, which included both close air support in South Vietnam and pinpoint bombing missions over the north. "We had hit a bridge north of the DMZ," he recalled. Heading back, his flight encountered heavy flak. "We leveled off at five thousand feet and headed for home. I saw some smoke in the cockpit, and a couple of red lights came on. I opened the window a little. I was on fire and there was a big hole in the right-hand seat, where flak came through. I had to decide whether to bail out or stay with the ship. I was way north of the DMZ, and if I'd have bailed out, I was likely headed for a POW camp—if I survived. My wingman got me to a marine base at Phu Bai, south of the DMZ, and I made a belly landing. That was a really hairy one, but we saved the airplane."

Deatrick flew 402 combat missions in Vietnam and was twice awarded the Distinguished Flying Cross. After returning from Vietnam, Deatrick became the commandant of the new air force aerospace research pilot school at Edwards. With this job came a promotion to colonel. During Deatrick's tenure at the school, his students received the long-awaited Lockheed NF-104A, a rocket-powered variant of the F-104 Starfighter intended to inexpensively train military space pilots.

In 1968, Deatrick was selected to attend the National War College. After graduation, he was assigned to the Joint Staff, Office of the Joint Chiefs of Staff. In 1972, he became the director of Test, Air Force Systems Command, Andrews Air Force Base, Maryland.

Gene Deatrick retired in 1974. During his twenty-eight-year career, he flew fifty different aircraft, including many as a test pilot, and made an incalculable contribution to operational flight safety in the US Air Force. He lives in suburban Washington, DC.

GUION "GUY" BLUFORD JR.

While NASA is a civilian agency, until 1986, all of its astronauts were military officers. And until 1977, every one of them was white. This may have been because, in order to sell space exploration to the taxpayers, NASA needed human pilots to glamorize its very expensive projects. That required experienced aviators in top physical shape at the flight controls, and only the military had them. The first military service to fully integrate was the air force, but not until 1950. Thus, when NASA was created in 1958, the most experienced military pilots were all white men. Guy Bluford didn't much care about any of that when he applied to become an astronaut. He merely wanted to fly in space and to utilize his hard-earned skills in aeronautical engineering. And NASA was the place to do it.

On the night of August 30, 1993, forty-year-old Guion "Guy" Bluford Jr. blasted into orbit aboard the space shuttle *Challenger*. Less than a minute into the flight, he was fifty thousand feet into the dark sky and subjected to the enormous pull of earth's gravity as his spacecraft was hammered by the jet stream and shoved to and fro, rattling the shuttle and its crew. Bluford, who had flown 133 combat missions during the Vietnam War, all of them in the F-4 Phantom and almost half of them over North Vietnam, was not at the controls. Instead, he was strapped into a seat on the crew deck with the other mission specialists. This was his first mission into space, but it would not be his last. Even so, Bluford was making history as the first African American in space. He had followed a long, hard, and perilous route to earn this distinction, but that was not on his mind as the *Challenger* went into earth orbit. His attention that historic night was instead on the mission, as it always was when Bluford was flying or anything else.

Known in his youth as Bunny, Guion Bluford grew up in a middle-class, racially mixed neighborhood in Philadelphia. Both of his parents came from distinguished families. His mother, Lolita, was related to Carol Brice Carey, a well-known contralto and voice coach, and his father was the brother of the editor of the *Kansas City Call*. Guion Sr. was a mechanical engineer until epilepsy forced him into early retirement. His mother was a special education teacher in public schools. She once confessed she thought Bluford the least likely of her three sons to be successful. She worked overtime to fund college for all three sons. His brother Eugene is a computer programmer and has a doctoral degree. And his other brother, Kenneth, is a teacher by profession, with a PhD in English.

Bluford was fascinated with his father's attitude toward work. "He would charge out of the house every morning, eager to get to work," he said. "I thought if engineers enjoy work that much, it must be a good thing to get into." He decided on a career as an aerospace engineer while he was still in junior high. Yet his indifferent high school grades gave no hint of the prodigious mental capacity he would demonstrate as an adult. After high school he enrolled in Penn State and promptly flunked freshman English, dropping his GPA below 2.0.

He did not give up but pushed himself to work harder. "My best year at Penn State was my senior year, because it took me four years to figure out how to study," Bluford said. "It was a challenging experience, and I thought, in the end, it gave me a lot of grit. That helped me throughout my career."

In 1964, he graduated with a BS in aerospace engineering and an ROTC commission as an air force second lieutenant. He went to flight school and earned pilot's wings in 1965. He was deployed to Vietnam in 1967 as copilot of a high-performance fighter. The F-4C Phantom II is a two-seat, twin-engine, all-weather, long-range supersonic interceptor and fighter-bomber originally developed for the navy. It was later adopted by the marines and the air force, and by the mid-1960s F-4C's had become a major part of their inventory.

The Phantom is a large aircraft with a top speed greater than Mach 2.2. It can carry more than eighteen thousand pounds of weapons on nine external hardpoints, including air-to-air missiles, air-to-ground missiles, and various bombs. Like other interceptors of its time, the Phantom was designed without an internal cannon. Later models incorporated an M-61 Vulcan rotary cannon. Beginning in 1959, the F-4C set fifteen world records for in-flight performance, including an absolute speed record and an absolute altitude record.

Bluford was stationed at Cam Rahn Bay as a member of the 557th Tactical Fighter Squadron. Most of the missions he flew were to provide air cover for the bombers. They encountered no enemy fighters—most of the North Vietnamese air force had been forced into underground shelters because of the bombing. A few fled to China and were rarely seen. The balance of Bluford's missions were primarily close air support for infantry.

When he returned from Vietnam, Bluford spent several years as a test pilot and flight instructor. For the next five years, as a T-38 instructor pilot at Sheppard Air Force Base in Wichita Falls, Texas, he taught both American and West German students to fly the sophisticated trainer as part of the air force's undergraduate pilot training program. This included takeoffs, landings, instrument flying, navigation flying, and formation flying. He served as an assistant flight commander and executive support officer to the deputy director of operations of the 3630th Flying Training Wing. He had more than twelve hundred hours of instructor pilot time in T-38's and was awarded Luftwaffe wings by the West German Air Force. Many of his German students went on to fly F-104's while his American students flew various aircraft.

While he was an instructor pilot at Sheppard, Bluford sought several opportunities to become an aerospace engineer within the air force. Unfortunately, the air force was critically short of pilots and needed his skills as an instructor more than as an engineer. The air force also indicated he would need a master's degree in aerospace engineering if he wanted to serve in that career field. "In preparation for going back to graduate school, I decided to take several advanced mathematics courses by correspondence at the University of California, Berkeley," Bluford recalled. "I elected to do preparatory course work that way, because there were very few educational opportunities in Wichita Falls. In 1971, I applied to the Air Force Institute of Technology (AFIT) for the master's program in aerospace engineering. In June 1972, I was accepted into the program and was assigned to AFIT, which is at the Wright-Patterson Base in Dayton. This was the break I needed to get into the engineering field. I was initially assigned to the air weapons program, but I was able to change my major to aerospace engineering. After three semesters, an AFIT professor recommended I stay on for the PhD program."

Bluford accepted that challenge, and in 1978 he earned a doctorate in aerospace engineering with a minor in laser physics. He ranked consistently among the top 10 percent of his class. While attending classes, he continued to work as a test pilot and a flight instructor at nearby Wright-Patterson Air Force Base. Then he was selected as branch chief of the aerodynamics and airframe branch. "I had completed my research for the PhD program and was in the midst of writing my dissertation. For me, at the time, being branch chief of the aerodynamics and airframe branch was a job I had always wanted. It was a great opportunity for me to use both my technical skills and my flying experience in developing advanced technologies for future aircraft. I led an organization of forty-five to fifty engineers, who were doing basic aerodynamic research in such areas as forward-swept wings, supercritical airfoils, advanced analytical aircraft design techniques, inlets, axisymmetric nozzles, and computational fluid dynamics. It was a great job, and I was really enjoying the work."

In 1977, the air force told Bluford he needed to return to a flying job. He needed to complete nine years of flying in his first eighteen years of service, but he had so far completed only six years of flying. Bluford began looking for a flying job. His background was primarily in tactical fighters and training aircraft. "I wanted to return to the fighter pilot business by flying F-15 or F-16 aircraft, but the air force wanted me to return as a T-37 instructor pilot," he recalled. Then Bluford saw that NASA was looking for astronauts to fly the space shuttle, and that opened opportunities for scientists and engineers (mission specialists) to be astronauts. "This looked like a great opportunity for me to fulfill my flying requirements in the air force, utilize my technical skills, and expand my technical knowledge all at the same time," Bluford said. "I could do it as a NASA astronaut. What a deal! So I applied in 1977. Meanwhile, I was still writing my dissertation with a plan on completing it by the end of 1978."

He submitted his paperwork for the astronaut program within the air force. Including Bluford, more than a thousand officers applied for both the pilot and mission specialist jobs. The air force selected roughly a hundred officers for consideration, and Bluford was chosen for the mission specialist position.

"I still remember a conversation I had with Tom Stafford, head of the air force selection board, many years later about my astronaut application," Bluford recalled. "He was impressed with my credentials and thus supported my application to be an astronaut. After the selection process was completed, the air force sent our names to NASA to be included with the applicants from the other services as well as eight thousand civilians. So throughout the summer of 1977, I wondered if I was going to make it or not."

Bluford survived a series of cuts to become one of thirty-five new astronauts. Among the others were two African Americans and a half dozen women, including Sally K. Ride. As no African American had then ever flown in space, reporters asked Bluford if he felt driven to break the racial barrier and be the first black man to leave earth. He said no, he was not ready to set another goal for himself. He simply wanted to fly in space and keep his personal privacy.

"It might be a bad thing to be first if you stop and think about it," Bluford said, addressing the mission's impact on himself rather than the opportunity it provided to speak for his race. "It might be better to be second or third, because then you can enjoy it and disappear, return to the society you came out of, without someone always poking you in the side and saying you were first."

When Sally Ride learned she would be America's first woman astronaut, she excitedly called her mother. Bluford was told at the same time that he had been scheduled for the next shuttle flight. He went back to his office and quietly finished some paperwork. He told his wife and their two teenage sons later that night. His two brothers heard the news on the radio the next day.

A few civil rights activists, long critical of NASA for waiting so long to put a black American in space, complained that Ride would precede him in space. That didn't bother Bluford. Instead, he was delighted. "She can carry the spear and get the attention," he said. "That relieves me." Bluford told a reporter he had never perceived his race as an obstacle to anything. "If I had any obstacles, they were self-made," he said.

Even now, long after his flights into space, Bluford remains something of a loner who says he has no best friends and no heroes. He describes himself as an average guy. "I felt an awesome responsibility, and I took the responsibility very seriously, of being a role model and opening another door to black Americans," he told the *Philadelphia Inquirer*. "But the important thing is not that I am black, but that I did a good job as a scientist and an astronaut. There will be black astronauts flying in later missions, and they, too, will be people who excel, not simply who are black who can ably represent their people, their communities, their country."

Bluford made four flights into space. On his first, aboard *Challenger*, he was responsible for the in-orbit launch of a communications satellite for the Indian government. He also assisted in a scientific experiment to separate live pancreas cells as part of a long-range biomedical project that NASA hoped would lead to the development of a pharmaceutical industry in space. After five days in orbit, *Challenger* dropped back to earth and landed at Edwards Air Force Base in the shuttle's first night landing. Shortly after that, the air force promoted Bluford to colonel.

After months of participating in public relations events for the shuttle program, Bluford returned to Cape Canaveral to begin work in an administrative position. Before he started, however, he was notified of his selection for the next shuttle flight, which included West German aviators. The training for this mission took eighteen months and was conducted in both West Germany and the Houston space center.

Mission STS-61-A, again aboard *Challenger*, was a Spacelab mission and required a crew of eight. Once in orbit, half the crew worked on a variety of space experiments while the other half slept in a soundproof compartment.

His third shuttle flight's mission was to study the upper atmosphere, cirrus clouds and the Northern Lights. In 1992, Bluford's fourth and last shuttle mission had a classified Department of Defense payload. He retired from NASA and the air force the following year.

In 1993, he became vice president and general manager with the engineering and computer software company NYMA Inc., later called Logicon Federal Data Corporation (FDC). It was purchased in 1997 by Northrop Grumman. The company was based in Cleveland, Ohio, and Bluford was responsible for overseeing FDC's aerospace engineering and research-related programs. Because the company provides support services to NASA as well as the Federal Aviation Administration and the Department of Defense, Bluford is still closely involved with NASA. In 2000, one of his projects was the support of the NASA Fluids and Combustion Facility.

In 2001, Bluford signed with The Space Agency, a public relations firm that represents former astronauts and space pioneers, thus ensuring that Bluford continues to inspire audiences, young and old, when he speaks at seminars, conferences, and corporate meetings. Among his favorite topics is the perspective gained by traveling into space and orbiting the earth. "I've come to appreciate the planet we live on," he told the *Philadelphia Inquirer.* "It's a small ball in a large universe. It's a very fragile ball but also very beautiful. You don't recognize that until you see it from a little farther off."

Today, Bluford runs a successful consulting business from a tiny office in suburban Cleveland. His job requires some travel, which gets him around the country.

Not long ago, after speaking at an all-black high school in Camden, New Jersey, Bluford was approached by a shy youngster who mumbled that he wanted to join the air force. Perhaps seeing something of himself decades earlier, Bluford looked at him knowingly, patted him on the shoulder, and said, "Go out there and buck it."

MARY COHOE

As egregious as stealing the lands and livelihoods of Native Americans were the long and mostly successful federal policies aimed at extinguishing their spoken languages and their native cultures. Despite more than a century (and counting) of these policies, a few Native American languages persist. Although teetering on the brink of oblivion, many native nations are fighting to preserve their language and enlarge the pool of native speakers, the seed bank of maintaining ancient religions and customs. Among the most successful are the Diné (Navajo) of the Southwest.

In 1944, Mary Tsinnajinnie Cohoe was born in Ganado, on the Ramah Navajo Indian Reservation in eastern Arizona. "My mother was a high school graduate," she recalled, "which at that time was very rare among Navajo people, especially women. She was asked by the federal government to be a principal teacher at Toyon, her home community, near Cuba, New Mexico, a village about sixty miles north of Albuquerque. In order for her to take that job, she gave me to my aunt and uncle in Arizona. I grew up with them until I was eight years old."

In 1966, Cohoe graduated from New Mexico Highlands University in Las Vegas, New Mexico, about an hour's drive from Santa Fe. "I started out with a major in music, but I ended up majoring in physical education," she recalled. For two years she taught PE in New Mexico's public schools. By 1968, however, Cohoe decided she must go to Vietnam.

"I just thought I needed to be there. There was so much news about it across the nation, and I thought, why is it so wrong to be there when we have friends and relatives who are not only being drafted there, they're enrolling, they're enlisting to go from the reservation. Young Navajo men were enlisting to go rather than waiting for the draft. And I had to know, really know what was going on. I thought it was the right thing to do."

Cohoe said she didn't believe what she saw in the newspapers. "It was not just my people, my relatives, my nephews, my brother, my Navajo friends, and young people who were being drafted. Navajo and non-Navajo people were being drafted or just enlisting. I was not that much older than they were, so I made it a point to find a way to Vietnam."

Cohoe did her own itinerary. "I was going to go on my own. How much was it going to cost. I forgot how much it was going to cost one way on flights to Saigon, Albuquerque to Saigon, and I thought, *Good grief, I'll have to borrow money from the bank.* But I did not have a cosigner and I didn't have a job. And what would I do when I got to Saigon? Then I remembered a brochure from a teacher placement bureau when I was being interviewed for a teaching position back in 1966. I found it, a particular brochure from the American Red Cross seeking volunteers for service in South Vietnam. I was eligible. I was a college graduate. I was between the ages of twenty-one and twenty-four. I was single and I was very healthy, so I applied."

The Red Cross invited Cohoe to an interview in Denver and paid for her transportation. There were forms to fill out, then a visit to a doctor to get the requisite immunization shots. Assured that she would be hired, Cohoe let her employers know she wouldn't be returning for the fall semester. Before she could start training, however, the Red Cross required at least one parent give permission, even though Cohoe was an adult. "My mother didn't want me to go. She would not sign for me. Somehow, I begged my dad to sign for me, so he did. I needed to get from Cuba to Albuquerque's airport. I could take the bus. However, they would not even take me to the bus depot," she recalled.

"I had to ask a neighbor to take me. I started Red Cross training in June. The supplemental recreational activities class, which lasted two or three weeks, was held in Charlottesville, Virginia, because Washington was full of antiwar demonstrators."

Her brother, a marine, was in a San Diego hospital, recovering from wounds suffered in Vietnam.

"Then we flew across the nation to San Francisco. Our orders were to get on a flight, military orders. We waited in San Francisco for maybe three days and finally were able to get on a flight from Travis Air Force Base," she recalled. Her flight took her to Honolulu, Manila, and then Saigon.

"We were asked not to raise our window blinds because the heat would come into the plane while we were still on the runway. It took some time to get all of us off the plane, but the blinds went up anyway. It was hot. It was very hot. Good grief, it was hot," Cohoe recalled.

Mary Cohoe was one of 627 Red Cross "Donut Dollies" who served in Vietnam during the entire war. "I understand there were at least 110 of us in the country at a time, and we were rotated. Over all the years of get-togethers, reunions, and big events, as far as I know, I'm the only Native American woman who did that," she said.

Donut Dollies was a nickname from earlier wars, when they sometimes passed out coffee and donuts. In Vietnam, they went from unit to unit, trying to bring a bit of home and good cheer.

"We had mobile units and recreation centers. My first assignment was all mobile units, which was up in Chu Lai. We were also trained to conduct audience participation–type activities. We planned them and had dry runs with each other. We took out our games, and the main purpose for us being there to take out the games was just to get the GIs to get their mind away from the war for just a little bit. A little time, anywhere from thirty minutes to two hours maybe," Cohoe explained.

Although American soldiers went to great lengths to protect these young volunteers from danger, it wasn't always possible. "We were sometimes in danger," Cohoe said. She was usually based at Cam Ranh Bay. "I worked with whoever took care of operations out in the area. If they were operations in heavy contact, we wouldn't go there. We served all the branches—the army, the air force, the marines. Not so much the navy. Up in Chu Lai were mainly fighting divisions, the army, and marine air groups, and the marines," she recalled.

In some ways, the presence of pretty, well-groomed, friendly American women was a problem to the vast bulk of fighting men they visited in the field or in garrison. "Look but don't touch" was the policy. Red Cross women were not allowed to date any of the men. On occasion, they would be invited, in small groups, to dine in a general's mess. Even there, the officers were ordered to keep their distance.

"We didn't go out there to hug and maybe not even shake hands. Maybe once in a while, but I don't remember doing those things. We always went out in pairs or groups of four or more." And because they were usually flown to and from the units they visited, danger was always present in a war zone. "I remember one time when we were in the only chopper in the area, we had to make a quick drop in. We were told to get in the middle of the passenger compartment. When we landed, they threw in a couple of wounded guys. One of them was NVA—an enemy soldier. He was blindfolded. His hands were tied in the back. I was right in the middle, and he was right in front of me. We flew away from there as fast as possible and went back to Chu Lai and got out and that was it. Then another time, at Cam Ranh Air Base, we had both units, mobile units as well, so recreation centers. Two recreation centers at Cam Ranh Air Base, and on a mobile one farther south at II Corps.

"Once we flew up to Bao Loc in a C-130, it was that far. We had to stay overnight because we were there in the afternoon, and then the monsoon started and there were no flights out. There were no proper quarters for women. They gave us a little shack with locks on the outside as well as on the inside. And we were given a couple of M-16 rifles. We were told, 'This is in case we have a ground attack.'

"I thought, *Good grief, I come from a hunting family.* At the time, I thought, *If I have to, I'll figure it out.* I knew those rifles were powerful. I thought, *Okay.* But my partner wanted to check it out. I knew there were two rules. If you don't know a rifle, don't touch it. Number two, we are noncombatants. Don't touch it. I was so upset with her because she was the one. . . . She was the leader for the day, and she was the one who delayed our flight. Our flight was ready to leave, but she had said, 'Oh, Mary, we'll take the next one.' The next one didn't come until the next morning.

"When I was in Chu Lai, we were often hungry. At least I was hungry a lot. We would have to be on the chopper by six in the morning. That meant getting ready earlier to walk over there and then fly somewhere and hang out all day long, come back, and the mess hall was closed by six. So we missed breakfast and dinner unless we had something back in our trailer. We did get invited to the general's mess every Monday evening. And at the general's mess in Chu Lai also. The food was good, and being in the company of colonels and the general. Afterward, we would go to the back door to the general's mess and take the leftovers.

"Then, when we were at Cam Ranh Bay, we were also invited to dinners by the navy. They had nice plates and linen tablecloths."

Before the end of her yearlong tour, Cohoe's mother became ill, and she was allowed to go home early. But when she got back to New Mexico, like many Vietnam veterans, she was unsure of what to do next.

"I just didn't know what to do," she recalled. "I was kind of lost. I decided to go back to school for a quarter, which was just a few months, just to do something. Then I was recruited by Highlands University to accept a fellowship to go into guidance and school counseling. The university had received a fellowship, and they needed a Native American person. I was visiting my grandparents on the reservation in Arizona, and the school found me. I accepted and stayed at Highlands University and earned my master's degree in guidance and counseling.

"After I got my master's, I went home and thought I'd just hang out there for a while. My mom told me I should go find work, go get a job. I wanted something different. I was offered jobs. I wanted to do something with Native American students, especially Navajo students. I was offered a job at three different schools, but they were bureau jobs, Bureau of Indian Affairs jobs." Many Native Americans do not care to work for the Bureau of Indian Affairs (BIA), because they disagree with its methods and goals.

"Then I heard about the Ramah Navajo Reservation. There is a big Navajo reservation and three satellite communities: Tohajilee, Alamo, and Ramah Navajo. I didn't even know Navajos were out there. Ramah Navajo people decided to start a school, which was unheard of across the nation the way they wanted to do it. I thought, *They're crazy people. I think I'll go join them.* I went to be interviewed, and that was another adventure, another uninteresting and long adventure in the way of distance from my home. I had to use a map to find the place, and I stayed overnight. I did not speak Navajo at the time, because I grew up in a boarding school."

Since the latter part of the nineteenth century, most Native American children were required to go to boarding schools run by the BIA or by Christian missionaries. They were not allowed to speak their native languages and were punished if they were caught doing so. The result was generations of Native Americans who could not speak the languages of their ancestors. Because language is culture, they were largely stripped of their ethnic heritage.

"When I came here to Ramah Navajo, I had not spoken Navajo for years and years, but I understood it. I had to have a translator. The Ramah Navajo school board interviewed me for over two hours, entirely in Navajo. They wanted a 200 percent commitment from me if I wanted to work here. I finally said I would, and I started in the fall of 1970 as a teacher and counselor. As the years went by, I inherited other responsibilities," she explained.

Ramah Navajo is a unique and exceptional institution. In 1968, the state of New Mexico closed the only public high school in the area. That left the children on the Ramah Navajo Reservation no way to attend high school except at a BIA boarding school. The vast majority of Navajo people do not want to send their children to such schools. So they started their own. "First, we were leasing old school buildings," Cohoe explained. "Then, in the fall of 1975, we moved up to Pine Hill. Not a dollar from the tribe. Not a dollar from the BIA. Not a dollar from the state. Congress appropriated funds for us to build our school buildings here.

"We follow the New Mexico Department of Education standards required to open a nonpublic school. At the time, we were called a contract school. We contracted with the BIA that we would operate our own school," Cohoe explained. "Any child who could get here by bus was welcome to attend. Then, in 1975, Congress passed the Indian Self-Determination Act. And we do things that no other native tribe in the nation experiences. Teaching is in both English and Navajo.

"In 1975, President Nixon said, 'Ramah Navajo is a model of Indian self-determination,'" Cohoe recalled. "Later on, the public law came about. Then we built a school with the following mission statement: Our mission is to nurture and develop students who will meet the challenges of today's ever-changing society while perpetuating their culture and language."

Each student is required to take the Warrior Pledge: "I believe in myself and my ability to do my best at all times. I believe I should treat others as I want them to treat me. I believe in the strength of my heritage that is the foundation upon which I stand. And so I dedicate myself to study hard and take pride in myself and my school."

Except for the years she left Ramah to get married and have children, Mary Cohoe has spent her adult life at Ramah Navajo. When her marriage failed, she took her three daughters and went back to Ramah, where she continues to live and work today. Now fluent in Navajo, she serves as the head K-12 school guidance counselor. "I've served here as the federal programs coordinator. I also gave myself the title congressional liaison in the eighties because I like working with congressional committees to get things done here, to get funding for different programs here.

"My daughters grew up here, and this is their home. I'm no longer with the father, with my ex-husband. We're good here," she said, pride in her place in Navajo society and her home beaming from every word.

MIKE
HEBERT

During the decades of the Cold War, no Americans were in more physical danger than the invisible-by-design ranks of the US intelligence agencies, especially the CIA. Working as a field agent meant constantly moving one's family and household, being on duty 24/7, even when supposedly on vacation, and always living a double life. Forget about James Bond. CIA agents rarely had much backup, worked for modest salaries, and lived to expect the unexpected. The best of these men and women usually had military training and a soldier's can-do attitude.

Mike Hebert (pronounced Ay-bear) is the son of a US Navy petty officer who spent most of his long career on aircraft carriers. Like most military families, the Heberts bounced from one base to another. Hebert started school in Bermuda, then spent most of his youth between Jacksonville, Corpus Christi, and Virginia Beach. Summer vacations were spent at his maternal grandparents' farm in rural Georgia, where he learned to hunt and fish and became a proficient marksman. "My mom's folks didn't have a lot of cash, but their property had a lot of game," he recalled. "My grandmother would say, 'I feel like cookin' squirrel tonight,' and I'd go shoot some squirrels. Or she'd say, 'We'll have rabbit tonight.'" At night he patrolled the fields with a shotgun to keep raccoons, skunks, rabbits, and other nocturnal animals from destroying the crops.

"By the time I wore long pants, wandering around in the woods with a gun at night was not a strange idea to me." This became relevant when Hebert went through SEAL training; many of his classmates were city raised and had never been in the woods at night.

Hebert's paternal grandparents spoke only Cajun French, which sparked his interest in languages. By the time he reached maturity, Hebert was comfortable in half a dozen languages and went on to learn many more. He can get along in almost any country in the world.

Hebert's parents divorced while he was in high school, but his mother had established a career in the Department of the Navy. Her long service included a tour in Vietnam. Hebert's stepfather, who had survived the 1941 attack on Pearl Harbor aboard USS *Nevada*, also had a long navy career, mostly in battleships. He retired as a warrant officer.

As for Hebert, he grew up wanting to follow in his father's footsteps, sort of. He enrolled at the University of Idaho and joined the Naval reserve Officers Training Corps. In 1972, between his junior and senior years, he spent the summer in Vietnam as a midshipman on USS *Newport News* (call sign Thunder), the world's largest heavy cruiser. His duties consisted of standing watches alongside the heads of each of the ship's various departments: engineering, deck, gunnery, communications, and others.

The *Newport News's* principal mission was gunfire support to US Marine and South Vietnamese units. Its nine eight-inch guns could hurl 335-pound high-explosive projectiles at targets up to seventeen miles away. In August 1972, *Newport News* joined USS *Providence* (CLG-6), USS *Robison* (DDG-12), and USS *Rowan* (DD-782) on a raid of Hai Phong harbor. *Newport News* shelled shore targets with its eight-inch guns. *Providence* and *Robison* provided anti-aircraft cover, and *Rowan* launched four AGM-45 Shrike antiradiation missiles at North Vietnamese radar sites. At least two North Vietnamese torpedo boats engaged the task force and attempted to attack the cruisers. *Newport News* was also very effective in the battle of Quang Tri. The ship and crew, including Hebert, were awarded the coveted Presidential Unit Citation.

In October, *Newport News* suffered an accidental explosion in gun turret number 2, at the cost of nineteen lives. By then, however, Hebert was back in school. In 1974, he graduated with a double major and was immediately commissioned and called to active duty. Although he was the best pilot in his class, Hebert volunteered for underwater demolitions–SEAL training (BUD/S). The first SEALS, who received additional training in parachute operations, came out of underwater demolition teams (UDT), and for several years the terms were almost interchangeable.

Most of Hebert's deployments were with Seal Team 2 while he was assigned to UDT-21. "Every time they had some mission where they needed extra men, they'd grab us," he explained. That allowed him to attend the navy's winter warfare school. Commanding a platoon, Hebert also saw deployments to the Caribbean and the North Atlantic.

His dream of a navy career ran aground when all US armed services began congressionally mandated reductions in force size. After serving in both UDT and ashore, he completed five years of active duty and was released to the navy reserve.

Hebert wanted to join the FBI. He spoke French, Russian, and Spanish, but the bureau required a degree in law or accounting. "I looked at the Naval Investigative Service, but they had a hiring freeze. Then I thought about the Secret Service and the Border Patrol. In the end, I joined the Central Intelligence Agency," he said.

"The CIA has a wide range of jobs, assignments, and specialties. A lot of stuff I'd done in the navy fit with what they were looking for," Hebert explained. "Many of the people they hired had advanced degrees. I had, instead, some time in Vietnam and some in Special Operations. I had command time. I had used scuba gear, parachute gear, various explosives, and weapons. I had more worldly experience than classmates who had advanced degrees in Russian studies and that kind of stuff. My interest in languages really helped too."

Hebert had one more thing: the military mentality. He would go anywhere he was needed, do what was asked of him, always cheerfully. "Many of my colleagues seemed prissy at times. They wanted to go to Europe, they wanted to go to nice, very civilized places. They wouldn't go someplace that didn't have this, that, or the other thing. I went with the needs of the service, and that helped me. It put me in some very crappy places, but it also gave me some really good jobs."

After training, Hebert began the first of a long series of overseas assignments in operations. He attended functions where he attempted, with some success, to recruit diplomats from the host country or from third countries, who could provide information vital to American national security.

As he traveled, he picked up new languages. "To use the verb 'to speak' means to be fluent in a language," he explained. "French and Farsi are my most current. My Russian is a little rusty, but it's in there. I had, at one time, very functional Greek. I can travel and get along fine in Spanish and German. I studied Hindi for two years and Bengali for two years. I've also dabbled in Macedonian and in Swahili, even in Esperanto, an artificial language based on Latin." But that wasn't the end. While earning a black belt in tae kwon do, he picked up some Korean. "Language proficiency opened a lot of doors, introduced me to a lot of people, and taught me a lot about different cultures," he explained.

Hebert's spy work was classified, but there are a few things he can relate. By inference, one can imagine the sorts of things he cannot reveal.

"As time went on, the type of targets changed. When I first joined, it was the big Soviet threat. There were certain KGB officers who were harder for us to make contact with," he explained. "During the day we would do our regular work. Often we spent evenings meeting with sources. But at the end of the day, we always drove by places where Soviets were known to hang out at night.

"If their car was parked near some restaurant, bar, or club, we'd sidle up next to them at the bar and buy them a scotch and start a conversation," he related. "They knew who I was. On one level, it was a game: a little teasing, a little jiving, that kind of stuff. But always there were rules, a gentleman's game. But not terrorists. Terrorists just want to cut your head off. They'll never have a drink or talk with you. The Soviets were almost always open to a little tit for tat. If something happened within their world, and maybe they were a little disgruntled, they always knew they could talk to us. This is what we were taught to do. Hard targets, they may not come over right away. The Soviets were tough. But some operations were ultimately very successful because everyone involved followed protocol," Hebert concluded.

With the end of the Cold War, the CIA shifted its emphasis to counterterrorism. Hebert's career followed along. He became a base chief a few weeks after the death of a local leader. "The country was in turmoil," he recalled. The political turmoil gradually resolved after an election and an inauguration.

Africa was a dangerous area. Terrorism was growing in many of the pro-American countries. Hebert ran counterterrorism operations against Hezbollah terrorists in West Africa. "Hezbollah is a tough nut to crack, but we had some success against them there."

This was around the time when al-Qaeda bombed the American embassies in Tanzania and Kenya. "There was a ripple effect. We had to bolster security in all our embassies, but especially in West Africa," he explained. Hebert spent his last years in the CIA training police and military antiterrorism units in countries throughout the region.

Hebert retired from the CIA in 2002, but he still serves his country. "It seems like I've been busier since I retired," he said with a smile. Today, he roams the world. It's a mixture of classroom and field work, a task that requires not only broad experience but also a facility with foreign languages.

Few, if any, handle both better than Mike Hebert.

SCOTT RATLIFF

The bane of Native American reservations is alcoholism. With few jobs and fewer prospects, many men and women fall into the trap of dulling their senses with alcohol or other drugs. Distrustful of outsiders, especially whites, Native Americans too rarely realize their potential unless and until they are awakened and led by one of their own.

It had been a hard winter on the plains of central Wyoming. As the sun rose in mid-January 1943, Catherine Ratliff realized her baby was coming. The Ratliffs, members of the Eastern Shoshone Tribe, lived on a ranch twelve miles from their nearest neighbor, and still farther from the hospital at Fort Washakie, on Wyoming's Wind River Reservation.

Scott Ratliff wrapped his wife in a thick blanket and set out for Fort Washakie in his battered pickup truck. Hours later, when he arrived at the hospital, a nurse told him it might be a day or two or even longer before the baby came. He said goodbye to his wife and returned to the ranch, where there were animals to feed and chores to do.

It would be two weeks before he returned to the hospital to learn his wife had given birth to a healthy boy, whom they named Scott but called Scotty.

Catherine was furious she'd been left at the hospital for two weeks. "I guess she forgave him eventually," opined her son, now in his seventies. Catherine, now ninety-seven and a widow, lives alone on her ranch.

"I was raised on that ranch," Scott Ratliff explained. "My extended family lived there, and besides my sister and younger brothers, I had nine cousins. Being the oldest, the responsibility of getting things done always fell on my shoulders, as it still does. If there's a family problem, it seems like they always come to me with it."

As a senior at Pavilion High School, Ratliff began to drink. Upon graduation, he enrolled at the University of Wyoming. "I dropped out several times," he explained. "I got married and I had a lot of family problems, mostly because of my drinking. That kind of thing wasn't as common on the reservation as it is today, but it certainly wasn't foreign. Alcohol has been a big part of my life, both sober or drunk. I spent many years drunk." He continued, "They were painful times because they severed marriages. I was twenty-four after my first divorce. And then, in 1966, I was drafted."

At twenty-four, he was the oldest in his training cohort and spared many of basic training's worst indignities and appointed to positions of responsibility. After advanced infantry training at Fort Polk, Louisiana, he shipped out to Vietnam and to the Twenty-Fifth "Tropic Lightning" Infantry Division's Second Battalion, Thirty-Fifth Infantry, then operating in the Central Highland jungles near Dak To. "I enjoyed seeing that part of the country. There were so many native people living there, and I liked that," he recalled.

Ratliff was an assistant machine gunner. Four months later, when his gunner was killed in a firefight, he did what he had always done: he took over. He grabbed the gun and began firing at the enemy. A little later a bullet tore into his right shoulder.

"It was kind of interesting," he explained. "When I got shot, it also took the top part of my lung out. It blew me over and I saw what looked like my arm flying off. It was just a flash. The bullet severed the main nerve instantly. I never felt a drop of pain from that arm."

Ratliff was quickly flown to a field hospital. "I was bleeding badly. They gave me blood and plasma, then put me on a plane and flew me to a big hospital in Qui Nhon," he recalled.

Doctors repaired a torn artery in his arm, but not before gangrene had begun to appear in some of his fingers. "In all the Western movies of my childhood, when someone got gangrene, they had to cut off a leg or an arm or something to save his life," Ratliff explained. "I did not understand gangrene. When I came out of surgery, I still had my arm, but I couldn't feel it. It was like I was holding some other man's arm. Then I saw that two of my fingers were turning black. I called a nurse over and she said I had gangrene. I said, 'Jesus Christ, get a doctor over here and cut them fingers off,'" he recalled.

The nurse explained his gangrene was only from a loss of blood. When they fixed his artery, the fingers would again receive blood flow. As it happened, Ratliff did lose the pads of his little and ring fingers.

From Vietnam, Ratliff was flown to Japan for more surgery, and then to Fitzsimons Army Medical Center in Denver, where surgeons attempted for the next eleven months to find a way to repair or regenerate the nerves in his arm. "There was a gap of about six inches in the nerve, where the bullet destroyed it. And they were never able to hook up the two parts," Ratliff explained. "The doctors asked if I wanted them to amputate my arm. I wrestled with that idea and finally decided against it.

"I'm a rough man and was kind of a worthless piece of crap before I went into the service, mostly because of my drinking. I continued with the drinking for years, but I realized I had to do something with my life. I had three daughters by then, and I had to support them. I knew I had to get an education, because I couldn't make it doing physical stuff.

"I got out of the service in Denver and stayed there while I went to Arapahoe Community College for two years. Then I went to Black Hills State University in South Dakota for two years," he continued. In 1973, Ratliff earned a master's in counseling at the University of Wyoming. Meanwhile, he struggled daily to learn to use his left arm as well as he had once used his right.

After college, Ratliff returned home to the Wind River Reservation and found a job as an Indian counselor at one of the high schools. Later, he ran the Department of Indian Education there for a year. "Indian education didn't differ a great deal from what the white children got. I worked at different schools, and I tried to train my students to treat Indian students as they them-selves would want to be treated," he explained.

Ratliff obtained some government funds and used them to hire home-school coordinators to work with at-risk children at all the schools on the Wind River Reservation. These students were struggling academically. The coordinators tried to keep them in school instead of becoming so frustrated that they dropped out.

For the next twenty-five years, Ratliff counseled Indian students at Central Wyoming College. "Their biggest problem was attendance," he explained. "Students fell behind and wanted to quit. Some of them were involved in petty crime and they'd get arrested or go into hiding. Or they'd just take a week off. It's hard to make that up. I had to talk to their teachers and see if I could get them back in class. Sometimes they'd have to change classes."

All the while he was teaching and counseling, Ratliff engaged with the reservation community. He sponsored the Veterans Club, the Rodeo Club, the Blue Sky Indian Club, and other student organizations.

In 1979, drawing on grim determination and what the Cody, Wyoming, *Star Tribune* described as "his strong spiritual belief in his Creator," Ratliff quit drinking.[1] "That's a long story," he said, "but never mind. Once I was sober. I discovered I had thoughts. A brain that could function. I'd been drinking for so long I'd forgotten about that."

Soon after achieving sobriety, Ratliff attended a community meeting with several members of the Wyoming House of Representatives. He didn't like what he saw. "I thought I could do a better job than they were, so I decided to run for office," he explained. "I didn't know anything about politics. Nothing. I couldn't even tell you who I'd voted for the year before. But I ran and I won."

Ratliff went on to serve six two-year terms in the legislature between 1980 and 1992. "I served on the appropriations committee for six years, and we made many important decisions about the future of our state," he explained. Of the many laws he worked to pass, he is proudest of one that required insurance companies to recognize alcoholism as a disease. "That was huge," Ratliff said.

After twelve years in office, he decided he needed to change his life. He and his wife divorced. "I was pretty well-respected and so was my wife. Many in the community were angry at me over the divorce. I decided I didn't want to go through another election."

The Wind River Reservation traces its history to 1868, and it's unique because it's the only reservation where two former enemy tribes live. The Eastern Shoshone Tribe, the original residents, share the land with members of the Arapaho. Each tribe manages its own affairs and has its own schools.

Ratliff has left a lasting imprint on his community. He founded and served as the first president of the Wyoming Cowboy Hall of Fame, whose purpose is "to preserve, promote, perpetuate, publish and document Wyoming's rich working cowboy and ranching history." A lifelong horse rancher, Ratliff has spent a lifetime in the saddle. He still has five hundred acres and raises what he describes as "petting horses." And he competes in rodeo and other equestrian events.

Since 2002, Ratliff has served as an advisor to Wyoming senator Mike Enzi, a lifelong friend. "I keep him up to date with all tribal issues, and I try to keep the tribe informed of federal issues," Ratliff explained.

Ratliff has served as a member of the Wyoming state board of education since 2011 as well as on the National Advisory Board on Indian Education. With several like-minded colleagues, he started Native Ed for All, which works to expose all students in Wyoming to Native American culture.

Ratliff is also involved in trying to reintroduce the Shoshone language to the younger generation as a means of preserving a vanishing culture. "There are about 5,000 Shoshones but only about 123 native speakers," he explained. "That's terrible. Part of the problem is there are very few educated people who speak the language. In years past, most people grew up hearing it spoken by their grandparents or parents. That's not happening now. The schools tried bringing these grandparents in to teach. They're fine people and know the language, but they are not teachers. They want to teach the children one word at a time. In successful language programs, students are taught a subject using the language. And they've had tremendous success with full immersion.

"I believe that the term *warrior* isn't just about the minutes when you're battling," Ratliff opined. "You are either a warrior or you are not. And if you are, it's a lifetime battle. I'm seventy-five years old now. I've made it this far. I call it good, living the life of this man. I've had some blessings," he said.

A proud Shoshone warrior, Scott Ratcliff continues to battle for his people.

VIET X. LUONG

The ethnic stew that is America has been seasoned and enriched by the tens of thousands of Vietnamese refugees who fled communism and sought a new life in America. In a time when some revile nonwhite foreigners, it is vital to consider the tremendous contribution of Vietnamese Americans to the national weal.

In 1933, Viet Luong's parents were born in North Vietnam. "My father was born in Son Tay and my mother in Nem Dang," he recalled.[1] "My dad served in the French commandos. When they went south in 1954, my father transitioned to the Vietnamese Marine Corps, becoming one of the first US-trained Vietnamese marine officers in South Vietnam." The elder Luong served multiple tours in the United States during the fifties, including training at Quantico, the amphibious landing school in San Diego, and Camp Pendleton, California. Between training abroad, he served as a captain and later a major in South Vietnam's First Marine Battalion.

"As a marine, he fought throughout the country as a backup or strategic reserve to the rest of the South Vietnamese Army along with the South

VIET X. LUONG

Vietnamese airborne division." The Luong family, meanwhile, lived mostly in Saigon.

In 1968, at the start of the Tet Offensive, Luong, the oldest son, was two and a half years old. He remembers a series of explosions throughout his otherwise quiet residential neighborhood. "Our house was burning, although I didn't see the fires. We were immersed in smoke. It was a typical house in Saigon, with large metal sliding doors locked from the inside with a big key. I remember my mom with all of us, at that time six kids, scrambling to find the keys to get us out of the house. Finally, we poured out into the streets. Some of her relatives came by and helped evacuate us to a safer part of Saigon."

Otherwise, Luong has mostly good memories of his childhood. "Compared to folks living in the countryside and actually exposed to the war, we in Saigon were in relative comfort. I remember meeting a few of my uncles' American comrades when they returned from the war zone," he said. "I also remember going to the movies once in a while. Mostly seeing Chinese martial arts movies, Bruce Lee movies, and so on. Life was fairly good for us in Saigon. We were pretty much sheltered from all the hazards and the violence of the war.

"My father had majored in English at the University of Saigon, and he spoke fluent English," Luong said. "When he was home from the war for a few days, we sometimes watched the American Forces Network. I remember watching *The Big Valley*, *The Rifleman*, and even *Combat!*, with Vic Morrow, when I was a kid."

By 1975, the senior Luong had risen to become the chief aide-de-camp to Gen. Le Nguyen Khang, the former commandant of the marines, then chosen to be vice chief of the army. "My dad became his executive officer, and so he followed him onto the army side but still retained his status as a marine officer. So we led very privileged lives."

In the months before the fall of Saigon in April 1975, the senior Luong accompanied his boss on a nationwide tour of South Vietnam's combat areas. "He came back disappointed," Luong recalled. "He doubted the country could last through the coming summer. My parents often discussed this after dinner. I was too young to participate, but I understood what was happening, and I was afraid. Then my parents involved some of my older sisters in their conversations. My oldest sister was already in college at the University of

Saigon. My other three older sisters were in high school. They had started to talk about possible courses of action, and of course, since I was his only son, he talked about possibly sending me out of the country to live with some of his marine advisor friends in the States. When he became convinced South Vietnam was doomed, he began talking about getting several of us out of the country. Then they began to talk about whether he should go back to a marine line unit to fight or, if the country were to fall, go into the jungle to continue the fight against the communists.

"I was pretty distraught at hearing some of that. I was only nine, so I didn't get to participate, but I knew exactly what they were talking about and was wishing for none of it to come true. My dad was a stalwart officer. We felt very confident whenever he was around, whether it was in terms of our safety, leadership, or direction. He was very influential to all of us," Luong continued.

"My mom was different. She was a supportive wife. She sacrificed her entire life. But my dad was our patriarch. So when he came home in March and said, 'We are in trouble,' I was saddened by that. I was willing to stay. I didn't want to be split up or go anywhere for my own safety. I was worried more about my family sticking together.

"Then came April, and apparently he had been talking to some of his friends. One of them was Michael Casey—he might have been a CIA guy, I don't know exactly how he knew my dad. My dad told me he would get the paperwork done to get us out of the country. This was in the last week of April, the country was about to fall, and then the Central Highlands collapsed and fell into North Vietnamese hands.

"The communists were on the outskirts of Saigon, so we didn't flee toward Tan Son Nhut airport until April 26, 1975. We shipped out pretty quietly. We were told to bring only a change of clothes and all the paperwork that Mr. Casey gave us. Our driver took us to Tan Son Nhut. The first day, there were issues with the paperwork, so we stayed at a hotel. The next day, April 27, we went through the gates at the airport.

"It was so crowded! We couldn't get inside the terminal, so we stayed out on the tarmac. Everybody was happy. But when they announced they were shutting down fixed-wing aircraft operations due to the threat of enemy artillery and missiles, we thought we were doomed. People there were completely dejected. Most folks were pretty much resigned to their fate.

"Then, the next day there was incoming fire. Artillery and mortars. We just knew we were doomed. I was really scared. Then we were bombed by a couple of captured A-37's. Later I learned one of the pilots was a turncoat. But when we saw that plane zoom by, my dad looked up and said to us, 'You're missing out on a monumental moment in history.' He was completely calm because he'd seen so much combat. But I was scared to death.

"I remember reciting my Hail Marys and stuff like that. I thought for sure we were going to die. My dad told us they're pretty close if they're shooting mortars. Then, a US Marine captain walked up. I'm sure he was the guy in charge, at least in charge of airport security. He asked, 'Does anybody speak English?' My dad started talking to them.

"I didn't speak any English then, so I don't know what they talked about. But my dad then told some of the men in the area to start clearing away the debris. People had suitcases and clothes and everything sitting everywhere, because they thought they were going to die. Some of the men became belligerent, because they didn't know who my dad was. He had to pull a pistol on them to tell them to get on with the work.

"Over the next couple of hours, people pitched in and cleared a landing area for helicopters. That night they started putting us in groups of sixty people. Then the first of several CH-53 Sea Stallion helicopters dropped from the night sky to load the groups and take them to the aircraft carriers positioned in international waters off the coast. Thus began Operation Frequent Wind, designed to evacuate South Vietnamese with strong ties to the US forces in Vietnam.

"After our helicopter landed on one of the carriers, many thought we were on an island, because we were disoriented. I remember walking out onto the huge deck and asking my dad, 'Where are we?' He said, 'We're on top of the USS *Hancock*, a carrier from the Seventh Fleet.' Still confused, I asked what that meant. He said, 'That means nothing can harm you now.' That's been etched in my memory for decades," Luong concluded.

The *Hancock* sailed to the Philippines. From there the refugees were flown to Guam. "We stayed at the Orote refugee camp for about three weeks. After we were processed, my family went to the refugee camp at Fort Chaffee, Arkansas," Luong recalled. They remained for about six months, waiting to be sponsored by an American family, a church, or some organization willing to be responsible for the health and welfare of each family member.

The French government offered to admit the Luongs in recognition of the father's pre-1954 service. But the family opted to stay in America, and eventually Michael Casey, who had helped the family escape Vietnam, sponsored them. They moved to Southern California, and for three weeks the family lived in Casey's home. They might have stayed longer, but it was evident that nine children and two adults, sleeping on floors, put a heavy strain on their host family.

The Luongs rented a house in Silver Lake, then a low-income, multiethnic community not far from downtown Los Angeles. Luong's father took a job as a security guard and his mother worked in a fast-food restaurant. For a time, the older sisters found jobs until their parents decided they should go back to school. When they graduated from college and found work, most of their earnings went to support their parents and siblings. They worked hard and lived frugally. Only three years after leaving Vietnam, the family bought a house in West Hollywood. All the while, young Viet Luong went to school, learned English, and excelled at his studies.

Today, every member of the family has built a life of achievement. About his eight sisters, Luong explained, "One of my sisters is an attorney. After law school, she practiced for about three years. Now she and her husband own their own business and do very well. My oldest sister is a CPA who owns a real estate brokerage. She's very successful as well. Another sister earned a PhD in computer science and now works for Dell. She also teaches. Another sister graduated from college but is able to be a stay-at-home mom. Another sister graduated from USC and UCLA and is now a nurse practitioner. Another sister is also an attorney. Another sister is a housewife married to an attorney. And my youngest sister works for Fox News as a segment producer."

What of Viet X. Luong, the once fearful nine-year-old refugee? He graduated from the University of Southern California with a bachelor's degree in biological sciences and then followed in his father's footsteps and joined the US Army. He saw combat in Iraq and in Afghanistan. Presently, Maj. Gen. Viet X. Luong is the commanding general, US Army, Japan.

"We have worked hard, but most of our success is about our nation, the opportunities we received," he said. "The freedom we have to choose the way to live our lives, I think that's been more instrumental in our family's success than anything. Our nation. It's the only one like it in the world."

ACKNOWLEDGMENTS

We wish to thank Henry Weiss, James Caccavo, William Albracht, Jim Graham, John Ahearn, and the late Don Hirst for suggesting subjects to profile for this book. In addition, it needs to be said that Marvin's daughter, Tomi Wolf, provided invaluable assistance both by relieving Wolf of many household chores and as an excellent sounding board when discussing the relative virtues of candidates to interview. We also thank Diane Carlson Evans for persuading a particularly important potential subject to cooperate and sit for an in-depth interview.

Doug Grad, our literary agent, worked above and beyond the usual bounds of his job description to find a publishing home for the manuscript. He also offered invaluable advice and insights that proved extraordinarily useful in researching and writing this book.

Jenny Baumgartner, our editor, worked tirelessly to turn our manuscript into a book and to make it better than either of us had supposed possible. Sujin Hong provided invaluable assistance in proofing and fact-checking our manuscript. And Karen Jackson put together first-class publicity and marketing campaigns to bring this work to a wide public audience.

NOTES

Epigraph

1. Sonnet, Copyright ©2018, Ron Vazzano, used with permission.

Foreword

1. The Viet Cong consisted of two fighting elements: local Viet Cong from hometowns and villages, and "Main Force" Viet Cong, the battalion- and regimental-sized units drawn from the entire country. Each had distinctive fighting methods and capabilities.
2. What we wrote were not captions, per se, but facts about the roll of film that an editor would draw from to write the captions for individual photos.

Introduction

1. In 1964, while living in Long Beach and still a civilian, I (Marvin Wolf) had a casual acquaintance with several junior officers of USS *Turner Joy*, the vessel involved in the second incident. After reports of the attacks were widely circulated, I separately asked the engineering officer and the gunnery officer about the encounter. Each immediately said, "That's classified." I was too naive to understand the implications of their responses.
2. Disclosure: Marvin J. Wolf collaborated with Ky on a wartime memoir, *Buddha's Child: My Fight to Save Vietnam* (New York: St. Martin's Press, 2002).
3. On November 17–18, 1965, during the Battle of Ia Drang, almost every man present for duty in that platoon was killed or severely wounded near Landing Zone Albany.

4. From US Department of Veterans Affairs.

5. Neil Sheehan, "At the Bloody Dawn of the Vietnam War," *New York Times*, November 13, 2015, https://www.nytimes.com/2015/11/15/opinion/at-the -bloody-dawn-of-the-vietnam-war.html.

Don Ray

1. According to Don Ray. See also "Reagan Friends Buy Him a Place to Retire," *New York Times*, January 24, 1987, https://www.nytimes.com/1987/01/24/us /reagan-friends-buy-him-a-place-to-retire.html.

Jan Scruggs

1. Several men involved in the My Lai Massacre faced courts-martial, but only First Lieut. William Laws Calley Jr. was convicted. In 1971, he was found guilty of murder and sentenced to life, but President Nixon changed his sentence to house arrest, and Calley served about three years. Calley apologized in 2009. See Peter Ross Range, "Only One Man Was Found Guilty for His Role in the My Lai Massacre. This Is What It Was Like to Cover His Trial," *Time*, March 16, 2018, https://time.com/5202268/calley-trial-my-lai-massacre/.

Jay Mancini

1. The Presidio Trust Act, Sec. 101(3), https://www.presidio.gov/presidio-trust /planning-internal/shared%20Documents/Planning%20Documents/EXD -502-TrustAct-19961112.pdf.

John Balaban

1. Lucius Annaeus Seneca, *On Benefits*, trans. Edward Gibbon (London: J. M. Dent and Company, 1899).

2. John Balaban, *Remembering Heaven's Face: A Moral Witness in Vietnam* (New York: Poseidon Press, 1991). For more information, go to the International Voluntary Services website, https://ivsgb.org, and the US Agency for International Development website, www.usaid.gov.

3. Ho Xuan Huong, *Spring Essence: The Poetry of Ho Xuan Huong*, ed. and trans. John Balaban (Port Townsend, WA: Copper Canyon Press, 2000).

4. See the Vietnamese Nôm Preservation Foundation at http://www.nomfoundation .org.

Oliver Stone

1. See "Oliver Stone," *Bill Moyers Journal*, December 4, 2009, http://www.pbs.org /moyers/journal/12042009/profile.html; and Mark Lawson, "Oliver Stone,"

Guardian, December 15, 2006, https://www.indiewire.com/2006/12/the
-guardian-interview-oliver-stone-75543/.

Paul Longgrear

1. FAC is a forward air controller; A-1E Skyraider is a heavily armed, single-engine
   attack plane.

Russell Balisok

1. Jordan Rau, "'It's Almost Like a Ghost Town.' Most Nursing Homes Overstated
   Staffing for Years," *New York Times*, July 7, 2018.
2. S1 is a staff department that includes a human resources officer.
3. MARS station is the Military Auxiliary Radio System that used shortwave radio
   to contact amateur stations in the States and could connect two-way voice radio
   to the telephone system.

Frederick W. Smith

1. The Vietnam Veterans Memorial in Washington, DC.

Eileen Moore

1. Betty Friedan, *The Feminine Mystique* (New York: W. W. Norton, 1974).

Hal Kushner

1. Many would dispute this in favor of Lt. Col. John "Bullwhip" Stockton, the
   previous commander of the 1/9.

Mike Hepler

1. "Track" is slang for an armored personnel carrier, which has tracks instead of
   wheels.

Grace Liem Lim Suan Tzu Galloway

1. Photo by James Caccavo.

John Padgett

1. The B-40 was designed to penetrate several inches of tank armor before it
   exploded. Many nevertheless exploded inside helicopters.

Barry McCaffrey

1. A saloon near the Pentagon was called The Chief Joint of Staff.
2. Joseph L. Galloway, *US News & World Report*, March 4, 1991.

Charles L. Siler

1. Harold G. Moore and Joseph L. Galloway, *We Were Soldiers Once . . . and Young:
   Ia Drang—the Battle That Changed the War in Vietnam* (New York: Random

House, 1992). *We Were Soldiers*, directed by Randall Wallace, screenplay by Randall Wallace (Los Angeles, CA: Paramount Pictures, 2002).

Colin Powell

1. Colin L. Powell, with Joseph E. Persico, *My American Journey* (New York: Random House, 1995).
2. Colin Powell, with Tony Koltz, *It Worked for Me: In Life and Leadership* (New York: Harper, 2012).
3. Powell, *It Worked for Me*, chap. 1.

George Forrest

1. Harold G. Moore and Joseph L. Galloway, *We Were Soldiers Once . . . and Young: Ia Drang—the Battle That Changed the War in Vietnam* (New York: Random House, 1992).

Marshall Carter

1. Marshall Carter Navy Cross citation, https://valor.militarytimes.com/hero/4425.

Max Cleland

1. Max Cleland, with Ben Raines, *Heart of a Patriot: How I Found the Courage to Survive Vietnam, Walter Reed and Karl Rove* (New York: Simon & Schuster, 2009).
2. Toby Warren, *A General's Spiritual Journey* (Lake Placid, FL: Wild Goose Ministries, 2007).

Richard Armitage

1. In this context, "pregnant" means planting the public notion of a mutual willingness to make peace.

Silvestre Reyes

1. Reyes read this to me over the phone, and I wrote it down verbatim.

Eugene "Gene" Deatrick

1. Bruce Henderson, *Hero Found: The Greatest POW Escape of the Vietnam War* (New York: HarperCollins, 2010).

Scott Ratliff

1. Douglas R. Cubbison, "They Served with Honor: Spec. 4 Scott 'Scotty' Ratliff, Wind River Reservation," *Star Tribune*, March 26, 2017.

Viet X. Luong

1. After 1954, the Hanoi government consolidated many villages to make administration more efficient, so small towns like Nem Dang may be found only on local maps.

AUTHORS' NOTE

A few words about our methodology and choice of subjects.

Both Marvin J. Wolf and Joseph L. Galloway, but especially Galloway, have a wide circle of friends and acquaintances who are Vietnam veterans. We approached most of these people, in some cases to interview them, but more often in search of others who might be suitable. We also looked for suitable subjects on the internet. A surprising number of those we approached declined to be interviewed. Our goal was to find forty to fifty men and women of every race and ethnicity who had served in Vietnam in each of the armed forces or as civilians and in some way had distinguished themselves, especially in their postwar lives. From the start, we also intended to include Vietnamese refugees who have made outstanding contributions to the nation.

Our goal was a group that represented the 2.7 million Americans who served in Vietnam. Readers will have to decide for themselves how close we came to that representative sample. It was an imperfect process, and we suspect some will find fault with it. If so, we are to blame and no one else.

We were unable to find suitable men or women who had served in every Vietnam environment. Probably because US troop strength in Vietnam peaked in 1968 and rapidly declined thereafter, nearly all the veterans we spoke with had served in Vietnam before 1971.